THE NINETIES

WHAT THE F**K WAS THAT ALL ABOUT?

Also by John Robb:

The Stone Roses and the Resurrection of British Pop
(Ebury Press, £9.99)

The Charlatans: We Are Rock
(Ebury Press, £9.99)

For more information on John Robb
access his website at www.johnrobb.co.uk

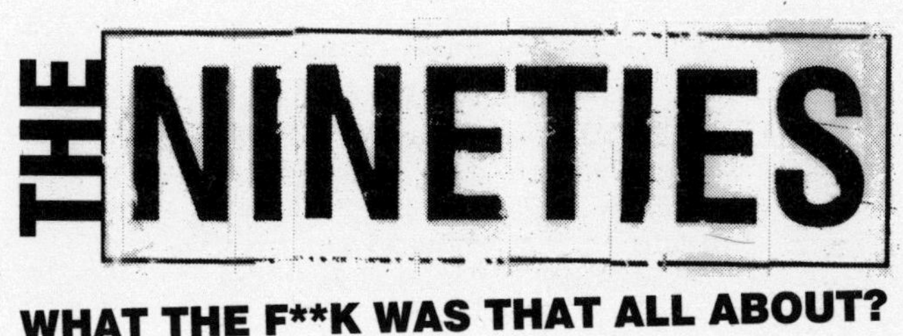

WHAT THE F**K WAS THAT ALL ABOUT?

JOHN ROBB

This edition published in Great Britain in 1999

1 3 5 7 9 10 8 6 4 2

Ebury Press
Random House, 20 Vauxhall Bridge Road, London SW1V 2SA

Random House Australia Pty Limited
20 Alfred Street, Milsons Point, Sydney,
New South Wales 2061, Australia

Random House New Zealand Limited
18 Poland Road, Glenfield, Auckland 10, New Zealand

Random House South Africa (Pty) Limited
Endulini, 5A Jubilee Road, Parktown 2193, South Africa

The Random House Group Limited Reg. No. 954009

A CIP catalogue record for this book is available
from the British Library

ISBN 0 09 1871352

Cover design by Sheridan Wall @ Stylorouge

Typeset by SX Composing DTP, Rayleigh, Essex
Printed and bound by Biddles of Guildford

Papers used by Ebury Press are natural, recyclable products made from wood grown in sustainable forests.

THE NINETIES

CONTENTS

PRELUDE

Just what is this slavering beast we call the nineties? This end-of-the-millennium psychosis decade whose music scene has lurched from one extreme to another? Extremes that include the heavy-duty guitar pain of Nirvana to the clean-arsed designer pop of Boyzone, to the fundamentalist rock-list bores and their deification of the so-called 'classics' to the kitschy ironic smirks of Brit artschool pop, from the grainy realism of Brit smack films, to the quirky slapstick violence of Tarentino, it's been a decade where good taste and bad taste swapped over and pop music fractured into a zillion tiny scenes – the niche nineties. It's been a decade of the supergroup touring purpose-built (in the nineties) arenas and superclubs; it's been a decade of hi-tech technology and lo fi records.

It's been a decade when every form of entertainment went pop: footballers swanned around like rock stars and rock stars looked like 1970s Third Division footballers. It's been a decade when everyone picked and mixed from the myriad of scenes for their own individual taste and then wore the same combat trousers.

And yet it's been a decade that's seen far more invention and sheer diversity than any before. It pisses all over the much hyped and fabled sixties – which is why I wrote this damned book . . .

If this version of events doesn't match yours then it maybe because my methods of research have had their own special flavour. Whilst you were putting your CD's into alphabetical order or making sure that you had all the classics neatly filed away – I've been out there waving the flag for rock 'n' roll. As I sit here in 1999 I find it remarkable that not only can ten years speed past so quickly but that they can be stuffed full of so much cool action . . . I'm also surprised that I can actually recall most of it.

This was a tough book to write. And I wouldn't have it any other way. In the course of writing this account I broke four computers, slept four hours a night, got into three fist fights and attacked the postman with a barrage of grade A invective after I caught him half inching a desperately needed royalty cheque.

I argued the toss with anyone who crossed my path and will continue to do so on publication. I fought with irate Beatles fans on a live TV debate, appeared naked on Polish TV, played more than a hundred gigs, saw half of Europe, spent half a day on the phone and the other on my portable Mac . . . I got thrown off TV for speaking the truth and ran three marathons, I also got on the shortlist for the first European astronaut to fly with the space shuttle mission.

In the course of researching this book I spent the nineties pissing on the Berlin wall, did scientific research on the love drug and wrote two hit singles. I was backstage at most major R 'n' R events, in the pit for the most exciting ones and actually on the stage for the most mental ones. I banished sleep from the equation, spoke to every wired up bohemian in the nation, and made love in the 'special room' of the pre-war Belgrade Town Hall. I've made a porn film, three albums, written three books and stared up the barrel of a border guard's gun. I've become a black belt and can knock off the 120K bench press and you still want me to mention your favourite sodding band? Waddya want – blood?

I've brawled, lived and loved my way through this freaked decade. If I was the person sharp enough to remember most of the action in the Manc fallout in my Roses book then, this time, I'm the only one dumb enough to actually try and get the nineties experience down into book form . . .

And before you enter this wild world that is the last decade of the millennium for one last time . . . remember one thing . . . Good taste is the enemy of er, good taste, to throw away your preconceptions . . . stop being so damned precious, burn those soddin' rock lists and blow your mind!!!!

WHAT THE F**K WAS THAT ALL ABOUT?

INTRODUCTION

The nineties was a time when the barriers came down. It was a time when you could cross pollinate and grab any scene you wanted. After acid house and ecstasy created a mood where anything goes, anything certainly did go. Pop culture continued to be fractured but you could smash and grab across all the different scenes. The age barrier disappeared, different generations pilfered each other's styles and sounds. New music rubbed shoulders with old styles.

There was a veneration of certain old school rock acts that was astonishing. Monthly lists of 'greatest records of all time' were endlessly published just to make sure that you were 'on message' (a very nineties phrase), this was something that Simon Price, author of the brilliant *The Manic Street Preachers . . . Everything*, noticed.

'There has been an extreme tug of war between people who believe in authenticity and the people who don't,' he says. 'Nineties rock culture can be best described as coming from a car boot sale. There's too much reverence, but at the same time music is going in many different directions although none of them are really forward . . .'

The total war of the post-punk era was no more, as Radio One DJ Mary Ann Hobbs – host of the excellent *Briezeblock* show which sums up the nineties schtick with a playlist dedicated to freaky electronics, post dance, drum and bass, lo fi and good old rock 'n' roll – explains:

'The most interesting thing, which relates to my show, I guess, is that it's no longer a tribal culture. The pop barriers have been smashed to smithereens. It's no longer a sin to own a variety of different records across different generations. When I was a kid you were either a biker chick, a mod or a punk. Having the wrong records was a grave social crime . . . It was totally illegal to have other scenes' records . . . It was a very strange time in that respect . . .'

This new freedom has seen lo fi luddites grab samplers while guitar-hating dance heads strap on six strings and form crossover bands. It has given musicians greater freedom to create, escaping the dark days of scene-orientated rock. After all, pop is meant to be some sort of adventure. You have to follow your nose and fuck all the rules off, otherwise what's the point?

Simon Price picks up on this theme that dominates the era.

'Collage has become a valid form of making music but there are people who still think that craftsmanship comes from the soul. Whereas I don't care how a record is made. It doesn't matter about the sweat and tears that went into the record, it's about how it affects the listener. It doesn't matter if the song is written by a committee or written by a machine instead of an orchestra, it's about how it affects me . . .'

Dance music fractured into a million different scenes while hip hop seeped into mainstream culture. The mid nineties gave guitar music a shot in the arm with Britpop but the fallout from that pinnacle has been long and slow. There is now a consensus knocking around the music biz that something has to change, that we are living, in the late nineties, in a similar era to that of pre-punk.

The big groups are getting fat and lazy, the lank longhairs are getting edged out by the pop stars. The shiny new pop scene is crushing rock and all its inherent dinosaur traits. While the guitar bands are becoming slothful, the pop saps are ruling the roost . . . John Harris, editor of *Select*, picks up on this thread:

'It was the way that Oasis released their last album with cassettes of it getting delivered in vans. It was so pompous. There's rock stars living in ancient castles . . . It's the death of the rock star. We need a punk rock . . . Oasis have killed themselves. They have become like a Ken Russell film – something like *Tommy*, over the top but not in a good way. For me the defining moment was when Richard Ashcroft refused to leave his table at the NME awards and the NME editor took them to him in a carrier bag.'

The nineties has certainly given us some great pop, some crazed, fucked-up underground music and a multi-styled cross reference of great new sounds. But in the late nineties there is a tired feel to some of the mainstream bands: they need challenging. They need their arses kicking . . .

Any takers out there?

CHAPTER 1

MADE OF STONE: SMASHING DOWN THE BERLIN WALL WITH A HAMMER

Who knows when a decade actually starts? Smartasses among you will point to the calendar and say 'Look it was right there, the first of January 1990.' But what we're talking about here is culturally – you know, when that shift occurs and things feel that they will never be quite the same again . . . For me, the nineties started when the Berlin Wall came down. The music scene seemed to shift gear and there was a rare spell of optimism around the world . . .

When did the nineties start?

Was it when acid house exploded out of the handful of tiny clubs that had been keeping it an E-fuelled secret? Was it when Manchester stopped raining and burst into party sunshine? Or was it when Nirvana suddenly exploded into the mainstream with a gut-wrenching power and influence?

Perhaps the key moment happened outside pop. And it was one of those moments when the real world seems to shudder.

The point when the eighties were crudely ended was when the Berlin Wall came down and the Russians' East European empire collapsed.

It was as rock 'n' roll as real life could get.

The grey days seemed to be over. The confused troops at the Berlin Wall poked their bayonets and dumb faces through the newly created holes in the Wall as the pissed-up mass of humanity on the other side laughed and jeered at them.

New Year's Eve, 1989, was a pivotal point in European history.

INTRODUCTION

After watching weeks of incredible news unfolding on the TV all that autumn it was a must-go location. The sight of whole populations who had just had enough of living in the Russian empire was powerful, overwhelming viewing. Every day saw another demonstration, another set of families walking up to the borders with their bags.

No one believed in the old ways any more.

Travelling to the tumultuous city with a man called The Lizard, we arrived in Berlin at seven in the morning. Slumbering on the slow overnight train we missed our stop. The Lizard was too deep into a bottle of cheap Polish vodka and I was pidgin-talking football with a stoned Yugoslavian gang of shell suits.

Missing your stop is not a major problem in most cities. But in Berlin it meant getting off in the old communist east side. Arriving there in the bad old days without a visa was asking for trouble so it was with trepidation – and for The Lizard a burning cheap vodka hangover – that we got off the Moscow-bound train and hit the streets of the former capital of East Germany.

In the grimy grey days of the Cold War, stepping foot on East German soil spelt big trouble. Even trying to get into the country legitimately was difficult. Three years before I had been knocked back for looking 'too punk' by a big, fat, surly army fucker who was in control of Checkpoint Charlie.

Apprehensively I dragged an ashen-faced Lizard across the grey morning platforms and into the main hall. The station was curiously dead. Wandering out on to the silent early morning streets unchallenged was a novel experience. The iron fist of totalitarianism seemed to have been pulled back. The fake communism of forty years had evaporated and there seemed to be no-one around with whom to celebrate.

That morning, East Berlin was silent in its splendour. When the city was split after the war, the Russians had ended up in charge of the original centre and most of the old municipal blocks. Huge old buildings stood in the crisp early morning light along the main slew of Berlin's Unter Den Linden. Some of the buildings were still pockmarked with bullet holes from World War II, the desperate last weeks of the Reich when the Allies finally stormed the city and crushed the evil Nazi empire.

Walking towards the Wall we expected to be challenged at any moment by the cops. But nothing happened. The sharp cold air of the last morning of the eighties hung unmolested by the officious waffle of the police.

Our plan was to climb over the Wall and wander over the former no man's land and back into West Berlin. After all the Wall was only a symbol. It didn't mean anything any more. Four weeks on since the collapse of East Germany had left a very confused situation. No one really knew whether it was an offence or not to clamber over its grey concrete slabs and cut across to the West.

The east side of the Wall was as stunning in its powerful rudeness as the west. The wall cut a huge gash across the city, interrupting the streets and driving through houses with its own crude logic. The only difference was that on the east side there was no graffiti. The crazed spray-can sprawl of decorations that danced across the western side was totally absent here. The bleak concrete of the east side was here for the sole purpose of keeping the crushed citizens hemmed into the rotting fake state of East Germany. While the West turned a blind eye to the constant repainting of the Wall, the East German government was not in the business of letting anyone near the Wall, let alone paint all over it.

The Wall was much taller than it looked in photos – by now any plans to clamber over and into the uncertainty of the old no man's land had to be abandoned. We stood there looking at the rubbish piled against the concrete and the weeds sprouting from the cracks in the concrete in this forgotten part of the city and started to laugh at how pathetic it was. All that was left to do was to piss against its no bullshit crudeness. I whipped out my cock and left the sweet stain of freedom against a wall that only weeks before you would have been shot for getting this close to.

It was a spooky and satisfying moment.

The wall that had imprisoned a nation was taking the full blast of an early morning slash. It was a sweet green stain against the last days of totalitarianism.

Post piss, I smirked at The Lizard and we decided to follow the wall round and see if we could find a way over. We both fell silent, concentrating on distant clanking.

In the early morning silence a strange sound was wafting over from the western portion of the Wall. The western half was a couple of hundred metres away over the deadly open space of no man's land. The West Berliners were up early and doing some DIY of their own. In the distance all that you could hear was the chinking of a thousand hammers on the now-pointless concrete slabs. Even at this early hour, the West Berliners were chipping away at their Wall with tiny hammers and their bare hands, striking their own tiny blows for autonomy against the hated Wall. It sounded like a whole mass army of freedom fighters and we knew we had to be in on the action.

Having finished my piss, we walked along the Wall. The streets were still empty as the weak early morning sun licked against the crumbling old buildings of East Berlin.

'I hope this is the right way,' mumbled The Lizard, a man who didn't like walking too far.

By following the Wall around we worked out where the back end of the Checkpoint Charlie border crossing was and wandered down to the narrow inspection huts that lined the break in the omnipresent concrete.

Of course we were worried. In effect walking through the Wall backwards, we could have been up for some awkward explaining. But there was just a brief cursory checking of passports and no difficult questions – it seemed like the guards were just pretending that they still had a job to do – whether this was still technically a border or not, no-one seemed to know. In their heart of hearts everyone knew that it was all over but the machinery of the state was still intact and it had not been totally dismantled as yet.

On the other side we were welcomed with a bizarre sight. In total contrast to the scowling emptiness of the east, the west was a hive of frantic activity: there was a large crowd of people hammering away at the wall. Already there were gaping holes in the concrete.

The people had been busy.

The Russian troops stood on top of the Wall, their guns cocked – ready, but impotent. The tide of history was turning against them. Weeks before, East Germany had been dissolved and they were now but a token force, a footnote in history, a lost army, powerless to prevent the people from exacting their revenge on the grey cruelty of a state once in complete control. The soldiers stood on the wall confused.

No one was in charge.

Under their feet the tiny hammers were gradually removing the very symbol of the East-West divide.

Through the holes in the Wall that were the size of a fist, you could peer through and shake hands with baffled soldiers. Blagging was in full force, some were selling army hats to the money-toting Westerners who were looking for chic and hip Russian army accessories. Cigarettes and handshakes were exchanged with some troops, while V-signs were being given up to those who, like their comrades on the Wall, were still trapped in the bad old days and stood sternly to attention, sneering at the crazed rabble through the tiny cracks.

Grabbing at the crumbling concrete with bare hands, you could pull away lumps of rock loosened by the hammers. Each piece of rubble felt like a physical chunk of oppression being pulled away. There were hundreds of people scrabbling at the concrete, impatient and not waiting for the governments to do the decent thing and just bulldoze the whole lot down.

On the street, capitalism was already moving in with vendors smashing up pieces of paving slabs, spraying them and selling them on to dumb tourists who had started to emerge in the afternoon and were looking for pieces of Berlin Wall to buy.

Celebrating the new year we returned to the Wall that night. It was a powerful celebration. We were sucked up by a huge tide of humanity as almost a million people swept across the city to celebrate the first new year of liberation. A whole city was getting out of jail: it was a powerful and liberating moment, intoxicating in atmosphere and chemicals. The euphoria was tangible, fireworks were being thrown in the air and landing everywhere as a huge mass of humanity scaled down to the wall. While some still ripped away at the holes, which by now had doubled in size, others climbed up on to the wall itself and were dancing and singing. Isolated pockets of gun-toting troops stood there, stoic and confused at this invasion, while others continued to sell what they had or kissed girls and attempted to party with their stiff limbs.

The epicentre was the Brandenburg Gate. The huge crowd climbed over the Wall. Ignoring the troops and the cops, the crowd surged on to the gate itself and burst through into the old East Berlin. The Gate had been the symbolic heart of Berlin itself and just running through it and on to the broad avenues of East Berlin was a liberating moment. That night the final fabric of the Russian empire crumbled. Pinch-faced politicians were being run out of town. The party was here and the people just wanted to get drunk and have a good time.

It was a great night. A celebration of freedom. There was some real raw emotion on the streets. Everyone genuinely believed that things were really on the up. The punters on the streets were telling the politicians to fuck off. Power to the people – it's always a beautiful sight and one that at the time seemed to be a marker for a brave new era. Looking over the crowd joyously surging around the Wall, it was like being at the biggest rave in the world.

For a few weeks after it really felt like the age of Aquarius had arrived early. And the nineties was going to be the decade of idealistic, hedonistic kick-ass action and astonishing political freedom.

Of course things would turn out very differently . . .

CHAPTER TWO

SEARCHING FOR THE PUNK ROCK SPIRIT AND FINDING NIRVANA

The photos show a pair of Converse sneakers snapped through a skylight window. In the room lies the dead body of Nirvana frontman Kurt Cobain. It was the end of the trail for the troubled rock star who, the night before, had cranked a whole load of smack, written a suicide note and blown his brains out . . . The saddest moment of the nineties . . .

Kurt Cobain's desperation and alienation had touched a raw nerve in the rock 'n' roll scene. His band Nirvana had spat out a rock 'n' roll that mattered, a heartfelt howl that stopped you dead in your tracks. It may have been inspired by a pained mind but it was also a celebratory rush. Just witness how 'Smells Like Teen Spirit', when it gets slapped on in an indie disco, drives the whole place wild. Easily the most important band of the decade, they shook the music scene out of its apathetic state. In Nirvana's wake came a whole generation of pale imitators, the so-called Grunge scene. It was a scene that Cobain would rightly despise.

In their early days Nirvana were treated as 'just another rock band', but it didn't take a genius to work out that with vocals like this, the band were truly special . . .

This chapter looks at the US underground scene that spawned Nirvana, and recounts a couple of early interviews with the band (one of their first ever with the European press and the other just before *Bleach*, their debut album, came out) . . .

New York, midsummer 1990. The stifling heat was overbearing.

Kurt Cobain was sprawled in the corner of the room. A roomful of wrecked bags and ratty sleeping gear. The band were on the shit circuit – the never-ending toil of rusty old clubs that is the cutting-edge circuit the world over, the stinking cesspits with snarling owners and rustbucket PAs that bands are meant to cut some mean and lean action on before they break out and become famous.

Nirvana were in New York for the New Music Seminar, the back-slapping music biz conference where delegates flew in worldwide, got out of it together and laid down the connections that would dominate the action for the next twelve months . . .

It was the beginning of the end of any idea of indie meaning independent – the wheels were clicking and the business machine was purring. 'Indie' had become a sham, a good way of selling you shit. The eighties had been declared a no go zone and rock was pretty well dead. Metal had degenerated into poodle rock and punk had all but disappeared. It was all a tad dispiriting. Rock 'n' roll has a habit of getting into these ruts but every now and then someone talented comes along and cuts through all the bullshit – the scare-crow hippie slumped disinterested in the corner of the room had that something about him . . .

Still virtually unknown (the gig they played in New York as a four-piece was performed to about twenty people) Cobain wasn't the hip totem of supercool disaffected worldwide fuckups that he has since become. He was just another struggling rock 'n' roller, considered by so-called pundits and experts as a singer in one of those crappy heavy metal bands that only *Sounds* would write about. In fact, Cobain was already displaying an extraordinary talent with that voice . . . the voice in the wilderness that could well save rock 'n' roll. On the way over, on the plane to the US to interview them for *Sounds*, we decided that Nirvana were really going to break into the big time and sell well in excess of 50,000 records – hey, they might even sell 60,000! The scene for great rock 'n' roll had shrunk so much that this was the limit of anyone's expectations.

Pre-Nirvana in the mid to late eighties American rock had been a constantly shifting landscape. From the intense and rigorous workout of hardcore, the stripped-down and hi-velocity American version of punk rock, some of the bands had developed their music into a new sonic landscape . . . the scene leaders were Sonic Youth, the New York based experimental outfit. Sonic Youth had affiliations with the hardcore scene but were rooted in the detuned guitar workouts of Glenn Branca. They formed at the beginning of the eighties but it wasn't until their third album *Bad Moon Rising* (1986) that the band had started to break through. Signed to the key US underground Homestead Records in America and Blast First in the UK, Sonic Youth were the plug on top of a whole heap of wild shit, wild shit that they often had a hand in getting signed on to their labels.

There was the Butthole Surfers, the sky-high freakout band who sounded like Jimi Hendrix on even more acid. Their music was great, check out 'Locust Abortion Technician' for wild and wacky stuff that still manages to be kickass rock 'n' roll.

Big Black cut intense drum-machine driven power tool guitar stuff with an awesome, machine-like textural rush. Typically, these bands were providing a route out of the post-punk hole for a whole bunch of outfits and Big Black were to become a highly influential outfit. Vocalist Steve Albini was soon producing a stack of bands including The Pixies' breakthrough *Surfer Rosa* album, a record that went on to influence a rack of bands including, eventually, Nirvana. Big Black offered punk rock an escape route but they imploded before they could reach a mass audience which, despite their obtuse heaviness, they could have easily embraced. Albini went on to form the uncomfortably monickered Rapeman and eventually Shellac, who by the late nineties have become, perhaps musically, his best project. Shellac are a scratching and scraping trio whose sound was one part heavy slabs of visceral guitar bass and drum grind noise and on the other the tense lo fi dynamic of the Albini produced Slint (who were a key inspiration to a mass of UK late-nineties underground from the likes of Mogwai).

Dinosaur Jnr were fuzzed-out guitar freakouts exploding out of the middle of tune-laden rushes. Husker Du had been doing this type of shit for years but Dinosaur Jnr somehow managed to twist the Beatles through a fuzzbox formula adding a Neil Young classic rock whine.

Built around the enigmatic J. Mascis, a man who mumbled through interviews and mumbled through his songs, Dinosaur Jnr seemed to write classic songs effortlessly: their signature tune 'Freak Scene' boasts their keenest melody and most explosive guitar solo. They were also cool enough to rent my back garden for a much needed hundred quid to make the video for the song. Their bass player Lou Barlow was kicked out of the band and took his already up and running Sebedoh project into the nineties with a series of very personal albums. He eventually cut a surprise big hit with his side project, Folk Implosion, and the raw-assed hip hop flavoured crossover big seller 'Natural One' from the film *Kids*.

It was a golden period of US underground action and started a tradition that still resonates today in 1999 with outfits like Mercury Rev and The Flaming Lips flying the flag for warped underground guitar action.

The fistful of Sonic Youth related bands were the scene leaders and were about as big as it got until Cobain burst into the mainstream.

New York in the summer is a monster. The heat rises out of the pavements and the place oozes street life in a way that British cities with their shit weather and scowling gangs of pissed lads could never emulate. The vibe is good and the reports of ultra violence are exaggerated. Manchester is a far meaner city to pace around all night than the big apple. We were holed up on Avenue B. There was me and photographer Ian Tilton and Nirvana's affable pressman Anton Brookes.

Avenue B is in the heart of the sleazed up bombsite buildings where the yuppies were only just beginning to dare to tread. Avenue B was still rough city. Sat on the steps I struck up a friendship with a kid who was dealing coke to flash gits in holy-roller limos sending out their drivers to do business with the bug-eyed street trash. He had a gun shoved down his sock and his stash was hidden in a plastic bag in a pile of rubbish. He asked about the Queen and how everyone was back in England. We talked the usual shit while waiting for the deals on wheels to make themselves known.

The noise of the city was incredible, a concrete jungle of shouting and whooping with the immense background hum and grumble of tons of traffic in the distance. You'd just sit there and soak it all up, the power and the beauty of the concrete city beast . . . and New York was the ultimate beast. British minds were always blown by the 24-hour nature of the place, STUFF STAYED OPEN! It wasn't a matter of getting bored to bed by the shite local regulations that straddled the UK – you could live like a normal human being. If you wanted to go to the shop after five o'clock – it was open!

We had been there for a day or so and the city was already seeping in. The night before, when we arrived we had been about chucking bags into a tiny room and checking out the floor space. Being from *Sounds* we were always dealt the short hand. Hotels were out of the question. Budgets were tight. Record labels didn't have the money. It was always dossing down on the floor, but that was cool. We could not be bought! It was better for us to be hanging out with the band. And crashing out on floors was something that punk rock had trained its combatants in for the last 15 years. . .

The only thing was: this flat was tiny – there was us, Nirvana, their mates and fellow Subpop band Tad all crammed into one tiny room. If you know anything about Tad you would know that we definitely had a situation here. Tad were big guys – the affectionate elder brothers to Nirvana's mad kids.

Cool guys but big guys. They were sleeping back to back in this hot room. With no ventilation we were going to get to know each other. We had no choice.

The piece was a front cover feature on the two bands. It was meant to be split between the pair of them but for some reason Tad eventually ended up on the cover!

Nirvana had been in my sights for a long time now. The first single 'Love Buzz' had blown my mind. A roughhouse raw garagey rush of punk rock sound, with a bug-eyed smudgy shot of some longhaired rock dude on the cover. It was a cool guitar rush but once that vocal kicked in you were instantly hooked – Cobain had the voice of the angels. A beautiful blemished, raw, tuff gnarl of a voice and it spoke volumes. It sounded like a world-weary old man with a Charles Bukowski throat coughing up the nine degrees of a heavy beer and tab abuse while trapped in a kid's body. He sang with such power, it knocked you off your tracks. This was a new and powerful voice in rock 'n' roll and no-one was really getting it yet. Nirvana seemed to be doomed to the underground, trapped by their brilliance to that netherland of fanatics and hungry journalists.

Just before its proper release in the UK, in his first-ever British press interview with me for *Sounds*, Cobain explained the inherent moodiness of his powerful rock 'n' roll that was already obvious from that one single.

'It's because we are a bit secluded, out on a limb up here. The local scene has always had an element of rock in it. But it's always been a gloomy element. That's why I reckon you guys in the UK like it, because your rock is on the gloomy side too. Maybe it's the weather – we have the same sort of miserable climate that you have.'

Seattle is famous for its rain. It rains there even more than Manchester. You can hear its dampening down of optimism oozing from the very pores of the bands that have flooded out of the city in the wake of Nirvana. The grunged bands with their slowed-down Black Sabbath riffola and Beatlish minor key melodies copped from Nirvana.

In the same interview Cobain raved about The Melvins, a band that he saw as the perfect group to emulate. That was about as big as he dared to hope Nirvana would be. He was going to be in for one hell of a shock.

By 1989 rock 'n' roll was running out of possibilities. The long slow fallout from punk had left a scene empty and bored. Everyone was looking for something to blow their minds with, and it was a three-pronged attack that was going to change everything and set up the music for the nineties.

Acid house had arrived without media permission. The Roses and The Mondays were swaggering their way into the mainstream and doing it in fine style. But the punk rock quest was demanding some raw edge action and Nirvana were the first band for a bunch of time providing the emotive guff that sated the hunger.

Sure there had been false alarms from Mudhoney, and Fugazi were a lean, mean riffing machine talking their inspiring talk and making me rethink the way I operated. Neither band was interested in dealing with the poisonous mainstream: Mudhoney seemed to just laugh at the notion of success and Fugazi were diametrically opposed to the system anyway. However, Nirvana had that pop thing, that spark that meant that they could go all the way.

All the way to 50,000 records!

In those far-off days of the eighties, the bands that ruled the rock mainstream were vile dogs with permed mullet haircuts who took too much cocaine and were tanned in the disgusting stain of fake suntans. Metal was in the hands of dim-witted fools and pop was dealt out by major label lackeys who were quite happy to suck corporate cock. For a band to bust out of the underground and into the Top Ten was unheard of!

The post-punk fallout had meant that it was pretty damned difficult for anyone to crack the pop mainstream. Now in the late nineties when there is a conveyer belt of cool bands getting the big payoff, the eighties seems like a far-off place.

Sonic Youth were quite often quoted as the yardstick to being successful and not losing whatever it was that made you special in the first place. They had signed to big bucks label Geffen and would eventually recommend Nirvana to the label.

None-the-less at this point Nirvana were still Subpop's secret weapon. They were the band that co-owner Jonathan Poneman felt was going to break big for them.

Staring intently across the table into the bar next door to the gig in Maxwells, the tiny venue in the New Jersey enclave of Hobokon overlooking the Hudson River, he was talking ten to the dozen about his protégés.

'Nirvana, they'll be the band the cracks it for us. A lot of people don't see it yet but they are going to be massive, the songs they come up with are incredible . . .' It may have been the usual label-boss talk, attempting to build the band up out of nothing, but you had to respect the man: he certainly knew his music and his enthusiasm was infectious. And in this case he was totally on the nail correct.

Subpop was making a good reputation for itself. It was releasing the great garage MC5 shakes of Mudhoney (they could have been so massive if they could have been arsed) and the dark guitar howl of Tad (an outstanding and underrated band). Most people considered Nirvana to be the weak link in the chain. When *Nevermind* came out and it all went crazy, people changed their minds with world-wearying predictability.

Before the gig, tall-as-fuck bassman Chris Novoselic was the most approachable. Standing in the bar at Maxwells he talked about the never-ending tour and how he was looking forward to getting back home again. He also talked about Yugoslavia and his roots. He was already aware of the tensions that were inherent in The Balkans and would spend time there in his post-Nirvana years attempting to make people aware of the situation.

At that moment in time, though, Nirvana were a well-kept secret. A few lost souls were wandering into the venue and when the band hit the stage there can't have been more than twenty in there. The tiny venue looked massive in its emptiness.

Not that it affected the band, they tore into their set with all the fervour of small town boys who have got the big city break. So what if there's no one here – this is New York City! We are in the big time! Guitarist Jason Everman was lost in a blur of long curls, while diminutive drummer Chad Channing clattered about on the kit with nowhere near the power of his eventual replacement, David Grohl but with an admirable fiery enthusiasm.

The tiny stage was imprisoning the lanky frame of bassist Chris Novoselic who was virtually stooping as he hung over his carrion bass. This did not stop him from leaping up into the air nearly grazing his head on the low slung roof when the adrenalin gripped his soul. Flanked by this motley crew was Kurt Cobain who was a bundle of intense energy and packed the most powerful gut-wrenching voice you'd ever heard. It was the sound of terror and celebration wrapped up in the fuzzed-out power-trip songs but it came armed with a ruff-arsed wall of melody.

The songs were so damned catchy: in all that melée of sound there beat a pure proud pop heart. Nirvana, even at this early stage, were definitely packing a pop punch. The sheer raw power of their music was captivating. Ignoring the sparse crowd they ended their set combusting with excitement, totally trashing their gear in a climax of pure rock 'n' roll exhilaration. Guitars flew everywhere, the bass was shoved into the roof and the drum kit was kicked over. It was a great rock 'n' roll pantomime and it gave you a real raw primal rush to be so close to such full on guitar carnage. Even the sound of the splintering gear and straining strings sounded awesome, a superb sonic explosion to end the set.

After the carnage the sound of a few hands clapping felt so strange and empty. Nirvana had arrived and had kicked some righteous ass. It's a shame that no-one was there to check it out.

That night we all huddled in the hot flat. After spending a riotous night out in the big apple, I crawled back into the tiny one-room apartment and slept on the kitchen floor under a coat surrounded by shattered sleeping bodies. The road can be hell sometimes but it makes sleep come very easily. The room was full of rock 'n' roll snorers, someone in the Tad camp had a neutron-sized roar of a snore. The heat was stifling as New York's nightlife ground on mercilessly outside the windows.

The following day I got to interview Kurt. Everyone else had gone out and he was huddled exhausted in the corner. It was the end of a long and mean tour.

'I'm just glad we're going home tomorrow. We're going to drive back in one go all the way and then get some proper rest . . .' he drawled through his mop of greasy, long, mousy-coloured hair that was streaked with bleach. He was wearing the generic flannel shirt and battered jeans, the mish-mash thrift torn look that would become 'le grunge' of the international catwalk within a couple of years. He spoke with a voice that was rough, raw and weary.

Kurt talked about his roots.

'I come from a town called Aberdeen. It is a logging town. That was all there was to do round there. Chop down trees and work in sawmills. I didn't want that sort of life. I was a real misfit. The place was full of jocks, meat heads . . .'

Cobain was the town outsider, the classic rock 'n' roll role model of alienated youth. He was not macho enough to fit in with the clichéd and ritualistic dumbed-down male lifestyle of his contemporaries. The only person he could empathize with was Krist (later Chris) Novoselic. The pair of them, inspired by the film *Over the Edge*, would run around town in a spree of vandalism, spray canning subsituationist slogans all over the beat-up streets.

The only escape route they could see was rock 'n' roll.

'I'd always listened to the Beatles. My mom and my auntie always played Beatle records. And then I heard Black Sabbath and that really connected with me. I finally heard punk records a few years ago. Stuff like The Sex Pistols and The Clash. I read about them in papers when I was a kid and I had a whole idea of what they sounded like in my head. It took years to get through to us up there in the sticks, it took forever, but when I heard it it felt really good . . . although they were never as powerful as I had imagined. It was seeing Black Flag that really made the punk thing for me. They were really inspirational.'

Music, the classic escape route. Cobain already had his sights set on rock 'n' roll. There was the local band called The Melvins who were inspiring him.

'They're such a great band. I would go to their gigs with them, do their guitars and stuff . . . I learned how to be in a band watching The Melvins . . .'

With Novoselic in tow, Cobain moved to Olympia. Back and forth they went, putting the band together with whoever they could find. Once they had enough songs they went into the studio and recorded a demo. The engineer was a chap called Jack Endinio.

'He loved the stuff that we were doing and he rang up Subpop and told them about us . . .'

Subpop, fired by what they had heard, quickly signed the band and released their debut 'Love Buzz' single. A song that sounded far more poppy than their just recorded *Bleach* album.

'The album is similar to the single in the way the songs are. But we've recorded it a lot rawer. It sounds a lot better, harder. The single seems so commercial now. But it's bound to be, since it's a cover of the Shocking Blue song!'

Cobain was curled tighter into the corner of the room. An introvert in an extrovert's world. Rock 'n' roll may offer an escape route from where you are from but it will never let you escape just who you are. At the time *Bleach* sounded powerful. It also sounded a long way from their contemporaries. The key was songs. Nirvana had a fistful of great tunes and Cobain's voice scars the songs with something far greater. This stuff really sent a shiver down the spine.

Later that day when their battered van disappeared into the New York night, you could sense changes were afoot. There seemed to be a distance between the band and their second guitarist, the affable Jason. He didn't seem to fit into the tight-knit core of the outfit. He looked too clean for a start! He wasn't as insular and was more into hanging out. So it was no surprise to find that a few months later he was no longer in the group.

The same with their drummer Chad. A competent enough player, he wasn't what Cobain was looking for. When he got the chance to poach hardcore band Scream's sticksman David Grohl he took it and it made a marked difference to the group's sound. Grohl was one hell of a powerhouse drummer and it pushed the songs to their potential extremes.

When *Nevermind* came out the band took off like a rocket. Their record label, Geffen, hadn't pressed enough copies in the UK to cope with the demand and the record sold out within a week, dropping out the charts. With a repress it started its never-ending charge. In the US it went mental, capturing the nihilistic spirit of the times. The record was a raw rush compared to the mediocre mush that passed for a rock music at the time.

Nevermind is arguably the most important record of the decade. It changed the way that rock music was made and listened to. Its echoes resound to this day and its lead-off single 'Smells Like Teen Spirit' has become rock 'n' roll anthem.

The record all but destroyed its creator though. Instead of wallowing in the mystic land of success, Cobain seemed to crack and buckle under the immense pressure that it brings. Being a full on rock star is no place for a sensitive soul and rock stardom didn't sit easily on his skinny frame.

He married Courtney Love, the extroverted Hole front woman. They had a child, Francis Bean, and the domestic situation, albeit a fairly volatile one, seemed to have settled Cobain down. But the demons were still there, a vicious portrayal of Love in *Vanity Fair* magazine caused the pair a lot of emotional grief.

The follow-up to *Nevermind* was the raw, gutsy and cynical *In Utero*. Recorded by Steve Albini, it's a magnificently powerful-sounding rock record, in many ways far superior to its predecessor. Its stark and powerful production seemed to mirror the increasingly fractured lifestyle that Cobain was living. Some figured that getting Steve Albini in to produce the record was an attempt to reclaim their underground cred by making a record that was as fucked up as possible. In fact in hindsight *In Utero* sounds far better than *Nevermind*. Albini perfectly captures the fluidity and sheer raw power of prime-time Nirvana and Cobain was still writing great pop songs even in his darkest hours. It also captured the downward spiral of its creator.

The stories began to emerge of guns, domestic arguments, the cops, heroin . . . Some were true, some were rumours, the usual rock star bullshit.

They toured the album but it was all coming apart at the seams. Nasty rumours floated around about the state of the singer's health. In Rome he collapsed in the hotel. Some thought it was a suicide bid, some said it was pills mixed with drink by mistake. Four weeks later in April 1994 Kurt Cobain shot himself. . .

It was a tragic fucking waste . . .

WHAT THE F**K WAS THAT ALL ABOUT?

CHAPTER THREE

LAD CULTURE

The laddism that apparently sprouted in the mid nineties was hardly a brand new concept. Lads into football, beer, rock and talking about 'birds' were hardly marking a new demograph. It was just that it had been ignored by the mass market mags for years. One long look in the mirror and dear old Blighty would be able to see that, especially post house, it had become a country of blaggers, dealers, yobs, drunks and hooligans. The media, initially, weren't comfortable with this.

Students tramped through Manchester pretending to be Liam Gallagher with *Loaded* magazine stuffed in their back pockets. It's a man's magazine that tells the truth. Instead of posh restaurants it understands that junk food is the domain of most of its readers. It was deliberately crap in parts, some of it read like it was written in the pub but it was witty and totally irreverent. It couldn't fail. After years of being told that they were slobs, men found something and somewhere to celebrate in and its most visible result was in the clothes that dominated the decade . . .

Casual clothes have been one of the stories of the last quarter of this century. Postwar UK high-street clothing meant starchy stiff suits and ties for all occasions. When T-shirts started to appear in the mid fifties people were shocked. Weren't they something to be worn under the shirt?

Mass tourism in the mid fifties had exposed the Brits to the looser European styles. The warm weather on the continent meant that the people were more relaxed. Bringing back the new casual styles and showing off their holiday tans in their loose fits the Brits were starting to get the casual bug. Throughout the sixties and seventies the sports market started to get a grip: slacks, golf gear and cardigans came and went.

The Brits were learning to dress down. In the eighties this would eventually result in the casual culture as the sixties generation's spawn took the look and made it into tuff urban chic.

In northern cities like Liverpool and Manchester the winding down from punk had been very different from that in London. A combination of football, crime, clothes and drug culture had sent the two cities on a very different route from the metropolis. A route that would eventually dominate the street culture of the nation in the nineties.

The much mythologized casual is the subject of a never-ending style row that now and then dominates pub barneys or the letters pages of style magazines like *The Face*. Where did it all start and who was first? Even in small-town Blackpool where I grew up there were signs of the casual style in 1978. I remember one kid, who was wearing a kilt Adam and The Ants style, suddenly turning up with a wedge, cardigan and brogues and becoming one of the key thugs at the football.

In reality the late-seventies street look was, for most kids, a leather jacket and docs, sort of like The Undertones near-miss version of the punk look.

In Liverpool, experts point to the Scotland Road end of the city for the birth of the scally culture. This tight-knit community of rough inner-city housing is never short of life's little luxuries and yet never seemed to be tied to nine to five. It was round here that the first signs of scally culture emerged in 1977. And it was to Bowie that they looked as the style king. In the seventies David Bowie was god. Theoretically he should have looked a prat in knitwear shorts but somehow the man who fell to earth pulled it off. He could look cool dressed in the most ridiculous outfits. It didn't do him any harm that he was also pumping out a fistful of great records to accompany his stylistic endeavours.

Strangely enough his art-school foppery hit an instant chord with the tough inner cities. There was something about Bowie that made sense to the wildest kids. Bowie clones would pop up here and there and watered-down versions of his look peppered the school yard. In the glam rock days he was The Man.

But Bowie was smarter than that. When glam went glum he

made his move. Reinventing himself as the plastic soul king and then as The Thin White Duke, and again in 1977 as the wedge-haired European based in Berlin cutting his nu dark pop on *Heroes* and *Low*.

On the front of *Low* Bowie stared into the distance, a stark image of his face framed in a side parting. It was the cue for the sharp kids to restyle their hair.

The haircut itself doesn't look much now but in the mid seventies with perms and lanky greasy hair the norm and the punk shock troop spike the alternative, a Bowie wedge looked plain weird and it started to catch on.

In Liverpool the Scotland Road boys managed to turn the effeminate Bowie look into something far tougher. Even in their mohair pullovers (already worn by the punks who copied them off the Essex jazz funkers) and plastic sandals (same route as the mohairs) they didn't look as camp as the look should have suggested. The style was completed with camel duffel coats.

But the defining part of the whole look was the lopsided wedge.

For years pop looks had been disseminated by TV. *Top Of The Pops* was one of the key trade-off points for pop fashion. Sure there had been street fashions before, teds, mods and punks had adopted their own versions of the main look.

But the scally look was going to catch on via a very different route. On the terraces at the start of the 1977 season the wedges at first stood out a mile and then as word slowly spread the idiosyncratic look started to catch on. The terraces in 1977 were a different world than they are now – the occasional punk mixed with the odd Bowie freak and a whole lumpen mass of greasy centre partings and flares.

The wedged up boys must have stood out a mile.

The key melting pot for this new clothes consciousness in Liverpool was two clubs, one called the Swinging Apple and the other called Checkmates. It was here that a punk-scally crossover started to happen. The soundtrack to this action was great: a real mixture of tunes . . . A typical play list of the time at Checkmates would be. . .

1. Dillinger 'Cocaine'
2. The Normal 'Warm Leatherette'
3. Iggy Pop 'The Passenger'

4.	Joy Division	'Transmission'
5	Steel Pulse	'Ku Klux Klan'
6.	Ian Dury	'Sweet Gene Vincent'
7.	The Damned	'New Rose'
8.	The Clash	'White Man In Hammersmith Palais'

Accompanied by this ace soundtrack the Bowie/Roxy kids and the match lads would hang out. Former Farm vocalist and documenter of the casual scene, Peter Hooten, was there.

'It was a great club. It was one of the few places where you could get in with trainers and plastic sandals. There was a split between beer-bellied boys from Birkenhead and the Bowie freaks in the rest of the city but in this club there were no squares. These were the hip match lads.'

Misty-eyed, some claim that this club was the true melting pot of a casual style that would echo through the next two decades. The art-school heads would hang out at Eric's and the punks and skins and footballers at the Swinging Apple while the beerheads had their own hellholes to get plastered in. The Swinging Apple was a space to exist in, a space that would reap dividends for both sides of the cultural divide.

In 1978 post-punk, electronic music started to make its first inroads into the scene. Spiky hair in clubs like Checkmates was being flattened down into fringes, termed the 'Cyclops wedge' by Kevin Sampson (ex Farm manager and currently author). By February 1978 the initial punk-influenced look (a look that owed a big debt to Bowie) was giving way to the new football fused style.

The match look was now defiantly the preserve of the wedgies.

The match lads were 'sporting a drooping fringe and straights' according to Kevin Sampson. They were carefully combing their hair into an approximation of the Bryan Ferry wedge, with a touch of The Beatles mop top. Some scenesters even claim that the haircut was influenced by Kraftwerk.

The look swiftly became the look of the city. It caught on like wildfire and a clothes obsession dominated Liverpool's culture. It was a look that other cities were at first bemused by.

Peter Hooten remembers the reaction of London football fans to the Liverpool contingent when they arrived in town. 'There was a real misunderstanding. They would shout "Fuck off soul boys" to us when we were really into stuff like The Jam, The Clash and reggae like Steel Pulse.'

In Liverpool the wedge haircut reigned in the late seventies. It was a look ignored by style pundits. A scene too far away from the cosy consensus to warrant any attention. Instead of the predominant straight leg jeans, Liverpool went for the drainpipes or 'drainies', and even then it had to be Lois drainies.

By 1979 there was a label war going on. Every month the key label was changed in a battle to remain at the head of the pack – Fiorucci, Lacoste, all had their frontline fashion moments before being discarded and given over to the masses. Left to its own devices the scene ran with its own rules in that gloriously elitist manner that dominates the best street fashions.

In the UK no matter where you come from you're a snob!

The look was now spreading across the UK: Kevin Sampson in *The Face* wrote of the London 'chaps' and the Manchester 'Ferries' as the style started to spread to other inner cities in the late seventies.

The London 'chaps' were now beating the scousers at their own game, mixing Nike trainers, frayed Lois jeans and Lacoste shirts worn with cashmere scarves and jumpers and, in the winter, Burberry raincoats.

The terraces were becoming catwalks.

The football fan of the early eighties was no longer a rattle-waving scarf-wearing wally or a toothless skinhead grunt but a mass of label-wearing style-coded casual-wear freaks, still available for a bit of violence but as interested in his wedged hair and his training shoes as in the next punch up.

The look, always restless, was moving on again.

In the inner cities of the north in the late Seventies kids were already wearing their Timberlands, buying up hard to get gear from specialist shops. It was a sartorial search that gave the look an exclusive edge, Pete Hooten remembers.

'There were only certain shops that you could buy the stuff from. A couple of places in Manchester and that was it. You had to really know where to look to buy the gear.'

As the shops got hip to the look they even began to understand its fast-moving nature: 'for one day only' stickers would be stapled onto gear hoping to con the aspiring casual into a veneer of exclusivity.

The look would change every week. It was fashion on fire. As soon as the wallies had copped the look then the hardcore would move on. And this was no more prevalent than in the training shoe.

Throughout the whole of the late seventies and into the eighties the training shoe was the ultimate symbol of casual culture. There was a tight code of hip around the sports shoe, a confusing race to get the most cutting-edge trainer. Peter Hooten remembers the moment that the trainer first made its impact on him.

'I remember seeing my first strap-over trainer which was unheard of at the time. Even now in England you don't see them much. When people saw them they stopped in their tracks. Someone had brought it back from Germany. That's where a lot of that stuff came from. The sports shops over there had a lot more stuff, probably to cater to the American army bases.'

The first trainer to get hip was the Adidas Samba – the black one with the white stripes. But there had been trainer action before that in 1976: the blue and white fake Adidas as worn by Starsky in *Starsky and Hutch* had given the shoe a cult status at school and Converse basketball boots had been hip in the punk days along with white canvas pumps copped off the back of Ramones sleeves.

It had been there on the fringes of fashion but now it was going to get serious. Pre Reebok and Nike's mass advertising the Stan Smith all-white tennis shoe was the flavour. Hooten, ever the shoe historian, looks up.

'The big one in Liverpool was the Puma Argentina in '78 to '79 after Argentina had won the World Cup.'

If you were really on the ball then you had the Puma Menotti, the red and white version named after the Argentina manager. When Liverpool went down to London on match day they caused much merriment with their new training shoe look, as Peter Hooten points out.

'They used to laugh at us and call us poofs, and they were stood there in their flying jackets or donkey jackets.'

What has to be remembered is that in the late seventies these trainers were pretty difficult to get. They achieved cult status because several of their permutations were only available from the continent.

You had to be really into your shit to own a pair, not like now – where they are high street staples.

In many ways the casuals were an eighties version of the mods: the quest for sharpness infused both scenes. The casual's sister scene – mod – intermingled and informed the look. A certain amount of cross-pollination occurred: the quest for sharpness infused both scenes, and both the nu casuals and the eighties neo mods loved The Jam.

Paul Weller's outfit was traditional enough to escape from the clutches of the punk audience and into the mainstream. The band was one of the first groups to cross right over to the football fan territory. Sure enough there had been bands with a legion of rowdy fans before, The Stones had been the flashpoint for riots, Mott The Hoople and Slade had raw street followings. The Specials and Madness had attracted some of the worst elements of the football culture with accompanying tedious yobbery at their gigs. But The Jam were one of the first bands whose following was football-styled. In many ways they were precursor of the mid-nineties Britpop bands with the same sort of fanbase and reverence for sixties mythology. At a Deeside Leisure Centre Jam concert, the Liverpool and Everton fans glowered at each other and punches were thrown.

Throughout the eighties and nineties the football fans' take-over of breakthrough indie bands would become a feature in pop. From Joy Division to The Smiths through Madchester and Oasis it would become a crucial crossover point on the road to the mainstream.

I can still remember the puzzled looks of New Order fans as their band was taken off their hands by the football mob.

The football/casual crossover was in its embryonic stages but the rucking on match day was already being caused by well-dressed gangs of youth. The media's skinhead stereotype had already been consigned to the history book away from football to the far right wilderness of politics.

By 1979 the Liverpool club scene had move on to the Harrington Bar where the soundtrack was a mixture as off the wall as Joy Division and The Crusaders. The jazz funk flavour that was the pre-punk Liverpool sound was inching its way back in and bringing with it its own style-conscious tips.

Early eighties

In the early eighties the clothes were starting to take on a sports flavour. Tennis shoes were worn with faded jeans and Adidas ski anoraks. In London, the look was still evolving with Lacoste and leather wear before tumbling into the all-encompassing sportswear that has dominated the last 15 years of street fashion. Meanwhile in Manchester, Adidas ruled.

By 1981 every city had its casuals: the dress code had been spread via the terraces. There were subtle dress code differences but they amounted to slight shifts to mark out the home turf. While the cockneys wore diamond Pringles the scousers wore green Peter Storms. The basic look for both cities was Slazenger jumpers, Lee jeans and Adidas trainers. Football culture was still evolving. Now a long way from the clichéd Neanderthal image, the fans would sit at the match instead of standing. There was also a dark side emerging with the increasing use of Stanley knives for swift and mean disfigurement of opposing forces.

It was getting meaner and more efficient out there.

By 1981 the casual culture was here to stay. Its nationwide status was building a foundation that has seen it become the key pillar to nineties fashions and attitudes.

One of the main tenants of the whole culture was its lack of reliance on American street culture to inform it of its codes of conduct. This was another link with the early sixties mod movement which had also taken several of its cues from Europe. And it was to the continent and, especially, Italy that the next flavours were to be found.

With Liverpool FC constantly winning in Europe their fans were continually exposed to the more sport-oriented look of Europe. One of the greatest ironies of the time was the Liverpool fans' obsession with clothes and their team's total style-bypass. The squad came complete with perms and crap moustaches and crazy too-tight shorts . . . they were a million miles away from the training shoe and label wars that were going off all over the terraces.

Fortunately for the fans the club was better at winning trophies than getting a cool haircut and the fans' eyes were opened by the new styles in Europe. Maybe more importantly they were also aided in their style quest by the far more lax security of the European shops who hadn't, as yet, got a handle on the Brits on the rob. It was a social phenomenon and one that commentators like Peter Hooten still chortle about today.

'People would rob stuff all over the place. I remember the European cup final in Paris in 1981, all the stuff that was robbed! Coming back to Liverpool, it was like an open bazaar . . . For the Real Madrid final everyone got there on the Sunday and the match was on the Wednesday. By Monday they wouldn't let you into any shops because everything had been robbed! . . . I don't like to go on about it because it reinforces the scouser stereotype! But at the time it was good enterprise. It was the economic situation at the time that caused it. I remember that Joe Strummer said that the robbing fans were like the vanguard of the English working class!'

More like the van load of English working class! As the sorties returned to the north with their haul of jewellery and sportswear the city was awash with gear and it started to change the way people looked. The street started to dress more European. Sportswear was coming in. Euro chic was in the frame.

'It was lifted off the shelves of European shops. No shops in town realized the sort of stuff that people were into wearing – and that's why Wayne Smith made the money. He had it sussed. It was a latter-day piracy. Everyone went abroad to Europe and came back with goodies like a tray full of rings . . . They were doing lots of jewellery. Not many people were harmed and it changed the culture of the city for ever.

'In Europe there were loads of scousers and Mancs in gaol! They thought the robbing was easy but the locals caught up . . . so I guess you could say that the true sports look was robbed from Europe.'

It was Thatcher's dream of private enterprise gone mad. Europe was awash with Brits on the rob. Alan X, a Manchester ticket tout, recalls the glory days of the eighties.

'We would spend the whole summer out there touting tickets. It was easy. There was no one else doing it. They hadn't cottoned on to it yet in Europe. There would be a whole crew of us just going round from gig to gig. Nowadays, of course, there's loads of gangs out there touting. It's pretty difficult to make a living.'

Britain was changing. As the eighties drifted into the nineties everyone was on a blag, selling a bit of knock off here, a bit of drugs there, robbing this and fiddling that. There was a huge black market economy going on. Go down the pub you could get yourself a colour telly and a bike for a tenner. They may have once been yours but what the fuck! You got them back! And you could always get stoned on some weed bought from the same geezer!

Clearing shops out of jewellery was good for paying the bills but it was the bagfuls of trainers that were returning to Liverpool that were styling the city's elite fashion squads. Empires were being built on the back of the trainers craze, as Peter Hooten remembers:

'Wayne Smith started this small shop in Slater Street after he noticed that training shoes were selling four times as many as they had done before. He had these two smart lads in there who understood just what everyone wanted to wear and the street culture that was going on . . . now Wayne Smith is like Harrods and those two lads don't work there any more!'

On the streets the label war intensified. Different trainers and different pullovers were craved and then discarded in a precursor to the late-nineties label craze. To be smart in the old days of pre punk was easy, Ben Shermans, Harringtons and Sta Press had combined neatly for the suburb thug. But the ground-breaking Liverpool lad was constantly looking over his shoulder at the latest look.

'One week it would be Stan Smith trainers and then they would be out. The tops would be Lacoste, then Benetton, then Fruit Of The Loom, whatever was in that week. Bubble jackets were a big thing – now they are associated with Harlem drug gangs but back then they were fashionable for about a week!' recalls Hooten. 'It was like a manifestation of conservative values that the underground accepted,' he laughs.

Timberlands were ubiquitous: not available in the UK, they were being imported en masse by the shoplifters. It gave them an added exclusivity, an added street edge. In London, the label was neatly captured by a piece by David Rimmer while visiting White Hall Clothiers in Camberwell:

'A school uniform shop has started stocking label gear and was swamped by mid teens spending whole afternoons going over the clothes. Pierre Cardin T-shirts, Diadora green flash kangaroo skin trainers and Fila track suits were eyed enviously and bought by parents twisted round little fingers. The shop has started stocking grey flannel Farah trousers, Lacoste T-shirts and Pringle diamond pullovers. They had sold out immediately after expanding into the wild world of labels and had suddenly became a fashion epicentre.'

The article went on to describe the cutting-edge look down Walthamstow Road of wedges or wetlook hair with highlights, Lacoste, Fila, or Ellesse tennis shirts, Pringle (squares or stripes but definitely not diamonds), Fila or Sergia Tachinni tracksuit tops, Lois or Fiorucci straight legs, sometimes with the bottom of the leg seam split by about as much as three inches . . . It was typical, with a few regional variations, of the way street kids were dressing nationwide. As long as the right labels were there from Lacoste's crocodile, Fiorucci's triangle and Pringle's Lion you were in. It showed that you were prepared to shell out for your clobber (or at least rob it).

Cheap this stuff wasn't.

Paid for by shoplifting, begging, stealing and borrowing, or even having the very shirt stolen of your back! There were fakes but they could be spotted a mile off.

In the mid eighties the intense style war began to change. The economic situation in the UK was starting to dictate the way people lived and the way people dressed; the iron fist of Thatcherism was smashing down hard on to the already blighted economic landscape of Liverpool in 1983 onwards.

With Thatcher in power there was a definitive and marked change of street attitudes between the more affluent south and the crumbling north. This was reflected in the two key centres of casual culture, Liverpool/Manchester and the capital. In London, casual was big time – the clothes were easy to buy and the style codes became entrenched in the city's urban folklore. As a reaction, Liverpool, a city never to follow anyone else, started to dress down.

The whole look waltzed downmarket. It tramped out. Labels were still the key but there was less of the intense bickering over the hippest label. It was down to the individual. Suede shoes replaced trainers. Lager was usurped by cannabis while Frank Zappa became the new Merseyside musical totem. Corduroy jackets with big pockets became de rigueur. The jacket was perfect for stashing stuff in. Perfect for shoplifting. The new look was more than just the latest eccentric wardrobe for young working-class flash. These were looks that were dictated by a lifestyle. A lifestyle of dope smoking, shop robbing, living on the edge hustling off the new black market Britain. The nowhere land – a million miles away from the cosy world inhabited by Thatcher and her Tory cronies.

In an attempt to document the ever-changing scene that was erupting around him, Peter Hooten started his fanzine *The End* in 1982. *The End* was unlike any other fanzine on the scene at the time. It took the piss and it was rooted on the terraces. Less about the usual 'zine fare of freaky underground groups it was into pop, the sort of post-Jam and Clash street guitar pop that was filling the post-punk vacuum. But what really defined *The End* was that it documented the rise of casual football culture. *The End* was always value for money, it was damn funny and it knew its shit. Its knock-on influence can be felt everywhere, from the football fanzines like *When Saturday Comes* that it preceded by several years to the laddish lifestyle piss-taking of *Loaded*. James Brown, the initial editor and driving force behind *Loaded*, was in regular contact with Hooten, turning up in Liverpool in 1985 with a Mohican carved into his head (by your author with a rusty bloodstained blade).

'James Brown came to Liverpool for this special gig that we

were doing where we invited loads of Juventus fans over after the Heysel stadium disaster. Ted Chippington was on with us [fab deadpan comic]. I remember that James was flabbergasted by the scenes. He didn't understand that sort of thing, he didn't know that it existed.'

The match lads rammed the venue and the place rocked. Hooten still laughs when he remembers the future *Loaded* editor's reaction.

'I remember James came up and said, "Peter don't you feel ashamed that The Farm are just a lads' band?" Ha! ha! ha!'

Hooten saw *The End* filling a gap in the scene.

'During the time there was only a couple of more serious music magazines in Liverpool. We wanted to reflect an attitude. We also wanted to take the piss. We were very anti-fashion. We were trying to get people to buy gentlemen's clothes, you know wear suede elbow patches and smoke a pipe!' Hooten cackles.

Perhaps the best thing in *The End* was its 'In and Out' column – two pointed lists that would deflate pomposity and give a rough guide to what the editors were thinking. An instant piss-taking style guide to the street.

As the eighties moved on, clothes manufacturers started to cotton (ha!) on to the fact that there was a big new look going down on the streets and clothes that they had virtually given up on were highly in demand. And there was a smattering of national press attention. The now defunct music paper *Sounds* had a cockney casual band on the cover as then *Sounds* journalist Gary Bushell was on a quest to find another street youth craze to write about after the collapse of his Oi movement. As the casual scene was getting bigger, the scene in Liverpool was starting to get stranger as a still-baffled Peter Hooten laughs:

'It was the so-called winter mountaineering look in eighties Liverpool. The old man look. There was the tweed jacket, crew neck jumper, suede boots, Clarke's originals. There was an attempt to revive the country squire barber look, the Norfolk look . . . the tweedy country man look with a seventies wedge, mohair, trying to look like an upper-class twit. But up to no good as Jack Straw would like to say . . . Wax barber coats were described as robber jackets . . . They were great robbing jackets for shoplifters.'

Liverpool was now dressing down, getting stoned and listening to Frank Zappa whilst following the likes of Groundpig round the city's pubs. Other cities were still dressing in the smartest

Fila track suits, Ellesse T-shirts – and Tacchini (Italian for peacocks) were everywhere. Adidas was brushed aside as the Nike Legend became the training shoe and this, in turn, was superimposed by the Nike Ace. The flash fans now followed Manchester City, Aston Villa and Middlesbrough and Aberdeen up in Scotland. 'Radical sports chic', as Kevin Sampson neatly terms it, was the rage at these clubs while Liverpool went off into its own weird world.

Out of this melée of street culture, *The End* was, in Liverpool, doing pretty nicely thank you. It was becoming the mouthpiece for a whole undocumented rush of street culture. And Peter Hooten was about to take a musical step as well.

By now he had joined The Farm.

'They used to rehearse in my house in Walton. One day the singer didn't turn up and as I was a pretty lippy sort of character they asked me if I wanted to have a go. The song I sang at the audition was in fact Iggy Pop's "The Passenger" and I knew that really well as that was one of the songs you heard loads when you went out.'

The early Farm were dominated by the songwriting of Steve Grimes who attempted to push the band towards his beloved Velvets, Patti Smith, Flaming Groovis classic seventies underground tastes. They may have been his songs but The Farm were always going to sound far more English than that as Hooten pushed the band in a more pop direction.

'In an act of Stalinism . . .' he jokes.

He'd barely joined the band when the press interest in the casual scene saw some bizarre offers.

'Bill Drummond [eventually to form the KLF] had a meeting with us and he was saying "I know what's going on" and went on to tell us that we should pose with bull terriers and go for the full look . . . we turned him down.'

It would be another six years before The Farm made it!

The other mid-eighties bands that were considered to be representatives of the lad culture, or maybe heirs to The Jam's throne, by the music press were the Housemartins (chiefly for frontman Paul Heaton's connections with the football subculture) and The Redskins who were considered to be a touch too close to the skin mod culture to be true representatives.

The Farm appeared on the Oxford Road Show in 1985, outsiders in the pop pantheon. They had a clutch of Peel sessions under their belt and a commitment to a tune-infused guitar rush but they were very much outsiders in the Live Aid-drenched mullet-rattling mid eighties.

Things were changing and the astute pop band was going to have to look for some added inspiration to crack the formula.

'We went to see Big Audio Dynamite and Don Letts was using a sampler. It made us think that we would have to do things differently. I was there with Simon Moran, who was sort of our manager, and I remember turning round to him and saying that was something that we should do.'

Moran himself went on from eventually managing The Farm to becoming the biggest promoter of the nineties.

As The Farm retreated to the rehearsal room in 1986 to work out how to get the new technology to work for them, the nascent lad culture was finding some key outlets for its expression away from the terraces.

Mid eighties

If Manchester was famous for the Hacienda, the club that was defining youth culture in Liverpool was the State. Key DJ Steve Procter was dealing a multi-musical mix that was combining all types of flavours.

This was the backdrop to scouse mid-eighties lad culture, a musical riot that included the king of soul, James Brown, The Clash's 'Magnificent 7', The Bunnymen and the Housemartins. It was an eclectic mix of pop. The club was packed with at least 1,000 people a time. It was spoken of in hushed tones but has dropped out of history due to a combination of Liverpool's lack of mainstream media connections and the city's keenness to keep itself to itself.

In the mid eighties Liverpool had entered a siege mentality. Politically further to the left than any other city in the UK, it took pride in its lone stance against Margaret Thatcher. Even if the people of the city were being somewhat duped by their council, the public themselves had real socialist hearts. Once the second richest city in the world just 70 years earlier, its dreadful decline since the Second World War had left it gutted and shattered, but it was still peopled with a proud population. No wonder it had its own way of conducting business.

Imagine the horror when the city down the road, Manchester, a mere 30 miles away, started to get hipper and richer. The former murky dark city of Manchester was now challenging Liverpool.

Since punk Manchester had had the biggest groups, the hippest club and their own big record label. At least Liverpool was still better at football and the fierce rivalry between the two cities manifested itself at the match – Liverpool and Man U matches were becoming fiercer and fiercer. It was the grudge match of the season and the tension was very noticeable. There were often rumbles. It was getting mean out there.

Away from the intensity of match day the dope-smoking scally scene was still holding sway. Groundpig were the key band. Dealing a set of Zappa and freakout out rock to a pot-smoking audience they became something of a phenomenon in the city. Playing round a tight circuit of pubs they caught on among the cognoscenti who were rebelling against the new casual uniform.

In Manchester there was a similar situation with the Happy Mondays. White scallies on dope! Times were changing. In the seventies, pot had been for hippies and freaks. Now it was filtering down to the street. After the 1981 riots the streets were awash with smack (conspiracy theories claim that this was deliberate to pacify the wild youth) but now dope was the key drug.

'People got into it because it was against the law!' laughs Hooten. 'It gave it a cutting-edge respectability.'

The dress code was getting odder: cord jackets were getting replaced by ski wear – all-in-one outfits – the precursors to the dreaded shell suit, usually one colour and emblazoned with motifs. It was a look copped from the streets of New York where the American city's sheer coldness demanded some extreme clothing. In Liverpool where it was nowhere near so cold, the clothes caught on because people liked them.

The Madchester explosion of '89 changed everything. It made the casual look, with a few baggy alterations, become the predominant look for the nineties. Manchester got the credit for the style and the swagger. It must have riled The Farm.

'Yeah, I remember *you* were on Radio Merseyside going on about the Roses and Mondays and how The Farm must be pissed off that the Manchester bands had stolen their thunder, you bastard!' cackles Hooten.

The Farm were galvanized into action. They could see that the Manchester bands were stealing their thunder. The street casual story that had been exclusively theirs for years was going thirty miles up the road to Manchester. The post Big Audio Dynamite electronic flavour to their music stood them in good stead when it came to cutting contemporary pop which dictated at least a nod to the electronic pulse of the acid house vibe.

'We already had "Groovy Train" together and a punkier version of "Stepping Stone". We even had "Altogether Now". We had the stuff. We were ready,' points out Peter Hooten.

They were in touch with Terry Farley, the London DJ who was making a name for himself on the acid house scene and was one of the faces behind London's hip as fuck *Boys Own* magazine. Farley had already been in touch with Hooten. After all, *Boys Own* was heavily inspired by *The End* – it had the same street culture interest. It was a clubs, good times, and football rock 'n' roll riot . . . except that it was from a Chelsea perspective.

'Terry Farley used to write to *The End* about how he wanted to start a mag like it and base it on clubs and fashion. *Boys Own* captured that moment in 1986 and '87 in clubs, fashion and records . . . At the time *The Face* would have it that everyone was dressing up when the opposite was true and *Boys Own* were detailing the club reality.'

The Farm went down to London to record with Terry Farley. The song they chose was 'Groovy Train' which was a twist on the Flaming Groovies' 'Shake Some Action', purloined by the band's tune writer Steve Grimes.

The Flaming Groovies are one of the great lost bands of rock 'n' roll. They cut a whole heap of great blissful pop songs like early Beatles guitar chimes with great harmonies. Somehow they were always out of time – the early seventies wasn't the place for this sort of palaver but if you like that sort of guitar pop then check them out and if your in a band definitely check them out as they have a whole heap of tunes for you to 'borrow'.

That February in 1990 Farley shackled 'Groovy Train' to a heavy heavy beat that he had half-inched off a then unknown import copy of Snap's 'The Power'.

In the studio the band were in a high state of excitement. They knew that they had a hit on their hands. They sat there with wide-boy manager Kev Sampson and co-manager Suggs from Madness conspiring how to blag the band to the big time. They didn't need to – the breakbeat was so damn infectious that after years in the doldrums The Farm found themselves with a big club hit. Especially in London where the trendy clubs were hammering it.

The Farm were now in. 'Groovy Train' made the Top 50. This was followed by a whole run of hits. They had to put up with accusations of jumping the bandwagon which was pretty ironic since they had been on this sort of tip for years but it wasn't something that unduly worried them.

'In the early nineties,' says Hooten, 'it was non-stop Madchester front covers on the NME. This made me really proud. It was great to see The Roses and The Mondays on *Top of The Pops* reinforcing what I'd maintained for years that this style can have a universal appeal. Not just in Liverpool – it had spread out. The Roses' debut is still one of my favourite records ever.'

The amount of Es getting dropped was changing not only pop, fashion and language but it was changing attitudes to football culture. There was a marked drop in the fighting at matches. It was nothing to do with the Tories' crazed schemes at crowd control. The pills were taking their effect along with different attitudes, as Hooten reminisces.

'During that period barriers were dropped. I do believe that something special was going on. It was a period when trouble stopped at matches. Hooliganism was not fashionable any more. I remember going to Manchester for a night out which would have been difficult in the mid eighties. I went round town with The Mondays contingent spending the night in dodgy clubs and instead of it being really heavy, people were just coming up and saying 'Alright scouse, ya bastard', just messing. It might have all been drug-induced but I'd rather have a happy pill than a load of violence . . .'

For a time the violence thing died out. It keeps making sporadic returns as a new highly sophisticated breed of hooligan takes full advantage of mobile phones, the Internet and pre-planning their rucks. Sometimes it's even good old-fashioned violence going off. Every now and then the tension returns but it seems a long way from the regular violence of the late seventies. As England found out to their cost during the World Cup in France when gangs of blubbery sunburnt guys regularly went on the rampage, the last true jobs are now supporting the national team.

The Farm fell apart in the mid nineties but the culture that they had championed for years in the previous decade was massive. Lad culture has become the dominant look of the nineties, swamping out rival cultures. It may have been pioneered in Liverpool but it took the Manchester bands to make it a national obsession. The non-stop run of groups from Manc all trading on their yob credentials and label conscious looks struck a chord in the UK.

John Harris, editor of *Select*, looks back on the lad decade:

'The nineties was about Oasis defining the way to be. We've had six years of it, being drunk and wearing ill-fitting sportswear. Everyone wanted to be the Manc male. It affected everyone – The Verve in 1992 arrived with an androgynous look, they fell in with Oasis and started looking like lads. They cut their hair and started wearing fishing hats!' he laughs. 'It affected everyone, every band. There's was no getting away! As pop pundit Jon Savage pointed out, "rock stars now have the same aesthetic as footballers".'

Casual culture rooted in the seventies and pioneered in the eighties has become the mainstream in the nineties. Baggied out maybe, a touch more designer labelled, but it's still the same schtick that Peter Hooten was writing about in *The End* nearly fifteen years ago. It's an aesthetic that was neatly captured by one of the big success stories of the nineties – *Loaded*.

CHAPTER FOUR

LOADED

'I wanna get loaded, I wanna get high' goes the dialogue that kicks off Primal Scream's generational anthem, 1990's 'Loaded'. Naturally the song became the title of the key magazine of the decade.

***Loaded* was a men's magazine that owned up to the truth. A truth that men's lifestyles were more concerned about good times than the stiff fake New Man crap that the other titles had been peddling in the eighties. By owning up, *Loaded* started a revolution . . .**

Subsequently it's been ripped off by nearly every magazine on the shelves, from fitness mags to women's mags to all the other men's mags . . .

Loaded editor James Brown's Britain was a country of football, pubs, all-night parties, cheeky quips, crap sitcoms, great pop, *Carry On*s, and endless in jokes – in other words it was the real Britain . . .

When *Loaded* was launched many thought it was going to be an obvious flop. But there was a huge yawning gap in the market for some beery irreverence. It just needed someone to actually get off their arse to fill that gap.

Loaded has became a nineties publishing phenomenon. Hardly a magazine gets printed nowadays without some of *Loaded*'s flavour, half-inched and slapped into it. From the funny, snidey picture captions to the lightweight yobbishness bleeding through the articles, it's become a snapshot of what nineties culture was really about. Spread the covers of *Loaded* across your floor – not only will it make your room look a bit of a mess but the run of cover stars will sum up the key cultural points that are dotted across the landscape . . . from Homer Simpson to Prince Naseem – many of these people never had magazine covers before, the olde world of men's mags was too stuffy to even think about the likes of the Simpsons being of any cultural worth.

But then *Loaded* was coming from a very different angle. The firebrand ex-music journalist editor James Brown had cut his teeth on his own excellent cut and paste fanzine *Attack On Bzag* in the mid eighties – a perfect breeding ground for wilful individualism.

At the time Brown was a spiky kid, brimful of enthusiasm and ambition. Sharp and intelligent, he would turn up at gigs in Leeds with a sackful of fanzines and a bigger sackful of attitude and spunk – from the start he would piss people off with his cheeky irreverence and full on gobshite style. *Bzag*, his initial assault on the world of media, was a rapid-fire rush of wit and enthusiasm covering everything from the underground assaults of the post-punk rock outfits like the 3 Johns, Nightingales, The Membranes, early Creation and post-punk rock, while taking in writers like Hunter S. Thomson and John Belushi. It was interspersed with crazed drawings and wackoid one liners and helped to hold the line against eighties' conformism along with Everett True's *The Legend* and your author's *Rox* fanzine in a self-styled 'clique against the bleak'. It was a cultural war and we were not going to be defeated. Brown moved from his hometown of Leeds and spent time in Manchester where he started stringing for *Sounds* before moving to London in 1987 and becoming the enfante terrible of the NME.

Looking back now, Brown sees the nineties as a victory for the staunch underground resistance we were all fighting at the time.

'Oasis were the victory at the end of a long battle. It took a long time but the non-manufactured pop scene was the result of people working a long time in the underground. People like Alan McGee had been working hard at breaking it big before Oasis with bands like Primal Scream and the Mary Chain.'

Writing a fanzine may have been good for cutting your teeth, but it wasn't going to start a revolution. Now on the NME, Brown was making a name for himself with an abrasive approach. He was nearly made editor in the early nineties. But his caustic attitude (occasional fisticuffs and a ready quip) had made too many enemies and he was looked over only to re-emerge at the helm of the much-touted new lads' mag *Loaded*.

Straight from launch, *Loaded* was an instant sensation. As Brown points out, its formula was an honest and sharp summation of the new fractured environment of the times.

'Loaded reflected the culture of the times. I wanted to create a magazine that was not there before. Create something that crystallized what a lot of people were feeling and when it went on to be a big influence on other magazines I was proved right. *Loaded* was the first magazine for a long time that was familiar with the way its readers felt.' Not since perhaps the *Sun* and primetime *Smash Hits* was there a mag that was in tune with its readers. Brown, when he moved on to the upper echelons of the men's mag world at GQ in 1997, was quick to blow his own trumpet. His detractors had to keep schtum. They knew that he was right. 'When I went on to edit GQ I told them that *Loaded* had had the same impact as when the electric guitar came out and made the acoustic guitar superfluous . . . it just couldn't be heard anymore!'

Mary Ann Hobbs, the Radio One DJ who used to work at *Loaded*, feels the magazine captured the flavour of the decade.

'The nineties started with *Loaded*. That was really interesting. All that desperate uptight eighties hypocritical rhetoric crashed. It would be really interesting to go back and look at old-style mags. You'd audibly laugh at the weary culture. *Loaded* fucked it up the arse! It detonated the whole thing in one fell swoop . . .

'There was nothing genuine about New Man eighties idealism. In the nineties you can be open about what you do. People have become a lot more tolerant. In the eighties pretending to be perfect was a total fallacy. *Loaded* exploded on to this scene. The magazines before were a joke! Who lives like this! No one I know! *Loaded*'s impact was the same as when the musical barriers came crashing down!'

James Brown sees the nineties as when popular culture went haywire. A decade when all different strands combined into one gloriously messy whole. He pinpoints the moment when he feels this all coalesced.

'The first key moment of the nineties for me was New Order's 'E For England' record. The mixture of a debauched comedian, a group that were a bunch of drug goblins and the England team. It pulled together three of my favourite interests. And that was what I went on to do with the magazine. Just putting together football, comedy, clubs and music and I had that New Order audience in my mind when I put it together. The sort of people who liked what was almost an effeminate sort of music, not like heavy metal . . . not macho music, but with a football mentality.'

Brown, along with magazine publisher Alan Lewis, had spotted a gap in the market. The nineties, like every new decade, had thrown up its own set of possibilities. Post acid house, the old rules didn't apply any more. The new generation were less interested in getting their information from specialist sources. If *Loaded* covered a bit of everything in a fast and loose manner, then perfect.

The post house generation were not just into one thing. Older generations had been into just punk or mod or football. But Brown could spot a new way of thinking that was emerging. Couple this with the old-style men's magazines that seemed so stuck in an eighties groove with their slavish, metropolitan West End worlds and out of touch witterings and you had the chance for an unexploded grenade to go off, as James Brown points out:

'It was now more acceptable to be into different things. It was about enjoying yourself whatever you were into. If you liked Kiss the band, pinball machines and rowing with a bottle of brandy and a pocket full of grass then that was cool and that was what we set out to write about.'

The Britain that *Loaded* launched itself into was a very different place than it had been in the mid eighties. There was a new confidence in the air. Britain was no longer the self-deprecating nation that it had been in the eighties.

Brown detected the vibe. 'Things had changed. Even in sport there had been some great moments. Instead of getting knocked out of the World Cup before the finals, England and Ireland had done very well in the 1990 World Cup. And Prince Naseem was a world beater. This was so different from the eighties when losers like Eddie The Eagle were national heroes.'

From Eddie The Eagle to David Beckham, from a wally that came last in downhill skiing who spoke shite and looked like a dick to a world-beating pretty boy who was hip, cool and married to one of the world's biggest pop stars.

The eighties sucked.

In the nineties life was more fun, the debauchery that had been for the elite few in the sixties was now on the streets. Of course some people got fucked up and of course there was still grinding poverty but for your normal fella times were a lot better. *Loaded* documented all of this and that's why it was massive. Britain was learning how to party.

There were cool clubs in every town and city. Brown recalls great nights in places as far flung as the Shetlands and Exeter. After acid house people were partying big style, drugs were floating around everywhere. In the eighties only rock stars and freaks took drugs. Now everyone was on that tip. Dope smoking, E popping, lager swilling, training shoe-clad Saturday nights in house clubs. Rock 'n' roll loving geezers who went to the football and shagged around. If that was the nineties for you then *Loaded* was your bible. It threw the traditional magazine roles into the air. The NME was primarily a music paper and the rest of the men's mags were still chasing the New Man myth.

Loaded was the men's mag that walked it like it talked it. It spoke in the language of the bars and clubs of the UK.

'I wanted the writing in *Loaded* to be like listening to the most entertaining bloke in the pub who had done a lot of interesting things and was really good at talking about them. I wanted it to be new writers who hadn't written for men's mags before and who would write with enthusiasm and in an exciting way. People who understood what was going on.'

Writers like Martin Deeson and Jon Wilde made their names on *Loaded*. It maintained the right enviroment for its irreverent creativity, the office was like a den, casual tomfoolery was the order of the day, most of the key decisions were made in the pub and there was a complete lack of earnestness. As hung over and 'mad for it' as their readers, *Loaded*'s circulation seemed to double every month. But then Brown was living the lifestyle of those readers, Like all the successful nineties mags he was not only knocking about in the same pubs and clubs as his subscribers but he was reporting it back to them in their language. A new language for a new decade.

'I was going to clubs like Back To Basics in Leeds and I noticed that it was full of men not covered in men's magazines. People were leading a hedonistic lifestyle. In the nineties the punters became the stars – it was a knock on from acid house . . . when dance music exploded all over the country it completely changed the way people thought and did things. Decadence and debauchery were in now. They were there for everyone and not just for Led Zeppelin! Britain was now being led by DJs and drug dealers!'

Loaded perfectly captured the vibe of the decade and it was paying off big style. Within six months it had gone from being the nineties mirror to nineties totem. 'Loaded lad' was a sociological term. Men and women's magazines were putting funny captions under their pictures (something Brown had been doing since his *Bzag* days) and nicking whole chunks of editorial from the mag. But *Loaded* was miles ahead, its stars were the people's stars – the front cover, always the key battleground in publishing, was a million miles away from the men's mag norm.

'Their covers were all – what was considered to be – very strong role models for British men at the time. We had people like Frank Skinner, Gazza, Suggs, Paul Weller and Oasis on the cover. Before that men's magazines had the likes of Will Carling or Tim Robbins or loads of American actors. They always had men who were smartly dressed. It was like they were living in a really stupid world.'

In 1999 the cutting edge of men's culture is sold through the men's magazines. Post-*Loaded* magazine success stories like FHM are even outselling the initial market leader and specialist magazines are trapped in a ratings war. The *Loaded* effect has been one of the key strands of the decade.

CHAPTER FIVE

IBIZA

If ecstasy was the fuel and acid house the soundtrack then Ibiza was the spark. The tiny Balearic island in the Mediterranean was the unlikely spot that completely changed British pop culture and music for ever.

Dealing in that escapist dream of drinking and shagging by the Mediterranean, Ibiza is the perfect escape from the too grey Blighty hometowns. It's not hard to sell a dream in these conditions. Throw in some hippie flavours and a dedication to hedonism and you've got some sort of ingredients for a youth movement.

Even with all these factors, it's still amazing how the whole thing coalesced and exploded from the Bland and on through a slumbering late eighties British culture.

For years it had been a holiday spot. A cheap bunk-up in the sun. One of those Blackpool in the Med style places where you could turn yerself lobster-red, drink lager and get laid with no strings attached. A one-week escape from grey days UK. Ibiza was just another one of those sleepy south European enclaves that from the mid sixties onwards was redeveloped to meet the demand of a new breed of jet-set tourists with little interest in the local culture.

Small villages were turned wholesale into concrete leisure zones heavily themed towards the sort of fun pub/chip-shop/Brits-on-the-piss backdrop that we as a nation curiously seem to enjoy. The island went from a backwater of 30,000 people to a festering holiday sweatbox of half a million sun and sangria worshippers. It was bawdy and wild and it was a sun-soaked escape.

Encouraged by Spanish fascist leader Franco, Ibiza was a money-making holiday hot spot. Not quite so encouraged by the old man was the looser attitude that would inevitably come in the wake of mass tourism. A motley crew of people were attracted to the island. Draft dodgers, hippies and the bohemians joined the gay scene in enjoying the laxer atmosphere (mainland Spain wouldn't even allow couples to kiss in the street!) and an undercurrent of boho action was established.

The hippies with all their free-love baggage gave the island the flavour that it still enjoys today. They would prattle on about Ibiza being on a fault line and having a bedrock of quartz giving it a 'special vibe'. The hippies dug free love and, well, free everything. They planted the seed that would eventually flourish in the last few months of the eighties – the least hippyish decade known to man.

A club scene had been on the up and up since the early seventies. Amnesia was considered the best, the main DJ was Alfredo, an Argentinean who had fled after the 1976 coup. His eclectic turntable tastes pretty much paved the way for what has become known as Balearic.

The club already had a long history. Opened in the early seventies, along with Pacha, it was a hip haunt. Freak guitar music and reggae were the soundtrack. They eventually succumbed to the disco regime of the late seventies albeit in an ostentatious manner. All fountains and extravagant decors, it was over the top and plain wild compared to the burger and chip joints of Doncaster High Street. The clientele were even wilder. Not for them the handbag shuffle. These were Euro show-offs. Flash and beautiful. Partying till the dawn. Making the clubs back home look dullard in comparison.

The music was upbeat and the drugs were wild. Stoned on acid, coke or mescaline (a warmer more natural buzz than the harsher chemical rush of E) the island partygoers were hip to any changes in the bohemian head trip code. Ecstasy started to infiltrate the scene in the early eighties and was a perfect accompaniment to what was going down. Groups of young Brits were cottoning on to the action as early as the mid eighties. The London suburbs kids started to congregate on the island getting off on the hedonistic good times in the boisterous 24-hour up-for-it party way that only the Brits can.

South Londoners Trevor Fung and Ian St Paul had been travelling to the island since 1980 and they were so enamoured with the place that they had set up their own bar, The Project, in 1987. The Project swiftly became the focal point for all the Brits who, by word of mouth, were discovering the action that was going down in the Med.

The word had started to filter out. There was a great party scene going down on Ibiza. The Project geezers invited some of their London mates over. Upcoming hip hop DJ Paul Oakenfeld (who had been started on the turntables by Fung back in '81) came over to celebrate his 26th birthday. With him he brought a bunch of mates, funk DJ Johnny Walker and Nicky Holloway (who was running soul weekenders with his Special Branch organization). Also along for the ride was Ibiza veteran Danny Rampling, an Old Kent Road soul DJ.

They arrived in Ibiza expecting it to be like the UK . All one club, one music, cool clientele and tight rules of behaviour. They arrived in the middle of a flood of Es. Swiftly turned on to the new drug they were taken to Amnesia.

They were blown away with the club's amazing MDMA fuelled atmosphere and DJ Alfredo's Balearic musical mix – perhaps the starting point to that very nineties thing – the massively eclectic music tastes that dominate the decade's record collections. In short, it was nothing like the clubs back in Britain. After spending their whole holiday getting blown away every night in Amnesia, Rampling for one elected to return home to London and recreate the same sort of atmosphere. Oakenfeld had already tried to do it before in the mid eighties but no one had got it, the music wasn't what his demanding clientele wanted and there was no E to soothe the troubled punter.

But this time maybe the conditions would be more favourable. Amnesia had definitely shown the way forward. It showed that the right music, the right people and the right chemicals could create an amazing party . . . for fuck's sake, who wouldn't be hooked!

The crucial four had had their minds blown. They couldn't just leave this dream on an island in the Mediterranean. They were determined to bring it back to London with them.

Sod the miserable weather, they were going to bring a bit of that holiday sunshine into Blighty.

Things were never going to be the same again. House music was already getting played in London but it took the full-on party vibe (and the added E) to pump it through the roof. The Ibiza experience was to ignite British youth culture. It has made Ibiza itself one of the buzz words of the nineties. The island represents the holy grail of house culture and it has benefited accordingly. After acid house exploded in the UK it was re-exported back to Ibiza. Especially after Flying's legendary jaunt there in 1990, when a combination of cutting edge DJs and bands (Farm, 808 State etc.) partied like bastards. From then on, throughout the nineties, it has become a totem for wild times, complete with the accompanying drugs shock horror headlines from the hypocritical tabloid killjoys of the Fleet Street press.

At the end of the decade, with clubs like the splendidly over-the-top Manumission, Ibiza has become the focal point for the Euro party scene. Some say that it has become tacky but the endless hedonistic tales that pour back from the island point to the good times of which the place has now become symbolic.

For the whole of the nineties ravers returned with a fistful of wild party tales, wild-eyed with enthusiasm and buzzed up on the decadence that everyone needs in their lives.

The magic of Ibiza had ingrained itself as deeply on them as it had done on the four mates from London. They may have gone to Ibiza for a week off but they were profoundly shaken up by the good times that were inherent there. Whereas most people come back from their Mediterranean holidays with a crappy hat or some badly taken photos, they had come back with a new way of life. When Oakenfeld and Rampling and their buddies returned from Ibiza in 1987 they did more than unpack their bags . . . they unpacked a social revolution.

CHAPTER SIX

ACID HOUSE

Pre acid, the house scene already existed albeit in a specialist underground sense.

There were associated scenes. Electronic music was already the club staple. B-Boy culture had made inroads, hip kids were digging rap . . . There were sound systems that had been in existence since the reggae days with MCs doing their stuff over records. There were key black dance collectives like Shock and Soul II Soul, and there was already a dance music underground.

But it wasn't like Ibiza . . .

It didn't have that crazed party edge to hook into. House music had made a few inroads – you could hear it in gay clubs where it fitted in neatly as the next up-tempo dance style after hi energy. At first you would hear it out and about in '87 and confuse it with hi energy, just a little less cluttered and a little bit more on the bass drum.

Underground radio stations were playing house. It was there seeping through. Already it had its own hit records with Farley 'Jackmaster' Funk's 'Love Can't Turn Around' (Top 10 in August '86) and Steve 'Silk' Hurley's 1987 'Jack Your Body' (No. 1).

As early as January 1988 London Records were releasing 'acid house' compilations, Graeme Park was playing house at the Garage in Nottingham and Mike Pickering was playing Chicago Trax and other early house in Manchester.

Graeme Park's DJ career tells the story of the subtle changeovers that would happen before the acid breakthrough. He worked in Nottingham's fab Selectadisc record shop (always worth checking out, they sell some pretty amazing records at even more amazing prices). Selectadisc ran a reggae night at the Ad Lib club in Nottingham and Park got his first gig DJ-ing there. As the years rolled by he would mix hip hop and electro into his sets before becoming one of the first house DJs in the country. He arrived at The Hacienda via Sheffield's Leadmill and it was here that he would make his name as one of the key pioneer DJs.

There were also DJs making house-influenced crossover hit records. Mark Moore with his S Express had had a run of great glam pop hits, starting with April 1988's 'Theme From S Express' (No. 1). Over the next year Moore's project were *Top Of The Pops* regulars, their colourful take on pop an obvious precursor to the house explosion.

S Express were part of a late-eighties scene of outfits that were taking advantage of the new technology which had dropped drastically in price. All the talk of the time was just what effect four-track samplers and computers were going to have on music when they hit the street.

Outfits like Coldcut, M/A/R/R/S and Bomb The Bass proved that you didn't have to get a band together to get your songs moving. Hip hop had shown the way with samples and breakbeats, proving that pop could be constructed from the scraps of other people's songs. Now with the same sort of technology on the streets, anyone with a fistful of ideas and a few hundred quid could assemble a song. And what a bunch of hits they cut.

The scenario was set. Music was changing. It just needed coalescing, galvanizing.

Acid house goes to London

The crucial four returned to too-grey Blighty from Ibiza on a mission, their mission was to keep that fantastic holiday vibe going back in London . . .

The club scene in the eighties had been caught in a spiral of exclusivity. The 'style' decade had been about trendy specialist clubs playing rare groove or soul. There wasn't much fun to be had in the nocturnal British scene. With their minds blown by the Ibiza experience, the crew returned to London. They were hooked to the house beat. They wanted to carry on dancing – but where?

They would go to gay clubs like Delirium because that was the only place they could find that played the records they craved. They looned about in the corner buzzing on the Es, dressed in their hippie casual crossover look, hair scraped back into pony tales, acting the goat, puzzling the style-conscious club clientèle.

They felt like outsiders. It was obvious that they should start their own clubs off to get the vibe the way that they wanted, to try and recreate a bit of Ibiza in sarf London.

Oakenfeld and St Paul started the Project Club on Streatham High Road, recreating the Ibiza vibe late into the night until they got busted by the cops. They invited down the posse from *Boys Own* magazine and starting to create the network of names that would dominate the early days of the house scene.

You just have to look at the names of the editors of *Boys Own* to see a rollcall of prime movers of the acid house scene: Andy Weatherall and Terry Farley, the two key DJs and remixers of the period, Steve Mayes and Cymon Eckel.

The influence of *Boys Own* magazine on today's dance press means that the mag still gets props from people like Ben Turner, editor of *Muzik* magazine:

'*Boys Own* magazine was really important. I worshipped everything that it was saying . . . their logos, their attitude and references.'

The new vibe was about to coalesce with spectacular results . . . In November 1997 Danny Rampling found a space at a fitness centre near Southwark Gym, billing it as Klub Sch-oom (as in the rush you get off an E). The first night wasn't purely house, they mixed it with funk, Rampling and Carl Cox played the house stuff. Within weeks it had mushroomed into Shoom, creating the whole acid house mythology. For starters they came up with the logo that would define the whole subculture. Their flyers were decorated with the smiley face taken from Alan Moore's Watchman comics.

The smiley became the symbol of acid house. It looked stoned. Pretty vacant. It even looked like a pill. The smiley was the perfect symbol for the E generation. Soon it was everywhere. On every flyer. On T-shirts. Spray-canned on walls. Even beaming out from the pages of the *Sun* before they realized they were backing the dreaded drug culture. If you want a snapshot of the times you can't go far wrong by looking at the smiley.

Shoom quickly developed its own mythology. From the football thugs holding hands cliché to the warm glow of being loved up, punters' inhibitions would literally melt. You could feel the childlike glee of the clubbers in the warm womblike cocoon of the E'd up vibe. Everyone was loved up. Christ, they were even taking teddy bears down there with them . . . This was quite a different club experience. Even the way that they danced – jabbing sets of shapes into the warm moist sweaty atmosphere, would become the dance of the nineties. If acid house had been bandied around as a term before, it now made perfect sense. This was fried. This was acid.

The clubbers were now togged out in that kinda hippie way, loose and baggy, hair getting longer. But these were nineties hippies, they could get their hands on the drugs with far more ease, and were far more cynical, more realistic than their dippy cultural forefathers. This was an inner-city take on the whole sixties ethic. Sure enough they were talking love and peace – that's what E did to you (*Boys Own* were even talking about handing out flowers outside their beloved Chelsea – surely the first sign of E chilling out the terraces).

From Shoom onwards in small clubs in London, house music was soundtracking something new and something strange. With ecstasy chucked on top it was mutating into a whole new pop culture . . .

The next key club night was opened by Paul Oakenfeld – Future, at Sanctuary kicked off in April 1988. Future (which became Spectrum when it moved to Heaven later that year), with its pyrotechnics, full-on special effects and laser beams, was the precursor of the acid house club experience and the superclubs of the late nineties.

In '88 Shoom and Spectrum were setting the agenda, creating the scene that virtually engulfed the UK in the next couple of years. From being well-kept secrets for the Ibiza bon viveurs the clubs were fast becoming victims of their own success. If there is a good party in town it's pretty inevitable that it's going to get oversubscribed. If you hear there's a place where some neat drugs, wild clothes and mad records are going down, you're going to be there aren't you? No messin'.

A Spring article in ID was the first national press the acid house scene had had. Its references to acieeeed and other slang terms chucked the phrases into the popular parlance. Before it had been a secret. Now it was in open territory. Acid house was on the verge of becoming a full-on pop craze with all the attendant press hysteria and misunderstanding that that entails . . .

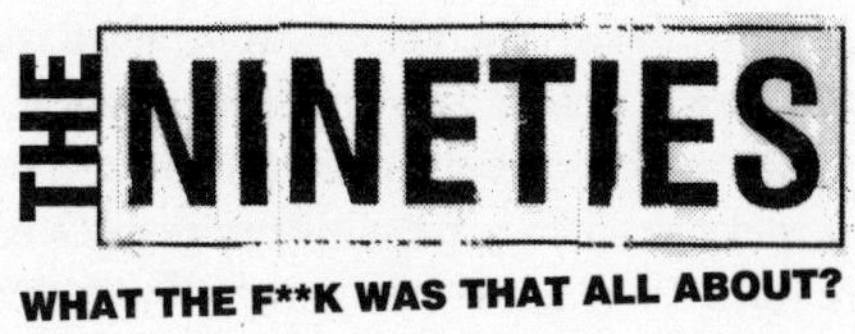

CHAPTER SEVEN

DRUGS

Greasing the wheels of the pop scene, drugs have always been a controversial lifestyle choice. In the nineties the drug culture went super nova. After acid house they became acceptable to everyone except for the authorities who had little or no idea about how to deal with this mass explosion . . .

When E finally arrived on the scene in the late eighties it created a cultural havoc not seen for years. If there is one thing that blew the pop complacency apart at the end of the decade it was the sudden arrival of the 'love drug' as a mainstream pastime in the UK. Shifts in youth culture come with shifts in drugs. Drugs are the key to any change in pop. They are the catalyst and the fuel. You switch your chemicals and the whole world will shift with you.

Ecstasy, when it finally arrived good and proper with its new attendant soundtrack of acid house, changed the very fabric of the UK forever. It transformed the way we thought, dressed, accessed music and it changed the way we fucked with our minds and bodies. Ecstasy blew the drugs wars into a fully blown big league that it had never contemplated before.

The key word in any debate about drugs is hypocrisy. It's about booze-swilling moral guardians busting and banning people whose choice of poison is different from theirs. From the *News of the World* exposing high-profile drug-takers left, right and centre to other media hypocrites on their puritanical soap boxes, they, along with other similar occupiers of the moral high ground, had destroyed the careers of people from *Blue Peter* presenters to

England rugby captains. It was a sign of how prevalent drugs were in the nineties that these previous bastions of so-called respectability were now hanging out with the chemical generation.

Meanwhile New Labour showed no signs of decriminalizing marijuana. It's like no-one in Parliament or the media has ever done any drugs. The fact that Tony Blair listened to Genesis in his 'wild' youth without ever taking in any drugs at all is totally terrifying.

The drugs don't work, or do they?

Pop music is about drugs. There, we said it. Got it out the way. It's about the drugs you take or the drugs you don't take. Drugs have affected every move or change in pop: hippies and acid, punks and speed, house and E, nearly every fake celeb and media whore in the late nineties and cocaine. A new chemical means a new culture. Whether that's good or bad or right or wrong is beside the question.

It's the way that things are.

The very sound and shape of the music and the attendant clothes are influenced by the chemical ingestion. The late sixties were tinged with LSD, while punk was speed and lager (and dope but no one mentioned that in case they got laughed at for being hippies). Drugs are part of human nature. Altered states: Blow yer mind. Just to go somewhere else. That's the appeal. From the boring suburb afternoons to the escape from the shitty hi-rise inner cities, they are an escape route.

For some people they are also a swift exit to an early death or mental illness, while for others they are the life-affirming turning point. For most they are a couple of fucked up years – a chemical passage of rites. Everyone takes them or talks about them and no one ever wonders why – 'just say yes' to the peer pressure and you're as big a schmuck as the anti-drug lobby.

Drugs have been filtering down to the mainstream for years from the sixties explosion onwards. School days in the late seventies saw a handful of druggies. Most people just got pissed on the legally available drug – booze.

In the early eighties after the riots the streets were flooded with cheap smack. It fucked a lot of people up but it stopped them causing trouble – that was the cynical theory anyway. Drugs were 'a problem' but not a mass phenomenon. If you wanted to go somewhere where people took a lot of drugs you would have to go to Holland. In the UK getting plastered in the pub was about as transcendental as it got. Alcohol brought its own problems with it:

chronic illness, violence, car smashes, wife beatings – all the sort of stuff that comes hand in hand with the 'respectable' government endorsed demon drink – raged across the nation.

Let's face it, you can't imagine a football riot fuelled by marijuana or even LSD. It was the legal drug that was fucking everyone up!

Society has got a funny attitude about drugs. While some drugs are the work of the devil – Satan's little powders – some are not only legal but virtually forced down your neck. From mid teens onwards there is a lot of pressure to drink and smoke. Advertising, coupled with pub culture (and let's face it, where else is there to go in the UK?) and peer pressure, demands a drinking mentality.

Try to be a non-drinker on a night out and you'll understand the constant pressure to booze it up like a 'real' man. Oddly our old mate 'getting pissed' is quite possibly the worst drug there is. Up to 30,000 people die a year from drink-related incidents and ask anyone who works in the casualty department of a hospital what a Saturday night is like and they'll wearily relate you tales of drunken blokes (and it is mainly blokes) wounded in fights. Fucked up in gutters, unpeeled from lampposts after drink-driving or their wives kicked to fuck when they get home sodden with drink. Worra laff!

Occasionally there may be a drug fuck up, a smack overdose or an ecstasy nightmare but, compared with alcohol's never-ending roll-call of pain and disorientation, it's a rare event. Coupled with alcohol is the nation's premier source of cancer, cigarettes. The two often go, quite literally, hand in hand. Heavy-duty advertising, insidious sponsorship of sport (hey, we're so healthy!) and an attached coolness make the products irresistible. People like getting smashed and people like smoking. That's cool. Whatever gets you through the night and all that.

By now you'd have to be a complete idiot not to understand the inherent health risks of the products. Alcohol has always been popular. It's part of the culture. The old British stereotype of the stiff-upper-lipped gentleman and his brolly has been replaced by the far more accurate image of the fat beer-swilling balding yob, staggering around in crap shorts and trainers with no socks at the big Eurofootball events. A sunburnt gut and fuzzy tatts.

That's booze for you, it makes you beautiful!

Strange then that cigarettes and alcohol are completely legal while all other drugs are still under the cosh. New Labour even went as far as appointing Keith Halliwell, the 'drug czar', to help conduct the vote-winning 'war against drugs'. A war that they can't possibly win if walking around my block of flats is any evidence to go by, with staggering smack heads and dope fiends the fucked up downside of the 'drug revolution'.

It was ecstasy that blew the whole debate wide open. Before its mass popularity drugs had been the preserve of the bohemian freaks and the smacked-out losers with fucked-up lives in the UK's dead-end estates. In the eighties, drugs were pretty unfashionable. Post-punk puritanism meant that drug-taking was something that was lied about in pop culture. It was something that people did but they didn't mention too much. Cocaine floated around some corners of the pop scene. There was the Apocalypse Now of acid and a small-scale interest in marijuana on the casual scene. Smack had been all over the streets after the 1981 riots but was again confined to desperadoes.

But drugs were for freaks. They were not a mainstream concern. After E the attitude to drugs on the street became massively relaxed. Everyone seemed to be smoking draw, cocaine was in the clubs, smack was casually used 'to knock the edge off the coke or the E'. The only drugs that didn't seem to have a renaissance were acid and speed which seemed to be the forgotten substance in the late nineties.

Ecstasy had been around for years. Like all modern drugs it enjoys a long and strange history from being formulated in the lab to hitting the streets . . . In the early eighties Mark Almond and a coterie of friends had experimented with the then unknown drug. It was known in clubs but via Ibiza the connection was made between house and the drug. It was a powerful bond that melded the two together.

The other drug of the decade is cocaine. In the eighties it was the yuppie drug, sneered at by most of the pop world (although there were plenty of sniffers). Come the nineties and going to the toilets has taken on a whole different complexion, cubicles are jammed with people sniffing and snorting. Anyone uncool enough to drop in for more traditional bog business was treading on away turf. Risking filthy looks from the new kings of the porcelain!

In the nineties there were codes that had to be understood! Cocaine seems to be everywhere. It's the bonding agent in the hurly-burly worlds of media and pop. It makes people with no confidence perk up with a fake swagger.

Coke makes you talk fast and loose. It also makes you talk shit.

Perfect in its context.

Crack, the cocaine derivative, hit the streets big in the early nineties. With its instant high followed by a mean low and its intense addiction, crack takes drugs to a new level. 'Once you're in the crack zone you're hungry for more,' related a friend. It created a hunger that could only be fuelled by getting more. Crack was associated with a big rise in the crime rate, especially in American cities where it was far more prevalent.

Mean drugs that fucked you up always lurked in the dark corners of club land. Ketamine – a powerful sedative (special K in club parlance), either shoved up your nose or down your gob – is the nastiest of the new breed of drugs. There was also GHB which was used on the eighties body-building scene to pump up muscles. Neither were much fun but still float around.

While some drugs became highly fashionable, some fell out of favour. It's a rarity in these chemical days to hear of anyone dropping acid or a bag of magic mushrooms. Maybe hallucinogenics were too difficult to party on. You can't swank around a designer bar with a head full of psychedelic visions. Drugs had changed their function. Instead of being 'mind-expanding' (now that's debatable: most acid heads I've met hardly seem to have had their minds expanded) club drugs were now for celebration or obliteration.

The smack heads cluttering up the stairwells of my flats are looking for a way out. Wrecked on the brown, they are blotting out the world. Smack has been on the rise since the post-riots drop in its street price in 1981 when, after the streets of the UK were alive with the near anarchy of the rioting youth, they were suddenly swamped in heroin in the aftermath. Since then it's been percolating through the generations.

Despite the array of 'just say no' campaigns and pretty laughable posters of spotty kids on drugs, the smack habit held strong. No longer the decadent preserve of rock stars, it was the ultimate fucked-up street-kid drug . . . Post acid house its allure has been as strong as ever.

In the rock world it was big on the grunge scene, hovering like an evil black cloud over many musicians. Famous for their habits were Kurt and Courtney: while the latter was tuff enough to break the spell, Kurt Cobain shot himself a week after absconding from a drug clinic. And still no-one learned! There were a whole shit-load of users who burned out under the spell of the drug. Nobody ever learns. It may be the most cosseted comfortable high in the world but the way it rips your life apart, the dreadful craving and emptiness that it leaves behind – fuck, is it worth it?

Is there anyone left in the pop scene who is innocent of the risks? Speed, which had been the big drug in the punk days, still hovered on the edge of the drug scene. The poor man's coke, though, was gradually usurped by the more readily available cocaine. Smoked in its crystalline form, speed is known as ice and produces an explosive and fucked up high, lasting for hours. The comedown is too mean to mention.

Drugs, which once had been the label of the freaks, were now the pastime of every Saturday-night piss artist. Ecstasy dominates nineties culture. It changed the way that people danced, dressed, socialized – it heralded bar culture. It changed the way that people went out. It had its own slang and it totally shifted pop into a new universe.

Without ecstasy, there would be no acid house, no travellers, no New Age protesters, no Madchester, no Prodigy, no Oasis . . . On the other hand there would also be no pointless teenage overdoses or no huge out-of-control drug culture.

Before ecstasy, Britain shut at midnight, clubs were for wallies and pop was jammed in a cul de sac. The cities were dead. There was fuck all to do.

Drugs are intrinsic to the human condition. People have always taken them. People are always curious about them, and people always get in a mess with them. It's got to the stage now when people think you're not rock 'n' roll if you don't take drugs.

Stupid talk! Choose your poison but don't let anyone else choose it for you.

The story of the decade is the proliferation of drugs. The debate rages back and forth. The only difference now is that the defenders of the moral high ground have probably dabbled as well. The only solution is decriminalization. It's time to face the truth – people take drugs and they like them.

Let's just make sure that no one gets fucked up on them.

CHAPTER EIGHT

HAPPY MONDAYS

I interviewed The Happy Mondays on their 1999 comeback tour. This piece expands on the interview and captures the sheer buzz of the 1989 breakthrough of the one band that really captured the E-fuelled acid house flavour for the 'indie' nation. Coining the 'Madchester' phrase, The Happy Mondays, ramshackle anarchic nature perfectly mirrored the vibe on the UK streets – the money-making, drug-taking, living-for-kicks and baggy-clothed UK of the decade . . .

It's hard to believe now but it's a decade since Madchester took the pop world in a surge of loose clobber, street swagger, wild drugs and great pop. It was the most important burst of rock 'n' roll action since the punk days and set the blueprint for nineties UK guitar pop. Its echoes still resound to this very day. And what better tenth birthday present for the baggy Madchester party than the ultimate freaky party band reforming.

The Happy Mondays were back out on the circuit, selling more tickets than they had ever done before. Selling out the Manchester Evening News Arena is a far bigger deal than the GMex shows of yore – the 9,000 tickets went in just an hour. In 1999 the Happy Mondays are big bucks. It's a combination of nostalgia, reputation and great rock 'n' roll that's putting those older, fatter bums on the seats.

It will also keep their label, London, happy. The greatest hits album followed hot on the heels of their comeback hit single, a loose cover of Thin Lizzy's classic 'The Boys Are Back In Town' and there is talk of cutting a brand new album.

In the late eighties and early nineties The Happy Mondays were putting a raw street funk into the charts. They were also a consummate pop group, knocking out classic singles with ease. They played gigs that were euphoric parties or neat excuses to get completely cained to a great rock 'n' roll soundtrack.

Their role in Manchester's musical evolution is of tantamount importance. Shaun and Bez, the working-class bohemians, doing drugs and bunking off around Europe, escaping grey old Manc and doing what the fuck they liked, were pioneering the Manc role model that would be the nineties male stereotype. Sat in their E corner in the Hacienda bringing the new drug into town. Turning people on. They were at the forefront of the city's dance explosion. Being the freakiest dancers on the scene, they ignited the Hacienda and the whole of the city. Maybe for The Mondays it was more a case of cashing in than turning on, but suddenly the city went all wonky and everyone was celebrating the powerful rush of this fab new drug.

The Happy Mondays made music that sounded like no-one else: a demented mixture of funkadelic, funk, northern soul, punk rock, indie and disco – a ragbag of influences all slapped together in a stunning whole. Shaun Ryder's lyrics were sheer ruff-arsed poetry: funny, mean, perceptive and always spat out in a north Manc vernacular. Some lines were swiped off other songs, while others could only be his.

The Mondays were true originals.

They were brutally honest about everything, including their drug use and rock 'n' roll lifestyle. These were no mere dilettantes but a full-on freaky dancing crew. The Mondays were raw people and that made their gatecrashing of the too-clean pop party all the more welcome.

Their return to the pop world in the late nineties has raised a few eyebrows . . . Can they still cut it and what's the point? sceptics wonder.

Shaun Ryder, for one, had pretty clear motives for getting the old gang back together.

'It was the fucking tax bill. It was the tax man that made me do it. I never wanted to do it. I just needed the money to fill a hole,' his rough ragged voice intoned, 'but as we started playing the stuff I really got into it. At first I was looking forward to the last gig, getting it over and done with but then I started to enjoy it. I'm looking forward to playing all the shows now.'

His partner in crime, Bez, nearly didn't make the reunion as he recounted.

'I wasn't sure about it at first. I was not having it. I didn't want to spoil the myth, leave it as it is . . . I didn't want it to be pure cabaret. But when we started rehearsing it sounded good and we had some new stuff to play like the single and different mixes of the classic songs . . .'

The Mondays without Bez is unthinkable. For sure it's Shaun's band and he calls the shots but without the crazed, skeletal, scarecrow dancer the band is meaningless. For many clueless pundits Bez may have been a joke figure. Cynics wondered just what he did. They didn't realize that Bez's dancing was the focal point of the band and provided the only visual on the stage. Bez's wild shapes were the cue for a whole pop nation to dance like wild-eyed maniacs. His onstage relationship with Shaun was like the best buddy movie on stage, the pair of them cut some great photo action. In pop, charisma is all and Bez had it. Not that he could give a fuck, as he related the week before the comeback tour.

'My motto is "do as little as possible". It's what I live by! I'm hyped up for these gigs, though, I'm driving everyone mad!'

Contrary to public opinion Bez hadn't been sat on his settee getting stoned. He's written an autobiography, done TV, recorded a dub record with ex-Clash man and good mate Joe Strummer ('It'll be out when Joe gets some money') and he'd been in training.

'I've been boxing, snowboarding and I play football every week. I'm the oldest one there, I turn up at the five-a-side pitches and I'm ten years older than everyone else. I'll tell ya what, though, I'm well fit for these gigs!'

Ryder is in it for the money and Bez is looking for the buzz. It's that brutal honesty again. It's the sort of honesty that makes people dig The Mondays and makes Ryder the unlikely spokesman of a generation – a generation of drug heads and crazy fuckers, the sort of people who aren't going to be listening to Steps or gasp with pleasure at Blur's new direction. The Mondays represent a whole pop constituency of their own and, along with The Stone Roses, irrevocably changed the face of British pop in the early nineties.

The Happy Mondays leering, lurching, freak funk had been ignored in the stainless eighties. What chance did anyone give their first album, 1987's *Squirrel and G-Man*, flatly produced by ex-Velvet Underground's John Cale?

The Happy Mondays seemed to be totally out of place in the late eighties pop plod. They scored some good press but mostly baffled looks. No one knew just where to place this palaver.

They were going to need a massive cultural change before anyone got a handle on their particular madness.

That sea change was the much-vaunted acid house boom and its attendant drug culture that frazzled the minds of a generation enough for them to make sense of Ryder's crew's paeans to street decadence and urban weirdness.

Before 1989 most of the rock 'n' roll weirdness had been dealt by art-school loons and bored rock stars. Drugs had been the preserve of the wealthy, the weird and the crazed. Ecstasy had blown the whole thing wide open. Drug virgins were getting laid by the seductive new drug and in its wake there was a big boom in attendant chemicals. Smoking dope was back on the agenda and the street scene took on a psychedelic hue, a psychedelia that was a long way from the dippy-hippie bed-in of the late sixties but a far meaner and harder take on the boho lifestyle.

For The Happy Mondays this was a godsend.

They were already soundtracking the chemical revolution. In 1988 The Mondays delivered the album that in many ways opened up the whole new pop era. *Bummed* is stained with the grubby new psychedelic. The album captured the fucked-up flavour of the times with its loping semi funk, lurching 'psycho'delic flavour, tuff 'n' funny street lyrics and was streaked with an innate pop heart that was capturing the street kids and the indie kids in the new post E fucked-up constituency.

Even the artwork is a brutal slap of raw freakiness. The leering shot of Ryder on the cover was painted by the north's answer to Gilbert and George, Matt and Pat. The pair, Ryder's cousins, under the monicker of Central Station Design, came up with a superb series of portraits of wacky northern personalities and did most of The Mondays' artwork.

Lurking inside the record's grooves was the same deceptively slipshod funk, northern soul propelled bass lines, underrated almost Beefheartian strokes of guitar and Ryder's madcap lyrics spat out in a sneering whine. It doesn't sound like a winning pop formulae when you write it down but just whack the record on and it all comes together and makes complete sense. Somewhere lurking in this foul beast of sound was an innate understanding of great pop. These songs were so damned catchy and they were telling tales of a drugged wild outlaw life that was fast becoming the new normality in Britain's council estates.

This time the record took off and hit the back end of the charts. The preceding single, the September 1989 Factory released 'WFL', a reworking of 'Wrote For Luck', had been seeping around the country and was becoming the anthem of the autumn. The end of set singsong, 'Wrote For Luck' was the call to arms to every drugged-up yob in the land.

The relentless remix by Paul Oakenfeld, piling on the massive groove, was a genius move. The Mondays were finally communicating with their potential mass audience. The people this time understood and when that November's 'Madchester Rave on EP' was released, it scraped the back end of the top twenty. Not only was it the Mondays' first proper hit, it also christened the scene.

By the autumn of 1989 The Mondays were on a roll. The autumn tour was a nightly celebration of the good times as the band stumbled into town and laid down the law on the nu street swagger. Clobbered up in designer baggy, dressing up to dress down, the loose fit was the new street style. The Mondays' gigs were packed full of drug-fried kids – many of them cutting loose on their first ever ecstasy.

The crowd was hyped up with excitement. Every fucker in the place just wanted to gurn like a buffoon or dance like a dislocated idiot.

The leader of the gurning pack was Bez. So often derided as 'just the dancer' by the flat-footed armchair crit, Bez's gangling stage moves and freaky dancing were instrumental in teaching a stiff-assed white boy generation how to dance. His bug eyes and general demeanour perfectly captured the chemical highs of the times.

Throughout 1990 the Mondays were in their ascendancy. 'Step On' and 'Kinky Afro' were top fives. The outsiders were not only gatecrashing the party they were pretty damn well throwing it. But there was no way it could last. Their third album *Pills, Thrills And Bellyaches* was a smash. But come 1991 and their star was beginning to wane. 'Loose Fit', despite being a great song, could only get to 17. They entered 1992 recording their fourth album, *Yes Please*, in the Bahamas amid media talk of drug binges, car crashes and wild behaviour.

Any band burning on the sort of hi-octane lifestyle of The Happy Mondays was inevitably going to implode. The last album comparatively stiffed at No. 12 and their final tour seemed like a slog. Checking out the shows there was none of the euphoria of the '89 celebration. Support band the Stereo MCs were mopping up every night and they were nicking The Mondays' crown from right under their noses.

Ryder walked out of a tabled deal from EMI to 'buy some Kentucky Fried Chicken', as they say. He disappeared, teamed up with ex-Ruthless Rap Assassin rapper Kermit, returned with Black Grape, put out one superb album and one so-so album and fell apart within a couple of years.

Black Grape synthesized The Mondays funk into a molten whole. Kermit was the perfect foil for Ryder, his sharp raps counterpointing Ryder's Salford drawl. But they always had a volatile working relationship.

Ryder hasn't spoken to Kermit since the split and there are reports that his former campadre's post-Grape outfit, Manmade, has since fallen apart after getting dropped. Ryder was last spotted writing a column for the *Daily Sport* before he stunned everyone by reforming the Mondays.

The rumours had been around town for about a year about the Mondays coming back. Did he feel like he may have left it a touch too long?

'I'm not dyeing my hair yet, not using the Grecian 2000, so it will work,' joked Ryder with the easy-going laugh of a man who knows he's got a good thing going. The Mondays never traded on youthful good looks so, perversely, they actually make sense making rock 'n' roll into their middle age. They never cleaned their act up. They've remained outlaws. They've still got the edge.

Ryder is well aware of the pratfalls that face any band coming back on to the circuit after years in the wilderness. He's got the motive cleared up and he knows even if the band was crap he would have his tax bill paid off but there is something stirring in his own personal pride that makes him want it to work.

'It could have been cabaret bollocks or hard as fuck and it's ended up hard as fuck. We've messed with the songs. Some of them will be versions of the old stuff. We went through all the remixes I never liked years ago ha! and found different versions to play. It stops it being boring.'

The Manchester show was great, a swaggering call to arms from the last gang in town.

Only it's not quite the same gang.

'There's a couple of different members in. We replaced the keyboard player and the guitar player,' Ryder informs us matter of factly, not using the original members' names, also neglecting to mention that Mark Day was one of the great understated strengths of the band with his thrilling skewwhiff guitar shapes – a prime factor in their sound.

Not that they have fucked up with his replacement: guitar man Wags, once of the underrated Paris Angels and of Black Grape, has his own cool style to add to the new Mondays. Ryder also had to iron out a couple of problems with other key members.

'With Paul [bass player and brother] we fell out five years ago and then made up about a year ago. Then we fell out again about a month ago, but we now nod at each other again. But the band is getting on great. Gaz and Bez and all that. It's a real laugh. It's like old times!'

Also drafted in is the previously unknown Nuts, whom Ryder met in Ibiza.

'He's not a rapper,' spits Ryder. 'He's a singer, right!'

Back in the ranks is Rowetta, the leather-clad diva whose extrovert whiplashing over-the-top sexuality was the perfect foil to Ryder's onstage lumbering, and who has spent the past few years singing on dance records.

There is this batch of dates and talk of festivals. How long does Shaun see this going on for?

'Nothing is planned. If I stop enjoying it, it'll stop, that's how I live my life. If we get offered any special gigs we'll do 'em. If anything interesting turns up in Europe we'll do it . . . but fuck touring the States . . .'

The Mondays were bound to be great at these shows. When Ryder has something to prove he always delivers. The first tour when Black Grape were out on the circuit was something special. The hunger for success always seems to bring something out of this ragbag crew. You can always be guaranteed some great party action. Huge gigs sold out by a band that only had two Top Ten hits. It shows the cultural importance of the band – their story has transcended generations. The comeback gigs gave the Madchester prime movers a chance to reap what they sewed at the beginning of the decade.

The Boys, as they will certainly keep telling you, are definitely back in town.

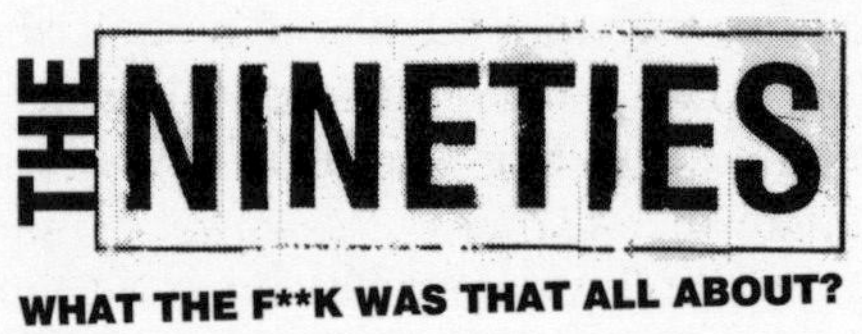

CHAPTER NINE

STONE ROSES

Caught at their peak, this interview with The Stone Roses in 1989 is printed out in full for the first time. The band had just played their legendary Blackpool show and were on the eve of their Alexander Palace gig. At the time the thought of an 'indie' band playing to 7,000 people seemed incredible. It shows how much the goalposts have moved now when yer average guitar band would virtually use the same gig as a warm up show . . . From this heady point when it looked like The Stone Roses would take the world, they seemed to stall, but even their slow disappearance could only add to their legend . . . But let's have a glimpse of the band at the height of their powers when they were casting the British guitar band template into stone for the whole decade . . .

1989: It's been a good year for The Roses.

Ian Brown and John Squire are sat in a Chorlton pub. Victory is theirs at last. Since 1985 they have been on the verge of something. Armed with the massive self-belief that has set them apart from their contemporaries, they had promised much and delivered little, the occasional single, the odd legendary underground gig, the sporadic piece of graffiti. As 1989 gathered pace they were recording an astonishing debut album and this year, the last year of the eighties, it's come out, grabbing plaudits and sales. They have been on the road most of the year, starting off playing to a handful of people and ending up with next week's sell out 7,000 show at Alexandra Palace.

No wonder the Roses pair look so pleased with themselves.

Not that they are getting smug about it. Ian Brown acknowledges the sudden change in their fortunes with a certain humility.

'We always said that we believed what we are doing is right. And that it would take time for the world to catch up and that's what happened . . . I don't get no satisfaction out of proving people wrong. We always thought that people were not going to get to hear us properly until we put an LP out. Most people hadn't heard anything by us at all till *Made Of Stone*. Up till then we were this established Manchester band that hadn't got out of Manchester.'

At the start of 1989 they were packing potential but no one was getting it, but at the end of the year they have become the biggest buzz in the country. Their debut album has been the soundtrack to a Mancunian and then a nationwide summer – one of the few albums that slotted in with the ecstasy buzz. It's a buzz which has culminated in the sold-out show in Blackpool. A night when the band made their definitive statement. Not that John Squire was totally pleased.

'I came off stage from Blackpool thinking that it had been shit, I wasn't happy with it at all.'

Apart from the guitar player's misgiving it was a classic rock 'n' roll occasion. The birth of a scene occurred that heady evening as the Manc baggy thing went nationwide. It was the start of a new pop epoch.

Across the land the pop wars have been raging. There is a new generational shift as The Roses along with The Happy Mondays have become the two bands that have best been able to reinterpret rock 'n' roll for the post-E generation. The music's different, the drugs are different and the clothes are different.

In fact, if there's one thing that's really getting people arguing it's flared trousers. There are the people who hate them, seeing their very existence as an affront to the great punk rock style wars and there are those that love them but claim that they wore them first (Liverpool or Manchester who had the first flares . . . the debate rumbles on!)

Ian Brown sits back and smirks. He's just enjoying the controversy that has flared (ha!) up in the wake of his sartorial decisions . . .

'You get a buzz out of it because people look at you and laugh because you're not wearing the same pants. It's weird how something really simple like that can make you feel really special. Cressa [the band's so-called fifth member and best mate] gave them up so I took them. I carried the flares because someone had to and now we've got all this [*referring to the flared trouser craze*]. Me and

Cressa used to knock around together a lot. Used to wear flares back in 1984 for summat to do . . . He got sick of wearing the flares and reverted to parallels so I started to wear them. I thought someone should continue.

We're as loose as the next man, with flares people don't actually get to see your legs. They think that wandering around in a pair of ridiculous high waistband loons is all that we are about and nothing could be further from the truth . . . the cut of our trousers is pretty vital to us you but you get misinterpreted, don't you. When you get misinterpreted like that it's worse than getting misquoted . . . that's the thing that keeps us awake at night. . .' he jokes.

'Some people look really good in flares but some people just don't. I remember getting my first pair of straight trousers and getting laughed out of town because I was not wearing flares, but now it's gone full circle, and I thought punk was about change . . .'

A couple of years ago The Stone Roses were more about leather trousers than flares, in a trouser choice that has mistakenly seen them called a goth band when they were far closer to the Creation classic leather look like Primal Scream and Jesus And Mary Chain. It's a look that Ian Brown still harbours a certain affection for.

'I wouldn't mind leather trousers now actually. Time's about right for leathers, there's too much denim about . . . you're going to get some people soon with semi-flared suede trousers and they'll look excellent.'

John Squire looks up.

'If you don't look like a city businessmen you're obviously making a statement. It's harder to look scruffy!'

Before we get bogged down in sartorials we'll switch to the music. There is a definite drug stain on The Roses' music. It reeks of psychedelia, but not in a retro sixties way – this is music that is awash with a late eighties feel. They've taken the classic melodic guitar wash and made it into a sound track for this year. They may not sound like an acid house band but their music has a warm ecstatic glow to it, it feels like ecstasy. They've made a guitar record that fits in with the druggy mood of the times but relates to a classic canyon of guitar euphoria.

So the clothes have changed and the drugs? In 1989 it seems like everyone is either on an E or talking about it. There's a stoned, immaculate feel about things . . . the band are understandably fairly taciturn on the issue. Ian Brown:

'They're pretty important is all I'm saying!'

John Squire adds, 'Anything that affects your brain has got to be pretty important.' Manchester itself, the city, has always been hip but now it's a totem of chemical cool. Droves of kids are pouring in at the weekend looking for some of the experience. Countless articles have recast the place as a sort of northern San Francisco. A drug-stained Northern scallydelic outpost of acid casualties. Locals are bemused; Ian Brown is baffled.

'If you didn't live here and you read all the things that were written about it, you would think that it was Christmas every day. You meet people from Northampton and Dudley and you see them wandering around in the street, wondering where all this sparkle and mystical magic is and it ain't there really. It's a few clubs on a few nights and a lot of people with a good attitude and that's about it . . . Manchester is compact and confined to a small city centre. Everyone knows each other. Everyone's always wandered in each other's scenes. Everyone's now talking about indie and dance coming together, well that's bollocks, everyone I know has always had dance records and rock records, it's not just a sudden thing that's happened. It's always been there . . .'

And the chants of 'Manchester' at the gigs – how does it feel to be the seen as the city's standard bearers?

It's something that bothers Ian.

'Yeah, it's strange, especially when most of the people doing it aren't even from Manchester. I don't like being part of that scene. You don't leave your area and start shouting where you're from. It's really stupid. What's the point? Who gives a fuck.'

'Patriotism of any form is stupid,' Squire cuts in.

Manchester, though, has always been swift to embrace its heroes. The city supports its bands to an intense, clannish degree. Parochialism is fierce. It's a matter of local pride. It also makes it difficult to get about town. The Stone Roses may have been a big band in the city for a lot longer than the rest of the country but in recent months even here the recognition factor has sky-rocketed. Ian Brown is trying to find his own methods of reacting to the problem.

'I still get the bus. It keeps your head together. People see you on a bus and they say "What are you doing here? You were on *Top Of The Pops*." I don't feel famous. I don't feel any different.'

John Squire is disinterested in the very notion of fame. 'It's a completely abstract term, fame, isn't it?'

Brown points to the weirdness of creeping pop stardom. 'It's a bit strange when your on Oxford Street and 14-year-old girls pull your arms and you're trying to calm them down. That's strange, but you can't complain about it, you shouldn't have started it if you're nor prepared to accept it . . .'

Maybe their ambivalent attitude towards stardom explains their media technique. The band have given a series of interviews where they have stonewalled the journalists. It's meant that many people have seen them as being arrogant. John Squire doesn't agree.

'If you're talking to a dickhead, you're not going to give much away, are you? It's going to be more of a chore, isn't it?'

Ian Brown is baffled by the surge of media interest.

'There's Stone Roses everywhere, so I can understand why people get sick of it. Because a lot of people are bound to be put off a group that's constantly in the press and on the radio. It's been crazy in the last few months and I'm sick of seeing myself in them as well.'

The Stone Roses are going to have to get used to this new visibility. *Top Of The Pops* has become a serious part of their agenda. A couple of weeks ago they were the classic 'Manchester night' when they appeared on the show with The Happy Mondays. That night was a big moment in the city's pop ascendancy. Ian Brown looks back on the performance – it was a great day out.

'It was a good day with Mondays and the roadies. There were about twenty Mancunians in one building. If you want to get to the top you've got to get there among them, against Kylie to have any affect.'

The tune they played on the programme, 'Fool's Gold', sees the band shift a gear. The single sounds like it's reacting more to the house thing than the album. Tied to a funky as fuck breakbeat and slapped around with a fantastic wah wah guitar lick and a fab driving bass line, it sees The Stone Roses reacting directly with the dance floor. Is this where their music is going?

'We try to make each song sound different from the last one,' says Ian Brown. 'I don't think that they all sound the same even on the album. Every time we write a song we try to make it different. "Fool's Gold" isn't a Stone Roses mark 2.'

Attempting to push on they are already throwing up question marks over the sound of the album. John Squire is worried about it.

'The sound is really suppressed on it. I know what was laid

down and what came through and it wasn't what I wanted exactly. I think it's important to change sound but it's not always that easy. We can't judge what we sound like. We can't judge anything about ourselves. It's just us. I can't take an outsider's point of view and listen to the record. In fact I've only listened to the album twice since it came out. You listen to the album more than I do, don't you Ian . . .'

He nods towards the singer, who mutters, 'Yeah, I like it. I thinks it's top, I think it's a good LP. I don't think it matters if it's a debut LP. We achieved what we wanted to a achieve. We still haven't recorded the ultimate LP, but it's not a bad start . . . We want to put out a second LP that wipes the floor with the first one and we're confident that we can do that.'

There is talk of a new single coming soon, hot on the coat tails of *Fool's Gold*. Ian Brown talks about the future.

'I haven't got a title for it yet, but we've got something that we've been working on that should come out next February or March. Again it's different, but it's more of a groove thing. That's the way we want to move, in a groove direction . . .'

We leave the pub and move back to John Squire's small terraced house in Chorlton. He lives round the corner from Brown who has just moved from West Didsbury to be closer to his song-writing partner. We stop at a kebab house so Ian can buy a grim-looking kebab. The vegetarian Squire remains outside. The pair of them, the inner core of the band, are so different from each other. They are chalk and cheese, but they plug in each other's gaps. John Squire is quiet – almost taciturn – and artistic, and prefers to stay in and work on his Jackson Pollock-influenced piece or play his guitar for hours while Brown, although he has a big creative input into the group, perfects his swagger and effortless cool while bumming around, a restless heart and a bohemian soul. Brown is always on the move. He even wrote the words to 'Made Of Stone' about it.

'It's about hitch hiking, being on the move. I've always been on the move ever since I lived in Sale. I never hung about there. I hung about with lads from all over the city. I travelled all over. I've been to every seaside resort in England before I ever toured. I've been to most of Europe, moving about. It's what I'm into doing.'

And the reason . . .

'I want to meet everyone on the planet and see every place that I can . . .'

While Brown is on the road, Squire is working on those great paintings, several of which have become Stone Roses record covers.

They may have been influenced by Pollock, but the guitarist is looking to move on.

'I'm bored with that dripping and splattering. I want to do more of my own sort of stuff now. I still think that it's important that we do our own sleeves though. If you buy a record you not only get the sound of the band but what was going on in their head at the time as well. You shouldn't let anyone else get in the way and dilute it . . . you shouldn't say "Here's the record, let's get some guy in London do the sleeves." It should be us all the way, because that's what people are interested in and that's what they should get and not some sleeve done by an advertising designer . . .'

This is a part of the band's drill, this stoic independence. It's such a northern thing, this like it or lump it attitude. It's something that Ian Brown firmly believes in.

'You should realize that you don't have to do anything you don't want to do. If you don't want to turn up, they can't make you do it . . .' he states, his punk rock soul still lurking just below the surface.

Brown like Squire, was fired by punk. While he liked the nihilism and anarchism of The Pistols and then the furious adrenalin provided by psychobilly and underground punk before moving into soul music, John Squire was a Clash fanatic, digging the cool chic, the romantic heart, that beat inside Strummers's gang before moving on to Hendrix and Led Zeppelin and on into the whole world of trad rock.

Today Ian Brown's taste is very different.

'Marvin Gaye at the moment and Isaac Hayes' "What's Goin' On" . . . there's a track called "Stars" by Mr Fingers. I've played that single every day for about six months . . . also a lot of house stuff . . . I play house records all the time at home. I get a buzz off them like it was a rock band. I don't think you have to listen to them in a club or off your head. I listened to Jimi (Hendrix) for about two months and a lot of reggae, a lot of Adrian Sherwood, he's my favourite producer. I listen to his stuff all the time, and all that On U stuff, those African Head Charge LPs are top . . . I went to see that On U thing live and it didn't work, it was like cabaret.'

And so, finally, to Ally Pally, the reason that we're all here, on the eve of the big one. Why play here? It's an old venue – not many people have played there for years. The place is more associated with psychedelic happenings than great rock 'n' roll. Maybe that makes it more apt!

Ian Brown has an agenda.

'We wanted to play a gig that was like a big party. Blackpool was perfect. It was summer and that really worked. We don't want to play established rock venues, so that's why we've played Alexandra Palace. It wasn't to get us up the ladder. It was what we personally wanted to do for our own enjoyment, knowing that people who were into us would be into it as well.'

The Stone Roses are on the threshold of a rock 'n' roll revolution. Can they pull it off? Could this be the biggest band of the nineties? Ian Brown certainly thinks so.

'We've shown our potential. It's up to us to fulfil it . . .'

It's going to be a long strange trip.

Postscript

What a strange trip it was. From this point things started to unravel. Alexandra Palace was marred by a booming muffled sound. The talked-about single 'One Love' was greeted by muted enthusiasm (although it was their highest chart entry at No. 4). They sold out the 30,000 capacity Spike Island outdoor gig the following summer but the gig was generally acknowledged as being a damp squib (although the band themselves played a great set). There was the series of tent gigs and then the retreat to the studio to record *The Second Coming*. By the time that came out Oasis had stolen their thunder and their audience.

In fact it seemed like every other band in Britain had fulfilled the Roses' potential for them. They set up the blueprint and everyone else followed it to the letter. They are easily the most influential British guitar band of the nineties.

Currently they potter around with solo careers. John Squire went on to The Seahorses, cutting melodic soft rock records; Ian Brown made an eccentrically produced solo record that contained some great tunes and then got locked up for a couple of months after an altercation on a plane; Mani plays for Primal Scream and Reni is in his attic writing cool songs that he never seems to be able to finish.

In 1999 there were talks of their reforming after the Seahorses fell apart. Reports indicated that most of the band were keen to do it but John Squire has thrown himself into forming another band.

The Stone Roses ended the decade as the band that never did fulfil its enormous potential but they did leave us with one killer album – the best British guitar pop record of the decade that no one has been able to match within that genre.

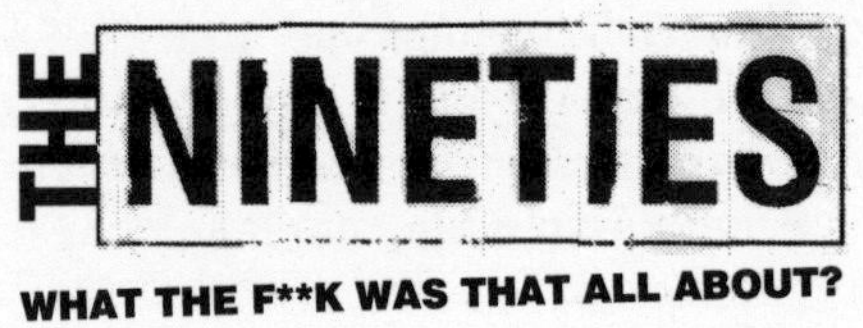

CHAPTER TEN

PRIMAL SCREAM – KNOW WORRA MEAN

In the slipstream of the Roses and Mondays, Primal Scream were one of the first indie guitar bands to react to the acid house thing. Regulars at Shoom and already living a full-on bohemian lifestyle, their rock 'n' roll antennae were already twitching to the possibilities of the dance scene. Pulling in Andrew Weatherall and Hugo Nicholson to remix them was a genius move, it sparked *Screamadelica*, one of the most loved and influential albums of the time . . .

Flashback 1: 1998

The backdrop is a Stuka bomber. The weapons are the twin Les Paul attack. The band a flurry of long hair, leather and rock 'n' roll shapes. Frontman Gillespie still skinny, still remarkably young-looking for a hard-living mid-thirties rock 'n' roll vulture, cuts a skinny ass cool. The two guitar players hog the stage wings; there's Throb, rock 'n' roll incarnate on one side, and on the other there is the slight figure of Andrew Innes, the musical genius behind The Scream – his amp festooned with Scottish regalia.

It looks great.

They're so rock 'n' roll they've even got Mani from The Stone Roses on a free transfer and he's brought his bass and he's revelling in it, yelling at the crowd and thrusting his guitar at them in a celebration of rock 'n' roll – Mani is the four-string yob who unfashionably revels in being onstage.

Brixton, 1998 and the Scream are on top form. Their last tour had been a shambles. They'd tried to pull it off with a drum machine. It didn't work. Now with a proper human drummer they are a drilled band. They are burning.

The Scream play tunes from every corner of their zigzagging career. From rock 'n' roll to dance. From dub to gospel. From pop to Stones swagger. They've been everywhere, pilfered everything and still sound like themselves.

Only this time they have lifted it up a gear. In Brixton they pull all the strands together and make it sound like one hot band.

It really rocks.

Tonight Primal Scream are awesome.

Flashback 2: 1990

Bobby Gillespie is being sick in a bin. We're sat in the park round the corner from Creation Records' Hackney base. It's a deep wretch but not much seems to come up. But the boy is so thin there's probably no food in there to throw. He sits back down ashen-faced and apologizes. He's been living in the 24-hour party zone for too long and he's paying for it.

Bobby and his gang live their lives like a crash course from the pages of dog-eared Rolling Stones books. Rock 'n' roll in the nineties comes complete with its own manuals. What Keef and Mick did in their glorious swaggering prime is what rock 'n' roll bands are expected to duplicate for ever. The only thing is the Primals seem to be living it and loving it a lot harder than their mentors and sometimes a man's gotta pay.

'Led Zeppelin sang songs about "California". About wanting to escape, and indie bands sing songs that are so dreary, so small time,' Gillespie sneers, wiping the bile from his mouth.

The Scream are on a mission. They are attempting to escape from the clutches of the underground. *Loaded* has given them their first proper hit. However, the purists don't like it. The band had been a totem for the fanzine anorak scene. Their interest in dance music is viewed suspiciously. Some cynics reckon it could be a case of handy bandwagon jumping. But these people haven't heard the album yet. *Screamadelica* is one hell of an escape route. It's more than just an indie band trying to play dance music. It's an indie band trying to come to terms with all the great music that's ever been made and using acid house as a spark, a catalyst or just an excuse. It's brave and it's bold. Inside its songs there are echoes of dub, dance, rock 'n' roll, free jazz, the Stones, garage psyche and the blues. It sounds like one of the most important records of the year. When this record comes out it will break down the boundaries between rock and techno paving the way for a whole bunch of young mavericks to reshape pop music.

The band had been some of the first people to hang out down at Shoom. Their interest in acid house was fired by their doctorship in chemicals and their wild-assed understanding of having it large. Being psychedelic heads they clicked into the second psychedelic era, digging the fact that this time you could dance to it.

Primal Scream, in hindsight, were perfectly placed to make the jump into the crossover. The stinking phrase 'indie/dance' does their music no credit at all. *Screamadelica* was a far better record than that piss-weak expression describes.

Screamadelica is a challenge thrown down.

When the album was released it was the third key rock album of the period (The Roses and The Mondays were, of course, the other two). It was another soundtrack for the crazed times. Another attempt by rock 'n' rollers to make sense of the fired-up dance scene. It was also another album to play after a night out clubbing. A bliss out record as the E wore off into the dawn. The album reached its high point with the band's third single, the transcendental 'Higher Than The Sun' where Sun Ra met a rock 'n' roll band on a blissful E high.

Punk rockers in the dance hall! Primal Scream were stamping their own freak vision on to dance culture.

Screamadelica saw two generations clash . . .

Flashback 3: 1986 – living on the toilet circuit

Primal Scream are playing Manchester Boardwalk. They've already been through the pop mill. Gillespie was the original drummer in Jesus And Mary Chain and a leading light in the Glasgow underground. They've got a small pedigree and already they are Creation's cornerstone band, a role they will continue to play through the downs and astonishing ups of the label.

Their debut singles are indie classics, 'All Fall Down' and 'Crystal Crescent', especially its B-side 'Velocity Girl', are slices of pure pop dripping melody and cool. Key songwriter of the original line-up, Jim Beattie has a handle on this sort of post-Love rushes of gliding guitar pop. They come complete in leather trousers, a rarity on Creation where every band seems to creak uncomfortably in cow hide.

The set is fashionably short. They rattle through their songs, some of which barely reach the 90 second mark. The band may play honey-coated pop but they play it with a punk-rock sneer. These are no mere lightweights. Primal Scream are Glasgow hard nuts throwing fey shapes. They are the Creation ethic distilled to its finest, far closer to what the label is about than the more successful Jesus And Mary Chain.

In the mid eighties they may be music press darlings but mainstream pop has little interest in this sort of behaviour. It looks like they are doomed to cult status.

Flashback 4: Making anthems – 'Loaded'

'Loaded' is more than a single. It's an event. Acid house is massive and indie is cowering. The Manchester bands have assimilated its groove, its drugs and its lifestyle into their own schtick. Everyone else is just plain stuck. Is there anyone else out there prepared to go with the flow?

The obvious candidates to make sense of all this are rock 'n' roll fanatics Primal Scream. They understand. They know about decadence, hedonism and good times. They've already been an influence on The Stone Roses (the debate still rumbles on about 'Made Of Stone' and 'Velocity Girl' sharing a chord sequence).

They've been doing their research. Being part of the Shoom crowd they certainly knew all about the rush of prime-time acid house. But they had been drifting out of fashion. They had even bizarrely been lumped in with the 'shambling scene', a patronising term coined for indie strugglers in the mid eighties. Their debut album *Sonic Flower Groove* had been an exercise in jangling guitar pop, Love and The Byrds put through the blender Glasgow style. Released on McGee's major label imprint Elevation, it hadn't taken over the world as they had hoped. It had come out and disappeared. The band seemed doomed to cultdom.

They had toughened up their sound for the eponymous *Primal Scream* follow-up. They had been touring like bastards. Gigging always makes a band sound harder. You can't avoid the adrenalin rush of pushing those guitars that bit more. It always connects with the crowd. These boys were rock 'n' roll fanatics. They were deeply in love with The Stones, the MC5 and The Stooges, as well as sweet Memphis soul and freaky seventies funk. You listen to that kinda shit all the time and it's bound to affect you.

They seemed to be on their own with this mission. The second album was totally against the grain – hard rock was hardly hip. As the record did its small fry business The Scream were too busy to care. They were getting out of it and surfing the new acid house craze that was kicking off in small clubs in London. They couldn't help but be enthused by the new youth movement. Stuff like that always affected them. They were relieved to find some like-minded people in the clubs. people who dug the same sort of wild ass rock 'n' roll that they did. Andrew Weatherall was one of them.

This is where the connections were made.

It was Alan McGee who thought of it first. Why not get Andy Weatherall in to remix 'I'm Losing More Than I'll Ever Have', the slow burning soul fuse off the album? Weatherall understood The Scream perfectly. From the same sort of post-punk rock 'n' roll roots, he'd also had his mind blown by acid house and he was making his way as a respected DJ on the nascent scene.

In the studio with the Primal's track he stripped it all away and rebuilt it with an infectious breakbeat and a battery of cunning samples, turning the song into a near bluesy instrumental anthem. Preceded with a sample of Peter Fonda shouting 'I just wanna get loaded, get high' from the classic biker movie *Wild Angels*, capturing the outlaw spirit of early acid house. The single was pure class. It dripped with the Primal's melodicism. It was stained with the blues. It had had Bobby's sexy bit in the middle and more importantly it had the groove.

The record was everywhere: reaching No. 16 in the spring of 1990. It was Primal Scream's first chart record. It was their anthem and arguably the first 'indie/dance' record. 'Loaded' paved the way for a pop revolution. Indie bands now 'got dance' . . . 'there has always been a dance element to our music' was the battle cry. DJs and remixers got the call up to save many bands' careers. There seemed to be a million remixes (the best of which were usually by Weatherall himself) and undergound pop switched from the bedroom to the dance floor.

Fired by the creative success of 'Loaded', the Primals were swiftly back in the studio. They sensed that they were on the verge of something really big. On the coat tails of 'Loaded' came 'Come Together', a mishmash of shuffling house beats, gospel melodies, Bobby's languid vocal and some neat steals from the MC5's 'Kick Out The Jams'.

The single set them up perfectly for *Screamadelica*. After that album Primal Scream were going to be one of the hippest bands of their generation.

Flashback 5: Rock 'n' roll!!!!!

Dance traitors, they squealed as Primal Scream burst back on to the scene with their 1994 foot-on-the-monitors rocking *Give Out But Don't Give Up* album, turning their backs on the indie dance shuffle that they had pioneered in favour of the rock 'n' roll that they couldn't help loving. Not that the warning signals hadn't been there before the album's release – 1992's 'Dixie Narco' EP oozed a bluesy flavour, a mooch away from the dance floor. The fourth album, though, was a total rock-out. The Es had worn off and the hard-rock heart beat just below the Primal's surface was again beating hard. People just didn't know what to do with the record. It didn't seem to fit in anywhere. Dismissed in many quarters, the album still crashed in at No. 1.

In fact Primal Scream had cut a great rock record. The lead track 'Rocks', released as the first single, was their first Top Ten hit. The single was dripping Stones riffola and rode high on a tempestuous Motown drum stomp. It may not have been acid house but it was one hell of a dance record, albeit of a more traditional variety, as a thousand UK dance floors would testify.

The group's reputation as innovators had taken a denting. They reacted by going back out on a limb with a track for the *Trainspotting* soundtrack and their very alternative song for the Scottish World Cup bid, 'The Big Man And The Scream Team Meet The Barmy Army Uptown', a joint excursion with Irvine Welsh and the On U Sound System. The post 'dance traitor' music was a return to their dubbed-out dance excursions. Only this time it was darker and freakier. It was a harbinger of what was about to come.

Flashback 6: When the going gets weird – Primal Scream really get going!

Stung by the 'dance traitor' mud-slinging, or just following their natural instincts into as yet uncharted territories, the Primal's 1998 fifth album is, to these ears, their best yet. *Vanishing Point* is a dark trip. A black-humoured scowl. A comedown from the relentless hedonism. There had been talk of smack infiltrating the Scream camp. Maybe talk is cheap and the rumours bullshit but the stain of mean chemicals has oozed into the vinyl.

The 'Kowalski' single is one of the most remarkable Top Ten chart records ever released, a bizarre sonic collage driven by a Jah Wobble styled heavy dub bass from newly arrived Mani. Bobby whispers breathlessly over the top. It's a trip into somebody's hell, no chorus no middle eight, no hookline and still a Top Ten hit. There we are, told you it could be done!

The following album is a weird mélange of freak funk, an organic rush of neo-psychedelia, dark dub grooves, blissful pop and militant lyrics. You can hear nods to Can and Lee 'Scratch' Perry, pebbles garage rock, US experimental underground and free jazz in its grooves – fuck there is even some space for some cool pop moves ('Medication' what a song! it even has The ex-Pistol's Glen Matlock on bass, weird!). Primal Scream always boasted of having great record collections and here was some evidence!

Recorded in their own eight track, all warm cracklin' valve gear and ancient reverbs, the record was always going to be flavoured with some of that dub wizardry. In fact the dub version ('Eko Dek') of the record is even better. This is a band doing just what the fuck they want and ending up with the bit of everything freakiness that perfectly captures inner-city living in the late nineties.

Not that it was a misery indie workout. There was also a stark daft humour in the grooves, as with the Scream's cover of Motorhead's classic theme song 'Motorhead' calling card, the sort of crazed post-session seven-in-the-morning humour that this record captures. The dark swamp of hedonistic comedown just before the next day kicks in with its recriminations and hangover.

Pop has never sounded this strange.

Primal Scream were back out on the parameters of pop, doing what they did best, documenting the highs and lows of the chemical generation.

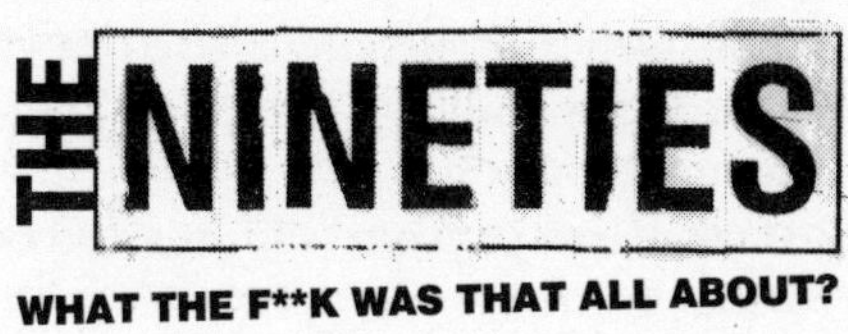

CHAPTER ELEVEN

THE MANIC STREET PREACHERS: PREACHING TO THE BLUE GENERATION . . .

It's hard to imagine Richey being in The Manics now. Every time I think of the doe-eyed kid with the frantic burning mind and messed-up soul I just feel sad. His disappearance, like Cobain's suicide, is one of the lowest pop moments of the decade . . . two sensitive souls who got burnt, not strong enough for the demanding regime of the nineties.

On 2 February 1995 the most troubled UK musician of his generation vanished. The band rightly carried on cutting some of their best songs. Weighed down for ever by the disappearance of Edwards, who for the core fans was their totem, they have survived and thrived, becoming one of the key British bands of the decade. Their story tells the story of the nineties better than most. At some points they violently opposed the consensus and at others fitted in better than they ever dreamed.

'Manic Street Preachers Will Always Matter' (T-shirt thrown on stage, 1999)

The Manic Street Preachers' story is one of the stories of the nineties.

It's a titanic story of rock 'n' roll dreams come true. A tale of heady idealism and sharp political suss countered with the nightmare of a young man who stared too hard into the dark heart of rock 'n' roll and got burned. It's a story of beautiful contradictions. A high IQ rock 'n' roll balanced with a superb dumbness. A pumped-up steroid-drenched metallic rock from a band that oozed a delicious femininity. A band who had a desire to conquer the world and an inbuilt self-destruction, a streak of musical conservatism and a revolutionary soul.

Fuck, what a band!

The nineties saw them go from wild-hearted outsiders with an agenda so sharp that most people didn't get it to the comfort of stadium rock. From gobshites with a stunning agenda; mascaraed strummers with a glam Marxist manifesto, to chart regulars in baggy pants.

They tapped into the underlying melancholia that stains the nineties. The misty valley melancholy that is inherent in the rusting Welsh industrial belt of proud people whose backs have been broken by vicious postwar governments. They took delicate minor key melodies and supercharged them with roaring fat guitar rock 'n' roll. It's a formula that works.

Originally their punk-rooted music sailed over most people's heads and their non-stop rhetoric and sky-high dreams left most mainstream pundits wondering if they were serious.

By the end of the decade they were the mainstream, singing their power ballads and rock 'n' roll missives in packed stadiums.

They had come a million miles from their starting point but somehow managed to retain the emotional kick and confused idealism that had always made them such a great band. They may have ditched the cool glam shapes and lost the guitarist that, for many, was the soul of the group but in 1998 as they rocked the Manchester Evening News Arena they were still a great band.

The Manics are pop's conscience, except that they are not sniping from the sidelines. They are right in there in the middle of the fray. They have the ability to be hilariously rude and disarmingly polite.

They loved The Clash but were smart enough to use Guns N' Roses as the chassis of their sound, adding The Clash's swagger and soul and subtracting The Roses' crass dumb rhetoric.

It's difficult to believe, now that they are constantly feted and groaning under the weight of music-biz awards, that when The Manics burst on to the scene in 1990 they were treated with contempt and a thinly veiled near racism that sneered at their Welsh background. In the middle of the baggy era they believed in skin-tight punk-rock togs, a vicious attack of socialist slogans and an outright contempt for their contemporaries. They were a long way from the stoned, play-dumb of most bands at the time and a long, long way from the 1990 zeitgeist but for a few of us who believed in their dream they were a welcome godsend.

I'd already reviewed them, mentioned them in dispatches, but it was getting them on to the cover of *Sounds* with their third single the Heavenly released 'Motown Junk' that still gives me the biggest buzz from my journo days.

Interviewing The Manics for their first-ever front cover that was published on 26 January 1991 was a different affair than now. Cooped up with the penniless band in the back of a transit van grabbing quotes, we were round the corner from Jeff Barrett's Heavenly record label, which was frantically attempting to sell the band to a sceptical music business.

Perched on their amps were four wired Welsh kids in love with punk rock – especially the smeared mascara end of the glam punk fallout, the power of metal c/o the warm Les Paul riffing of Guns N' Roses – and the non-stop polemic of the crucial hiphop guerrillas Public Enemy.

They were rock culture freaks with dog-eared volumes of r 'n' r history, well-thumbed Orwells and related literature. They seemed to have read everything related to pop culture and would speak about it with the intense authority of true believers who have been cooped up for too long and are ready to tell the world what they feel. They may have been ear-marking certain journalists to expound their myth to, but we were not dupes. We wanted the band to make it almost as badly as they did. All we did was to add to their myth – after all there has to be some sort of romanticism in these too grey times.

Instead of having qualms about 'selling out' or cowering under the Indie Law, The Manics were already thinking big.

They were also distancing themselves from the crippling indie thinking that was crushing most post-punk guitar hustlers of the time.

'You've got to reach out on a massive level,' claimed guitarist Richey James Edwards in the ice-cold shit-heap of a van. 'Once we've done that we will fade away. We want to make ourselves obsolete as fast as possible. It's no good just inspiring groups. People go on about The Stones inspiring the Paris riots in '68 which was fine but they just carried on. That's so obscene . . .'

Richey spoke in a quiet, appalled voice.

To him rock 'n' roll stank.

All the heroes had gone. A rock 'n' roll romantic, he was sickened by the greed machine that the music scene was. The Manics were the last band on earth that believed in the power of rock 'n' roll. They really thought that it could bring change.

And that's why we loved them.

'We can put a song out like "Repeat",' intoned bassist Nicky Wire. 'It's like five lines repeated over and over like "repeat after me fuck queen and country" and if you're in a position of power it will go straight in at number one. I think that it would cause a lot of problems because of the nature of the lyrics . . .'

The pre-fame rock 'n' roll loving Manics were, conversely, disdainful of the rock 'n' roll myth. They had a puritanical streak. A disavowing of the trad rock pastimes that Nicky still adheres to right up to this day. Speaking then he sneered at the myth.

'Cheap hedonism. It's always been exploited all the time. Every government must be happy with feeding people alcohol and drugs. It's like people say I hate society so I'm going to be bombed out of my skull . . .'

These were sentiments that the band would return to for the monumental 'Design For Life'. Nicky, a lanky bag of bones, had that sort of too tall frame perfect for cradling a bass and was huddled inside a blue padded anorak. Wire was disarmingly polite as he spat out his anger and disgust at the music scene. And he seemed to hate every band on the scene.

He also broadened his disgust to the world at large.

'It's really frustrating – people can't articulate their anger, they just attack each other. If they ran down the street and smashed up Tescos or the job centre that would be perfect. I'm not snobbish about these people though. These are the people that I hang around with when I'm back home . . .'

On the other hand The Manics had high hopes for their pop generation.

'The revolutionary class is every kid that's pissed off. You're just not going to get old people involved. They have too much to lose. Young people, though, have got no fear. They don't care what happens to them. Like at football matches. When you've got no fear you can do anything.'

Having no fear in 1990 included wearing make-up and glamming it up. At the height of the baggy wars the very sight of The Manics was enough to trigger a very negative response in most people. For Wire their image was a deliberate statement of intent.

'When we play everyone knows that we are pissed off. You know that. You can feel it. But we don't want to reflect that by looking really grey. We put on stacks of eye liner, spike our hair, spray our clothes. We want to be the perfect mix between politics and beauty . . .'

Richey peered up, nodding his agreement with his bashful yet fierce eyes. He and Nicky were glam on the dole. Dressed to the nines even their clothes spat polemic. Stencilled with slogans and snarling with pop art reference points.

They were wardrobe with attitude.

Such a stance was unheard of in the early nineties and it was a stance that made them feel very alienated. Their contemporaries left them cold. If they didn't fit into The Manics' idea of perfect rock 'n' roll they were the enemy.

'You look at other bands and think . . . it's so obscene that fat people are allowed in groups. It's like when I saw The Charlatans on TV and their audience had moustaches . . .'

To get a real picture of what The Manics were up against you have to have a swift look at the music scene at the time. The pop mainstream was, as ever, crap, while the so-called alternative scene was dominated by the loose-fit clobber and attitudes of baggy. The Manics with all their Clash-inspired spray paint slogans and skin-tight white Levis and their super-sharp rhetoric were clashing decisively with the playing-dumb indie rockers of the time. Instead of keeping schtum they slagged off rival bands.

Inevitably they were hated.

But they were taking their all-out pop war to the people.

Having supported Flowered Up on a Heavenly Records package on 16 November 1990 they were ramming their new art riot right at the baggy kids. Wire was pleased at the connections being made.

'After those gigs the kids were coming up and saying they were really into us. They had never seem a band like us before, you know, jumping up and down. They don't want to know about the past. They want to know about something that is happening in their lifetime. Bands like New Model Army are too wrapped up in a political manifesto. Their singer comes over just like a teacher.'

They were disgusted by everything but offered no solutions apart from themselves. This was a culture war and they were pop art suicide bombers.

'It's important that people don't see us as a dogmatic band,' worried Richey. 'We're just like them. We can't write a thesis on reviving the world's economy like The Redskins. We are a product of these times.'

Their shooting from the hip polemic and wired, intense pop socialism was at a direct contrast to the dope, shagging and football in the streets roots of the new laddism that was busting out all over Blighty.

The Manics, it seemed, cared.

They cared about everything. Clothes, politics, rock 'n' roll and life, while everyone else just got stoned.

It was a refreshing and thrilling contrast and made their first series of incendiary interviews the perfect launch pad for their career.

They hated everything that was gross and flabby in the current music scene. They talked with the incendiary fervour of rock 'n' roll zealots, lips unbuttoned and eyes burning with a righteous intensity.

'We're nihilistic,' they lied. 'It's a really positive thing. We want to destroy the hierarchy in this country, the monarchy, the house of lords. Homophobia. Racism.'

Lofty aims for a showbiz troupe but noble aims for any man.

Richey, in his quiet voice, would zigzag through a whole heap of cultural targets. His kohled eyes shyly hidden below a bird's nest of died jagged black hair, his post-teen fading pock-marked skin and handsome face, Richey was a kid blossoming into a pop star.

The Manics knew that they didn't fit but they were coming out fighting. They would spend the whole of 1991 gigging the fuck out of the UK in front of sceptical audiences, who were denying their swagger . . . locked into the grey. Sometimes it was violent and sometimes it was ecstatic, but out of the debris of the UK music scene they were picking up a hardcore following.

The band was a classic mix between two almost earnestly talented musicians, James and Sean, and the two maverick souls of Richey and Sean, the onstage wingers who wrote the words. Words that James would shoe-horn (occasionally there were just too many words resulting in a few slurred lines!) into his music and bring to life with his powerful rock 'n' roll voice. It's one of the key strands of The Manics, the way that James makes sense of Richey's pain or Nicky's anger and, along with criminally underrated Sean, makes the songs into classic slices of nineties pop.

A division of labour only possible in a band that knew each other inside out.

All four were immersed in pop culture and very close.

They had shared the same bedroom back home in the Welsh mining town of Blackwood in Gwent. Like kids everywhere they played football and Nicky excelled, going on to captain the Welsh under 16s and getting trials for Arsenal, an early sign of the football and pop crossover!

While Nicky was thriving at football, Sean was the youngest trumpet player in the South Wales Jazz Orchestra and James was into drama. James and Nicky went to Swansea University to study history. The young Manics were winners; everything they touched seemed to turn to gold.

They had known each other for years, Sean had even moved in with James, his cousin, after his parents had died. All four had the same music tastes and the same dreams when they were growing up. Dreams that could only result from a tight brotherhood forged from spending their intense youth cooped up together. They were a tight unit, endlessly debating rock 'n' roll, refining their tastes into a purist whole. Grabbing what they needed from the indie scene, they were fired by the sharp-as-fuck polemic of bands like Big Flame which they crossed with the supa cool punk rock of The Clash and the melodic metal of Guns N' Roses.

They religiously read the rock press.

They were smart.

They were hip.

They were angry and they had a plan.

Rock 'n' roll, though, at first seemed a tough proposition. After leaving university Nicky put together Betty Blue with Sean and James and a mate of theirs called Flicker.

Flicker soon left and the three-piece, complete with driver and tactician Richey, put together their dole cheques recording their first single 'Suicide Alley' as the newly christened by James, Manic Street Preachers.

Already they had sent out demos of their fierce pop polemic to the right sort of heads on the press. The tape arrived complete with the song's slash and burn lyrics and a biroed ranting letter slagging the sorry state of the indie scene.

The seven inch was a short slice of razor-sharp punk rock and landed them in the no man's land between the transit van punk of

Mega City Four, the out and out hardcore of the US underground and the cranked guitar pop of the indie scene. Basically there was nowhere for the band to go.

By now Richey was also out of university and was designing the band's artwork and it wasn't long before he would join as the band's auxiliary guitarist. His sense of style and finely honed idea of what a band should be were the final pieces in the jigsaw.

Richey started hustling the band in earnest – the usual round of sending out records to everyone who could possibly give them a break. Chasing a gig at the Horse and Groom in London, he sent a single to Kevin Pierce, who, himself, had spent years as a pop iconoclast with his own series of fanzines and missives.

Pierce was fired by what he heard and gave the band their first London gig. Typically it was playing the capital that sparked the band's next break. One of the punters at the gig that night, Ian Ballard from the indie Damaged Goods label, offered them a one-off singles deal.

They cut the 'New Art Riot' EP, another rush of punk-rock pop songs. This time they were getting a lot more attention, grabbing singles of the week and some press action. But the big break was their future manager Philip Hall who, on hearing the single, drove to Wales with his brother Martin to check the band rehearsing at a local school. The Halls were hooked and were the important connection that would change the band's lives. The band moved to London and moved into Philip Hall's tiny flat. Here they started breaking all the rock 'n' roll rules by hoovering the place and tidying up to the nth degree.

Here was a band that was quite definitely breaking the mould!

Even at this early stage they were looking to make a big impact. As Nicky related:

'The eighties were really crap. Before we heard Public Enemy we had to go back in time before we found any inspiration. There was no contemporary stuff for us. I mean the fact that they've had to resurrect a band like the Velvet Underground is so pathetic . . .' He spat out 'pathetic' syllable by syllable, underlining his hatred. 'When we started it was bands like Echo And The Bunnymen, Simple Minds and the Wedding Present . . . it was the most horrid time.'

After the Damaged Goods one-off single, they were signed by Heavenly Records. It was a perfect combination, Heavenly's boss Jeff Barrett was a walking talking music maniac who loved The

Clash. He was, alongside the Halls, the hippest press agent in London. The band with the quotes were surrounded by the PRs with the influence. This whole thing was going to go. The press were slowly beginning their intense love hate affair with the group. Out on the circuit things weren't so easy.

At the early gigs the band would be met with a bemused silence. Their first shows in Manchester at the Boardwalk, in deathly dull colleges on the outskirts in London (Friday, 11 January at Royal Holloway College at Egham in Surrey where they played one of the best gigs I have ever seen them deliver to a room of bored students, in other words a typical student union circuit night) or supporting Flowered Up at the now defunct International One in Manchester, were exercises in confusion and confrontation.

Bemused pop kids would rant on about the band being a 'hype' and that they must be crap because 'they wore make up'. The arguments I'd have on the band's behalf in the Boardwalk bogs!

The Manics were hardly ingratiating themselves with the early nineties pop kid.

They were too flash. Always a cardinal sin in UK music scene. You win no friends from the indie sector or the twilight world of John Peel where there are strict rules about what makes a valid group. A self-proclaimed broad-minded scene where men couldn't wear make up, the indie underground is defiantly conservative.

They released two singles on Jeff Barrett's Heavenly label to whom they signed in August 1990. There was the 1991 released fast shots of 'Motown Junk' and the anthemic 'You Love Us', a response to the music media who felt that the band was cartoon punk. The Manics were meeting the massive wall of indifference head on. So far, apart from their coterie of dedicated fans, no-one seemed to be getting it. But 'You Love Us' was kicking up enough press fuss and gatecrashed the Top 75 grabbing No. 62.

They toured the UK hard that winter. After the Manchester gig there was a party at the Brickhouse and The Manics were more like tired kids on the road than fire and brimstone dealing pop fanatics.

Nicky moaned about having boils on his neck and started listing all his tour ailments. A full-on hypochondriac, Wire was about a million miles away from the rock 'n' roll archetype, just a tired lanky bassist loving and hating the rock 'n' roll on the road experience.

But their innate pop talent was already showing itself. James had one fuck of a great voice and was an effortlessly talented guitar player. His white Les Paul spat a superb fat melodic rock that was at once traditional, soaring and celebratory but tinged with an epic sadness.

To many they were a joke band. Not the sort of rock 'n' roll that you could take seriously. They just weren't drab enough to be dragged back into the great gutter of 'real' music.

The Richey arm incident put a different slant on things. You can see how the band, stung by accusations of not being 'real' by the anal 'proper music' Gestapo of the indie world, were driven to desperation. Being interviewed by Steve Lamacq backstage at Norwich Arts Centre on 15 May 1991 pushed the fragile guitar player over the edge.

Steve was a fan but was not one hundred per cent convinced. He sniffed an element of the cartoon band about them and pushed this line in an interview for the NME. Putting to the band the thought that some people thought they weren't for real, Lamacq unintentionally opened up a hornet's nest whilst the guitar player opened up his arm. Richey produced a razor blade and carved '4Real' into his forearm. He may have been committing a desperate gesture, but it makes for a powerful statement as the scarred guitar player holds up his ripped-up limb to the shocked NME photographer, Ed Sirrs, minutes after carving one of the slogans of the decade into his forearm. His slashed arm and kohled eyes make him look like iconic.

It was a great rock 'n' roll gesture – irresponsible, sick and glorious, and loaded with meaning. It could also be the point that the soon-to-be icon started his descent into a mental hell.

A week later they moved up from Heavenly to the parent big bucks Sony/Columbia organization. The Manics now had the machine behind them. Accusations of 'sell out' were laughable. It was the nineties. Time to get real. Time to get the music out to more people than the underground scene who were suspicious of them anyway.

Their first release on Sony was the July 1991 single 'Stay Beautiful' (No. 40 in the UK charts), followed by October 1991's 'Love's Sweet Exile' (No. 26); the major label backing saw them inching towards the mainstream. The re-release of 'You Love Us' (No. 16) early in 1992 finally saw the band in the Top 20. The Manics were on a slow upward curve. That March the crunching, stunning 'Slash And Burn' headbutted its way to No. 20.

Their molotov missive-stuffed debut album, *Generation Terrorists*, released in 1992, had scraped the teens of the album charts. This was fine but hardly the multi-million-selling event that they had boasted they would release and then split up afterwards when their work was done! The band were hit by the truth: rock 'n' roll was a long, slow grind and their ecstatic fantasy of selling ten million records and then splitting was starting to look like a pipe dream.

Real life is always tougher than the romantic vision. So they started to grind it out. If this was going to be a war of attrition then so be it.

Throughout 1992 they were hammering home the mini hits. Their fan base was growing. For all their polemic and at odds defiance of the musical trends they could play great pop music. Track after track was being pulled from the *Generation Terrorists* album and hitting the Top 20 . . . the powerful 'Slash And Burn' (No. 20), the anthemic 'Motorcycle Emptiness' (No. 17) and then that September they finally scored the big breakthrough with the cover of 'Theme From M.A.S.H.' (No. 7) putting them into the Top 10.

At last they had been accepted. They now had their own core fanbase – a coterie of leopard-skin-clad desperadoes who looked like the coolest pop kids on the circuit. The Manics' gigs were a flurry of flamboyance and feather boas. Their fans oozed sex and situationism. The Manics were attracting the same cabal of intense letter writing fanatics as The Smiths had in the eighties but somehow flasher in their intensity.

I interviewed them just before they hit the stage at Birmingham Aston University in the summer of 1993 and the band were as combative as ever. In the tiny motel room they were still gunning for the same targets as they piled on the pre-show make-up. Already there were signs of the sort of wear and tear that being on the road can etch on to the psyche. Richey was by now drinking and Nicky was relating tales of his partner's post-gig back to the hotel love life – not hard to miss when you're sharing a tiny room.

While Richey threw on his fake leopard print coat, Nicky related that his love of beat literature came from his elder brother Patrick Jones. They piled into the car outside the hotel in a blur of fake furs, make-up and teased hair. They had the star swagger – living out their rock 'n' roll dream.

The second album, *Gold Against The Soul* (June 1993, No. 8), had just been released. It was a record that seemed intent on putting the group on to trad rock trajectory. They were still spitting alienation and pain but the songs were now almost normal rock. Musically they could have passed for Queen (hardly an insult). For many it was too smooth, the sound of a band desperate to succeed at all costs. I remember banging on to one of the band about how they should cut a rawer album, not get lost in corporate rock world. Mind you, that road never worked for me!

The album contained some great singles ('From Despair To Where', June 1993, No. 25; 'La Tristesse Durera', July 1993, No. 22; 'Roses In the Hospital', September 1993, No. 15). The pop heart was still beating strong and Bradfield, the band's principal tune-writer was still banging out great melodies.

Just when the band seemed to be finding an even keel, disaster struck. On 7 December 1993, their manager Phillip Hall died after a two-year battle against cancer. They were devastated. Hall had held the band together throughout their frequent bouts of self-doubt. His belief in the band had been tantamount. It was a fucking tragedy.

Post *Gold Against The Soul* The Manics were locked into a dangerous journey. Nicky Wire seemed to retreat from rock 'n' roll as Richey went further out there. Richey's obvious deterioration became the focal point of press attention on the band, adding to the intense pressure that the young guitar player was already under. They were becoming proper pop stars and the pain and pressure of the big time for a band that was as sensitive as this was beginning to hang heavily on their bony shoulders.

They started recording their new album *The Holy Bible* in a back-street Cardiff studio during 1994 against a backdrop of Richey's descent into mental illness.

You would read about the band's tour of Thailand and shiver at the personal degradation that was a million miles away from the rock pig motives that usually accompanies drinking and shagging exploits. You would hear gossip, read snippets of stuff in the press, or just look at the guitarist who was looking more and more like a ghost.

Against this backdrop it is hardly surprising that the album was the band's bleakest work.

Working fast, they had the new album in the can. An intense and wired affair, it was the logical culmination of the way the band were heading. The first single off the album, 'Faster' was released in

May 1994. Richey was finally admitted to a clinic that August. When Richey was released from the drying-out clinic, The Priory, near Northampton, they toured hard, culminating in a live performance at the London Astoria that December where they trashed all their gear.

They were the last gigs that Richey ever played with the band.

Richey's disappearance

In 1995 there were plans to go to the States. Richey and James were booked into a bunch of interviews over the water. America was (and still is) impervious to The Manics' charms. Probably seen as an English 'haircut band' by tight-arsed lo fi pundits or too plain weird for the rock heads, The Manics don't stand a chance.

On 1 February, just before the scheduled trip, Richey slipped away from the hotel. He left a shoebox full of artifacts and drove back to his flat in Cardiff where he left his passport. Two weeks later his car was found, the battery was flat and there were cassettes lying on the floor. It was clear he had been living in his car but where he went after that and how long he was there is anybody's guess. Those desperate hours in the car are painful to think about. As he slipped away from his car he disappeared into thin air – some say suicide, some say he just got away.

Ironically, Richey's disappearance put The Manics into the spotlight that they had once craved. They were in the mainstream press. The story started to roll. But it was under the spotlight in a way that they had never wanted.

They were getting taken seriously and their delayed dignified return to duty, slipping back into the limelight supporting Oasis at Maine Road and The Stone Roses at Wembley Stadium, was handled with the respect that it deserved. A low-key gig in the gay Traitor bar underneath the Hacienda saw Nicky Wire break down, the emotional punch of playing without Richey had just struck him.

The new Manics seemed a changed band. Gone was the glam guerilla look, the extreme images. Live, they left an aching space on the stage where Richey had once played, a poignant vacuum. It was just them and their music. A music that was going to be a bolder and bigger sound. The initial punk rock rushes or the skewered heart of darkness of *Holy Bible* was in the past, replaced with anthemic soundscapes. They were set for the big crossover. It was a similar scenario to Joy Division going into New Order after the suicide of vocalist Ian Curtis.

The Manics were no longer in the business of alienating the average rock punter. They were now embracing them and the results would be spectacular.

Just over a year after the disappearance of Richey, The Manics returned to the vinyl frey. In April 1996, they released their landmark single and one of the best ten singles of the decade, the monumental 'A Design For Life'. A stunning anthem, it was a powerful summation of working-class Welsh culture, an attempt to reclaim the territory from the dumbed-down Britpop version of the British working class, the anti-intellectual grunt that is worn as a badge of pride by musicians far smarter than they dare to let on.

From its 'Libraries gave us power . . . then work came and made us free' opening lines to the 'we don't talk about love' DUN NUH NU NUH 'we only wanna get drunk' chorus, the song was a lyrical masterpiece. Nicky Wire, in the best set of lyrics he'd come up with, was touching so many nerves all at once. That 'libraries' line will always make me think of wandering around Newport, Gwent and the socialist murals inside the indoor market. Make something out of your life, knowledge is power! Don't piss it all away . . . What a powerful statement . . . Perhaps the most revolutionary thing a rock 'n' roll band can say and one of the key tenets of the most articulate musicians since the fallout of punk rock twenty years previously.

Watch them play this at one of their enormodrome gigs or when they supported Oasis and listen to the crowd singing along. It sends a shiver up yer spine! Powerful stuff!

The single was the biggest hit yet. Boosted by the band's unfortunate high profile and powered by the fact that they had just released their most emotive and passionate song, the anthemic 'A Design For Life' crashed in at No. 2. It was easily their biggest hit. The song becoming a pub jukebox favourite, a karaoke classic and, like the Specials 'Ghost Town' years before, a politically and sociology charged anthem played into the very heartlands of the UK.

The Manics, who had spent their youth being sneered at by the beer monsters, were now soundtracking their lives. They had gone from being the outsiders to the mainstream. They had finally pulled off the pop plan that they had detailed in the back of that van in 1991.

Swiftly following on the coat tails of their biggest hit was their fourth album, released on 20 May 1996, *Everything Must Go*, which is arguably their best. Whereas *Holy Bible* was an addictive and suffocating desolate descent into introspective hell, the ultimate Richey experience and an album that the band's core fans will always love the most (and a great record to boot), the new album was an explosion of pop colour as Bradfield finally moved into the spotlight, not just handling more of the interviews, but putting his stamp on the record and finally copping some of the credit for his musical talent.

They had negotiated the emotional landscape and come back with an album that has been criticized for being too trad. Bullshit, what is this fear of pop? Even the *Holy Bible* was made up of great songs. It was one of The Manics' key strengths, writing great traditional rock songs and then twisting them with fierce and powerful lyrics. This time they'd just upped the trad ante.

The album was a massive seller, its dark soul may have been superficially disguised but it was still there. After all, there were five Richey songs on the record, from the anti-Americanization of the UK of the opening 'Elvis Impersonator: Blackpool Pier' (lyrics finished by Nicky) to the harrowing tale of the American war photographer in the eponymous 'Kevin Carter' (Carter committed suicide, weighed down with a dreadful guilt after winning the Pulitzer prize for photographing a vulture preying on a dead baby in the vile hell of the mid nineties war in Rwanda). Some felt that the song was about Richey and it went on to be a Top Ten hit on its own in September 1996. The title track was a kiss-off, an apology to the core fans who hadn't wanted the band to carry on, a cathartic release. 'Small Black Flowers That Grow In The Sky', a song title that sounded like a Yukio Mishima short story was about animals, desperate, trapped in their fearsomely small zoo cages – another analogy for its author's condition? Who knows? You could look through the writer's last few lyrics looking for clues or you could sit back and let the powerful rock 'n' roll make you feel good.

The album, dripping a commercial edge, catapulted The Manics into mega-stadium success. The band that had once sneered at festivals seemed to be on at every summer bill and were starting to get comfortable with the stadia shows. Their show at Manchester's NYNEX was a triumph for the band, selling out the 17,000 capacity stadium.

The original fiercely loyal coterie of fans were beginning to feel betrayed. The song had broken The Manics to a whole new audience of laddish beer monsters – the sort of people that gave the core fans hell in the small towns and suburbs that they strutted out from. The letter pages of the music press were filled with the same sort of vitriolic missives that had filled postbags when the eighties icon of sensitivity, Morrissey, had slid from the top of the greasy pole of credibility.

For many it wasn't just the music becoming more commercial. The band were also losing the look and the rock 'n' roll glam swagger that had complemented their music in the Richey days. Only Nicky ever seemed to make the effort, still camping it up in dresses, Elvis sunglasses or any other weird get-up that he could get his hands on. Maybe getting dressed up in your punk rock party frocks didn't seem right any more to the band's muso core.

With their fifth album, the No. 1 *This Is My Truth Tell Me Yours*, they completed their crossover process. The new stuff was touched by the hand of mainstream. There were dark mutterings about the lyrics and the tunes. But to dismiss the album is to do it a disservice. The album proves that The Manics can write great ballads and that they still pack the punch with stomping tunes like the Top 5 'You Stole The Sun' single or the album's first release 'If You Tolerate This Your Children Will Be Next'.

The December 1998 return show at the Manchester NYNEX was a superb display of effortlessly great rock 'n' roll, the band as ever treading the fine line between trad and the ridiculous (Nicky Wire camping it up in a tiara and skipping). The politics and the situationism were still represented in a stark light show flashing up slogans and the leopard print army were still at the front huddling for shelter while the incurably square crowd (the sort of people who would have hated the band's make-up and glam era if they had known that they had existed!) filled up the rest of the huge hall.

For two hours the band ran through a whole slew of great songs. It may have been slick and it may have been a million miles away from their spiky roots. The band's glam style had been further binned. The musician wing were starting to dress designer casual, in effect looking like a normal nineties band. Merging in with the morass of baggy nothingness that was 1998/99, now the songs were doing the talking.

On 'If You Tolerate This Your Children Will Be Next', The

Manics have become what only a handful suspected at the start of the decade, a quintessential British rock band. One of those groups like The Who that everyone learns guitar along to or gets pissed in pubs to. Soundtracking the lives of the people that used to laugh at them, The Manics have quite definitely crossed over. In doing so they have become, quite possibly, the sort of group that they would have spat vitriol at back in the van all those years ago.

But that's growing up for you, kids! And at least they did it with dignity.

Turning into everything that you once were perceived as despising and doing it in style is one thing but getting past that into the middle-aged hinterland that destroys all bands of their ilk will, perhaps, be The Manics' next great challenge. It's one that they seem more than capable of rising to.

CHAPTER TWELVE

WELSH POP

'Every day, when I wake up, I thank the Lord I'm Welsh'

(Catatonia)

The Manics' breakthrough opened up the whole Welsh music scene. Single-handed they had made the principality hip in nineties terms. They were like the battering ram. Having to take the blows, the insults.

Before them there had been a very healthy but small-time Welsh language scene, the odd spark of action, the odd whiff of pop. Not much to write home about.

Post Manics, though, there is a rumbling volcano of Welsh bands of all different shapes and sizes. Far from being uncool, some bands even flaunt their Welshness – a delicious V sign to the years of being considered a backwards pop region.

By the late nineties, Wales was *the* centre for guitar bands in the UK.

As it was making its first faltering steps towards some sort of nominal political independence, the ancient nation was propelling a whole feast of bands towards the top of the charts. From Catatonia's blissfully exuberant guitar pop to the Stereophonics' hook-laden laddish rock, from Super Furry Animals innate indie weirdness to The Manics themselves becoming bigger than ever . . . Welsh pop was on a glorious high.

Fuck, even Tom Jones and the divine Shirley Bassey, two of the greatest voices to ever come out of the UK, were hip again!

It was a scene that has its own roots. Its own tradition. Its own politics.

Before The Manic Street Preachers, who formed in their own carefully created vacuum, there was a whole host of bands rooted back in the Welsh language scene of the early eighties. The scene was highly politicized, attempting to bring the Welsh language bang up to date by fusing it with modern pop culture. It was waving the flag for an ancient tongue that had been persecuted mercilessly by the mean-assed Victorian English. In the nineties the language revived itself to the extent that it was being taught in schools. It's no longer considered a dying language. The fiercely independent music underground had its part to play in making the language seem more modern, more relevant.

This was the time when Sons of Glendawr were blowing up English holiday homes in the Welsh villages. There was a whiff of anarchy in the air.

'We don't want to hurt anyone, we just want our villages back,' claimed X, someone who was linked with the organization. Fortunately the Welsh have never had to take the terrorist route. The ballot box decided it all for them. In 1999 the referendum voted 'yes' to some sort of self-government and in the following elections the Welsh Nationalist party, Plaid Cymru scored heavily. Fifteen years before, all this seemed as unlikely as one of their bands ramraiding the charts.

In the eighties the vibrant Welsh language pop scene, centred in the north around Bangor, was a rumbling collection of countless outfits creating a multi-styled assault of Welsh music. Most of the scene's profile had been bulldozed by the rugged shoulders of Anhrefn. Their nonstop talking up of the scene made them the first point of contact for English music media interested in the cause.

The band played a powerhouse punk rock and sang all their lyrics in Welsh. Everywhere they went they spread the gospel. In 1988 music paper *Sounds* did a double-page spread on the Welsh scene, painting a vibrant picture. A whole host of bands were singing in their mother tongue in a vastly differing bunch of styles.

There was the Fallesque landscapes of Datblygu, the electronic weirdness of Plant Bach Ofnus, the twisted hip hop of Llwybr Llaethog, the techno indie pop of Ffa Coffi Bawb (some of whom would become The Super Furry Animals), the noise manipulators Traddodiad Ofnus, the indie weirdness of The Fflaps and a thousand others.

It was a powerhouse of a scene – they even had their own record label Ankst Records who were committed to pushing the whole scene towards the mainstream. A mainstream that, c/o John Peel, was becoming ever more receptive to what was going on. Ankst also had two bands on its books who would help to bust this whole thing wide open in the nineties, Gorky's Zygotic Monkey and Catatonia. None of the hardcore Welsh bands has ever made it in commercial terms but they left behind a whole catalogue of intriguing records. Datblygu, especially, really had something but their fear of travel made touring difficult and their profile suffered accordingly. Anrehfyn could mount a fearsome roar of a punk rock gig but were only ever big in Czeckoslavakia. Post house Anrehfyn moved towards a dubbed-out kinda style cutting some interesting records.

Proving that the ancient celtic tongue could work in a modern context, the Welsh language scene was just one part of a national band scene that was far more frenetic than given any credit for.

In towns like Newport the Welsh language scene had very little bearing on local bands. In the early nineties Newport had its own little thing going on, to the extent of being dubbed the 'new Seattle' by a press greedy for some action. Bands like Novocaine, Dub War and Sixty Foot Dolls all waved the raw guitar flag while just up the valleys a few miles away in Blackwood, The Manic Street Preachers had already emerged.

Newport has always been a great rock 'n' roll town.

The focal point being TJ's, the sweatbox club run by the amiable John. TJ's itself is almost worthy of blue plaque status as the club where Kurt Cobain proposed to Courtney Love after a riotous Hole gig there. There had been classic gigs here for years. Cheap Sweaty Fun, a local crew of promoters, had been bringing in freaked out underground bands since the post punk days.

Outfits like Butthole Surfers, Sonic Youth, Husker Du and Big Black all scored their initial followings here a long time before the trendies got on board. TJ's had a classic crowd, a wild mental audience, a surfing crew of crazies oiled by copious gallons of alcohol.

TJ's really rocked. So it was no surprise then that years later there was a generation of youthful bands chasing this crazed creative energy. None of the bands, apart from maybe Dub War and Sixty Foot Dolls, have ever managed to break away but for a couple of years there seemed to be an inexhaustible supply of attempts.

In South Wales The Manics were the first band to break big from all this intense grass roots activity. A grass roots activity that, ironically, they had had very little to do with. In their early interviews they shunned the Welsh language scene. Like a lot of bands in Wales they felt that the scene had too much control over the country's culture and who actually got played on the radio or on the specialist local pop TV programmes.

The Manics looked to London for their escape route.

Their success meant that being a band from Wales could, at last, be taken seriously. In their wake came a whole bunch of bands that have stamped their presence on the nineties. The next band to make some sort of escape were Catatonia.

A phone call from Anhrefyn's Rhys, now at Ankst, alerted me to the band in 1992. The cassettes he sent over sounded good. They were more pop than the usual stuff that came out of Wales and right from the start Cerys's powerful vocals cut through giving them a definite edge and I did their first national press interview for the *Melody Maker*.

The band had roots deep into the Welsh scene. Hailing from Cardiff, all the group except for Cerys (who they had found busking outside Debenhams in Cardiff) had been in local bands. Bands like Y Cruff, The Hepburns, The Crumblowers and U Thant.

With Cerys on vocals, the group swerved towards a far more poppy direction. With a voice like that you know that suddenly that the jumble of chords on your guitar will explode into life. Their first single, 1993's 'For Tinkerbell', was a single of the week in the NME. They were on the map.

The band set out on what seemed a never-ending tour. The press was full of stories of Cerys being a pissed-up rock wild child. A few drinks and suddenly you've got a reputation! A good story.

1996's 'Sweet Catatonia' was their first low key hit (No. 61). The hard work was beginning to pay off. The follow-up, 'Lost Cat', landed just outside the Top 40. They were on the brink, playing on the club circuit for what seemed like years. They were one of those bands who always seemed to be grinding out their indie pop at the Manchester Roadhouse and similar venues. Somewhere deep in the fug of the venue you could hear a powerful pair of lungs over the solid backing. This was the trump card. Cerys Matthews had one of those voices. She could really really sing, a rarity in the independent sector. Their debut album, *Way Beyond Blue*, was released in September 1996. It only reached No. 40, a disappointment for the band as they had been building a big and loyal fanbase on the circuit and had had two near-miss singles, 'Bleed' (No. 46) and 'You've Got A Lot To Answer For' (their first Top 40 hitting No. 35) which had crossed over into the tough fortress of daytime radio.

However, in 1997 they finally broke big time.

The first sign that there was something good coming was with the 'I Am the Mob' (No. 37) single, a stomping slab of power pop which got in the charts just before Christmas. Catatonia followed this up with a brilliant album featuring a non-stop run of killer tunes, *International Velvet*. What a treasure trove. No wonder they spent the year rather noisily becoming big stars.

The album was doing fine in chart terms but it was the next single 'Mulder and Scully' (No. 3) that catapulted the album to No. 1 and the band into the big time. Single after single ('Road Rage', No. 5; 'Strange Glue', No. 11; and 'Game On', No. 33). In between all this Cerys also found time to hit the Top 5 with 'The Ballad Of Tom Jones', an arch duet with Tommy from Space.

What a year!

Their new album, *Equally Cursed And Blessed*, is not quite as vibrant as its predecessor but it hasn't stopped them from becoming one of the biggest bands in the country and Cerys from becoming one of the true pop stars of the time. Her extrovert wardrobe and big-hearted persona shone when surrounded by too clean pop bands and dowdy indie outfits.

Catatonia's very Welshness is one of their key flavours. It oozes through each record. Matthews's vocals twist and turn with an innate Welsh flavour, an accent that adds even more sexiness to her powerful lusty voice. When welded to the hook-laden songs, it's an addictive formula.

Running neck and neck with Catatonia's rise were The Stereophonics, a band that captured all those classic pillars of Brit rock that endears them to an adoring fan base. With a commitment to passion, guts, sweat and trad melodies, The Stereophonics are that rarest of things: a people's band. . .

Signed to V2, they released their first single 'Looks Like Chaplin' in November 1996. It was flipped with 'More Life In Tramps Vest' which has become one of the band's classic tunes. The song, a small-town vignette detailing a boring job in a fruit stall, has become a firm live favourite. It was re-released the following May as their third single and was their first Top 40 hit.

The month before they had had their first mini hit with 'Local

Boy In A Photograph' about a boy planning his suicide. Hard gigging and songs about people's lives that reached out and touched their audience were having an effect. Some people dubbed them as a version of The Manics without all the latter's emotional baggage, but that would be unfair. The Stereophonics write street lyrics, real-life dispatches, without having to resort to The Manics' slash and burn situationism.

Their songs are stripped down simple. A trio creates powerful rules. There is no time to mess around. No pointless solos. No one can sit back and take it easy. With no interest in drugs, they are firmly in the tradition of beer bands, no weirdness, no fucking about. It's like acid house never happened. They are the first post house band – untouched and untainted by the dance scene which itself is over ten years old and can hardly be described as new or cutting edge any more (old teds, old hippies, old punks and old ravers . . . time, as every shining new pop generation discovers, is such a bastard!).

The Super Furry Animals were quite definitely the jokers in the pack. Unlike the big three of the Welsh scene they harked back to a weirder, freakier music – the sort of stuff that the late eighties Welsh language bands had immersed themselves in.

Their own roots lie deep in that scene. Vocalist Gruff Rhys and drummer Dafydd Leeuan played in the aforementioned Ffa Coffi Pawb (say it quickly to get its full-on 'naughty' meaning) cutting two albums, *Clymhalio* and *Hei Vidal* in the early nineties. They toured the Celtic language circuit in their home country and in Brittany (the Celtic corner of France) with Anhrefyn.

The Super Furry Animals, since signing to Creation, have honed their sound down to an eclectic weirdness; a freaky pop that nods at techno, the post-punk stuff from the early eighties and the outer reaches of psychedelia. Analogue keyboards give their twisted guitar pop another texture with wackoid keyboard sounds and bizarre drones. Armed with mental lyrics, they take their out of space pop that one step further. Somehow, like The Happy Mondays before them, they found some sort of discipline in their madness and reined the whole crazed collection of influences into a pop whole.

It serves them well. Their debut album, *Fuzzy Logic*, was a neat snapshot of their freaky beat. Its sleeve was a montage of photos of Welsh drug-runner Howard Marks, author of *Mr Nice Guy*, (an autobiographical tale of drug dealing and pro-spliff politicking that would inevitably make its fifty-plus author one of the spokesman of the dope generation). The wacked grooves inside saw them embraced by the new spliff rock scene, making the band one of the prime movers in a late nineties psychedelic revival.

Tucked in somewhere just behind SFA were Gorkys Zygotic Monkey whose fungal weirdness has seen them score quite heavily in the world of late night radio. Fucked about by their record label, Gorkys have not yet managed to break out of the shadowy hinterland of 'big in the indie charts'. Maybe their music (and the very name of the band) is just that bit too strange for the mainstream.

In the wake of these bands comes a whole legion of new outfits. The Welsh, who were always famous for having a bit of a singsong, now have an army of bands fulfilling that role.

One sign that the South Wales/Newport scene is moving from hip into the mainstream is the making of two feature films set in the region – *Twin Town* was billed as the region's reply to *Trainspotting* when in fact it was more a twisted dark comedy and *Human Traffic*, the first street film to deal with the all encompassing nature of acid house culture.

However it's for its bands that Wales will be remembered in the nineties and they've made one fuck of an impression.

The dragon has roared.

CHAPTER THIRTEEN

DREAMING SPIRES – FROM OXFORD TO RADIOHEAD

While Manchester was raving and Wales was going into pop overdrive, Oxford became the last bastion of late-eighties Indie. The so-called brave new world glimpsed by London's My Bloody Valentine – a multitextural dream pop was seen as an escape route by many indie guitar outfits. By the early nineties Oxford was one of the focal points for the indie scene. A studied guitar drone coupled with an introverted stage presence that quickly had bands like Slowdive, Chapterhouse and Ride labelled 'shoegazing'.

By the mid nineties the college city was also host to the stadium-filling crafted rock of Radiohead. It was one hell of a legacy . . .

The dreaming spires had never really been a rock 'n' roll town. But in the nineties there was a whole explosion of activity in the city. There are so many reasons why something finally went off here, it's hard to imagine why it had never happened before.

A big student population. A close proximity to the big smoke. A tight small infrastructure – with Cowley Road, the heart of student bohemia, seeming like an endless row of venues – and plenty of money sloshing around on the leisure front.

Nevertheless it wasn't till the tail end of the eighties that there were any stirrings on the music scene to be arsed with. Sure enough they had their own share of local celebs before. Gary Glitter was from just up the road, the outrageously naff Mr. Big were locals, Slade had filmed their video for 'Goodbye To Jane' in Oxford and Lonnie Donnegan had recorded 'Does Your Chewing

Gum Lose Its Flavour On The Bedpost Overnight' at the Oxford New Theatre.

Mmmmm, let's face it there was not much happening, was there?

In the punk days Oxford was built into the national circuit and all the bands went through there but there was very little local action. It was never really a town where punk was going to catch on.

By the mid eighties it was one of the key ports of call for the anorak end of the indie scene. Oxford even had its own band, Tallulah Gosh, who belied their 'cutie' tag with some fierce guitar-driven records and an equally fierce commitment to the indie underground ethic. Live, especially in their early days they could barely play. Their early gigs would collapse into chaos, the drummer's kit would fall over, but they existed because of pure punk rock spirit. It was about getting up there and saying something, doing something. Make a statement. Its the purest form of pop music. Self-expression. Have a go reader, don't be daunted by the supergroups in the mega arenas, grab some mates, grab whatever instruments you want and go and make some noise, fuck you might even be good at it!

In the late eighties Tallulah Gosh's lonely sojourn as the only cool local band was ended with the arrival of Swervedriver whose droning guitar workouts were a precursor to the shoegazing scene, a scene that has come to exemplify everything about the city.

Swervedriver signed to Creation and were one of the label's priority bands in the late eighties/early nineties. Their multi-layered guitar workouts were out of sync in a mainstream UK scene that was under the spell of the baggy/Nirvana/house axis, but they made some pretty good inroads into the States. Ten years later and they are still in existence, probably trading on that respect abroad.

At the same time as Swervedriver's mould-breaking workouts a mod scene was emerging. Spinning off from this were 5.30 who in many ways were a Britpop band five years too early. The outfit were more than a straight mod band. They plied a jaunty guitar pop – kinda like an aggressive updated Kinks. 5.30 could sell out the Marquee but were passed over when the Britpop scene, that they had in many ways instigated, eventually broke big.

Both Swervedriver and 5.30 had shown that there was a way out of the local scene and in their wake a whole cacophony of local bands was starting to appear. Local journalist and scenester Mark Seargent looks back on the late-eighties emergent scene with a certain affection. 'You could see that there was a scene bubbling up at the time. Then, like now really, the bands would be at each other's gigs checking each other out. It was pretty close-knit. If someone had a really good idea you could be sure that someone else would be using it pretty soon after! I guess the best venue at the time was The Jericho Tavern, that was a great venue and a key place in the development of the music scene.'

Inspired by Swervedriver's very existence, a bunch of kids formed a band called Ride and were also swiftly snapped up by Creation. They burst on to the scene with a music paper frenzy. Some of their early gigs were mesmerizing, they may have had one foot inside the introspective – for want of a better word – shoegazing scene but they played with such a youthful conviction that their music would take off. They fitted very neatly into Creation as the latest in a long line of textured guitar bands. They also bridged the gap between The Stone Roses ultra melody and the nu skool of sulky student chiming guitars.

It served them well: pretty soon they were hitting the real grown-up charts with their monosyllabic run of debut EPs 'Ride EP', 'Play EP' and 'Fall EP'; in 1990 but their biggest hit was 1992's 'Leave Them All Behind'.

The creative tension between their two frontmen, Mark Gardener and Andy Bell, saw them fall apart in 1996. Bell went on to form the far more trad, almost Oasis-sounding Hurricane No1 who grazed the back end of the charts with a series of singles in the late nineties.

Perhaps it was no surprise that Oxford was going to be shoegazing central. The dreaming spires were perhaps evocative of dreaming music. (Mind you, the housing estates that surrounded the city including the notorious riot torn Blackbird Lees estate were having no truck with all this town centre action. They were into banging techno.)

In Ride's wake came Slowdive, also signed to Creation and Chapterhouse, both plying a moody introspective guitar music, a post My Bloody Valentine guitar drone rock. The press loved it, pushing it as a post Manchester wave but the music made very little connection with the public.

The bands, through no fault of their own, were seen as a hype and were resented before they could hit their stride.

Just when it seemed that Oxford was going to be the shoegazing capital of the world, a journo wet dream of a scene, a local indie band who had been around for a couple of years as The Jennifers changed their name to Supergrass and recorded a fab rush of fuzzy guitar poppy punk called 'Caught By The Fuzz'. Supergrass are one of the great understated British pop acts of the times. Even if their joyful exuberant pop leaves them lagging behind the serious stadium dinosaurs in terms of mega sales.

Nonetheless they cut great singles. Singles like the teenage guitar rush of their 1994 debut 'Caught By The Fuzz' and 1996's 'Alright', dealt a boisterous good time melody. Their debut album was choc full of youthful excitement and caught the optimistic wave of Britpop. Supergrass from the off seemed highly accomplished. The band seemed to be able to bang out class pop with ease. Live they were a confident celebration of the best things about the form, dealing out simple tunes that made you feel so fucking alive.

One of the bands that seemed to play all the time in the late eighties and got overlooked were called On A Friday. Mark Seargent was not that impressed. 'They were a bit boring really!' he laughs. 'Just one of those local bands that no one was really that bothered about.'

On A Friday, though, were to be making their own impact on the decade. The band would become Radiohead, the biggest group yet to come out of Oxford and one of the few British bands to actually make any impact outside the UK in the past ten years.

Nowadays Oxford boasts a highly eclectic scene. The superstar bands have regally elected to stay in the city, and cruise along the Cowley Road checking out the new bands. It's an easy-going scene. New bands are generally clustered around the Tricky Disco label, the best of which are the dissonant Nought playing a multi-textural layered guitar freakout that is far too heavy to be confused with some sort of shoe-gazing revival.

Walking down Cowley Road past the venues and the walls caked with peeling posters advertising gigs you know that you're in one of the creative hubs of guitar band UK – it oozes that low-rent bohemia that is the perfect backdrop of the form. As we enter the new millennia Oxford has become one of the key towns in the UK music scene . . . So cool that it is the home town of James Lavelle, the head honcho of one of the best 'dance' labels of the decade, Mo Wax.

Mo Wax has become a nineties bi-word for supa cool. A meeting point for house, hip hop, funk, soul and even punk rock (attitude). Within a razor sharp run of releases and a championing of some neat street action, Mo Wax ends the decade sitting pretty, an internationally renowned conduit of cool.

Sat in a big office in the centre of London is the man who is a portrait of the total fan as music biz mogul. A portrait that is more likely to be a spray-canned graffiti job.

Understanding the cutting-edge popular culture has always been something that the major label dinosaurs have never been that good at. And imposing your own vision on to the music scene takes a combination of an iron nerve and blinkered fandom.

Mo Wax's discography reads like a riot act of great action. Involved in putting out music that deals in a whole myriad of styles and textures.

Hailing from Oxford, Lavelle left school at 16 and started by worked in a record shop and started his own club. Through his Mo Wax nights in his hometown he swiftly hooked up with the right sort of names on the scene – Galliano, Gilles Peterson and the acid jazz posse were guests at the club. They swiftly noticed the teenage enthusiast, seeing a fresh new face on the nu jazz scene.

In the nineties the jazz tag is pretty all-encompassing, taking in all elements of sampling culture. Mo Wax is in love with the stylish element of the jazz pioneers and the new textural possibilities of post sampler music.

The label was formed as the young Lavelle saw an opportunity for a new cutting-edge take on what the acid jazz boys had been dealing out since the late eighties. Borrowing a bunch of money from mates, he set up the label. Relying on his own vision based loosely on the hip hop style, he grabs elements of several different scenes. It's eclectic, it has no respect for musical boundaries and it makes perfect sense in the niche nineties.

CHAPTER FOURTEEN

ACID HOUSE GOES MENTAAAAAAAL

It was too good a secret to keep. Anyone who visited those early clubs wanted some of the flavour to themselves. Inevitably, the scene was going to burst out all over the country. By the summer of 1988 the best-kept secret of the Ibiza originals was appearing everywhere: acid house was begging to turn into a full-on rampaging youth cult – with all its attendant problems . . .

The story was out. There were some wild times going down. Shoom was turning hundreds away. What had been a private concern in the autumn of '87 had now turned into a full-on craze by the summer of '88. Acid House was going nationwide and the culture was changing fast from a bunch of mates recreating the holiday vibe to a national obsession. Like followers of a band that goes from playing the toilets to the stadia in a few short months, its original fans felt cheated.

What had once been their own private blast of hedonism was, by now, nudging the mainstream.

Shoom had moved to the more central YMCA on Tottenham Court Road attempting to cope with its popularity. Spectrum was mobbed by what *Boys Own* termed 'acidteds', daygloed wardrobed new arrivals on the scene picking up on the scene clichés, pissing off the originals and having a great time.

It always happens in youth culture. You can see it in punk. The elite few set up the scene and everyone else marches in, reinterprets the culture via the mainstream press and creates their own version. It loses its originality. It loses its edge. However, nothing should ever be exclusive – if the people want to party, let them!

Nicky Holloway, one of the Ibiza party crew, emerged on the scene in June 1988 with 'The Trip' which he promoted at the Astoria. For many of the inner acid sanctum this was the moment that house went commercial, went overground. The club made no effort to remain underground and catered full-on for the 'acid teds'.

And it was enormously successful.

The scene was certainly swinging, the daily papers were full of shots of bandana'd youth in smiley regalia monging out to the new beat. It was getting so massive that it was becoming a full-on pop movement defining the year.

1988 was termed the 'second summer of love', as a far-reaching rush of youth culture that hadn't been felt since 1977 gripped the nation. It was a case of whether you were on the bus or off the bus. It created a generation gap. The music press ignored it and Fleet Street, at first embracing what was going on in the hope of flogging papers on the back of the craze, beat a hasty retreat when they realized the dread drugs were involved.

Frontline clubs Spectrum, RIP and The Trip were the front-runners, each having their own unique interpretation of the craze. In their wake came a whole run of illegal clubs and warehouse parties. Acid house lent itself perfectly to an underground culture. Setting up a sound system was quick and relatively cheap. There were plenty of takers for the nights and everyone seemed to be looking for the party. The drugs angle had scared off the mainstream (there had already been two E related deaths) and *Top Of The Pops* (just to show how Cliff Richard they really were) had banned any record with the word 'Acid' in the title after D Mobs's Top 5 hit.

By the autumn of 1988 acid house was the street craze of the UK: the culture's framework was well in place, warehouse parties, club nights, weekends on the E, smiley shirts, baggy clothes, a new slang, shock horror headlines. It was a classic youth culture experience.

From here it would go mega. From the small clubs it would burst into raves, the sheer volume of people and the hunger of the new promoters meant that massive illegal events became the only practical way to promote the music. (And make pots of money.) Clandestine phone calls, pre-recorded answerphone messages combined with word of mouth would pass the crucial party information on: out in the middle of nowhere there would be some massive action going down. Thousands of kids would turn up to dance all night. The motorway services were chocker with cars and baggied up ravers, their eyes booming out of their heads.

The M25 became one big party roundabout as the search was on for that night's big rave. Motorway service stations were hives of gossip and the newly arriving mobile phones were a vital connection as well as the queues outside the services' call boxes. It was a buzz, driving around looking for the action, giving the cops the slip . . . outlaw pop culture, it's always the most exciting. Score your drugs, talk crazy shit, stumble through Farmer Brown's fields, hear the distant rumble of the acid house and then get lost in the pop oblivion of crazy sound, wild lights and E-fuelled camaraderie . . . what a great escape from the inner city or the dull suburbs. Fall in love with complete strangers, melt with a chemically fired loved-up warmth and dance like a wired up maniac . . . it was the purest expression of the pop dream.

The authorities eventually clamped down. It took them time to understand just what the fuck was going on. Eventually police raids and new legislation crushed the rave scene.

The big outdoors raves, the illegal warehouse parties, were pushed back deep underground. By 1991 the whole scene had generally returned to the clubs where it has since prospered, totally redefining what the club environment is all about as well as pop culture itself.

CHAPTER FIFTEEN

POP WILL EAT ITSELF

Is not only the name of a band that was managing to combine hip hop and indie about five years before anyone else without any credit but is also quite an astute term. Dave Quantick from the NME came up with the phrase in the mid eighties when he was trying to describe the way that pop was becoming more and more self-reverential.

Even in his blackest nightmares in those far off days he couldn't have envisioned a live circuit where there were few new groups, just bands pretending to be old groups. In 1999 pick up a live listing for any small-town venue and that's the story. Coupled with this was the bands from the past going one better and reforming. Mind you, after twenty years in the wilderness they look less like themselves than the covers bands! Pop was now choking on itself . . .

Pop is now old. It's no longer the noo scene daddio. It's been around forever. It's more than forty years since Elvis checked into the 'Heartbreak Hotel'. Pop is no longer the fast-moving lithe yoof of its past.

In the nineties there were a couple of new phenomena that could only have been a result of the longevity of the form.

One was the covers band and the other was the band reformed.

A whole mob of creaking old relics decided to tread the boards again in the decade. At one time the news that a band was going to go for it for one last time was greeted with horror by the pop world.

But in the post-post-post-modern world anything is allowed.

Even bands that had been trapped in the amber of pop history as shiny totems of youthfulness were back out on the boards. The Velvet Underground were one of the more bizarre reformations, ending up playing a strange set at Glastonbury. Vocalist Lou Reed was singing songs that had always worked because they sounded like they were recorded in a shed and played to a hundred people. Now they were getting blasted out to thousands of people and sung in a bored karaoke voice. But then that was one of the cool things about the nineties – the debunking of myths or at the very least the cashing in on them.

Cashing in were The Sex Pistols who decided to make some of the money that everyone else had been making out of their legacy for years. The band sauntered around the world for most of 1996 to mixed reviews. I found myself playing with the Pistols at Finsbury Park, being in one of the support bands on the day. Like most people who actually liked the Pistols our crew firmly expected it to be a bloated load of old crap. But the band were great, opening with the craziest song, 'Bodies'. They sounded spot on, playing their furious powerful songs. It may have had no sociological value and anarchy was not really in the air, but at least it proved once and for all that Cook and Jones were great musicians.

On that warm afternoon in Finsbury Park the Pistols rocked. Thank God they didn't put any new records out!

New Order returned to the fray after five years playing gigs that made grown men weep for their lost youth. Their glacial pop always sounded timeless anyway so they had no problems just returning from nowhere.

New Order, along with Echo And The Bunnymen, was one of the more successful comebacks. They didn't really lose any of their cool: sometimes when you're ten years ahead of the pack if you come back you still won't seem dated!

Perhaps inspired by New Order's effortless return The Happy Mondays re-entered the pack. Their gigs were surprisingly slick (well, the Manchester one was). It was just like they had never been away! Perhaps they hadn't left it too long for the comeback. Five years is about right to pick up from where you left off. No matter how grizzled you are you can always remember the names of the rest of the band, even the road crew if you're that together . . .

Despite this there were still a clutch of bands that eternally resisted the clarion call of the tax man and didn't regroup in the nineties but will forever be dogged with reformation rumours: The Smiths, The Clash and The Stone Roses. The Roses reformation story was fired up when The Seahorses fell apart. There was talk from insiders that they had nearly decided to do it but John Squire opted for getting a new band together. These three classic English rock 'n' roll groups have one thing in common and that's unfinished business. The Smiths' reunion, like The Clash, must surely be on permanent hold. The Manchester group were dogged by court cases, inter-band wrangling and Johnny Marr's continued success with Electronic, but the lure of the Yankee dollar can make even the most firm mind wander. . .

Still, why bother with waiting for the real thing to reform, when you can go and laugh at a bunch of chancers aping your fave band down the local? Made up of usually hotshot local musos who never quite got the break, these bands are often more capable of remembering the songs than the originals!

The gig circuit was now chock full of covers bands. Beer heads and losers who were getting paid the full whack for pretending to be Oasis, The Beatles, The Stone Roses, The Who, Mott The Hoople, Pink Floyd or anyone. By 1999 if there wasn't a band covering your set then you were a failure. The bands were slowly choking the life out of the live circuit.

The covers band phenomenon was imported from Australia where it had been popular for years. Down in Aus there is a huge live circuit in bruising pubs where experimental frontier-mashing rock is hardly the sort of gear that's going to go down well with beer monsters. Bands swiftly realized that cover versions placated the roughest of crowds. Eventually they just went one step further and became the famous band – getting happily doshed up and out of the venue without a broken nose.

Unfortunately like the tiresome karaoke machine imported from Japan via the Nissan plant in Newcastle, the idea caught on like wildfire with people who can't really be arsed if pop goes forward or not, preferring to wallow in the glorious past (even if it was a shallow copy).

It's a sobering thought but the John Lennon in The Bootleg Beatles, who are perhaps the biggest of all the covers bands, is actually ten years older than Lennon himself was when he got shot . . .

CHAPTER SIXTEEN

FROM RIOT GRRRL TO GIRL POWER

The music industry hasn't changed. It's still selling sex, whether its a knicker-wetting boy band or a wank fantasy girl band . . . It's the world's largest legitimate porn industry.

Sex sells. That's what it's about from Elvis to Madonna . . . Icons have used sex to sell records. In the late nineties the male singers and female singers know this and have a bit more control over their bodies. You'd have to be a total fool to enter the pop game and get pissed off because you were expected to thrust your crotch into some slavering camera in a TV studio. You'd have to be fairly sad to be in a full-on pop band (boy or girl) and want to get 'taken seriously as an artist' when your audience were more likely to get serious about your crotch.

And it's this atmosphere that has always made it more difficult for women artists with their own agenda to get taken seriously. With the man-made market rules dictating the rules on purely sexual terms, the pop scene is sometimes the last bastion of maledom, a men-only club like some sort of faded men-only bar in a dusty old cricket club. But that's slowly beginning to change . . .

From the early days of pop there have been people who have stood up against the conventional scrum and this process has accelerated in the nineties. By the end of the decade there are female artists who have managed to break free of these barriers. They can play with sex and still have something serious to say. Or they can ignore sex completely and do what the fuck they like with pop (ironically the reverse process is becoming true in male pop which is getting increasingly bimbo orientated) and set their own stall with groundbreaking music. The likes of Björk, PJ Harvey, Courtney Love, Lauryn Hill and Madonna and countless others are proving that you can have it on your own terms – and that's a powerful message.

For women it's always been a lot more difficult than for men to break out of this constriction. Generally looked on as sex objects, women in the pop world have always had more to fight against. But in the nineties fight they did, from the full-on assault of the Riot Grrrls to the more subtle methods of other artists of getting control over their own music and their own careers.

The Riot Grrrl scene in the early nineties was a brief moment, an explosion of intensity reacting against the rugby club mentality of the music biz with a creativity and intensity that matched the early punk days. The movement made a fair old dent in the underground. Opinions were re-evaluated and arguments raged.

The rumbling debate that always lies at the heart of rock 'n' roll has threatened to explode a few times, since the beginning of the nineties. Women's role in the blatantly sexist music industry was called into question time and time again. The male-dominated music scene in the first half of the decade was bombarded by the Riot Grrrls, who threw up a vociferous and vocal opposition to the age old way. It was an explosion of bands and fanzines. A surge of creativity. Unfortunately the movement fizzled out before any of the ideas it threw up could have been resolved.

The tiny chink of space that it created could have been a launching pad for its leading UK light, Huggy Bear, but they never grabbed the chance and fizzled out, leaving a clutch of fab wild punk records. When Huggy Bear came along, a lot of people got very pissed off. They may have never broken out of the intense cult underground, but they made their point. They burst out of the London fanzine scene, ignited a music press debate and disappeared and within six months the lad revolution was in full swing. It seems bizarre now that a band like Huggy Bear could exist in the UK pop scene. They went on a limb and they damned well nearly pulled it off. Their single, 'Her Jazz', was a great rush of punk rock pop . . . it got them on *The Word* and provided them with a platform . . . a platform that they gratefully stormed. Your author was an eye witness to the riot.

The main US outfit, Bikini Kill, went the same way, leaving a couple of great records and memories of some killer gigs.

Ironically the biggest success that came out of all this was the all-male band Cornershop who had found a space to exist in the initial days of Riot Grrrl, playing on many of the same bills as the bands and signing to Wiiija records, the label that was releasing most of the stuff at the time.

Unrelated to the movement, PJ Harvey also found a space to exist in the new post-Riot Grrrl scenario. But with her startling, stark take on the blues, she quickly created her own world, cutting some great albums including the powerful, raw Steve Albini produced *Rid Of Me*.

Courtney Love had dabblings in the Riot Grrrl scene but was always too much of a powerful set of contradictions to stay in any place for too long. Currently wooing Hollywood, it is difficult to remember that in the early nineties she cut some firebrand records with her band Hole – powerful rushes of post-grunge sound that hit an emotional intensity. Married to Kurt Cobain, she was widowed when the troubled Nirvana frontman committed suicide, but her bloody-minded determination to exist and create remains undimmed. Her 1999 UK gig appearances were a reminder of how powerful her presence is when you cut away all the bullshit.

After the explosion of *Loaded* and lad culture the Riot Grrrl issue was dampened down. Rock returned to its past and dredged up a lot of the old values. Except that now there was a new consciousness in the air. Women were no longer treated by buffoons like puppets or accessorized as baubles to decorate their chosen media with. By the late nineties you could get somewhere on your talent. There were pop singers doing it their way from Madonna and Courtney Love to PJ Harvey, Sleater Kinny and Björk. Certainly there were more women in key roles in the music biz, from radio expanding on its base of one woman (DJ Annie Nightingale) to a whole host of women from Mary Ann Hobbs, Jo Whiley and Zoe Ball. They, like the pop stars, all had their own agendas. They may not have been necessarily political but they were operating on their own provisos, not on anyone else's.

Even The Spice Girls' glib appropriation of the riot grrrl slogan as 'Girl Power' was vaguely empowering five year olds in the schoolyard. A confused mixture of received PC and new lad, the nineties offered no solutions to the age-old argument. It wasn't presented as a big deal. That's the way thing are now. If you were the right person you got the job.

On the pop scene there was a whole mixed bag of various women musicians with a completely different set of motives.

Mostly they just had a strong personal presence. Like the aforementioned Björk, the idiosyncratic Icelandic vocalist who quit her indie band The Sugarcubes to carve out a dance-flavoured pop that reaped big dividends in the early nineties. With her powerful and very individual voice she produced a run of hits, starting with 1991's 'Oops' where she sang over Mancunian dance pioneers 808 State's slab of great electronic sound, and spent the whole decade peppering the charts with her new dance-fused sound. A long way from the lumpen indie of The Sugarcubes, Björk fast became a fashion icon in the mid nineties, scoring big hits with 'Army Of Me', 'It's Oh So Quiet' and 'Hyperballad' – she was a powerful presence at the chic end of the club scene.

Her three albums from 1993's *Debut*, *Post* and *Homogenic* had a nimble inventiveness and invention that saw her never settling on one set style. She had the knack of working with the right producers and mixers from her debut dabblings in dance with Mancunians 808 State and later on with Bomb The Bass, Underworld and Nellee Hooper.

Lauryn Hill first caught the wave of fame as the singer from moody hip hop outfit The Fugees. She has gone on to a solo career that threatens to eclipse her initial group, bringing a powerful message of empowerment and a strong streak of humanity to her laid-back grooves.

More than a mere pop survivor, Madonna has managed to retain her hipness deep into a decade that should have really finished her off. A totem for eighties pop, she should have found it really difficult to survive in the nineties. But it's a testament to her ability to reinvent herself that she has survived this far.

At the beginning of the decade it wasn't looking very exciting. *Evita* was a pretty dull albeit successful project – there was a sniff of po-faced middle-aged seriousness about the whole thing.

Ray Of Light, though, is a great comeback album and her best record by a long chalk, her previous high points being the effortless bubblegum of her initial singles and the breathless sex of *Erotica*. Madonna 1999 seems to change with every month with every video – from New Age hippie chick who's into yoga and the Kabbalah to sci-fi Japanese chic to psychedelic vamp. There is humour and a sassy camp about her now, like she's enjoying the star stuff. She's also making great records. 'Frozen' is a deep dark ballad complete with fab gothic video.

'Ray Of Light', the title track, is the finest moment – an endless swooning rush of supersonic house doused with a spectral 21st-century edge. The album itself drips late 20th-century sounds c/o Brit producer William Orbit's musical input. The record has sold millions. It has everything that most mainstream records lack: it's funny, it sounds like nothing else you've ever heard, it's bold, it has great tunes and loads of style.

This is pop.

As mentioned before, The Spice Girls' 'Girl Power' slogan could well have been an appropriation of 'Riot grrrl' – a reaction to the underground? It's an intriguing thought . . . It became their battle cry, their slogan, empowering ten year olds everywhere. The Spice Girls have become the biggest band in the world in the late nineties. Every week they are expected to flop, to burn out, but they seem to go from strength to strength.

Superbly planned, they were the girls next door, that old pop cliché that works time and time again. Bold and brassy, they captured the new flavour and they were releasing great pop. They survived an astonishing outburst when half of them came out in support of the Tory party. Some of them even went as far as to claim that Baroness Thatcher (boo! hiss!) was the originator of girl power.

When Ginger Spice quit they were expected to fall apart – after all, she was the big-mouthed perceived leader of the outfit, but they survived once again: being a four-piece gave them the opportunity to make themselves more of a serious proposition.

Now they are smartly realigning themselves into solo careers while still working under The Spice Girl banner. There will be no getting rid of them into the 21st century.

The Spice Girls broke the boy band mould, turning the form back in on itself. The teen band – for years the preserve of the boy band – was now blown wide open. You could have all-girl outfits like All Saints, who were sold as a hipper, sassier version of The Spice Girls, or Bewitched who were presented as Boyzone's hip young mates or Steps who were a boy/girl band aimed at an under-five audience.

By 1999 there were girl bands that really were bands, playing their own instruments, like Hepburn or 21st Century Girls, managed by the ex-Spice Girls manager.

So, business as usual then?

Again, it's up to you the reader to change things. Get that band together or learn some studio skills and become a back-room person. There has never been a better time to get involved, so stop moaning and get creating . . .

CHAPTER SEVENTEEN

OASIS V BLUR: THE DECADE'S GREAT STAND-OFF

Some might say (ha!) that this is a story of north versus south, of the toffs and the yobs, of Manchester and London, but then it's far more blurred (ha! ha!) than that. The great pop rivals have dominated the decade: Blur have certainly triumphed with the critics and have also managed to survive teenybop massiveness to weird out and still have hit records. But in terms of the world record market Oasis are the real champs, with Top 5 records around the world whereas their arch rivals have yet to make any serious inroads into America or the rest of Europe.

As arch, clever or just plain experimental as Blur got, Oasis remained a hit-making machine, deviating only slightly from their path. Whether this will be their eventual undoing only their crucial fourth album, released in the new millennium will tell . . .

Early nineties: Come Together – Noel drills his troops

In the bowels of the Boardwalk they were there every day. Grinding out the riff to 'I Am The Walrus' over and over, stop start stop start. Instead of knocking off the live set and trying out a few new riffs like everyone else in the damp stinking rooms this band was serious. To some they were laughable – no one, just no one could make it playing this sort of stuff. For the music business down in London, the whole thing was a joke: the Manchester scene was dead and the world hardly needed another version of The Stone Roses, albeit one with all the edges knocked off.

Noel Gallagher had been around for ages. He was the skinny little guy with the long mop that hung around with the Inspiral

Carpets. Always polite, witty and a touch shy, he was like the hippest one of the Carpets camp. Some claimed that he was the band's roadie, but he never seemed to do much work for them.

Late night in the New Mount Street offices, the Manchester music biz nerve centre, he'd be hanging around in one of the studios, lurking around in the Inspirals office. He was always around, backstage at GMex gigs, whatever shows were going on in Manchester, whatever gigs were happening in those far-off days of the late eighties, early nineties when the city buzzed on its own freak electricity . . .

And now here he was with his brother, an even skinnier more youthful version of the Gallagher mould and three other guys holding guitars or hunched behind drums in the shittiest room in the Boardwalk, the one with the leaking pipe and the never-ending dampness. A bit of decoration on the wall by the band resulted in a massive union jack being painted on the shitty old bricks.

There was also a running graffiti battle with the Man U loving Medelark 11 with City and United graffiti etched on to the respective doors of the bands' rooms.

It was in this stale air that the biggest British band of the decade learnt their chops under the eye of bossman Noel. A demo with the word 'January' felt-tipped on it was thrust into my hands outside the Manchester Cornerhouse. I took it down to London where I nearly taped over it doing a Suede interview.

The demo, heavily influenced by the Stone Roses, was a collection of jangling John Squire/Johnny Marr guitar licks and unsure vocals from Liam who sounded not a million miles away from Ian Brown. Liam had seen The Roses at the International 2 and was blown away with Brown's onstage nonchalant cool. He was still seeking his own voice, the distinctive confident sneer wasn't in place yet.

It soon would be.

Blur

Originally from Colchester, Blur were hardly your typical Essex lads. Vocalist Damon Albarn and guitar player Graham Coxon met when they were singing in the school choir at Stanway Comprehensive School. The pair both had idiosyncratic upbringings, Albarn's father had a beat background, hanging around the sixties art rock scene that had spawned Soft Machine while Coxon had been born on an air base in Germany. In the late eighties Graham went to Goldsmiths College in London where he met the Bournemouth-born Alex James.

In 1988, along with Colchester-born drummer Dave Rowntree, they put together Seymour who played an angular art punk, sort of a post-Fall weirdness, the sort of stuff that had been Peel session faithfuls in the mid eighties.

They played a shambolic handful of gigs in the backroom pub circuit of London before signing to Food Records. They were signed by Andy Ross, who was working for *Sounds*. Ross, a late arriver in the music biz, was making some smart moves. Always bolshy and smartly self-confident, he was quick to work with his new protégés.

Not that they were that green behind the ears. Albarn had spent a couple of years working in a London studio in return for free time. He put together a keyboard-styled duo – a decade later pictures of the project emerged in the press with the future Blur frontman looking like Howard Jones.

Seymour changed their name to Blur in 1990. That October 'She's So High' reached No. 47. The next single was the Roses-influenced baggy infused 'There's No Other Way'. At the time they looked like they were the latest baggy bandwagoners, a sort of southern Soup Dragons, their geeky too clean-faced video only added to this suspicion. On the other hand the record was damned catchy and there were already signs that Coxon was an excellent guitar player with his squelchy guitar lick driving the tune.

The single was the first time that they were produced by Stephen Street, one of the master craftsmen producers of the British pop scene (his production credits include The Smiths, Morrissey and a whole gamut of key English pop bands). Since then Blur have worked with Street on most of their records.

In August 1990 they had released their debut album, *Leisure*. The album captured the confused mishmash of styles that were bouncing around the UK music scene at the start of the decade. Songs were tinged with a sixties psychedelic edge, hints of the poppy edge of Pink Floyd were given a nineties feel with swathes of freak guitars in the style of current big indie influence My Bloody Valentine slashed across the songs. Another key element that would be one of their main assets was the tight Beatlish harmonies that underlined the songs' innate melodic nous.

The album went Top Ten. Food had done a good job, Blur were established as a full-on chart entity.

In 1992 Blur had a quiet year with only the 'Popscene' single released that April which stalled at No. 32. The record had a harder punkier sound, hinting at a change in direction for the group.

A change in direction that would surface in 1993's *Modern Life Is Rubbish*. The album was a deeper trawl into the English pop archives twisting late Seventies new wave pop with the sharp social commentary that dominated prime-time Kinks. The album's title was taken from some graffiti on London's Marble Arch. The band had, by now, dumped their baggy look and were dressed like nineties neo mods. There was a defiant Englishness about the whole project, a V sign to the then dominating American grunge scene of the time. The record was a critical success but the band were slipping down the greasy pop pole, the three singles culled from the album, 'For Tomorrow', 'Chemical World' and 'Sunday Sunday', were all small hits, landing and then getting stuck somewhere just outside the Top 20. The sign of a loyal fan base but a disinterested general public.

It's the curse of indie, the hardcore of fans, the lack of daytime radio play. You get your own way, make your record the way that you want it, but the general public is looking in the opposite direction.

Not that it pissed Blur off. Press darlings, they returned back to the studio to work on their third album. They moved deeper into their English pop with an added classic songwriting touch.

By the start of 1994, Blur were the great indie survivors. Most of their contemporaries were burned out or 'between albums'. They had some sort of rivalry with Suede – Damon Albarn's girlfriend Justine Frischmann had once been in a foetal version of Suede and had had a fling with Suede vocalist Brett Anderson and there was bit of tension between the two bands. They had roughly the same audience – indie kids – and the personal politics added fuel to the fire.

After Justine had left Suede she had set up shop in Elastica. Frischmann's Elastica were a different kettle of fish from Blur. They cut a neat, wiry, angular pop with a fistful of hooks 'borrowed' from 1978 punk new wave bands like The Stranglers and Blondie. They even had to pay up a bunch of royalties to the men in black. In fact, it was a measure of just how hip Elastica were that they managed to make the Stranglers seem quite trendy, taking one of the most underrated bands in UK pop history's bass sound, sneering style of vocal delivery and tough melodic pop sensibility and turning it into hip mid-eighties indie listening.

Elastica's brash swagger took them into the charts for a run of hits – 'Line Up' (1994, No. 20), 'Connection' (1994, No. 17) and 'Wake Up' (1995, No. 13) – and saw their eponymous debut album become a UK No. 1 and also sell through in the States.

The success of their debut put pressure on their follow-up and rumours of drug problems and inter-band friction saw the album delayed for years. It looks like it will eventually emerge in 1999 but it's a very different band that will be promoting the record now that Frischmann's fellow frontwoman Donna Mathews has left the group to pursue a solo career.

The stand-off between Blur and Suede was one thing, a Page 3 music paper battle, but it was hardly mainstream fodder. All this was going to change in the next year. Indie argie-bargie was a small-fry falling out compared to the large-scale row that would break out with a band from Manchester that was starting to grab good reviews.

That autumn Oasis signed to Creation.

1994: Oasis sign to Creation

April 1994: just as Blur's great comeback single 'Girls And Boys' was sliding out of the charts where it had been a triumphant Top Ten, Oasis first anthem 'Supersonic' was making an impressive start, hitting a high of No. 31.

Oasis have made having hits look easy but when they broke through the pop scene was looking the other way. Manchester was dead. The Roses were half asleep in the Welsh hills and The Happy Mondays were in a chemical daze. The world was hardly demanding another Manc band.

Noel Gallagher was one of the faces on the Manc scene. He had been stockpiling songs while on the road with the Inspiral Carpets and he needed a band to bring them to life. He returned from touring to find that his kid brother Liam had put a band together. This was the perfect situation. It turned out that Liam Gallagher had hi-jacked the group from a bunch of Burnage mates (read this up in the band's initial vocalist Chris Hutton's pretty good account of the early days in his book, *Look Back In Anger*) who had played a handful of gigs and had received a helping hand from The Smiths' Andy Rourke.

Gatecrashing a gig in Glasgow they were signed by Alan McGee who arrived early, on the piss, celebrating his birthday with his sister. Blown away by a band that was everything that he had been looking for since the start of Creation, McGee signed them fast.

It was the perfect marriage. It gave Oasis an indie cred and it gave Creation a street band – their own Stone Roses. McGee had been looking for the big breakthrough band for years and here it was. This was The Mary Chain who were going to play the game. No sullen sulking or self-destruction, this was buoyancy, up for it rock 'n' roll, a celebration of life in raucous rock anthems that was going to appeal to the indie kid and the terrace lad in equal measures.

Oasis caught the times perfectly. Their rise seemed supersonic. One moment they were supporting Greenock band White Out on tour and the next they were selling everywhere out. Gigs at the likes of the Marquee were packed. Pundits who had been slagging this Manc shit off were sudden converts. It was an unstoppable rollercoaster.

Just when rock 'n' roll seemed dead, crushed by acid house, here was a band that remembered why it had ever worked in the first place.

The combination of Noel's great songs and Liam's classic gritty rock 'n' roll voice and effortless charisma was scoring heavily in their favour. Add to this the hilarious squabbling interviews where they played up the laddish sibling rivalry and you've got a potent rock 'n' roll mix. Their first release had been a thousand only pressing of 'Columbia', reprised and re-recorded from the 'January' demo. 'Columbia' was a good enough tune but the massive guitar power was not yet in place. Their first single proper, 'Supersonic', was the dogs bollocks – a massive swaggering rock 'n' roll anthem.

After that breakthrough Oasis spent 1994 knocking off Top Ten hits: the catchy as fuck 'Shakermaker', the stunning 'Live Forever', 'Cigarettes And Alcohol' (their personal manifesto) and the formula-breaking 'Whatever'. With their debut album, *Definitely Maybe* on the way to being one of the biggest selling albums of the decade Oasis represented Creation's shrewdest signing yet.

McGee's master plan was paying off. The Creation boss had seen beyond the premature talk of the death of Manchester and laddish bands. He saw that the shoegazing scene was for a small student market (he should know – he was putting out one of the bands, Slowdive). He wanted to get Oasis out before The Roses returned – a smash and grab raid on their audience.

Oasis put the swagger back into rock 'n' roll. They played the bad ass thing to the hilt.

There were rock 'n' roll escapades like getting thrown off ferries. The Gallaghers' rowing grabbed loads of press, constant column inches, but what was really telling was Noel's songwriting, a commitment to sheer quality. Not only knocking out class A-sides but flipping them with great B-sides, sensitive melodic workouts that showed both sides of the band's prodigious output.

Oasis always get the rap for being a Beatles copyist band. Apart from the obvious accoutrements, like the carefully cropped mop tops, Liam's John Lennon style swagger and a few half-inched tunes, it does the band a great disservice to dismiss them as a mere Beatles revival.

Noel Gallagher is a far shrewder operator than that. For sure he likes The Beatles, but there is a lot more going down here than that. Noel Gallagher is the curator from the great museum of British pop, his memory filing away a whole run of classic British pop moments from over the decades. The key to the Oasis sound is their Britishness. Most of the wicked pop roar that they spew out comes from a whole slew of influences.

The huge wall of guitars comes direct from The Sex Pistols whose music Noel grew up with when as a pre teen he sat on the fringes of punk in love with Johnny Rotten's crew's huge boisterous pop (never forget the Pistols were a great pop outfit) and surly two-fingered attitude to the world – something Noel and Liam have made a career out of. You can also hear echoes of primetime British glam rock, the most underrated music that this country had ever produced. Great 'people's bands' like Slade and their terrace anthems are direct precursors of Oasis's non-stop singles assault.

There are also echoes of Ian Hunter's Mott The Hoople, the pre-punk punks with their great mine of forgotten songs (especially Bowie's 'All The Young Dudes' which he gifted on to the struggling band, giving them their greatest hit and according to Noel at least three Oasis songs) and T Rex with their simple but devastatingly effective three-chord riffology.

It could be argued that instead of being just a Beatles revival, Oasis are in fact a direct descendent of the glam rock bootboy bands, churning out brilliantly and deceptively simple three-minute pop anthems that stomped the terraces, with a yobbish simplicity to their attitude and the all-important people's band touch. This would leave them with an uncomfortable relationship with the rock hierarchy who have always been suspicious of the 'people's band'.

While Oasis's astonishing rise may have been the story of the year, Blur were easily holding heir own. Their disco pastiche 'Girls And Boys' was their best single yet – a catchy as fuck almost daft chorus intoned over a bouncing bassline. It was an indie dance-floor smash and put them back in the Top Ten for the first time since 'There's No Other Way'. Hot on the heels of the single was the *Parklife* album. Stuffed full of songs about English life, it was the Kinks taken one step further. The album smashed in at No. 1 and was a critical rave – they won four Brit awards for the record.

The three singles pulled off *Parklife* were not as big as the Oasis juggernaut. 'To The End' hit No. 16, 'Parklife', No. 10, 'End Of The Century', No. 19. The best of these was 'Parklife', a rollicking good tune with actor Phil Daniels handling the cockerneee vocals and the band breaking into the very Kinks-like chorus. It had everything that summed up mid-nineties Blur: witty observational lyrics, third-person character playing, tight as fuck harmonies and great guitar shapes from Graham Coxon.

1995: Let battle commence . . .

August 1995 and *News at Ten* reported the pop battle of the year. The race for No. 1 was on between Oasis, whose swaggering ascendancy was starting to take on mythical proportions, and Blur, the band that was in danger of getting left behind. Already Oasis had scored a No. 1 hit in '95 with 'Some Might Say'. Their album was still in the charts. They were shifting vinyl big-time.

Oasis and Blur, they were chalk and cheese, they represented both mythical wings of British pop as John Harris, editor of *Select*, points out:

'Blur wanted to position themselves in that art-school ethic much more than Oasis. There are two wings in British pop . . . the art-school market and the yobs! It's the chasm that always divides music. The battle lines were drawn way back in pop. In the punk days you had Sham 69 and the Jam against the art school Banshees and Wire. In the glam days Slade against Roxy Music. There are always two sorts of British music – working-class black-influenced music against white art for art's sake stuff. Bands like The Manics straddle the divide. They are very working class with a strong political standpoint but they also have the self-improvement through education thing, which is quite different from Oasis's escapism. The Manics have the scum factor and the dream pop factor, ha!'

In the UK the pair off between two rival bands has been at the heart of pop culture. Hyped up like two Saturday afternoon wrestlers, unrelated bands are pitted against each other. It's a popular pub pundit pastime.

In the sixties you could have joined the debate between The Beatles and The Stones; in the seventies T Rex and Slade, The Osmonds and David Cassidy . . . whichever side you took would speak volumes about the sort of person you were. In the punk days it was The Pistols and The Clash and in the eighties they tried to pit Duran Duran against Spandau Ballet but no one really cared enough about either band to make it work. In the early nineties it was The Mondays versus The Roses but since both bands would give each other regular props, intense debate was again difficult.

The nineties key stand-off that summed up the pop war of the decade was between Oasis and Blur, both bands keen to put their imprint on the era.

And now the battle was well and truly on. The week that both singles were released (Blur having moved their single 'Country House' to match Oasis's release of 'Roll With It') was the most exciting chart week for quite some time. These were opening shots in the key battle of the mid nineties, a battle that Blur would win when their jaunty even more Kinks than usual single would crash in at No. 1, pushing Oasis's 'Roll With It' to No. 2.

In the end it was down to the sheer marketing power of Food's parent company EMI crushing Creation. The real battle, the battle over the albums, was a different story. Oasis's second album would go on to become one of the best-selling albums in the history of British pop, while the fourth Blur album, *The Great Escape*, although a No. 1 million seller, would lag far behind in the super league stakes.

The Great Escape was, like its title suggests, the sound of Blur slipping out of their pop straitjacket. With an experimental edge and multi-instrumental flavouring, it confused some fans but still saw the group grab major crossover appeal, appearing on both *Mojo* and *Smash Hits* front covers. The album, though, still dripped art-school whimsy and was soaked with that English pop flavour.

The runaway Oasis album had none of this. *(What's The Story) Morning Glory?* was streetwise, a sheer exhilarating celebration of simple rock 'n' roll played by a band at the height of its powers. Every track sounded like a single and when 'Wonderwall' seemed to hang around at No. 2 for ever during Christmas 1995 the album sales went through the roof and as 1995 slipped into '96 Oasis were on a journey that would leave them as one of the biggest British groups of all time.

The stand-off between the two bands had pushed guitar music back on to the front pages. It was at this point that Britpop bust into mainstream pop parlance. Indie was now big-time news, a whole host of bands began to crash the charts (see the next chapter on Britpop).

The escalation in the sheer size of Oasis's popularity can be measured by a series of landmark gigs. From the toilet circuit to the big venues to Manchester City's Maine Road stadium and then finally to Knebworth, the biggest gig ever put on in Britain. The gig was a major event. As *Loaded*'s prime mover and editor at the time James Brown points out:

'When I stood at Knebworth next to Alan McGee, it was the first time in a long time that the biggest band in the country was the best band. Into the eighties the biggest bands had been shit, the last great group to be really big was The Specials. But now for the first time since the sixties by far the biggest band in the country was also everywhere. The Smiths and New Order had been big in the eighties but their records never got played on the radio, but in the mid nineties Oasis were all over the place and that meant a lot.'

As the nineties panned out both bands would travel along very different roads. Oasis's third album *Be Here Now* saw them lose some of the magic. Their three-minute songs were stretched into longer and rockier six-minute workouts. They were still good songs, it's just that they didn't half go on – they seemed to be losing focus, the hunger that comes from being on the way up. When the album came out it got rave reviews everywhere – it was like people were too scared to say what they really thought of the record. In the following months even Noel would air his disappointment with the LP (which was still a huge seller).

As the decade ends the band are in France working on their fourth album. It is their chance to redeem their reputation.

Blur, with their next two albums, zigzagged on yet another

change of style. Abandoning their anglophile pop that had dominated their sound since their inception they started cranking up their guitars. Guitarman Coxon had long talked of his love of the US underground outfits, and the heavier more discordant approach of these outfits was starting to colour Blur's sound.

The first sign of this was the 'Beetlebum' single which sounded like *White Album* Beatles scored with a lo fi consciousness. It gave the band their second No. 1 in February 1997. The follow up, though, 'Song2' has become the band's signature tune, a massive explosion of a tune with shades of Nirvana. It was their breakthrough song in the USA where, although they have never scaled the heights of Oasis, they were starting to fill bigger venues. Blur's album was their rawest yet, a band rediscovering the joys of dislocated rock 'n' roll that had been one of the prime concerns of their pre-Blur Seymour days.

In 1999 Blur returned with yet another change of style, this time the critically acclaimed *13* (partly inspired by the breakup of the relationship between Damon Albarn and Justine Frischmann). The songs were strikingly more personal, 'Tender Is The Night' the first single going to No. 2.

And by this time both the Oasis/Blur rivalry and Britpop itself, with its by-now somewhat discredited Blairist associations, seemed like ancient history . . .

CHAPTER EIGHTEEN

BRITPOP

The Roses and The Mondays had kick-started an explosion. Within a year there were a whole host of kids monkeying around like Ian Brown, dancing like Bez, getting as stoned as Shaun Ryder. The bands were creating the blueprint for how British guitar bands would operate in the nineties. Stir into this mix a return to rock 'n' roll fundamentals, a digging out of Kinks and Small Faces albums, the neo mod scene in the upstairs rooms of Camden pubs, a revitalizing of the grass roots gig circuit post acid house by the likes of SMASH and These Animal Men . . . a full-on return to guitar pop . . .

By the mid nineties baggy had given away to Britpop.

In the late eighties *Sounds* did a feature on the British hardcore punk thrash scene, running under the title of Britcore – a pun on Hardcore. Within days, one of the freelancers had coined the crappy phrase Britpop, skitting the term. It rumbled through the papers for years until one day it found a scene to attach itself to . . .

In the post baggy fallout there was a clarion call for a new pop nationalism. Let's do what we do best! Let's make rock 'n' roll British style! From Camden to Sheffield, from Liverpool to Wales, all the different strands were combining. It was the biggest rush to form guitar bands since the latter fallout of punk rock. And if there were not enough bands around then ones that had been around for years could fill in the gaps.

Acid house had threatened to kill the guitar band. But there is something quite magical about a band kicking six string ass. In the early nineties the doom mongers were out in force. There was talk of the death of rock 'n' roll. There were plenty of 'new rock 'n' rolls' to fill in from comedy to computer games, from TV chefs to politicians . . . Christ! everybody got their turn.

The gig circuit was dead. The Manchester bands were fucking up or falling out. Blur were surviving but they were back on the college circuit playing to a few hundred fans. Guitar bands looked fucked.

1992/93 was the low point. But the fight back was under way. In the hands of the so-called New Wave of New Wave, a collection of bands like SMASH, These Animal Men and Compulsion were back out on the shit circuit gigging hard and packing out again for the first time for a couple of years.

Sure enough The Roses and The Mondays were big league but the small clubs had been overlooked. The new wave bands' determined hard gigging set the building blocks into place.

Punters were getting interested again.

Some pretty unlikely bands were getting lumped in with the NWONW (New Wave Of New Wave) outfits. I saw Shed 7 supporting Compulsion in Norwich, the York outfit having been erroneously included in the scene. Pretty soon they would break out and tour with an upcoming Manchester band called Oasis supporting them!

SMASH would fall apart after a disappointing sounding debut album, leaving a legacy of some great gigs and a brace of cracking singles. These Animal Men soldiered on, their MC5 fixation saw them burn bright before being snuffed out. I checked one of their last shows in Amsterdam and it was a killer – the band had never been so hot.

While NWONW attempted to rally the troops in the post-Madchester vacuum, there had been an attempt to launch shoe-gazing, a scene which sparked little interest. Meanwhile all over the country there were bands starting to come through, all different shades and styles, but they would eventually be linked up as Britpop.

As the new bands began to emerge, they found that the climate was changing. It was suddenly getting a lot more receptive bands. *Top Of The Pops* had a hip new producer and Radio One was starting to open up. After years of being a closed shop full of pipe-smoking buffoons stroking their own egos, a new generation had moved in. The playlist was opened up and a whole slew of guitar bands were pushed to the fore. The national exposure was going to make a massive difference to the sorts of bands that would be grabbing hits in the mid nineties.

The music press was now hot for any action. They had originally dismissed Manchester but they were making sure that they were not going to miss anything this time. All the different strands were starting to get picked up on. It just needed one spark to ignite the whole conflagration.

Many people have staked a claim to have been the instigators of the whole dominating mid-nineties UK guitar pop scene. Blur have a good case, but they have changed style so many times that it would be difficult actually to credit them with being the full-on innovators. Their then arch rivals Suede were always operating in a world of their own. No, the one band that took off and created a huge space for everyone else was Oasis.

There may have been a whole shed load of bands operating before the Gallagher brothers but not to the level that they were zooming towards. Their astonishingly rapid rise opened up a hunger for guitar music. People were back into the idea of **the band** and there were plenty of bands ready to fill in this space.

Britpop may have had little or no long-term cultural importance like, say, punk or acid house had but it had been damned good fun and it left a legacy of great pop songs. It's too soon in the recent past to be able to measure its productivity. Already you can see some great pop moments dotted about there in the middle of the lumpen mass of nothingness that always comes with a mass pop movement.

Some of the bands that broke through had been deserving a bit of luck for years. One of them was a bunch of eccentric geeks who had moved down from Sheffield to London called Pulp.

The summer of '91 saw their demo passing through frantic hands in the London A & R community. Years of rotting away in a shambolic manner had left Pulp a no-record-selling outfit, loved by a tiny coterie of journalists. Frontman Jarvis Cocker had moved to London to go to film school and the band looked dead on its feet.

Closing in on 30, a bunch of geeks and a crap history, they should have been, theoretically, write-offs. But sometimes the pop dream is worth pursuing and this band had enough life experience to write rich dark-hearted pop songs full of sleaze and low-life love.

And the demos that they were knocking out suddenly sounded great.

The new climate was looking for bands. Bands in any shape or form that fitted the new bill, no matter how slightly. A touch of irony and you were in. Some evidence of sixties hero worship – 'Come on down!'

Signing to Island, Pulp released a run of classic singles, from their first proper hit 'Do You Remember The First Time' in April 1994, to the following year's mega anthem 'Common People', the track that they will go down in history for. The song neatly dissected the class system with a witty lyric from Cocker, and was a huge roaring anthem. When they replaced The Stone Roses at that year's Glastonbury they got an incredible reception. Within two years they had gone from being the sad outsiders to Saturday night at Glastonbury rabble-rousers, something that they seemed to be made for. All those years of dreaming about being in a big-time band had paid off. Pulp knew perfectly what to do with their space.

The album, *A Different Class*, was one of '95's big sellers. *Different Class* was one of the records of the mid nineties. Smart and witty, it detailed the seedy undertow of the UK as well as detailing telling commentaries on class, drugs, the backdrop of then contemporary UK life. Jarvis (he was even christened with a pop star's name for God's sake) was the perfect pop star, a godsend for the Sunday supplements with his art school wit and geek chic.

Pulp, after years in the wilderness, were bumbling into the limelight. A limelight that was to brighten quite considerably at the 1996 Brit awards when Jarvis staggered on to the stage and waved his bony ass at the camera during Michael Jackson's cringeworthy set.

Jacko had been playing god in a staggeringly obscene stage show surrounded by a whole host of adoring schoolchildren, a typically tasteless stunt in the wake of his (unproven) over-friendly to children allegations.

It was the sheer pomposity of the spectacle that drove Cocker on to the stage in one of the decade's great pop moments. Everyone in the country apart from Jackson supporters cheered him on. It was a neat poke in the eye at the superstar's tragic arrogance. Cocker unwittingly became tabloid fodder and Pulp were in the big league. It was their notoriety high water mark.

The follow-up album. *This Is Hardcore* was a darker, brooding more personal, sophisticated piece of work. Lacking some of the pop edge of its predecessor, it struggled comparatively saleswise. The end of the decade sees Pulp at a creative crossroads. With Jarvis fronting a one-off series on TV on obscure artists and the band silent for a good stretch of time it will be interesting to see just where they can go next.

Pulp were the eccentrics of Britpop. They didn't fit in with any prevailing trends (after all, they had been going for years before the whole damn thing kicked off). Most of their mid-nineties contemporaries were fired into action by the Manchester outfits.

Closest to The Roses were The Bluetones, whose deceptively lightweight jangling missives occasionally hit the melodic heights of their mentors. Suburban boys from Hounslow, The Bluetones inspired a fanatical fanbase. Their gigs were devout experiences. The people buying into this stuff were fanatical lovers of guitar pop relating to the band in a manner that The Roses had demanded from their fans. In short these boys were adored.

It also scored them a run of hit singles including February '96's 'Slight Return', their biggest hit, which came armed with an ever-changing melody. It was a great song. There have been other brushes with the Top Ten but they seem to be losing their grip on the post-Britpop world, the late-nineties pop scene where guitar bands are having to struggle for acceptance again.

Cosmic scallies, Liverpool's Cast delivered a rizla'd series of interviews where singer Jon Power would free associate over any given topic. In any given tangent. His dope-wacked mind was capable of firing out an amazing machine-gun burst of ideas. Power, once the bass player in the legendary La's, knew all about motormouth strangeness. Coming from the same classic pop corner as cracked genius Lee Mavers (the man who should have had the Britpop crown but took his own strange route instead) Cast hinted at bluesier roots, namedropping the king of quirk Captain Beefheart but settled for a simplistic anthemic geezer guitar pop.

A pop that would reap them dividends. Every single they put out seemed to be a dead cert Top Ten. The mixture of dope weirdness and simple pop connected instantly with the new post baggy audience. The football-digging lad washing his car on a Sunday afternoon now had a spliff in his hand. He still dug the simple things in life like guitar pop and Cast dealt in all those things that have always scored heavily with this mob. Simple heartfelt songs dealing in honesty, passion and with the merest hint of escape.

The king of the new swing was of course Paul Weller. If there was someone who was completely embedded in the new lad sixties mythology it was the modfather himself. Weller had been through the wars. Writing the soundtrack to a good few pop generations since The Jam had busted out of the punk thing in 1977.

Imbued in suburban mythology and with the knack of getting it down into the three-minute songs, Weller was always going to get revived. If The Jam had been the biggest band in the country in the late seventies, dealing in real-life vignettes and rousing teen anthems with staccato guitar and sharp lyrics, they had spent the eighties with the diminishing returns of Style Council. The Style Council had started off well before hooking up on their own idiosyncratic route of jazz-tinged Gaulois pop. It was a personal crusade and one that looked dashed when acid house burst upon the scene.

Weller looked as washed up as the rest of his generation.

But the early nineties saw his canonization. The new generation of guitar bands starting to come though had grown up with The Jam. The increasingly mod-tinged scene in Camden was placing him back on a pedestal.

Ocean Colour Scene had been around for years. In the late eighties they were a mod-influenced outfit from Birmingham, before adding a Stone Roses flavour to their sound. They even had a mini hit back in the heady baggy days of '91, with 'Yesterday, Today' which scraped in at No. 49. Their guitar player Steve Craddock played in Paul Weller's backing band throughout the mid nineties, keeping the wolf from the door. Ocean Colour Scene were going through a bad patch at the time. But with a gritty resolve and in a more friendly post-Oasis climate, those Paul Weller connections served them well. By the late nineties they were knocking out the hits, becoming one of the biggest bands of the time and, perhaps, the band that the whole Dad Rock tag was built around.

Dad Rock was a press tag slapped on bands with an unhealthy love of all things from the past, groups that sounded like a summation of their parents' record collection. From Noel Gallagher's Beatloid love affair to the Small Faces fixation of smaller UK outfits there was the rank air of nostalgia floating around.

Britpop, the great catchall, was capturing all sorts of smaller fry into its nets, Echobelly and Gene were both flavoured by The Smiths before pushing their schtick into their own direction. Manchester's Marion were plying a stadium pop and could have been contenders before their vocalist fucked up. There were the Scottish contenders, Geneva, Travis . . . The list is endless. Sales of guitars went through the roof and every chancer and dreamer took the jump, most failed and are back in the suburbs all grown up with their Beautiful South records . . .

The new bands looked on the broad palate of pop to pick and choose from. Unlike the punk generation who sneered at whole areas of music, the new kids on the block were re-assessing rock history. Riffs were being lifted from an unlikely array of bands. History wasn't sneered at any more. All rock was laid out ready to pilfer from.

Sampling had already destroyed the fear of being caught red-handed with a pocket full of riffs. The Roses and The Mondays showed how blatant steals could be assimilated into their own very individual takes on rock.

In the mid nineties the bands just kept coming. Supergrass sounded like everybody and yet nobody. They also seemed to be able to knock out tight three-minute pop rushes with ease. There was something quite definitely special about their quintessential English pop.

Shed 7 emerged from the New Wave Of New Wave scene and were instantly caught up in the Britpop rush. The York outfit rooted back to the Manc classics-bands like The Smiths through to The Stone Roses were key players in their world.

First spotted as outsiders at a Manchester 'In The City', with vocalist Rick Witter waving a plastic doll about, the band grabbed instant good press, fell out with Oasis, but still held on to a pretty big following, a following that would always put their singles on the edge of the Top Ten.

And after all that? With guitar bands a marketable concern again, record labels reinvested in the band scene. Major beneficiaries from the new scene were bands like Glasgow's Travis or the raga rock Kula Shaker and even bands like Catatonia who profited from the new hunger for guitar-based pop.

There were always going to be bands that could get their fingers burned. The fantastically named Northern Uproar were that rarity in guitar pop – a band that was still in its teens. Stuffed full of youthful exuberance and a touching naiveté, they briefly flickered in the warm glow of the post-Oasis talent rush. First spotted as a gang of cocky 16 year olds sat around waiting to play at the Manchester Boardwalk they were too young to be spotty but too cocky by half. Front man Leon Mayer was a kid without nerves and they played a rickety fast youth club teen pop. The demo that was floating around boasted the fab 'Rollercoaster', a bouncing great teen pop anthem. They signed to Heavenly records and never seemed to quite capture their excitable youthfulness on vinyl.

A couple of mini hits later and they were discarded by the mean mutha of pop, bored of kids with northern accents. Just like Northside and The Paris Angels in past Manc fashion waves, they were crushed by the wheels of fashion before they really had a chance to state a proper case for themselves.

Now older and wiser they are still beavering away under different monickers, still writing songs, still seeking that magic pop moment. Still enthralled like moths to the flame to the bright burning fire of pop nirvana.

Like all pop moments Britpop found itself massive and then it was gone, its long-term effect on popular culture negligible. A lot of records had been sold, some great records had been made but it seemed to have hardly scratched the surface of popular culture. It just seemed to be a big empty vacuum. Lawrence, head honcho of the Lo Fi label Domino records has a point when he says:

'I despise the success culture that was so prevalent after Oasis. I mean they were a great band when they started. What it led to was bands being validated because of their scale of success. It became a blank canvas that plenty of bands were willing to hurl themselves on to. And the third division Britpop groups were terrible.'

It had been the soundtrack to the mid nineties, the so-called 'Cool Britannia'. When the fashion went, some of the bands crashed. But a surprisingly large number of them are still there at the end of the nineties, banging out the hits.

Britpop! It may have been a naff term but it was a hell of a launching pad for a whole gamut of British guitar pop action.

CHAPTER NINETEEN

CREATION

Every era has its key record labels. The sixties had Motown, Glam had Bell records, early indie Rough Trade, the mid eighties PWL. Whatever's going down, there is always someone who can stamp their identity onto an era.

In the nineties it could be argued that Creation did the job . . .

Creation captured the spirit of its times quite perfectly. Not only was it the home of Oasis, the decade's largest homespun band but also Primal Scream whose multi-styled music perfectly captured the proliferation of flavours of the times. Not content with these two definitive bands of the times it also released Teenage Fan Club whose trad guitar pop was supreme in its melodicism and sheer human warmth, Super Furry Animals' warped Welsh pop and Boo Radleys' intelligent pop classicism.

Not only was Creation the label pumping out the hippest guitar bands of the era, it seems to have reflected each stage of the decade. From the drug-guzzling acid house haze of the early part of the decade to the swaggering Britpop era of the mid nineties, to the hobnobbing with New Labour in '96 and then to nu technology statements of 1998 that put label boss Alan McGee back on to the front pages of the pop press. Constantly maverick in spirit even when it was releasing its most trad guitar music, the label still has that electric crackle of the punk spirit to it.

First and foremost Creation is a fan's label. Alan McGee, who, along with partner Dick Green, has built it up from the humble backroom background of the mid eighties, is a fan. He oozes enthusiasm. Even now, sat in his varnished office, he still looks like an overgrown kid who's managed to indulge in his favourite hobby and do it damned well. Truly this is a fan's paradise. For where most of us settle on buying Dexy's Midnight Runners' classic albums, McGee gets to sign Kevin Rowland to his label.

Virtually unchanged in the 15 years that I've known him, McGee is still in love with rock 'n' roll, but he's still got that business streak in him that has propelled him to the forefront of the late nineties UK music industry.

Born in Glasgow in 1960, he was just another going nowhere kid in the big city. At 11, McGee bought 'Get It On' by T Rex and ran through the whole pack of Brit glam before ending up as a Bowie freak.

'Then I had a dodgy period going to see stuff like Deep Purple and heavy metal stuff,' reminisces McGee talking fast in his Glasgow-stained brogue. 'I was just into going out and seeing bands. Actually I saw some pretty good bands at the time like Lynyrd Skynyrd and Thin Lizzy.'

It was, in fact, this Lizzy gig that started off one of the crucial friendships in McGee's life.

'Bobby Gillespie, who was about 14 at the time, came round to my house and asked if I would go with him to the gig. So I took him along.'

Alan went to the same school as Bobby. They knew each other from a distance. Being a year older McGee had initially kept his distance. A year is forever when you're at school.

'Bobby was always in the gang. He was never a fighter, he was just smart enough to hang with the gang. I was always more of a loner at school.'

Like most cool people of his age, punk was the total epiphany for him.

'Punk came along and that was it. I saw The Damned's Captain Sensible just fall on his bass on "So It Goes" and I became a punk. I never had peroxide hair but I looked like the Buzzcocks bass player, you know, drainpipes and Oxfam shirts. I never thought about the music business but it made me want to be in a band.'

Working in a factory making shirts and then drifting on to the building sites McGee was in that post-school hopeless world of crap jobs. It was after an experience on a building site that he knew that he had to get out.

'It was a horrible building site in Cumbernauld and there were all these Neanderthals basically, working there – not that everyone who works on a building site is like that – it's just that these guys were horrible guys. One Friday they decided to strip me naked and paint my bollocks bright red. I took it at first. I thought that this is what happens, like an initiation. I took the humiliation. They tried to do it to me the following week and I picked up an iron bar and started whacking them. After that they left me alone.'

Already disillusioned with the world of cheap labour McGee continued drifting. By late '77 he was burning with curiosity at the punk thing and pissing about as an apprentice electrician who hadn't even been shown how to wire a plug by his employers. Hearing the monumental 'Complete Control' by The Clash on Radio One sent him into a total head fuck.

'Imagine hearing that on Radio One! One of the greatest records ever made! That made me want to be in a band. I had to get up and do it!'

He joined a band called H20 as a bass player. The group who would eventually go on to score a couple of hits as a smoothie rock band were a far more interesting proposition at their birth.

'It started off as the New York Dolls type of thing but quickly moved away from that. I stuck it out for six months . . .'

It was here that he met another long-term campadre, Andrew Innis who is now the guitar player and the master creator in Primal Scream. Leaving H20, the pair of them formed Newspeak with Neil Clark (who went on to play guitar in Lloyd Cole & The Commotions).

'We were like the Scottish XTC, who were by the way a brilliant band. Everyone else was trying to be Bowie and we were somewhere completely different . . .'

Innis, even though he was only 16, urged the rest of the band to move down to London, threatening the 18-year-old McGee with the sack from the group if he didn't join him. So lock, stock and barrel they moved down to the Smoke.

'Me and Innis being spiky characters were either going to beat each other up or bond. We were geeky characters who were outsiders. We liked being in London but the rest of the band were missing Glasgow and moved back.'

Innis and McGee, cast adrift in London, did the only thing possible. Their band had disintegrated so they regrouped as the Laughing Apple, whose wiry guitar pop made it on to a few singles and a battered flexi disc that still has that vibrant urgent rush of youth stamped all over it when you whack it on the deck today.

'Govan CND gave us the money to start this label and put out a single. Bobby Gillespie designed the first three sleeves.'

Innis left the group when he caught a nasty bout of hepatitis. Regrouping with a guitar player called Dick they put out a single and toured the UK with Eyeless in Gaza.

It was a struggle like it always is in rock 'n' roll. But there was an incident that, for McGee, took him off the road to Damascus. A near-death experience pointed him in a very different direction.

The group had been struggling, three singles in and no real sales. They had just played a gig and McGee's bass had been stolen. Returning from the gig their van hit a patch of black ice and spun out of control. The crash was the icing on the cake.

'Luckily no-one was killed. We were spinning upside down like it was a tumble-drier. The mad thing was this kid called Nick Lowe who had big ears that were pinned back. After the crash one of his ears was unpinned and flapping around. We got out of the van in a state of shock and all I can remember is this guy's ears flapping around . . . We were just pissing ourselves.'

It was a turning point.

After the crash they chucked the band and Alan gave up on music. In 1981/82 he settled down, married and worked for British Rail. But that's the sick thing about rock 'n' roll. Once it's under your skin there's no getting rid. He had to find a way back in. If it was not playing with a band it would be something else as close as you could get to the excitement of the R 'n' R frontline.

'I thought, I'm not a musician so I'll put on gigs instead!'

He started the Communication club at the London Musician collective. Putting on Eyeless In Gaza, Go Betweens and Patrick Fitzgerald may have massaged his musician soul. But it was draining his bank balance. Every single gig lost money.

'After eight weeks I lost every penny I had.'

But the bug was still there and year later he started off the Living Room. The same sort of deal, small back room of a pub and a bunch of cutting-edge indie bands. I remember his frantic calls persuading the band I was in at the time, The Membranes, to come down and play a show for him. You couldn't refuse the insatiable enthusiasm of the man. The club was great, a dingy back room of a pub full of underground movers and shakers, pop fanatics. It was a vocal PA, sweat and beer and long rambling conversations about the spirit of rock 'n' roll. Everyone seemed to be doing a fanzine or in a band or putting out a record.

The place really buzzed.

Bands that passed through its doors were the likes of Three Johns, Mekons, TV Personalities, The Nightingales, Eyeless In Gaza and The Pastels – the building blocks of Creation. The first band on was The Nightingales who came down for a thirty quid guarantee. No one could refuse McGee's firebrand enthusiasm. It was the mid eighties – the music scene was lame and this was the fightback.

Running the club four nights a week, McGee was sat on top of a nascent music scene. Soon realizing that most of the bands either had crap record deals or were out of contract he started to think about the next step.

'I thought that this is small time but I could sell a couple of thousand records by each of these bands worldwide and break even.'

Getting the money from the profits from the club, McGee pumped it back into his new label. Inspired by Dan Treacy of the TV Personalities pop art Whaaam label, Creation was born and a flurry of seven-inch singles were released complete in their idiosyncratic bags. He released records from the likes of The Pastels, The Legend, Andrew Innes's new band Revolving Paint Dream. The singles all grabbed good reviews. The Living Room had its own coterie of music journalists 'hanging out'.

'If I let them in for free they would become mates!'

It gave the label instant access to the media. McGee was fast learning the ropes of survival.

Creation never seemed to sell any records but it was hip as fuck. And this sort of hipness can only eventually be traded off against something big time. The label spat attitude. With his co-partner in crime Joe Foster, McGee was rattling off terrorist press releases guaranteed to grab attention. And in the mid eighties where bland was the king, attitude was grabbed at with open arms.

'At the end of the day we were going to get noticed.'

All they needed now was a group good enough to cash in on all the hype they were creating.

And that first big break came with The Jesus And Mary Chain.

Everyone else was either too old, too fat or just plain too weird to fit into the tight rules of what constitutes pop success. The Mary Chain had the correct quotient of sex, style and subversion (especially after McGee had coerced them into wearing leather trousers and smashing their gear up, a plan of action that came after a particularly demented Membranes gig at Reading University and a whole bunch of drunken talk) but they also had the tunes.

'Nick Lowe (the pinned ears guy) ran a club in Glasgow putting on bands. The Mary Chain had given him a tape of their stuff with a Syd Barrett tape on the other side. Bobby Gillespie, who by now had got Primal Scream together with Jim Beattie playing guitar along with Beat boxes, being a big Syd Barrett fan borrowed the tape and heard the Mary Chain stuff. He loved it and phoned them up. He was the first person who had ever rang them. He told them that his mate ran a record label up in London and puts gigs on.'

McGee, getting the call from Bobby, rang up The Mary Chain and offered them a gig. They thought that he was bullshitting. He decided to put them on on a Friday and Saturday at the Living Room which was now at The Roebuck pub.

'They nearly kicked each other's heads in during the sound-check. I thought that this was going to be mental. They did an amazing cover of "Somebody To Love" and "Vegetable Man" and I was blown away with their covers. I offered them a record deal and that's how it started.'

It was that informal. All the way up to 1990, Creation did deals on a handshake. This was punk ethics. There was meant to be an element of trust. And bizarrely this system worked. Even now years later, after our album came out on Creation, I get the occasional royalty cheque, no contract, nothing, just the molten bond of enthusiasm.

The Mary Chain took off big style. With a careful bit of press manipulation McGee had a riot of his own on his hands. The band had a carefully cultivated wild image but in reality they were far more sullen, oozing a deadpan broodiness. For their first interview Alan brought them up on the train to Manchester, where I was living, for a piece in *Zig Zag*. We wandered around the city centre, with McGee clutching a plastic bag full of beer, trying to get the band as pissed as possible. They seemed to get quieter and quieter, ending up in the Hacienda at a Lee Scratch Perry show. They finally loosened up with a tirade of bitter hatred against the music scene. Most of the talk came from bass player (and now top video maker) Douglas Hart.

It was this dark-hearted bitterness that was the attraction of the band, combined with the constant warring of the two brothers. You just can't help wondering if McGee saw the Mary Chain part two when he stumbled in on Oasis at that now legendary Glasgow show.

The Mary Chain's success (their debut single 'Upside Down' sold in its thousands) totally changed the label. Instead of being hip outsiders, they were part of the big four indie labels in the UK – along with the likes of Mute and Factory. Alan was now a power player.

He was offered his own label, the major funded Elevation, to run with Creation and took some of his acts there with him. The Mary Chain signed to Blanc Y Negro with McGee, the leather-trousered philanthropist, as manager, released 'Psychocandy' – one of the rock 'n' roll moments of the decade and then drifted, post Alan, into the nearly men of rock 'n' roll – selling records worldwide but always trapped by their explosive entrance on to the music scene. The big-time move up to Elevation, though, nearly destroyed McGee.

'I wasn't bright enough to handle the big label people,' he now claims, years after the debacle that nearly saw him off. Returning to his roots, he started to give Creation his full attention again.

They regrouped in 1988 and signed the House Of Love (who moved on to a major with Alan managing them) and Ride. Along with long-term Creation outfit Primal Scream, they started to have hits, small hits, just inside the Top 40 hits and then bang! proper Top 20 hits. Creation was getting there. They signed My Bloody Valentine who made *Loveless*, one of the most critically acclaimed albums of the late eighties, an album that nearly bankrupted Creation with its enormous expense (rumoured to be £270,000 – one hell of a sum for an indie label). Sometimes the enthusiasm was outstripping the assets. But somehow they always seemed to survive and as the nineties approached it looked like McGee was going to be settling down to a nice fat cigar-smoking middle age running a moderately successful mid-sized label with a roster of hip guitar gunslingers.

But pop has the fab habit of suddenly changing its clothes, drugs and music every now and then. And McGee, being particularly sensitive to the fluctuations in the pop battle field, was soon in there.

In 1989 Alan went up to Manchester for the New Order gig and its legendary aftershow Disorder party. It was going to be a night that was to change his life.

'I'd already done E but that night there was pure ecstasy going round. I'd been going to clubs for ages but I'd never really got into acid house. I was just going round clubs with Primal Scream and trying to pick up women. The Disorder party was unbelievable. I remember at seven in the morning I was absolutely off my tits and I bumped into Shaun Ryder who gave me a fantasy tablet. I was talking to this girl who was a model who ended up being a singer [Eilidh from the Solar Race]. I was getting on well with her. And I was totally off my tits and I just said to her, you know Eilidh, you look like a green diamond! Her body looked like a diamond . . . At that point I think I lost it for ever!'

McGee wandered into the cellar room of the Hacienda where they were blasting out acid house, off his tits on the fantasy tablet. McGee suddenly got dance music. After that he upped sticks and moved to Manchester for nine months, becoming a regular at the Hacienda. It was a typically intuitive and crazed move.

Becoming mates with Mani and Ian Brown he also became part of the Hacienda scene.

'Acid house and punk were the two huge cultural movements in this country. People go on about Britpop. I mean that was good for my bank balance but culturally it was not important.

Raving from 1988 to '91 McGee was having the time of his life. Somehow he was also running a record label.

'I became a professional drug taker. But oddly enough it was the most creative time for the label ever. I put out *Screamadelica* and Swervedriver and incredible records from Ride and stuff like that and we had a dance subsidiary putting out Fluke's first album and a load of other records.'

They may have been putting out great records but as the nineties kicked off Creation was constantly battling the bank manager. Almost permanently a million quid in debt and with bands like the aforementioned My Bloody Valentine piling up the studio bills seeking the perfect record (they almost found it as well), Creation was up against it.

Sure they were having breakthrough bands. Primal Scream's *Screamadelica* had been one of the key records of the period, perfectly articulating the rockers' take on acid house. It was a record that had became a hipster soundtrack, detailing the highs and lows of rock 'n' roll club life in the late eighties. There was also Teenage Fan Club's *Bandwaggonesque*, witty guitar songs played with such an infectious joy that it had to break through. McGee was pushing the right buttons but he wanted something massive. He needed something massive. It was not only a question of survival it was a question of going for the big one.

In fact this is nothing new for him. From the day I'd heard him rant down the phone he had been looking for a huge band, every band McGee signed to the label, no matter how weird, he saw as a breakthrough (and The Membranes, even though we were fucked up as shit, he still wanted to break massive).

But schemes and dreams don't sell records. Creation's financial lurching meant that it had to be put on an even financial keel.

'I always managed to sell something to keep the label going and in the end I had to sell my shares to Sony.'

The financial situation sparked a change in direction for the label.

'It went from trying to sign the most revolutionary band in the world to trying to sign the biggest band in the world.'

The search was on. McGee was looking for something to sell shit loads of records. He had now changed his attitude to what he was looking for.

'Having said that I wasn't sure if Oasis were that band. I knew they were good but I wasn't sure where it would go.'

False alarms littered the search. The closest he got to fulfilling his vision he feels, was with World Of Twist. Dropped by MCA The Twist were looking for a deal. They asked for too much money and the deal was nixed. It was a damned shame. They were such a great band. Fronted by Tony Ogden, their smart psychedelic-tinged tuff northern soul pop would have been massive. Instead they fell apart and had to watch contemporaries Pulp pull off the same trick and become big time instead.

He stumbled in on Oasis at the now legendary Glasgow show. He was in the club early getting plastered for his birthday with his sister. Oasis were in town and threatened to beat the support band up if they couldn't play. They went on stage and McGee was transfixed. From Liam's studied nihilistic stare and stock-still charisma to the great songs, it was obvious to him that there was something great going on here. They managed to combine the Mary Chain's static cool with classic pop songs.

McGee instantly knew he had the band he was looking for.

And for Oasis, Creation was the perfect label to sign to. It gave them a hip indie edge, but a hip indie with major backing through Sony.

Hindsight, of course, makes Oasis look like the most obvious band in the world to sign at the time. But you've got to remember that in 1992/93 the stock of Manchester bands was really really low. The idea of signing one and claiming that it was the future of rock 'n' roll was laughable to most people. But McGee had a plan.

'I saw that The Stone Roses were taking forever to make their second album and I thought that if I just nick in there I could take some of that audience.'

It was a master stroke. While The Roses struggled with the completion of the *Second Coming*, Oasis burst on to the scene with the swaggering street touch that matched the rise of new laddism and the tunes that would soundtrack the generation.

In pop, timing is all. Even if things don't look right on paper, there can be a massive groundswell going on that just begs to be tapped into. Britain was coming out of acid house culture. The kids wanted to rock! Guitars were back in fashion and it just needed someone to come along and grab at this nu electric that was in the air.

People wanted the laddish/scouse Manc brash cheekiness, that raw edge, they wanted the wide-boy swagger of house and they wanted it in a rock 'n' roll band.

And Oasis had in bucket loads.

This was the real deal, they weren't taking the piss. Liam Gallagher was not a plastic pop star. They cut through the bullshit. They also released a series of great singles.

They took off big style and Creation was on a rollercoaster.

'I thought I could sell 200,000 throughout the world, Oasis were a good version of what The Stone Roses were doing. I never thought we'd sell 27 million albums! At the time my biggest band were Primal Scream.'

Just when Creation was breaking into the big league with Oasis, its commander was at his most fucked up. The years of intense partying and drugs had taken their toll. Collapsing on a jet bound for LA, McGee had a nervous breakdown. He took time out, dried out, packed in the drugs and booze and waited to get better.

'I tell you the first time that I ever felt better was at the Oasis gig at Maine Road. I arrived with Graeme Le Saux and people outside were throwing bricks at him and Graeme Le Saux is mad. He was shouting at them calling them wankers. It was the start of a great weekend. I soon realized that I had got over my problems.'

Returning to the raw real world. McGee found that his label was stuffed with sub Creation acts. Other people had signed groups to his label while he was convalescing. His vision had become diluted, he wielded the axe and dropped acts and staff. The only band that he kept on were Super Furry Animals.

'One of my A & R people was well into them and took me to see them. I thought they were great and I said "Sing in English and not Welsh, you could be massive." And they told me that they were singing in English!'

By now Oasis were the biggest band of the nineties. Creation was massive. They moved office from Hackney to Primrose Hill, the money was pouring in, the label's profile went through the roof. Oasis had changed the geography. Instead of being a man who ran a hip indie label and was big news in the narrow world of the rock press, the opinionated McGee was thrust into the limelight.

In the 1996 high water mark of nineties pop culture, a year when everything seemed to come together, he found his left-wing leanings were being called upon by the New Labour party. Seeking funds and personalities they were quite definitely going to be liaising with Creation. McGee was a high-profile figure in the early days of Tony Blair's New Labour, Cool Britannia regime. He got involved in a few committees, attempted to have his say and found the clandestine world of politics to be far murkier than the music business that he was used to.

'The New Labour thing damaged me but I'm still a member of the Labour party. I still believe that it's better than the Tory party. I was 36 years old and I had to do something I believed in instead of doing something that's just cool. Ultimately it did damage my reputation. At the end of the day it's good for the Labour party to have me involved in it, to have a spiky person in there with an opinion. When Noel Gallagher told the kids to vote Labour, it must have had an effect. I'm not saying that he won them the election or anything like that, but it must have made it feel hip again to get involved. That year millions of kids voted for the first time. That's got to be one of the things that won the election for Labour.'

The glory period of Britpop saw a boom in the British music industry – Radio One was playing guitar records, music papers were selling and bands seemed to break through every week. Creation was practically a major label and in the late nineties Creation is still stuffed full of guitar-playing pop classicists.

There is a new raft of acts and some old regulars. Primal Scream released their come down *Vanishing Point* album, a superb collage of freaky dark weirdness, Teenage Fan Club still release solid gold harmonized tunes, ex-Suede guitarist Bernard Butler fills in the singer/songwriter role that was always close to the heart of the label. There are new faced like Mishka and Trashmonk, a swerve away from the guitar band that has paid good dividends for the label.

With the approaching millennium Creation is in robust form. Its commander can only just believe it.

'I was thinking the other day that I had been running this label for 15 years which sounds amazing but now I want to run it for 20 years and then retire to the Welsh hills.'

Yeah, right! Somehow you sense that retiring is just not an option here. That once they have made sense of the Oasis explosion, Creation may find that it has just started on its maverick role. In terms of the nineties, though, it is the label that personified guitar pop in the era, on the one hand a fractured multi-styled workout and on the other a slavish respect for the past.

But through the ups and the downs it waved the flag for rock 'n' roll.

CHAPTER TWENTY

POP'S DOWNING STREET ADVENTURE

In the nineties politics has become pop. Like everything else smart PR flogs stuff. A neat image and crisp script and a ready smile – it wins votes, it sells records. New Labour are like a boy band, they don't put a foot wrong, the grins turn into gurns, there seems to be a desperate lack of humanity. Terrified of the old days of Labour when inner divisions made the party unelectable they have swung the other way.

One night early in their new term they threw a much-publicized party to celebrate their return to power. The reactions to those who went make interesting reading . . . New Labour was sniffed at for trying to 'get down with the kids'. Noel Gallagher was castigated for going, Liam Gallagher didn't get an invite, Alan McGee was tutted at and Damon Albarn turned his invitation down . . .

While for a whole host of other pop people there was barely an opinion either way . . .

Politics and rock 'n' roll have always been uneasy bedfellows. Cynics raised an eyebrow when Harold Wilson gave The Beatles MBEs . . . and who could forget the Tories lining up their showbiz supporters in a sorry roll call of personal greed?

Along with kissing babies and pretending to look concerned on the stump, showbiz schmoozing is a part of the territory with politicos.

The night that Tony Blair invited a whole heap of nouveau pop and showbiz figures to his party in 1996 was both the high water mark of Britpop and the beginning of the unravelling of several reputations.

Innocently enough it was just a schmooze, an attempt to grab the Britpop ticket by a New Labour party hungry to be seen as hip and bask in the reflected glory of the class of '96.

As they entered the hallway of 10 Downing Street the hip young princes and princesses of the so-called 'Cool Britannia' were entering the hallowed portals of the chic New Labour government. It was an opportunity for both sides to grab some respectability.

1996 was the high point in the Britpop explosion. Things had quite definitely changed. The stuffy Tories were out of office, Labour's victory had been a genuine buzz. There were virtually street parties when they got into power. Only a few years ago it had felt like the Tories would be in for ever. After all, if people were dumb enough to keep voting Thatcher in and sad enough to back John Major, what hope was there?

Of course New Labour being in power has ultimately meant little to most people. The sight of the Islington lackeys of the Labour party poncing around on TV reading the party line from a script isn't exactly what anyone had in mind when they went to the ballot box.

But at least it was better than the damned Tories.

The soirée at Downing Street was an attempt to showcase the explosion of new talent in Britain, the pop-loving PM (well, prog-rock loving PM) could rub shoulders with some of the mid-nineties movers and shakers. It's never cool for rock 'n' rollers to press the flesh with the establishment, but fuck this was the Labour party, at least it wasn't the other lot, so the invitations were carefully sent out, and the some of the nation's highest profile pop and showbiz personalities trouped down to Downing Street.

In the end the whole exercise made New Labour look clumsy in its attempts to grasp the youth vote and the pop people look uncomfortable in their unlikely party environment. Within a year 'Cool Britannia' as an advertising slogan was subtly dropped and Britpop was on a slide.

CHAPTER TWENTY-ONE

EPITAPH: THE PUNK ROCK LABEL

Showing the diversity of nineties music, American label Epitaph became the biggest independent label of all time – by releasing punk rock records. It was a delicious revoking of the rule book . . .

When ex-Epitaph act The Offspring hit No. 1 in January 1999 it was a shock. A shock despite the fact that the band's third Epitaph-released album had sold well over ten million copies in 1996 worldwide.

In fact their mega-selling *Smash* album underlined one of the big hidden scenes in the UK. Punk rock has been long written off by the courtiers of pop's inner circle when in many respects it was the most vital of all guitar rock musics in the nineties.

Epitaph has put punk rock into the mainstream. In selling high-energy guitar music to the mall rats, it's maintaining a vital music presence into the next millennium. By astutely tying their bands in with the adrenalin sports craze (getting The Offsping on to snowboarding videos massively boosted their sales) they have taken punk out of the ghetto and into the mainstream.

For punk rock to survive in the nineties it was going to have to get hip and get organized. The flag had been carried throughout the eighties by the underground hardcore scheme, a Byzantine clandestine world of specialist bands, tight rules and a tuff code of conduct necessary to survive when the world is against you. Spurned by fashion and the raging pop argument around them, the hardcore scene developed its own specialist codes of defiance.

EPITAPH: THE PUNK ROCK LABEL

In mainstream terms the music was dead. Ignored and pushed aside. The underground may have been raging, with bands easily capable of pulling 1,000 a show all over the world, but the glitzy world of pop had erected huge walls of indifference to anything that spat soul and conviction.

After mutating Stateside into hardcore in the eighties, punk was more than ready for the battle in the nineties. Grass roots, gutsy, committed to touring outside the established circuit, the form had settled down for the long haul underground. It was a scene that had its own rules and its own lifestyle. Compromising with the mainstream machine was neither what the bands wanted or were going to have any chance of achieving.

The original clarion call in the late seventies in the UK had mutated into something far fiercer and more committed in the States.

Fast, furious and full-on, hardcore was taking the punk rock into new areas via bands like Black Flag, fronted by a young Henry Rollins, who joined as the band's third vocalist and stayed to the bitter end). Rollins has gone on into the nineties fronting his own band, releasing an endless stream of books (some poetry and some great rigorous accounts of life on the road and all with a brutal realism and an iron discipline). Moving out there after joining Black Flag in the early eighties, Rollins and The Flag took the music to the furthest emotional extremes and the furthest extremes of the US in their legendary never-ending tours. Tours which Rollins excellently documented in the book *Get In The Van*.

Minor Threat flew the flag for fierce intelligence and driving music all across America. While in the UK, punk was in terminal decline with crap third-wave bands and depressing right-wing outfits, in the States the spark of punk rock had ignited a diverse and varied scene.

The space it created allowed bands like Sonic Youth to develop with their detuned guitar fuckeronics and the Butthole Surfers LSD laced Hendrixisms. On the other end of the scale were the straight-edgers, the non-drinking, non-smoking, sometimes vegetarian bands inspired by the brief thirty second song written by Ian MacKaye of Minor Threat, 'Straight Edge'.

Epitaph is the label behind the astonishing runaway success of The Offspring, the continued rise of the awesome Rancid, and the stubborn survival of No FX, Pennywise and a whole host of other bands. It is also bankrolling the continued careers of old timers like

The Cramps and the MC5's Wayne Kramer, as well as the comeback of Tom Waits.

The label is also a champion of artists' first style contracts that heavily favour the bands. It is all about loyalty and integrity as well as organization and sheer tough shitwork.

In other words, it's all about the stuff of hardcore.

The band that created this space was Nirvana. The astonishing success of Kurt Cobain bust open a huge territory. A demand was created for guitar action, a yearning for the pure, simple and direct honesty of punk rock. At first it was the charlatans of grunge that capitalized on Cobain's success when the real echoes of his muse were to be found in the US hardcore underground of bands like Black Flag and left-field guitar indie. The two eventual main benefactors of Nirvana's shattering success were thankfully punk rock and lo fi – the two main tenets of Cobain's vision, a million miles away from the dullard rock bores of Pearl Jam and their ilk.

As the new generation of teens started to get into rock, the nineties saw a whole proliferation of bands grab some of the action. Despite reports to the contrary and patronizing write-ups by tired old goofs, rock enters the end of the decade bigger than ever. Sales of *Kerrang!* and *Metal Hammer,* the leading rock mags in the UK, are on the up and up, and rock clubs are filled to capacity, in some cases drawing in a lot more people than any hip night club.

When Nirvana burst through in '89 it created a lot of space and confusion, the sheer rush of energy unleashed by this one event threatened the scene. A scene that had stabilized and survived on its own terms for years. Major labels moved in and signed bands by the bucket load.

It looked like punk-rooted music's brief flirtation with the mainstream was over. But in California, comfortable California, there were people with a different idea of how this pack of cards was going to be shuffled.

It is into this melée that Epitaph, set up by Brett Guerwitz to release his own band Bad Religion's records way back in the early eighties have stepped, mopping up the fast, poppier end of the punk rock scene. Purists may sneer at the out and out good time rush found in the grooves of several of their bands but Cali (fornian) punk has found a ready market with the teens.

Their first mass success was with The Offspring's *SMASH* album which has now sold over ten million copies worldwide and launched one of the biggest bands in the world (in the late nineties they are now signed to Sony).

With Offspring at the top of the charts, a whole wild tribe of Californian punk broke through. It just goes to prove that if the stiffs that control the radio ever bother to play what is considered patronizingly to be underground music, then it will sell.

Epitaph's own history lies deep in the bowels of US punk rock history and one of its most political bands Bad Religion. Punk rock hit the US slower than the UK but by the early eighties it had developed into its own firebrand version that was closely chucked together under the flag of 'hardcore'.

After Black Flag fell apart in the late eighties Rollins put his own outfit the Rollins Band together. Again they toured heroically but it is the spoken word and his never-ending series of books documenting his continual touring and emotional despair that have made Rollins famous in the nineties.

His spoken-word shows last for hours. No reading from sheets of paper for the punk rock warrior – two hours of endless stories off the top of his head, witty and incisive clashes with dark and dangerous, cool observations and an insight built from years on the rock 'n' roll front line, balanced with an unlikely sensitivity from his human pitbull frame pumped by years of body building. Rollins is the great punk survivor and well worth checking out when he's in spoken word mode.

There were also The Dead Kennedys and Minor Threat (who unintentionally kick-started the straight-edge scene before front-man Ian MacKaye went on to form Fugazi). The bands toured relentlessly, building up a live circuit that would create the foundations of most of the best American rock. Bands like Nirvana and the grunge mob, even REM, through to the lo fi contingent and on to the Beastie Boys (who began life as a hardcore band) owe a massive debt to these workaholic bands who played against the prevailing poodle rock stranglehold of the mediocre mainstream in the eighties.

Bad Religion were just one of these bands. Inspired by punk they were seeking their own interpretation of the form.

'The whole idea of Epitaph was to put out Bad Religion records back in 1980,' remembers Jeff Abarta, one of the key players in the Epitaph label. 'It was not really a full fledged label. There were a few releases of stuff like the Vandals record "Thelonious Monster"...

'In 1987 Epitaph became a fully fledged label, putting out stuff like the first L7 record, "No FX" . . . it just grew from there . . .'

When Epitaph broke big on the back of Offspring it looked like it was a piece of piss. In reality it was a combination of hard work, excellent organization and great songs.

'It was a case of right place at the right time with the right song . . . but it was also a hell of a lot of work. I remember when it happened it started to get big on LA radio play and it really went off. For 15 hours a day Brett and I were in the mail room filling boxes with records. We were putting in a hundred per cent. It was sick.'

Oddly enough when the label hit the big time, the band that it was set up for had already left . . .

'Bad Religion had left to join Atlantic three months before Offspring took off. They were such a great band, for me they could do no wrong till they went to Atlantic. It was very short sighted of the rest of the band. I don't want to talk shit about them but they would have been better riding the wave with Offspring than going to get major distribution. . .'

The punk scene is never happy when its bands get taken by the majors. Only this time Epitaph was fast turning into a label that could compete with the majors on their own terms.

Epitaph was the first punk label to go big time and by the mid nineties the biggest independent label of all time. It was an independent punk label making millions of dollars and putting it back into the scene – a dream come true. Of course there were criticisms – something as clannish and idealistic as the punk rock community is always going to be uncomfortable when one of its labels becomes a major player.

Epitaph, though, has survived – an inspiration to the punk rock community. Handing the baton of punk rock energy to the next generation.

Rancid have cut several albums of highly melodic punk that hints at the razor-sharp tautness of The Clash and the gutter poet lyrics of Shane McGowan. Somehow they have made this ancient mix sound really modern. Their big breakthrough album was their third, And Out Come The Wolves, a record that is a non-stop rush of great songs.

Their infectious cross of punk and ska makes them the latest in a long line of platinum punks. Madonna tried to sign them to her

Maverick label, sending nude pictures of herself to the bemused band. They turned down a million and half dollars to leave what is now the world's biggest independent label, Epitaph, to hook up with a major.

'We like Madonna, we think she's cool, but at the end of the day Epitaph is our home, it's the label that looked after us when no one else would.'

Close on 4,000 teens have stormed New York's Roseland for two nights checking the slash and burn dynamics of the Bay Area our-piece. And it's live that you really get hit full force with just how good this band is. They bang out the songs with a passion and a fury, rushing through a set of songs that are already ingrained on your memory from the three albums. Rancid can thrash out a cool tune and the audience are going berserk for them.

Rancid really are sound tracking their lives. 'Punk rock is even more relevant now that in the late seventies. You just have to look at the state of the world and what we are going through. Being young in America is probably a lot harder now than in Europe.' agrees Rancid mainman and mentor Tim Armstrong, eating an hourly meal that prevents his fucked up system from collapsing. He looks up and adds, 'In America punk rock never died. In the media's eyes it may have disappeared but it just went underground and remained massive. . .'

Armstrong is 29 and is a survivor, he's the one with the proud Mohican V signing from his shaven head. An intense and intelligent man, Armstrong belies his fierce look with a gentle intelligence. There's something of the romantic outlaw about him which combines with a streak of artiness. He directs the band's videos and live shares vocals with guitarist Lars Fredriksen. In the late eighties Armstrong was the leading light in punk/ska crossover Operation Ivy – who were the house band at the legendary Gillman Street venue in San Francisco. They had their fair share of fans, some of whom have become pretty famous, including Billie Joe, the lead singer of multi platinum punks, Green Day, who along with The Offspring are the other key band in this whole caboodle.

The success of Rancid has shocked the pundits. They have burst in with no hype. They are the people's band – sticking true to the much maligned principles of punk rock past – an oddly moral code that has served them well for years.

'Punk rock is different now, the kids just want a place to go.

They want a sense of belonging. That's what it always was for us as well . . .'

The audience at Roseland goes right down to mid teens, their hair soaped up into cool mini mohawks. The punk clobber is brand new, it's not like in Blighty where the punk kids got old, got drunk and hung around city centres slurping cider and cadging ten pences. There is a multifarious explosion of styles: cool zoot suits, gangsta punks, trad punks, skaters, long hairs. They go mental for Rancid who reciprocate, exploding with energy on the stage. The enthusiasm and lust for life is infectious.

Even detractors are forced to agree that this is a band that come armed with songs with rousing tunes. In short Rancid are actually pop. They also snarl great lyrics from their fucked up lives – snippets of stories and adventures, songs of gutter life and redemption. There is a positive message going down here: get your shit together kid, these are hard times and survival is the key.

'People used to sing about revolution in punk rock but everyone is more concerned with just surviving these days,' explains Tim.

CHAPTER TWENTY-TWO

GLASGOW

In the niche nineties every city in the country has provided its own musical flavour. The music business may have become more centralised in money and power terms in London. But the rest of the country has drifted further and further away in pursuit of its own musical vision.

The current way of doing things means that cities like Glasgow breed bands that have a disregard for the machinations of the music industry. The spirit of independence is still strong. And the music is all the better for it.

With an ever increasing highly identifiable indie rooted style the Scottish city seems to be moving on a tangent of its own. Looking west towards America and consuming more country and western than any other city in the UK the city generally ignored the Londoncentric music scene. Unlike Manchester which always saw itself as a rival to London, Glasgow just got on with its own business.

Speak to the bands and they will always drop names like the Velvet Underground, the New York loft pop scene, Love, Jonathan Richman, The Stooges . . . the roll call of American underground outsider rock 'n' rollers. The fierce independent spirits and wild hearted believers who were stamping their own definitions onto rock 'n' roll.

It resulted in a city stuffed choc full of guitar hustlers playing a melodic guitar pop that combines noise, sweet melody and cranked guitars in all sorts of angular shades and shapes.

Bohemian pop has poured out of Glasgow for years with

bands like The Pastels, Jesus and Mary Chain, Orange Juice, Aztec Camera, The Vaselines and The BMX Bandits and labels like Postcard waving the flag for pop purism.

The late eighties and early nineties saw a frenzied explosion of bands in the city. Teenage Fan Club, The Soup Dragons and BMX Bandits came out of the Buckfast triangle town of Belshill. The three groups were committed to a highly melodicised guitar pop that saw them scoring quite different levels of success. The Fan Club leant heavily on a well harmonised very guitar pop classic sound, The Soup Dragons started off sounding like a Buzzcocks speed rush of sweet punky pop then transformed into a baggy band. They scored one massive hit 'I'm Free' which saw them, briefly, as one of the biggest baggy bands in the US.

In the nineties lo fi dominated the city's underground, and a freewheeling creativity hit the headlines early in 1999 when Belle And Sebastian, perhaps the ultimate Glasgow band saw off Steps to the best new band at The Brit awards. They won by utilising the clannish spirit of the underground. Combining this with email lists, their well informed supa loyal fan base was on the case and pulled off one of the best pop pranks in recent years.

Belle And Sebastian fitted firmly in with the tradition of playing fey indie pop but carrying a big club behind their backs. They turned their backs on the music business rarely doing interviews and became the ultimate indie band inspiring the same sort of devotion that the Smiths had in their hey day.

Just behind them was a roll call of warped genius and classic underground pop including Mogwai's textural guitar work outs and (Falkirk's) Arab Strap and their guttural lowlife workouts.

Mogwai are the firey young brats on the Jock block. Its hard to believe that a set of textural guitar instrumentals can have such power but live they can create a hypnotic atmosphere without the usual rock dynamics of volume, speed and bludgeon riffing.

In the world of post rock, most of the bands can be a pretty studious bunch but Mogwai were young men on a rock 'n' roll mission. Their interviews were littered with neat outbreaks of yobbery, flying the flag for Kappa wear, rubbing the sensible indie face into the dirt . . . tales of drunken good times and impassioned defences of the spirit of rock 'n' roll. In one memorable interview in the NME they stuck the boot in on Blur and a whole host of other critics choices. Stuart Braithwaite smirks at the shit they kicked up.

'It is is something I regretted when I saw it printed. It was one of those rants where they just printed the mad parts! But I stand by what I said. People like Blur do make me fucking sick. Those stadium bands like Radiohead are terrible. It's so fake!'

Not that they are at odds with the decade . . . Stuart digs the nineties but believes that you have to dig deep to find the real action.

'In the nineties lots of special music has been made. Nirvana blew away hair rock and added realism to music and then you get people like Placebo coming along . . . Fucking terrible. But there has been lots of special music like Aphex Twin. Its there . . . you just have to look for it.'

Hailing from Hamilton, a less than salubrious suburb of Glasgow, Mogwai are hardly prissy college boys. They ooze punk attitude and spent their youth devouring carnal closes from The Stooges to The Velvets and then Seattle grunge fallout as well as highly influential outfit, My Bloody Valentine . . . whose name constantly enters the roll call of indie underground outfits.

In the late eighties My Bloody Valentine were releasing records that offered rock 'n' roll an escape route. Languid vocals dripping in post-coital sex could just be heard over a huge rush of guitars distorted into all manner of weird textures and sounds.

Cross this with the taut sinewy jazz punk instrumentals of Slint and you've got the ingredients for underground rock in the late nineties. Slint were also having a profound effect on a young musician from Falkirk, Pixies fanatic Aide Moffat who would eventually go on to put Arab Strap together.

'I first heard them in 1989 when I was 16/17. I remember getting their first album from the Falkirk record shop sleeves. It had a countryside feel to it. When their second album "Spiderland" came out in 91, it sounded timeless. . .'

Aiden's Arab Strap were starting to take their own definitive route.

'I was into stuff like Ivor Cutler as well, I heard him and sang songs in a Dictaphone, then we added drums, then kazoos it was real bedroom stuff . . . songs about girls. We recorded six songs and put a nice picture of the drummer's girlfriend on the cover . . .'

Released on The Delgadoes key Chemical Underground label, Arab Strap have been embraced by the Glasgow pop underground and have become one of the pillars of the cities assault on the new millennium pop scene.

An assault that sees the city firmly placed on the cutting edge of pop possibility.

CHAPTER TWENTY-THREE

BRISTOL

Re inventing hip hop, the city of Bristol came up with a whole new way of dealing with the break beat . . . An astonishing array of uniquely original talents emerged from a city that has, for so long, been seen as a backwater for pop music . . .

Bristol has always been an odd spot on the British music map. Not quite big enough ever to support its own sustainable music industry, there have been the odd flashpoints of action. But until this decade nothing has come out of the city to totally dominate the cultural landscape.

When Roni Size's Reprazent won the 1997 Mercury awards they were the latest in a long and twisting line of nineties talent from the city. Musicians who couldn't neatly be packaged in anywhere with their startling and original music.

Roni Size's Reprazent plied the sort of drum and bass that didn't sound like any one else. This was his own sound. They seemed to have twisted the formula and come up with something quite startling and different. This stark, inventive spirit is typical of the town where the collective is based and which has given rise to some of the nineties best and most original music.

The backbone of the city's music scene is Massive Attack, an outfit who have totally changed the concept of what a band is meant to be. A core of three members pulls in various vocalists that suit the tracks, creating a fluid music that can reach out in any direction and pull in a whole gamut of influences. They captured the sombre undertow of the nineties perfectly and made a far better job of the 'new seriousness' than most of the guitar bands whose territory this normally is. Jon Harris, editor of *Select* magazine, sees them as the band's band of the decade.

'The group who defines the nineties are Massive Attack. They are what the white musician wants to be like. Their rolling groove music sounds cinematic and evocative. Everyone wants to be like them . . . moody and difficult, playing dark and introspective music.'

Key indie bands were remixed by Massive Attack or collaborated with them or just let their sound symbiotically merge with their own. Their stark, dark music and laid-back, slowed down breakbeat chug could be heard everywhere from film soundtracks to Britpop bands looking for an escape route. They virtually created a whole new genre of music, the painfully titled trip hop, a hip hop influenced vibe that British musicians could feel comfortable with. At last, instead of copying the Americans' style, the breakthrough had been made: a multicultural, multistyled melting pot of sound – a proper reflection of the British street – had been brewed.

Massive Attack were one of the decade's true innovators.

The story of Bristol's take on pop is the story of a multi-ethnic sound clash. A vibrant cross-cultural melting pot of cultures that in Bristol, like any city with the same sort of mix, creates a great heap of tunes and some kick ass club action.

The attrition of styles soaked the city in the aftermath of the punk fallout, from the blues clubs in the city's predominantly West Indian St Paul's area to the newly inquisitive punk rockers looking for different flavours across the city. From one of the quieter corners of Blighty came some of the key outfits of the decade, cutting tracks that were utterly original in their sound. The Bristolian outfits' atmospheric mishmash of styles was a moody soundtrack to the dark decade.

From Massive Attack's supreme fusion of styles from hip hop, dub, soul, post punk and just their own sheer imagination to Portishead's extension of this moody polyglot into a 3D film soundtrack cinemascope of breathless imagination to Tricky's claustrophobic percussion-driven loops of smouldering madness, the city's inhabitants were working at the very boundaries of pop, where imagination ruled and being a slavish follower was irrelevant.

Not only that – even Goldie, the very public face of drum and bass, passed through the city along with Jazzy B of Soul II Soul.

The roots of the Bristol music scene go right into the heart of the St Paul's area, just near the city centre. It was here that the endless blues clubs flew the roots flag high. Combine this with the hunger for new rebel sounds in the wake of the punk rock explosion and you've got a volatile mix of young minds looking for some cutting-edge action.

The punky reggae party had been sung about by Bob Marley and was The Clash's Westway dream come true. The punk band had been one of the first to try and pull together all the various strands of revolutionary youth sounds in the late seventies and on the streets of Bristol people were getting the message as Barney, born in Bristol to West Indian parents, points out.

'In Bristol the punk thing was a big turnabout for a lot of us. The Clash would play in town and everyone would go to a punk gig but get off on the dub records that they were playing in between the sets. A lot of black kids and white kids were into John Lydon's Public Image Limited. We were getting off on Jah Wobble's heavy dub bass. I remember this guy Milo Johnson, who ended up in The Wild Bunch, who was a key person on the scene having a leather jacket with Public Image's logo on the back.'

The cross pollination was already kicking in. Black kids listening to post punk and white kids checking out dub and funk, soul and blues. It was a crash course in all the cool rude boy sounds, a most crucial education. Some had better access to what was going on than others. Daddy G, who would end up in Massive Attack, was well placed to get connected to new sounds working in the city's key underground shop of the time, Revolver Records. Other faces were already on the scene: Nellee Hooper, who has gone on to be one of the hippest producers in the world after his big break with Soul II Soul, working with the likes of Madonna, U2, and All Saints, was an early face as well as eventual Massive Attacker 3D, digging his punk thrash and getting into the early hip hop and graffiti scenes as they broke in the first couple of years of the eighties with Willy Wee (who still hangs with Massive Attack).

Barney looks back on the chaotic crossover with affection.

'My musical diet was made up of going to the blues, listening to dub plates and a lot of dub-orientated dancehall, lovers' rock on the heavy sound system. One particular club was called Ajax – we used to go to it a lot. It was the only one with a Qualitex sound system. You used to get people like Jah Shakka down there . . . He used to go to Bristol a lot. A friend of mine, TC, used to promote him . . . The whole roots thing in Bristol was held at the Malcolm X Centre or at the Ajax in St Paul's.'

St Paul's looms large in the legend of the city's music scene. Afro-Caribbean and bohemian, it was the crucial melting pot, the part of the city that was providing all the flavours.

'St Paul's is really important for the city,' explains Barney. 'The carnival held on the 1st July is an important event . . . It's like a better version of the Notting Hill carnival . . .'

It was at another club in St Paul's that the whole Bristol flavour started to coalesce. The Dug Out. Everyone who has ever played in some sort of wild assed' fucked up band in the eighties will have been through there. I certainly have and after the gig you could slip downstairs into the club and chill out to the heavy dub or reggae that was going down in there. The music was as idiosyncratic as it was varied. Barney spent virtually all his youth in there.

'The Dug Out was the key place. It was built after World War I. In the fifties it was always known as an illicit dive. People's parents would go on about it. There was talk of reefers! That sort of stuff! It eventually shut in 1986 . . . The music there was amazing. There was a bit of everything. They had a punk night. They played ska, disco, electro leading up to early Chicago house . . . There was a venue upstairs and video bar which was well crucial. It was there that everyone got massively into films, something that has really affected a lot of the groups . . . The Dug Out was always full of students, hustlers, people from St Paul's and the rest of the city all joined . . . The Wild Bunch played there from 1983/84 . . . This was where they literally learned their stuff.'

The film connection is crucial in the city's lineage. You just have to check out Massive Attack's amazing artwork or stunning videos for evidence of that. Same with Tricky or sonically you just have to get lost in Portishead's 3D soundscapes.

'The whole scene was made up of creative people. It was really multi-flavoured. Everyone was really into films – stuff like *Taxi Driver*, all the Scorsese films like *Mean Streets* . . . We made connections with those kind of films . . . Lots of it came from being like a kid on Saturday morning matinées. We grew up in cinemas . . . Bristol's key players, like early Massive Attack, were very film orientated. They were very influenced by Scorsese. Delj (aka 3D) is very creative . . . He's getting back on to the canvases and his artwork . . . But hardly any one has seen it . . .'

*

The first sign that there was something quite different going on here than the rest of the country was with the ironically monickered Pop Group.

While the rest of the country was in the throes of punk rock and getting safety pinned to the hilt and forming youth club three chord thrashes, Bristol's main punk export was a band that captured the intense fractured energy of punk rock but wired it to a quite different chassis. The Pop Group were an intense whirlwind of funk. There were shades of James Brown's Famous Flames here cranked through an extraordinary frenetic wall of sound. Fronted by the wild Mark Stewart, The Pop Group were operating on a quite different planet than the rest of the punk consensus. They were one of the first bands to break away from the straightjacket formulae of the times. Moving on into the brave new world of the post-punk experimentalists.

Their bass player Gareth Sagar went on to form the free jazz freakouts of Rip Rig And Panic. They made improvised chaos into an art form in the early eighties. Their gigs were a loose assemblage of riffs and soul power. Rip Rig were quite fab. I saw them in Liverpool supported by local outfit Frankie Goes To Hollywood playing their first ever gig. Rip Rig And Panic played music that went all over the place and they had stepladders on the stage that they kept climbing up and down.

Bizarre.

Neneh Cherry also had connections with the city's nascent new scene: she had sung vocals with Rip Rig And Panic and on a spin-off project from Rip Rig called Float Up CP cutting a divine near disco stomp of a single. There were also The Cortinas who played fast and simple punk rock and were famous for having a record sleeve with someone throwing up on it.

The Cortinas were the first in a long line of Bristol cider punk action with bands like Vice Squad and a whole scene of travellers and squatters. There was also a disparate avante underground. Barney points to another key band who have never got mentioned in dispatches.

'The Insects have been around for years. They were a strange avant garde set-up quite important in the scene. They are still going. The whole performance relied on a visual aesthetic with sound and animation . . .'

In 1980 another of the key names on the scene and a name

that is never given much credit was starting to emerge.

'Restriction was a UB40 style band from around 1980 led by Rob Smith,' says Barney. 'I reckon Rob is the genius person responsible for the whole scene. He was the guitarist who led Restriction. We all lived at 155 Cheltenham Road. It was *the* gaff in Bristol. Rob had a studio upstairs, everyone asked him questions about studios and he showed how it's done . . .'

The moment when everything really coalesced was when the 1981 Riots kicked off. The lingering discontent and frustration in the British inner cities snubbed by Thatcher was going to explode in the end. All over the UK the tension had been rising: newly politicized youth, bored teenagers, hooligans and normal people fed up with the heavy-handed authorities was a volatile enough mixture to really blow.

The most famous riots were in Manchester, Liverpool and London but it was in St Paul's that the initial sparks went off, inspiring the whole country into a frenzied weekend of anarchy.

After the riots there were the usual token attempts to put the sticking plaster back onto the gaping wound. Walking around the same areas today, there is evidence of change, but they are still ghettos – people are excluded from mainstream society. Perhaps that's the way the powerful want it.

Who knows?

In some cities the post-riot aftermath saw the price of heroin drop drastically on the streets and hard drugs hold the inner cities in a mean grip. It also saw the opportunity for the more idealistic to attempt to get something more creative going. This was certainly the case in Bristol where the new creative opportunities spurred important scenesters into the fray.

'There was a bunch of schemes to get youngsters off the street . . . YOP schemes, art opportunities, that sort of thing. In St Paul's they had this play called *Freedom City*. It involved Dave McDonald, people like that, and toured in Europe. It even got on TV. A lot of people met up and learned skills. Dave McDonald learned engineering skills. He's gone on to do Santa Cruz and Mogwai . . . He's like an extra member of the bands that he works with.'

According to Barney, *Freedom City* is certainly crucial in the city's musical infrastructure.

'The St Paul's riots were the catalyst for people moving on. Rob Smith produced Smith and Mighty. Rob Smith is the most crucial person. Everyone in Bristol owes Rob Smith . . .'

Hip hop was already making an important in road into the Bristol scene.

The early stirrings of hip hop and B-Boy culture were having their powerful effect in Bristol, just like any other British city.

'The Rock Steady Crew was going on, crews were coming together. Prior to "Walk This Way" people were doing hip hop crossover stuff. Doing mixes of Hendrix riffs, doing hybrids. Everyone was well into Hendrix and then Bacharach . . .'

The emerging scene revolved around the Dug Out and the Special K cafe just down the road.

'The Special K cafe was run by a Greek guy,' says Barney. 'It had a pirate station upstairs. Everything revolved round there. That's where everyone met. It was only five minutes from The Dug Out.'

The Wild Bunch had began to develop their idiosyncratic dub heavy atmospheric sound, developing out of the sound system scene. Key members Milo Johnson and Nellee Hooper along with eventual Massive Attack members, 'Mushroom' Vowles and 'Daddy G' Marshall were cutting occasional singles of slow stark atmospheric soundscapes. Chiselled with a craftsman's perfection, cuts like 'Fucking Me Up' and 'Tearing Down The Avenue' were building the foundations for a sound that Massive Attack were going to take overground. The Wild Bunch's sound systems at The Dug Out have gone down in legend. Everyone in town was there soaking up the vibe. A 16-year-old Roni Size cut his musical teeth in the packed rooms. The Wild Bunch were to have a profound effect on the city's music scene, tying together loose ends in a powerful and influential manner.

The Wild Bunch were getting a worldwide reputation, even getting as far as Tokyo where they fell apart. Barney picks up the tale.

'Wild Bunch turned into Massive Attack after they visited Japan – they were the first UK hip hop graffiti crew to go there. Milo stayed in Japan and that was that. Miles was the soulful backbone of the Wild Bunch . . .'

Post Wild Bunch, Nellee Hooper would take his vibe to both Massive Attack's debut *Blue Lines* album and to London's Soul II Soul's classic early nineties cuts, including the huge 'Back To Life' hit.

Hooper is the link between these two very similar operations, both Massive Attack and Soul II Soul had their roots in the sound systems, the Bristol-London connection was strong with Hooper working in both cities' sound system scenes.

The vibe would transport backwards and forwards from Bristol to London. A connection that is important. A quick 90 minutes on the motorway and you're virtually there. There was inevitably going to be some sort of cultural connections between the two places.

Barney explains. 'In the early eighties there seemed to be a parallel between the scenes in London and Bristol. Soul II Soul's Jazzy B moved from London to Bristol for a time. Everyone would go on a coach to see the Wild Bunch play London along with early electro pioneers Nutriment from Bristol in about 1985. A lot of Bristolians lived in Portobello . . . London feels close. London is just there. It's only 120 miles . . . That's not too bad on the motorway. This has caused an affinity of ideas going backwards and forwards. It felt very close . . .'

In 1987 Massive Attack started to come together. Robert Del Naja (3D) an ex punk and local graffiti artist who was doing community service after getting busted for his art (an art that he would later get lauded for with exhibitions) joined up with the ex-Wild Bunchers Mushroom and Daddy G with the specific wish to create 'music around art'.

In 1990 they released their first single 'Daydreaming' featuring Shara Nelson on vocals and newcomer Tricky's rapping. It was a crucial record. Introducing some of the key faces on to the nineties battlefield, Nelson's Aretha Franklin Motown – stained voice would be one of the early Massive Attack's special flavours. She would leave soon after and emerge occasionally throughout the nineties with an intermittent solo career, her great voice still cutting through as powerful as ever. Tricky's guttural growling raps were something very different indeed.

The debut *Blue Lines* album was a classic. Boasting the same great collaborators as well as the sweetest voiced reggae singer Horace Andy, its soundscapes perfectly captured early nineties Britain. Everything was in the melting pot here – from dub's luscious bottom end, classic soul's emotional kick and melody, the street suss of hip hop but from a uniquely British angle, all put together in a totally unique manner. As a record its crossover was huge.

Massive even!

The singles, 'Safe From Harm' and 'Unfinished Symphony',

were moody, powerful pieces that came complete with stunning videos (who could forget Shara Nelson's one shot vid walking through the street in LA for 'Unfinished Sympathy'? The Verve certainly couldn't and they pastiched it on 'Bittersweet Symphony'.)

Massive Attack had broken away from the trad focal point syndrome. The music really did do the talking. The album was ground-breaking and has become one of the key influential albums of the decade.

By the time Massive Attack released 1994's follow-up album, *Protection*, a whole music scene had appeared in their wake, and trip hop saw a whole host of imitators. Some felt that *Protection*, despite being a fine record, had been overtaken by the musical style that they had helped pioneer. This is doing the record a grave injustice. With cuts like 'Karma Coma', *Protection* is yet another stunning album with new singer Nicollette and Everything But The Girl's Tracey Thorn being used to full effect. A remix of the whole album by Mad Professor is even better, stripping the songs down to their dubwise bare essentials. It's a mean and moody collection.

Between albums Massive Attack were remixing the likes of U2, Madonna and Garbage, building on a massive reputation . . .

Their third album *Mezzanine* saw them restored as critical as well as a commercial faves. The album was darker yet. Its powerful force nearly pulled the trio apart while they were putting it together. Starting off with a clutch of samples taken from idiosyncratic post-punk guitar weirdness and then dropping all these but keeping the dark flavour of the period Massive Attack were moving deeper into a musical heart of darkness. Collaborators this time included ex-Cocteau Twin vocalist Liz Frazer, and newcomer Sara Jay. It was a great record.

Hip as fuck Massive Attack have cast a long shadow. Their ground-breaking music has opened up a big space for similar local creative mavericks to appear through.

The first of these was Tricky. Getting known through his collaborations with Massive Attack, gruffly rapping on their debut album, he was soon branching out on his own.

Tricky, real name Adrian Thorne was born in 1969. Growing up in the rough end of town, Knowles West, with the usual itinerant school CV of the artistic, Tricky drifted through his youth. It was hearing The Specials that got him deeply into music and Public Enemy who consolidated his new passion. Fired by the Wild Bunch he drifted into the early Massive Attack project, recording a couple of raps for their key *Blue Lines* debut.

He started working on their follow up *Protection* but left after recording 'Karma Coma', feeling that Massive Attack were making music that was not 'true to the streets'. He'd already released his first single, 'Aftermath', which he'd put together with ex Pop Group vocalist Mark Stewart.

He moved to London, signed to Fourth And Broadway and kicked off a solo career that saw one of the true originals of the decade on a splendidly erratic rush of releases. From the off, his music spat an uncompromising combination of influences with clattering percussion that hinted at his love of Tom Waits's rhythmic oddities and growling off-kilter blues stories. The booming bass end of dub, the Bristolian fucked up breakbeats and his own definitive personality grinding through his crackling gnarled voice – which neatly contrasted with co-vocalist and girlfriend Martina's vocal.

His debut album, *Maxinquaye* is a true nineties record. It sounds like nothing that has ever gone before. Tricky has taken all his influences and forged them into something totally original. From his rock cover of Public Enemy's 'Black Steel' to the dark psychosis of 'Hell is Around The Corner', Tricky had made a powerful debut statement.

The rest of the decade released what seemed a never-ending stream of tracks under different guises that sometimes worked and sometimes didn't (he also cut 'The Hell EP' as The Tricky Vs The Gravediggaz. The record – a crackling, suffocating slice of heavy duty hip hop cut with the distant relatives of New York's Wu Tang Clan – is my personal favourite of Tricky's idiosyncratic canon. There was also the Nearly God side project, a series of releases with different vocalists including The Specials' Terry Hall), as well as two more albums, *Pre Millennium Tension* and *Angels With Dirty Faces*.

He staggered through a whole bunch of controversy, falling out with fellow artists, attacking journalists backstage at Glastonbury. The weirdest fallout was with Finley Quaye who claimed he was Tricky's uncle. Tricky went as far as doing a rap refuting the claim – the pair who had once worked together on a track with Iggy Pop fell out.

Finley himself was another major maverick talent of the period. His debut album *Maverick A Strike* was a massive seller, stuffed full of upbeat reggae-fused songs sung with a honey-sweet voice. Finley had been planning the record for years. I remember him as a confident kid sat on my doorstep (he lived round the corner from me in Hulme, Manchester) looking for production tips, asking about records from the underground guitar scene, learning, hungry for information. He even asked me to write a bunch of lyrics for him, but I had to go on tour so I never got round to it . . . fuck I would have been a rich man now if that had come off!

Portishead

Tricky and Massive Attack – that's not a bad strike rate for any town, but the breakthrough of Portishead in the mid nineties consolidated the whole scenario.

Portishead took the so-called trip hop scene into the mainstream. Crossing the music over from the hipsters and into the living room of the thirty somethings who would have normally run in fear from anything labelled dance.

The band's main mover Geoff Barrow was brought up in Portishead near Bristol (hence the name). Barrow had worked as a tape op at Couch House studios where he met Massive Attack, started working with Tricky on a track for the Sickle Cell charity album and then went on to writing a song for a Neneh Cherry album. In 1991, while getting himself a cool reputation as a remixer working with the likes of Depeche Mode, Paul Weller and Primal Scream, Barrow started his Portishead project .

He'd already met vocalist Beth Gibbons on a job creation scheme. Gibbons had spent years singing in pubs, her powerful idiosyncratic voice was just what Barrow was looking for. It would perfectly spook the tracks that he was thinking of. They spent the early nineties writing tunes bringing in jazz guitar player Adrian Utley to help out.

The project took shape, introducing dark, evocative and atmospheric sounds that were near to film soundscapes. To compound the film theme Portishead made their own film – a pastiche of sixties spy films, *To Kill A Dead Man*, which Barrow and Gibbons acted in. An exercise in *film noir*, it underlined their musical intentions perfectly.

Released in 1994, on Go Beat, the *Dummy* album was perfectly timed. A low-key media profile resulted from the outfit's reluctance to do any interviews. Leaving their atmospheric videos to do the talking added to their mystique. At first the album slipped in and out of the charts, their reluctance to play the normal media game was working against them. But word was out and amazing press reviews sent it back on a long chart haul.

The album was record of the year across most of the music press, won the Mercury Music Awards and spent months in the charts. It even crossed over into the US, being a big MTV smash.

In 1997 their second epynomous album was a far more lavish and detailed version of the debut. The record had been a killer to make, Barrow, like anyone who has spent a long time in the studio, was a perfectionist and tinkered with the project till he achieved perfection. It was worth the graft. The record was a perfect follow-up to the ground-breaking debut.

In the same year, Roni Size won the Mercury Music Awards with his *New Forms* album. It was a stunning result. Instead of the usual music paper guitar band the judges had gone for something really different. Some cynics suspected tokenism. But this record is quite brilliant. Taking drum and bass and turning it into something quite different.

The fluid rhythms of the form seemed to be stretched longer. They felt like they were getting played live. The live session on Mary Ann Hobbs' show is a dizzying display of electronic music played with the adrenalized live edge of the very best guitar music, you can feel the musicians' sheer excitement at creating their music. The songs went over time, there was no point in stopping them. It was awesome stuff. At the end of the session Mary Ann is gasping at the audacious excitement of it all. A couple of years later and she's still a a major fan.

'I saw Roni Size play a 9,000 capacity tent and it was so intense. Loads of kids were going completely mental. He knew how to blow up a room. Watching Oasis is nice but it doesn't move me . . . When they played Earls court it was *pleasant* . . . It felt like an event but Roni Size in a tent . . . That was a show!'

Reprazent know how to rock a house. At V98 they DJ'd a set before James Brown came on stage. It was a sublime moment, the kings of the future and the king of the past, meeting virtually head on. It was as if both ends of the history of dance were colliding. A crash course in the history of the form.

Reprazent is a collective made up of Roni Size, Krust, DJ Die, MC Dynamite, Suv and Onallee on vocals. The Bristol-based collective came together in 1992 when Roni and Krust met up. Their roots of course go back to the Bristol sound system scene. Roni Size, who had got into hip hop after seeing the *Wildstyle* film, mixing his new love of hip hop with his childlike interest in reggae and soul which provided the base for his musical taste, and who had been at the Wild Bunch's neo legendary clubs, had by the early nineties got his own sound system together. Krust (whose roots lie in 2 Tone and seventies funk and soul) had hired a hall and booked in Roni Size's sound system. They hit it off, hanging round Bristol and travelling up to London to check the rave scene.

The collective started to come together round the pair. Suv had known Krust since their school days. DJ Die, a hip hop and skateboard freak, knew Roni Size from the days when Size worked in Bristol's Replay records, They spotted Dynamite MC-ing at a rave in Oxford.

Reprazent wasn't the first release from any of its members. Krist and Suv had already had a hit as Fresh Four with their version of 'Wishing On A Star' (a Top Ten in 1989). Roni, Krust and other members of the collective had already released a whole gamut of underground releases.

Gathered under the Reprazent banner, these disparate talents gained a national platform. Just another great tune-making crew from Bristol proving that the music scene was in a constant state of flux and evolution.

No longer a backwater, Bristol entered the new millennium as the provider of vital cutting-edge post dance music.

CHAPTER TWENTY-FOUR

RAGGA

Yet another style that burst from the never-ending reggae breeding ground, Ragga was the form's answer to the digitalization of studio technology. Its influence can be felt on the fringes of the pop scene and it has created its canyon of classic trax . . .

Flip on a pirate station and you can hear some amazing music going down. Fractured beats, heavy bottom end and garrulous cracked vocals, this sounds like true nineties music. Rooting back to Wayne Smith's 1985 'Under me Sleng Teng', a track that was put together after someone in Prince Jammy's Kingston Jamaica studio found a preset rhythm pattern on a Casio keyboard and, linking it to a keyboard bassline, came up with the first fully digital reggae backing track. With Smith's added vocal, a whole new form of music had come about.

Reggae, one of the most influential forms of music in the world, has seen some spectacular innovations absorbed by the mainstream musics, from dub plates, remixers, 12-inch singles even to rappers. It's been there first – an incredible rush of ideas from one small island in the West Indies. With the new electronics that were pouring into studios head on, it was inevitable that reggae would eventually fuse with the possibilities of digital. The key reggae/dub studios were hives of experimentation: even if these guys hit on a successful formulae and knocked out as many versions of it as they could get away with, they would always be looking for some way to change the form, go somewhere else.

When that Casio rhythm pattern kicked in back in '85, you can just see them working out the possibilities. a whole new genre of music created from one afternoon's messing about.

Not bad work for a day!

Ragga has entered the musical mainstream, touching on all sorts of variable areas of pop. The Prodigy are a band that have obviously been influenced by the manic break beats. The Essex outfit just speeded up the loops, giving their music an even more demented freak beat edge. Rapper Busta Rhymes has copped some of Ragga's flavours in his manic vocal delivery. With its sparse rhythms and aggressive vocalizing, Ragga picked up dancehall, the early organic version. Yelloman, Barrington Levi, General Echo, Junior Reid, Josey Wales were the prime practitioners of the form, full-on vocalizing often with leery lyrics over stripped-down simple rhythms, quite often recorded at Prince Jammy's studio. It was a raw development on the reggae front.

All Ragga was the same kinda guff cranked with a digital edge instead of using established dub plates. The new electronic form just cranked things that little harder.

The new form made big localized stars of Shabba Ranks, General Levi, Cutty Ranks, Beenie Man and Bounty Killer, as well as fuelling the distinctive sounds of records by Buju Banton and Sizla.

Banton himself has quite often been the centre of controversy, with his pointlessly homophobic lyrics creating a media storm. His coarse vocals and tuff street commentary have made him a reggae superstar and he has released a series of albums that are peppered with some great hard-edged cuts although not strictly ragga. Sizla is the new rising star of reggae, name dropped constantly by ex-Stone Roses vocalist Ian Brown, he is starting to achieve some sort of crossover success. The charismatic young star has the potential to go all the way in the new millennium.

Ragga was a great escape for reggae. Its tuffness and aggression have helped to make it sound cutting edge in the general blanding out of late nineties pop. The question now is: in which direction will reggae twist next?

CHAPTER TWENTY-FIVE

TRAVELLERS

**'The punks and the ravers and the drum and bass crew . . .
We love our noise that's what we do . . .'**
Gold Blade, 'Strictly Hardcore' (No. 64, 1997)

It's 1999 and the middle of the afternoon. Someone has dragged a generator over to Manchester University and is about to get an illegal rave going. It's sunny, the vibe is good, the music goes on and from nowhere, heavy, heavy looking cops arrive – the Tactical Aid Group. The party heads run into the nearby busy Oxford Road and block it for an hour as the big surly cops stare down at them. A girl skips gaily in front of the police. Their moustaches bristle with indignation. They can do nothing.

They eventually push the party back into Hulme, all the time getting trailed by their multi-million pound helicopter. Some rich old bag who has parked her car in Hulme to a save a few quid on a parking fee asks the cops what's going on. They describe the scene and go on about 'those sort of people'.

When it's a question of taking sides, it's pretty obvious that the police have theirs well worked out.

They are the frontline in the war between the underground culture and the mainstream. The curious war that smashes up rave parties and allows the centre of Manchester to become a piss head paradise, a place where sullen lad gangs can threaten passers by.

But that's Britain for you alcohol = OK, E and dope = danger. It's a war of attrition and it shows no sign of ever ending. Battered buses parked up, paint spattered, cracked windows, TV aerials hanging off the roofs, piles of wood for burning in the stoves, wild dogs and feral people. For most of the nineties, Hulme was Traveller Central, a bohemian outpost of freakiness and heavy manners. The soundtrack was techno, occasionally interspersed with punk rock or folk. In the summer the wild parties would cruise the night. The severe concrete blocks of the inner-city estate gradually becoming encased in wild dayglo paint.

It was the most extreme statement of punk utopia.

The punk connection had been forged by Crass who had taken the cry of anarchy and made it into a lifestyle. In the early eighties the band were huge. An invisible force outside the charts selling records so cheap they didn't register in the world of *Top Of The Pops*. Their following, dressed in a mashmash of combat gear, dreads and shaved heads, were swiftly moving into their own style.

Rooting back to the hippies in the late sixties and even to the beat philosophy of the fifties, the travellers were the new itinerants. They terrified middle England because they had no interest in the lifestyle shackles of the suburban dream. They had been in their buses for years and had enjoyed an upsurge in popularity as some elements of the punk scene started to branch out into a hardcore form of hippiedom.

For some, the only logical route out of the inner-city shit was to get in a bus and get on the road. By 1983 the travellers were known collectively as the Peace Convoy after some of their number hooked up with the Greenham Common anti-nuclear protest camp after Stonehenge Festival in 1982. A ramshackle army of highly intelligent itinerants revoking the British way.

The word was out: there was a place to go beyond fashion where, despite a tough lifestyle, the much talked about pop dream of total freedom was a possibility. The People's Free Festival at Stonehenge was the focal point of their year and by the summer of 1984 the numbers attending had swollen to 60,000.

Their increasing high profile and diametrically opposing lifestyle to that of the Tory Reich was inevitably going to lead them into confrontations with the Thatcher government. Summer of '84 saw the first skirmishes between the cops and the travellers at Nostell Priory and there was the faintly ridiculous image of Michael Heseltine thundering around in his flak jacket during the Rainbow Village evictions from Molesworth air base.

The 'Henge Festival of '85 was inevitably doomed. And when the authorities diverted the traveller convoy en route to the festival site, tensions were raised. English Heritage, the owners of the Stonehenge site, had slapped an injunction on the ancient monument and surrounded it with a whole heap of barbed wire. The local police force were instructed to stop the travellers at all costs.

The result was the notorious battle of the Beanfield as the police went in hard on the travellers. It was shocking, although hardly surprising, evidence of just whose side the police were on. The scenes of over the top cop violence were carefully doctored for the news but there was still enough there to show how ruthless the so-called free society was prepared to be to protect its own interests.

The Tories gloated as the travellers' honeymoon was over. Some hardcore travellers either turned to special brew to become the special brew crew or eventually smack and everyone else attempted to keep the flag flying.

The vibe moved on. Into inner city parties or on to Glastonbury.

Glastonbury became the rallying call for the travellers, initially allowed in free by promoter Michael Eavis. In 1989 the first sound system (Hypnosis) was dragged down to Glastonbury Festival. It started a new tradition. People like Nottingham's DIY collective and Cambridge's Tonka. These crews were a whole new tradition of music and merry-making. Collectives from all different areas of the musical battlefield, committed to the all-night freakout collectives like DIY, were putting on free raves on in the deep south of Wiltshire. It was one in the eye for the rave culture which had so far been a money-making machine. Thatcher's children had been bleeding the new utopia for every penny possible while outfits like DIY were just in it for the communal celebration.

It was a new strand in the dance wars. The idealism of the punk hippies and the soundtrack of the ravers uniting into a new whole. And the likes of DIY were key players in the new way. They were organized and smart and at the festivals like Glastonbury they were hooking in with all the different strands of underground culture. The punks, ravers and hippies were getting together. . .

Perhaps the best known of the new crew of urban dance guerillas were London's Spiral Tribe. Named after the spiralling shape of an ancient fossil shell, the Spiral Tribe were a loose collective of Henge veterans and club fiends. Inspired by the collective free-for-all and sheer fun of acid house, they put together their own sound system. With shaven heads and black gear they cut a very different image than the clichéd dayglo look of the scene and with their choice of tracks leaning towards the harder, faster and wilder shit available they swiftly became the freaks' choice.

Their first events were back in the inner city squats before they took their schtick in 1991 to Longstock, the alternative to the now sealed off Stonehenge. Firing up a full cylinder, they blew the minds of all present and stayed out on the road all summer, travelling from festival to festival, site to site, bringing their own wild party with them, bridging the gap between rock and rave, building the new way, bringing the travellers into the dance thing. Wild talk of shamanic rituals and pagan vibes were the order of the day as the Spiral Tribe took their music to the people a million miles away from the accepted machinery of the music world.

Pretty soon the hard-ass techno that the Tribe and their spin-off crews like Bedlam and Adrenalin soundtrack of combat techno was the aural backdrop of the freak show. In Manchester's Hulme, pounding techno parties were the order of day. The squatted flats were getting knocked together and made into party scenes. Long weekend parties would boom into the night, sound systems cranked hard, no cops or hassle. Every weekend would be spent inside the dingy converted flats listening to wild music till well into the next day.

Rooms full of wild-eyed travellers and inner-city kids getting off on the hedonistic pulse. The music was a tough techno a million miles away from the handbag house of the city centre clubs.

A wilder, rawer, music for a wilder rawer world.

Into this nationwide melting pot, this seething mass of different experiences, wild ideas were bound to form. The techno pagan crossover of new gurus like Terence McKenna were brought over the Atlantic with their wild theories of emancipation through drugs, magazines like San Francisco's *Mondo 2000* and its espousal of hi-tech weirdness in the shape of smart drinks, the web and brain machines were getting circulated.

When this paraphernalia started arriving in the more enlightened clubs in '92/93 it was obvious that dance music had moved a long way from the Saturday night discos of the eighties. Crashed out in the back room of a club with a brain machine strapped to your head watching the pulse of the red light was a pretty disconcerting experience and the smart drinks would be like drinking a thousand coffees all at once. Fired up by the new tech weirdness you would then look through weird bags of semi-legal dried up vegetation. Some of it, like Guarana, seems to be everywhere now and some of it seems to have seeped back to the underground. Some of it seriously disorientated the senses and some of it just gave you gut ache.

Spiral Tribe's wild-eyed enthusiasm had really started something. House music was no longer the preserve of weekenders. The freak show was changing the very nature of techno music. In their wake there was a whole host of similar sound systems.

But if 1991 was the honeymoon, 1992 was when the iron fist of the state was going to come down hard. A Spiral Tribe rave in West Acton was ruthlessly crushed by the cops and the police were getting on the travelling sound systems' cases. The Home Office started discussing laws to crush the culture. The storm clouds were gathering. Pop culture was lining up directly against the state.

But there was still time to stick one right into the eye of the authorities. In May 1992 a heavy police presence in the west country was squeezing out many attempts at parties. Somehow several hundred vehicles broke the cordon and ended up in a field in West Mercia. Within hours all the sound systems including Spiral Tribe were there. As the news broke on national TV the clarion call went out, the big party was on. The last stand was being enacted as thousands hit the road and the number of people at the site swelled to 25,000.

The ravers and the travellers partied across the weekend. Unbeknown to them this was the high water mark of the culture. The rest of '92 was a story of road blocks, police harassment and a media war against the travellers.

There were attempts to re-ignite the flame, like Spiral Tribe's breathtaking audacity in mounting an event at Canary Wharf. Inevitably the cops busted the party like they did at Smeathorpe, The Torpedo Town festival and Kerry in Wales. There were thousands of people out there looking for a party and there were as many police out there stopping them.

By the end of the year Spiral Tribe, despite having a neat record deal, were hounded out of the country by the authorities, relocating to Paris. A whole heap of court cases were piled up on their backs.

The party was over.

Now the authorities were going to make sure that they had the whole thing nailed down properly.

The Criminal Justice Bill was John Major's Tory party's reaction to what was going on. By 1993 the traveller rave community was estimated to be 50,000 strong. The powers that be's idea of society was falling apart. It seemed like droves of people were ignoring their tame vision of culture, that they were blatantly disinterested in Major's laughable vision of warm-beer-drinking, cricket-loving action and that their money was going somewhere else.

The Criminal Justice Bill was an affront to civil liberties. It seemed to be a pretty discriminatory attack on all points of the counter-culture and when the so-called people's party of the opposition led by Tony Blair refused to vote against it, it couldn't fail to make it through Parliament. It was the first time that a government had ever attempted to legislate against the counter-culture. For many pundits who had considered that nineties pop was a political wasteland and represented no threat to the powers that be, this was proof that the opposite was the case. Techno rave culture had trodden on establishment toes and was now feeling the full force of the reaction to their endeavours.

But instead of destroying the movement the publicity was fuel to the fire. Malcontents, dropouts and rebels were rallying to the traveller cause and with a new soundtrack in acid house and a whole new set of drugs to freak out with, things were going to change very quickly in the real underground.

In the late eighties Club Dog started its nights in a back-room space in Willesden that gave it a youth club feel. A mishmash of travellers and dayglo freaks hung out at the happening with the pre-house non-discernible soundtrack – of world music, dub and esoteric sounds. There was no hint of the freaked bedlam that would ensue in the nineties as the Club Dog ended up in huge venues in Manchester and London, becoming a rallying point for the local freaks.

Club Dog was just the latest event in a rumbling anarchic scene that had its roots back in the Crasstafari punk days. Crews like the Mutoid Waste Company had been putting on wilder and wilder parties with backdrops of huge scrap metal sculptures that they had built.

These clubs were pre-rave raves, weird scenes in the capital. Alternative lifestyle rallying points. Eventually, when they would pick up on the house explosion, it would become their soundtrack.

The travellers, armed with their militant punk hippyism and the

The Berlin wall, the best urinal in Europe, was removed in 1989 reuniting Germany and kicking off the Nineties.

Acid House changed the clothes, changed the drugs and changed the music. In 1999 the music scene is begging for a similar sort of revolution that wipes the smug look off the corporate pop world and its cloyingly dull music.

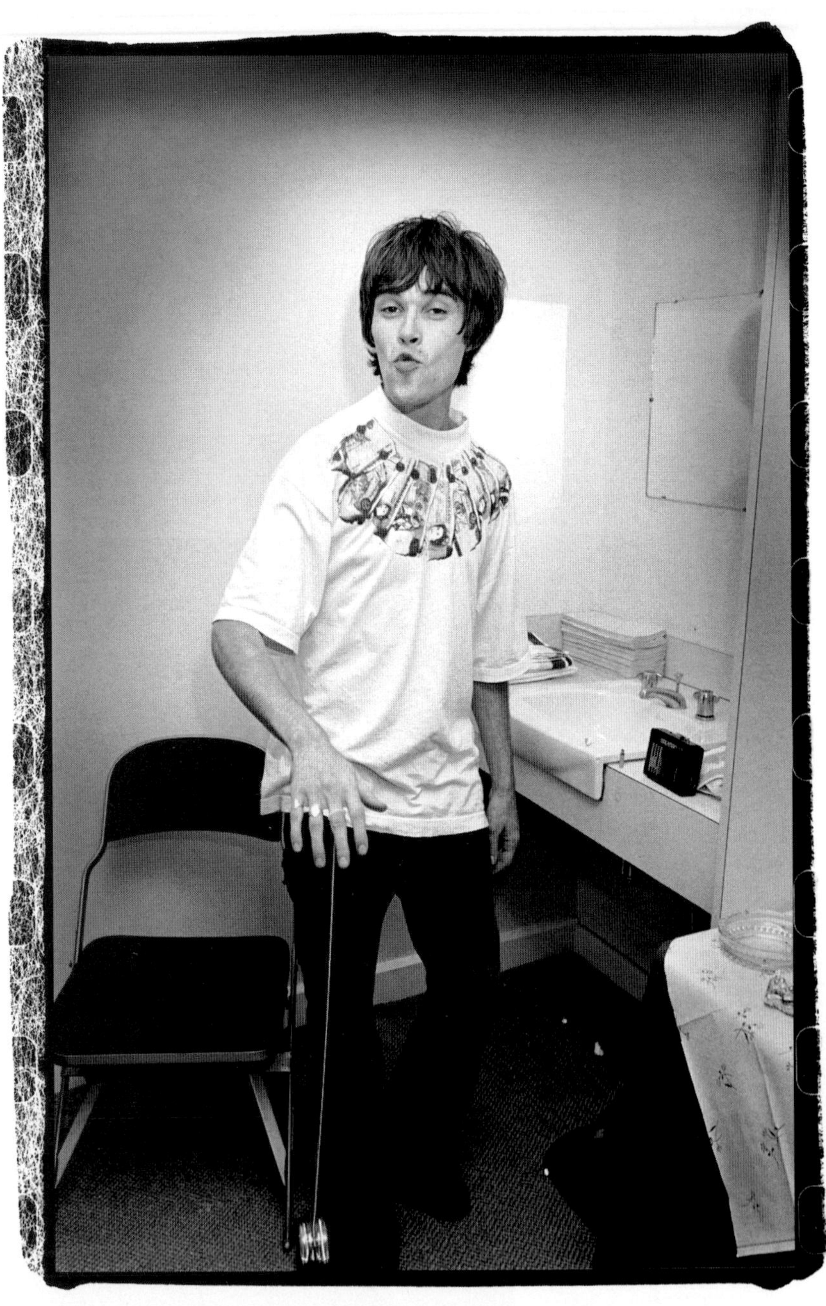

Ian Brown practises his yo-yo before taking the Indie hordes into the mainstream at Blackpool Empress Ballroom, summer of '89. Ten years later The Stone Roses still sound like the best band of their genre.

He may not have lasted the decade but his music will last forever. Kurt Cobain, the tormented rock star with the most amazing voice, found that the fame most musicians crave is a poisoned chalice.

The Happy Mondays, the Godfathers of the Chemical generation and not strictly in the beats sense.

Nicky Wire and fellow glammed-up members of the Manic Street Preachers caught backstage at Birmingham University in 1993. The band's situationist anger is underlined with deftly applied eye-liner and machine-gun guitars.

All grinning, all-dancing, cheery yesmen — nope its not New Labour but the boy band phenomenon of Take That; now known as the band that spawned Robbie Williams.

Quite literally knee-deep in shit, Swampy became a media icon in the mid-nineties and Fleet Street focal point in the protest movement. Party politics may have been dead but issue politics were the key to the decade.

Like the Beatles and Bowie before them, Blur changed faster than the pop consensus but still managed to stamp their identity onto a never-ending run of hits.

They've been called everything from 'dance traitors' to 'The Greatest Band in the World' but Primal Scream were always a band who knew how to be rock stars.

The Prodigy released some of the most crucial mid-nineties records, crossing metal with techno and then slapping on the punk attitude in full effect (just how weird is 'Firestarter' for a number one!)

Massive Attack burst through the nineties with their spot on, multi-styled journey from dub, to soul, to slowed down hip-hop and even a punk edge thrown in for good measure.

Loaded took the fine art of pub conversation and made it into the most influential magazine of the decade.

Jerry Springer, constructinng his moral high ground as the punters come and throw abuse at each other on the TV.

Once the preserve of cloth caps and rattle-bearing fans, football has become a yuppie past-time for designer threaded city oiks in executive boxes. As the predominant culture of late nineties Britain with stars such as David Beckham, 'it's not who who know, but who you support'.

Oasis re-invented the rock'n' roll swagger whilst remembering to bring along a fistfull of great tunes.

As the UK's most successful pop export of the decade, the Spice Girls flaunt their Girl Power credentials.

'Didn't you use to be in The Housemartins?' Big beat guru Slimboy Cook meets Fatboy Slim. Whilst Cook was grabbing the cred. and the sales, Beautiful South's Paul Heaton had a greatest hits compliation with some of the best selling British records of the nineties.

'Born Slippy' was one of the great anthems of the nineties — albeit due to its chant of 'lager'. The song's key role in the 'Trainspotting' soundtrack propelled Underworld and their cutting edge dance music into the mainstream.

Armed with a million dollar grin, Goldie was the first drum n' bass superstar cutting some great vinyl before becoming an unlikely supa-celeb in the soaraway stratosphere of the late nineties.

The Chemical Brothers revolutionised pop music, paving the way for big beat and finally removing that imagined barrier between rock and dance.

house movements drug and trance edges, attracted all sorts of soothsayers and acid profits. Fraser Clark, who had been on the acid trail since the late sixties, was invigorated further by a night out in Shoom. In the new bedlam he saw a revival of his beloved hippy schtick. Through a series of interviews and his new magazine *Evolution* he was one of the first people to redefine the dance explosion as a shamanic ritual, a pagan freakout – as something tribal and primal.

All sorts of heads were getting turned in this new melting pot of strange drugs, repetitive beats and wild clubs. The Shamen had been pottering around on the edges of the rock press scene for a few years. Their psychedelic pop, armed with heavily politicized left-wing lyrics, seemed out of place in the stiff-arsed eighties.

But when the band encountered acid house they saw hints of their version of counter-culture and how the new beat and lifestyle could be fused with their schtick to create something powerful.

Their interest in alternative lifestyles, technology and psychedelics saw them jumping wholeheartedly into the house thing. Things were moving fast. The Shaman now made sense. Swiftly fucking with their music, they were one of the first bands to break down the barriers between the DJ and the band. Their sets soon become a blur, great Dj-ing merging into the band's electronic psychedelic workouts.

It went under the banner of Synergy and they toured up and down the country with their version of the future, taking DJs like Mixmaster Morris and Paul Oakenfeld and support bands like the emerging Orbital on the road with them, breaking down the barriers between indie and dance, pulling the rock kids into the brave new techno world. The saddest moment of their history was when their key visionary member Will Sinnott was drowned in Spain after making a video for their 'Move Any Mountain' video. The band went on to mass success after the death of Sinnott but it was the key Synergy tour for which they will be remembered.

At the time The Shamen must have thought that they had found a way out, and that they were helping to finish off rock 'n' roll but now, at the end of the decade, their shenanigans seem to have been largely forgotten and post-Oasis rock 'n' roll is as big as ever.

CHAPTER TWENTY-SIX

NEW RADICAL POLITICS

You've got to party for your right to fight: taking the fight to the frontline . . .

The crushing of the traveller culture failed. It failed because it politicized the outsiders in a way that had obviously not been expected. Now instead of chasing up and down the countryside looking for parties and weekend-long freakouts, the culture moved on to direct action, opposing the government juggernauts on ecological and political issues. It seemed like an obvious next step.

Utilizing the same sort of tactics as they had in organizing their raves, if the Battle of the Beanfield had been the point when traveller culture knew that there was no turning back, Twyford Down was the birth of a new radical culture. . .

The death of mainstream politics meant that issue politics was thrust to the fore. If you want to change things, get on the streets or, to be more nineties about it, dig deep in a burrow or build a tree house and stop the corporate swine from carving up another chunk of countryside.

In 1989, at the tail end of the Thatcher years' the Poll Tax March in London had gone off big style. The understandably unpopular tax (the Community Charge, as it was known, meant that the comparatively poor would be forced to pay an equal amount of tax on their property as the comparatively rich, even though the latter might own several much larger properties; it was blatantly discriminatory and further evidence of the evil divisions that were being created in British society between rich and poor by Thatcherism) had been causing rumbling grief and discontent since its introduction in Scotland. It was bizarre enough experimenting with the unpopular, almost medieval, tax north of the border and when it was introduced nationwide it found itself heavily resisted.

There were all sorts of irritating catch-alls. If you didn't volunteer your name for your poll tax your name dropped off the electoral register – which was handy as most objectors were hardly going to be Tories! When the law finally caught up with you they forced you to pay it back in small doses. Some of us are still being docked two quid a week for our poll tax from a decade ago!

Not only was mainstream politics seemingly detached from real life, it also seemed to be about nothing other than staying in power. On the rare occasions it decided to wield any political clout it seemed to deal in a politics that was against the people. The Criminal Justice Bill and Clause 28, John Major's ridiculous pronunciations about the family, seemed completely out of touch with what people were really thinking and feeling.

Most of the time people weren't thinking and feeling very much. But these were issues that were inspiring direct action.

Twyford Down was the first high-profile protest and one that inspired a whole new style of protest. The nineties had seen the price of road-building go through the roof. For Thatcher the car was god, running down public transport and building roads at great cost.

One of the bypasses they planned to build in 1992 was at Twyford Down, building it through one of those rare corners of beauty in the UK.

For years they had been getting away with building their roads unopposed. But in the new politicized climate of rumbling discontent, when the contractors' bulldozers turned up for the routine dig, they were met with a ragbag of protesters – an unlikely alliance reflecting all strata of society.

First in were the Dongas, road people who were already dug in and prepared for the long haul. Bringing the all-night party spirit, they were at the frontline of a new style of protest. They turned into a party.

They were quickly joined by local middle-class home-owners, the old and the curious. Together they put Twyford Down on to the front pages.

Of course they didn't win – the bypass was eventually built –

but they put the issue into the news, created a national debate and inspired a whole host of similar protests.

As the nineties panned out the nu protest took hold everywhere. There would be a mixture of travellers and posh people protesting against the cruel way animals were being transported, pointless road-building found itself blocked by protesters, ancient trees were camped in by highly organized freaks. Increasingly sophisticated, they made tunnels, digging themselves in for the long duration. No longer easy to dismiss as dope smoking layabouts they were highly politicized and making a point.

By 1997 they even had their own superstar in the shape of one Swampy, who became a media celeb and even got offered a big record deal before disappearing down another tunnel. . .

Swampy, for the mass media, epitomized the lank-haired protester. As ever attempting to personalise any issue and trivialize it, they made him into a national celebrity. Within months he had been turned into a pin-up. How nineties can you get, from the barricades to pop star in a few months. In the nineties everything is pop!

The press, realizing that these people couldn't be written off as scum, but were actually getting a whole ton of support from middle England, seemed to change their tone. Swampy and his colleagues were being treated like heroes, their radical policies and environmental concerns in line with the way that a hell of a lot of people were thinking in dear old Blighty.

The tradition of passive protest had, of course, been around for a long time. Its prime proponent, Mahatma Gandhi, had refused to budge and waited for the British to leave India half a century ago; Greenham Common saw mainly women camped outside the fences of the American base in a protest against nuclear weapons being on UK soil; Animal Lib had been around for years but were now getting increasingly more militant.

It was just that after the government had declared war on the party scene it seemed to coalesce all these strands. In the mid nineties there was a whole host of radical fronts to be fought on. Issue politics was the rule.

Bizarre that even now the pundits chunder on about how the nineties generation is the most apolitical since pop culture began, only interested in designer clothes and drinks, and how they fought the glorious political battles of the sixties and listened to their fucking Bob Dylan records, or even the punk generation with its I

Wanna Be Me politics. The nineties saw righteous attrition on a whole gamut of fronts.

One of the rallying points was the anti-Criminal Justice Bill campaign. The ridiculous and unpopular law was being resisted in a variation of events. The anti-CJB campaign united the nu radical. The Freedom Network, based in Brixton, united all the different strands of dissent. The 1994 Criminal Justice Bill curtailed many basic freedoms primarily aimed at the rave crew. It was a catch-all that covered most areas of underground activity. Naturally there were protests.

Fighting for your right to party is one of the fundamental tenets of pop music and when the government is passing laws that breach civil rights then protest is the only answer.

In May '94 10-20,000 marchers took part in the first good-natured demonstration – a march from Hyde Park in July. A follow-up in March took place with twice as many people. It was a lot less good-natured this time. The frustrations were starting to boil over. Marching past Downing Street saw some demonstrators attempting to climb over the barricades. There was a stand-off as the mounted police galloped in under a hail of missiles. Things were getting increasingly tense.

In October, with the Criminal Justice Bill on the verge of getting through Parliament, the Advance Party organized the last demonstration – a good 100,000 turned up as a show of strength against a bill that they knew they had no chance of stopping. When the march attempted to get into the sealed-off Hyde Park, there were scuffles, stones were thrown and the police went in hard. It was an ugly day for democracy. Agitators were blamed by both sides and pundits pointed out that this scenario was what a post Bill Britain could be full of.

Despite all the protest the Bill was passed on 9 March 1994. The free party scene was effectively smashed. There were minor protests, a rumble of discontent, the scene went back underground to the squats, the inner-city shitholes that the cops didn't bother with. Every now and then the boom boom boom of the sound system team crashes across Hulme. As long as it doesn't cross the magic boundary into the nearby city centre's hallowed university turf then it's left alone. A lot of the crews left for Europe, their battered buses taking to the road for one last time, creaking to Spain or France where there is more space and more freedom.

*

Single-issue politics has become the key to the nineties. Every now and then an issue would swell up fit to burst, dominating the headlines. A road would get blocked, a planned runway would find itself facing highly organized eco-warriors whose romantic beliefs went beyond demonization by the press and started to take on Robin Hood-style characteristics. The British love of the underdog and inbuilt dislike of greedy corporations favoured the dug-in anarchists. Couple this with the fear that your house may be the next one to find a bypass getting bulldozed through its back garden then its understandable how this gang of outlaws was popular.

Animal Lib went further and further underground. Dressed as urban guerrillas they took their fight to the frontline, releasing mink from mink farms, copping ridiculous long sentences.

So much for the apolitical nineties! Everywhere you looked there was a pressure group here, a pressure group there. New radical politics is the voice of the disenfranchised, and to many it's the only way forward against a government that always seems to be detached from what the people want.

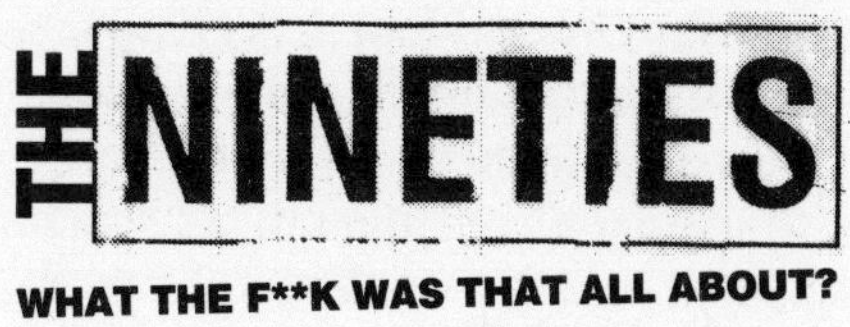

WHAT THE F**K WAS THAT ALL ABOUT?

CHAPTER TWENTY-SEVEN

FASHION

Fashion stalks the nineties like it has any other decade. The nineties was a story of designer chic: designer labels, designer music and designer football teams. It didn't matter if you weren't that sure what to wear – if you had the right label you would be OK. Nice 'n' tidy. Against this backdrop there was a mass explosion of sportswear reflecting sport's status as the primary mass leisure activity of the late twentieth century. Pop was further pushed back from the frontline as sports stars became role models and everyone started to wear training shoes.

There were also important intrusions from hip hop culture, the skateboarding scene and the tattoos and piercing end of the underground . . .

It didn't start like that.

Acid house had changed the rules.

The eighties had been about 'style' but the sheer physicality of the new clubs meant that baggy loose fits were an inevitable choice. The leisure age was creeping in and with it came leisure clothes. Mind you, for most people the leisure age meant being sat around on the settee on the dole smoking dope. In fact by the late nineties they weren't even on the dole. Careful massaging of the figures that had been going on since the latter days of the Tories meant that dole-heads just disappeared off the register altogether.

Despite that, this was the glorious new leisure age. Shell suits, track suits, easywear – it all came in hand in hand with the new culture.

On the edges of mainstream fashion skateboard culture has gradually seeped through to the high streets. The voluminous baggy-trousered wallet chained look has criss-crossed with hip hop culture and British street fashion has mashed together.

The skateboarders themselves first appeared in the early sixties when, to practise their surfing moves, someone came up with a surfboard that you could use on the land. It was a smart move: it quickly became its own subculture, with some practitioners going nowhere near the sea.

It crossed over to the UK in 1977 where it became a massive craze: a million skateboards were sold that Christmas in an astonishing boom. The whole scene quickly became very uncool, looked on as a bit of a naff youth fad, but a hardcore stuck to their guns and as it began to revive in the mid eighties with a smaller board with fatter wheels, it brought a hip baggage with it.

Developing through the eighties, skateboarding was now seen as an adrenalin sport. It had its own soundtrack of underground punk rock and hip hop, and somehow it went from being a little kid hobby to being a rebel sport.

The music, the clothes, the slang were all imported from America. Clothes were from the hip hop scene in New York. Stuff like low riders, hooded tops, training shoes, airwalk tops and shoes . . . the sort of fashion styles that are massive now.

The crossover has been incredible. What were once hip labels worn only by the élite at the heart of the scene have become everyday wear. Labels like Stussy and Mambo have become high-street fashions. Chains like Gap have appropriated the look, watering it down.

The breakthrough of the Beastie Boys into the big time has dragged the whole associated culture with it. With skating in their videos, their albums mixed hip hop and punk rock, selling the whole lifestyle to the mainstream. The fixation with Kung Fu, Bruce Lee, Hong Kong cinema and Japanese animation comes from the scene. The Beastie Boys' own magazine *Grand Royal* pummelled the message home with articles on all these esoteric items of cool.

The loose-fit skater look – a necessity because the high-energy lifestyle demanded such clothes – pushed army fatigues on to the agenda. It may have been one of the reasons why combats have become so ubiquitous, pushing jeans into the unlikely position of being high fashion . . .

But even while this was happening there was a very different fashion world grinding mercilessly on. Designer labels have been one of the key booms of the decade. A new catwalk glamour swanked its way across the globe. There were model superstars, skeletal super waifs, which caused a sharp increase in anorexia in teenage girls.

Impressionable girls were far more interested in the fleshless figures than the fabrics. Some nineties girls found themselves dangerously dieting, attempting to keep up with the stereotypes. Eating disorders were the ugly flipside of fashion as the impressionable tried to emulate the unobtainable.

The pressure to stay beautiful in the nineties is more intense than ever. Billboards spit cruelly unobtainable role models. Both male and females, because if there is one key trait of these times it's that men have become as obsessed with clothes as women. Manchester last year became the first city in the UK where men's clothes outlets overtook women's, and several other cities are about to follow suit.

There was an increase in male suicide and diet problems as, for the first time ever, men were subjected to the same physical pressures as women.

High fashion has became more exclusive. Super models swaggered up the catwalk, emaciated skeletons flogging freak gear. British supermodels like Naomi Campbell and Kate Moss were hyped as the faces of the decade. Campbell broke the mould, a black girl exploding the fashion world's white stereotype blue-eyed blonde-haired girl.

Moss was literally plucked from nowhere, spotted when she was 14 at JFK airport by Sarah Doukas, the owner of Storm modelling agency in London. The famous series of photographs that propelled her to stardom were snapped by Corinne Day, whose groundbreaking anti-fashion schtick was primarily responsible for the key elements of the nineties look. Day deglammed fashion. Her photos were of scrawny girls in cheap clothes in shitty locations. It was a hyper street look, a million miles away from the hyped-up glamour world of the catwalk and, alongside other key photographers like David Sims, propelled the superwaif/heroin chic and the misappropriation of the grunge look into the centre of the fashion storm.

Moss, pushed as the Twiggy of the nineties, was labelled the 'superwaif'. She opened the door to the far thinner skinflints that would push the physical envelope to the furthest extremes. Her anti-designer look and natural dressed-down style had her hooked into the fashion world's clumsy restyling of the grunge look. It was the launch pad to a career that has seen her dominate the decade's fashion catwalk. She has became one of those ubiquitous faces of the nineties' paparazzi wasteland.

The designer revolution has even started to challenge the ubiquitous training shoe in terms of street wear. Canadian-born shoe designer Patrick Cox redesigned what was basically a shoe that had been around forever and everyone was bored with – a lightweight summer shoe – and came up with the revamped loafer on his own Wannabe label in 1993, based on the white loafers worn by Yank funnyman Pee Wee Herman. The shoe became one of the defining items of mid-nineties dance culture. His black, red suede and green python skin Wannabe finding fame.

Sportswear's near relative casual wear had been riding in tandem with the boom. The crocodile logo of Lacoste had been crossing over on to the terraces since the late seventies as the 'casuals' dressed smart, flaunting their new relative wealth and sharpness. Like sixties neo mods they started to become obsessed with the minor details of their clothes, minor details like labels. It was part of the label revolution that would dominate men's wardrobes into the nineties.

Lacoste, perhaps the company that more than any other pioneered the label boom, was formed by a French tennis star, René Lacoste, whose nickname was 'La Crocodile' after winning a crocodile-skin suitcase in a bet. In 1933 he got a mate to draw a crocodile and had it embroidered on to the jacket that he wore on the tennis courts. Bizarrely the design caught on and became the first example of sportswear as fashion. Lacoste rapidly expanded across a whole gamut of casual and sportswear and has become the ultimate blokeish item.

Lacoste is a family firm and very much concerned with quality. Still produced in a small factory in Troyes, France, they started to distributed to posh clobber shops in Britain in the mid seventies. The casual revolution caught them on the hop, snooty shopkeepers couldn't comprehend the snotty-nosed kids appearing in their shops hunting down the Lacoste gear and the company were getting fairly pissed off having to chase down imitators through the courts. It was something that they had not bargained for! A spokesman for Lacoste in the mid eighties was disdainful of the 'football element' picking up on their gear and shook his head in bewilderment when he described punters taking a razor blade to their clothes to cut off the crocodile logo while in the shops (to stitch on to a cheaper shirt at home). Fashion fetishism of this extreme was not what 'Le Crocodile' had initially bargained on!

Lacoste, though, was a revolutionary concept and it was bound to spawn imitations from its successful thirties debut. It set the foundations for the way that people dress in the late nineties and had many rip-offs including our own Fred Perry (the last Englishman to win at Wimbledon way back in the thirties!) who launched his casual wear business as a direct copy of his French contemporary.

In the nineties, casual wear has become street wear. Labels are the totem of fashion, dictating what to wear to the not so sure. And if you are looking to join the dots between casual wear and label wear with a dash of the freedom of access that sportswear throws in then US giant Tommy Hilfiger is the name to drop. Hilfiger is the key name in streetwise sportswear. His big ass logo turns his customers into walking billboards. It's the perfect scam – the name is more important than the gear.

The bold logo was a reply to the bootleggers who were taking the tiny logos of his rivals and enlarging them on baseball caps and T shirts. Hilfiger came up with the distinctive big blue white and red logo, selling the idea back to the streets. His designs were dominated by his logo and his name was soon solid-gold hip. Hooking into the hip hop scene, Hilfiger was being name-checked in rap songs. Getting hooked with the most cutting-edge pop culture of the nineties wasn't going to fuck his career up.

The nineties saw a proliferation of label wear. If you weren't sure what to wear you could invest heavily in the 'right' labels and feel that you hadn't cocked up. Footballers and 'blokes' could swagger around town in their Armani, expensive well-cut and ultimately naff suits that hooked the punter in with their promise of some cod cool Italian chic.

Born in Piacenza in Italy, 1934, Giorgio Armani took the stiff suit and cut it as a confident yet relaxed item, capturing the smart yet relaxed aura of the laid-back styles of the Mediterranean. Armani started his career as assistant to Nino Cerruti, the Italian designer who specialized in luxury wear. Armani broke through in the money-grabbing eighties, designing clothes for women before crossing over to the men's market. His big breakthrough came in 1980 when he designed the clothes for *American Gigolo*, the narcissistic film starring Richard Gere which seemed set up deliberately to showcase his clothes, making them the virtual star of the film.

Armani's suits became the ultimate clothing for the new yuppie chic and in the nineties have become the second skin to every pro footballer and wine bar rat in the country, a sort of false sophistication that can be bought off the peg. Armani had opened up a whole new market and blazed a trail for the likes of Calvin Klein, Donna Karan and Jil Sander.

Calvin Klein virtually created the modern designer label, producing branded jeans in the early seventies. This, combined with relentless smart advertising and a knack for having the perfect understanding of the mass moment, propelled the brand to the forefront in the heavily label-conscious era.

Other designers at the forefront of the nineties clothes wars included the Austrian Helmut Lang and his downbeat modern styles; and Alexander McQueen, who broke the mould since leaving St Martin's in 1992 with a deliberately confrontational series of collections that brought accusations of bad taste, although that didn't stop him from following John Galliano into fashion house Givenchy.

Like Armani, Italian designers Dolce and Gabbana sold their idealized version of their homeland as label fashion. Their clothes were a mix between forties screen sirens, Catholic dressed-up Sunday best and stereotypical images of Italy from the pinstripe Mafia suits to the peasant look with religious details.

It wasn't just the young upstarts that were coining it with the nu Italian chic. Gucci has become a byword for sophistication. You could buy into chic by shelling out for their handbag. The Spice Girls' film featured a running joke with Posh Spice's inane love of the label. Gucci had made its breakthrough as long ago as in 1932 with the snaffle loafer which became the byword in Euro sophistication.

Riding almost in parallel with Gucci was the Italian designer Miucci Prada, whose penchant for the simple and the stylish hit a nerve. Her bags became a synonymous byword for style. Again rooted in the luggage business, she took over her grandfather's leather luggage firm in the seventies and brought it completely up to date, experimenting in new fabrics. Famed for its signature black nylon range, Prada has meddled in all sorts of colours and fabrics and has become one of the most desired labels in the curiously label-fixated times.

While most of these labels dealt in the nu square, dressing footballers and the Saturday night crowd, there was still some space for maverick spirits. Northerner Wayne Hemingway's Red or Dead label propelled extrovert threads to the cutting-edge club crowd looking for some freakier threads for their freaky dancing. Hemingway, rooted in the punk of his youth's multi-style conflagration, designed clothes that were an explosion of shapes and fabrics. A celebration of the much-mooted crazier side of street fashion that seemed to have been dying out in the late nineties as clothes became more uniform.

But the nineties wasn't all about label gear. On the other side of the card there was grunge, the dressed down rock 'n' roll look that crashed into the mainstream on the back of Nirvana, best exemplified by Kurt Cobain's almost genderless look of bleached hair, occasional dresses, raw make-up, cheap sunglasses and heroin chic. Kurt looked like an angel and a junkie and he looked fucking cool. The look was rooted in punk but updated by years of thrift-store cross-dressing. His death photo, taken through the skylight of his outhouse where he blew his head off, had his feet stuffed into a pair of Converse trainers. It can't have done their sales any harm.

Grunge may have become synonymous with Seattle but the look had been around for years in the fallout from punk rock – more of a suburban appropriation of the look than the heavy-duty city version. The look was filtered through second-hand clothes, Oxfam chic, imagination and a knack for matching up bric-a-brac for a total look. Most post punk rockers in the eighties carried it on and it sprawled through the rock scene in the early nineties and was bizarrely picked up by the catwalk major fashion scene as a plaything. Nothing that they could claim they had invented like they routinely do when they swipe something off the streets. It would only be a couple of years later in the mid nineties that they were claiming that they had destroyed it as well.

Like anyone really cares what those schmucks think!

Grunge became the wardrobe for the so-called Generation X (even that term was hardly original, being a book about nascent sixties youth culture in 1964 and being the name for a great punk rock band in the late seventies before its nineties usage).

Generation X were disaffected, over-educated baby-boomers who had everything and wanted nothing. Grunge was the soundtrack and the look. Fashion, of course, chewed up the latest street look and spat it out all wrong. Misappropriating the look, they sold it back as catwalk grunge and then as 'heroin chic'.

If Cobain was the totem of the male grunge look, his wife Courtney Love was used as the female icon. Her 'baby doll' look which she arrived at via Kate Bjelland from the now defunct Babes In Toyland was ripped dresses and big boots. In fact, again, it could be argued that this was a look that went back about twenty years as well. Groups like The Slits were dressed to kill in the same sort of garb in the post punk fallout.

The rock scene splintered after the grunge look. For some the look got heavier and heavier into body piercing and tattoos, for others they remained grunge fundamentalists, the look mellowing out into the lo fi scene where you could dress like Woody Allen like a lo fi nerd and be a star. Rock! took it all to the other extreme with the Marilyn Manson smudged eyeliner black PVC ghoulish chic that gangs of teens have adopted for the metal night out in town . . .

The street fought back. For years fashion houses have taken their inspiration from the Saturday afternoon kids swaggering into town . . . 'When I'm stuck for ideas I just go and see what the kids are wearing in London when they walk past . . .' sniffed one fashion house mogul before stealing another street style.

One thing puzzles me though. What did happen to those space suits that were meant to be the clothes of the future?

CHAPTER TWENTY-EIGHT

TRAINING SHOES AND SPORTSWEAR

From the casual wars to the nation's favourite footwear and back again, the training shoe has become ubiquitous in the nineties. It's only in the last couple of years that their rise has started to slow down. Everyone has got a pair – some people even use them for training. Their explosion has seen incredible profits for their parent companies and a revolution on what people put on their feet . . .

Likewise in sportswear, the much-vaunted leisure age has seen people decked out in leisure wear. Conversely, the lazier and fatter everyone got the more likely they were to be ensconced in sportswear . . . it was one of the anomalies of the decade . . .

Sport is the true art form of the twentieth century: Way ahead of pop and even in front of cinema – nothing gets the people's blood boiling more than sport. The new *Star Wars* film may be a money-making machine and everyone will go down to the multiplex to check it out but they won't be partying in the streets like they did in Manchester when Man U won the European Cup.

Sport now holds our attention more than any other so-called 'pastime'. And we are now dressing the part as well.

Sportswear has now become everyday wear. Dressing the sort of people who would never dream of lifting a finger in a sporting event – lardy-arsed couch potatoes, knackered smackheads, the elderly pub pissheads, as well as rainswept Saturday afternoon families – was a major achievement for the key companies in this phenomenon.

As sport gradually became the dominant leisure pastime of the globe, the fashion has followed suit. Maybe the fans thought that they could get fit just by decking themselves out in the tight fabrics and the hip shoes of the sporting star or they just craved the body-hugging comfort that sportswear is designed for.

By the end of the decade you would be hard pushed to find anyone who wasn't bounding around town in a pair of training shoes. The sports revolution was complete. The training shoe was king and the sexless track suit was dominant as the street fashion of the last few months of the millennium.

On the street it was sports gear that ruled the roost. Doughboys were crushed into figure-insulting track suits. The shell suit was superseded by look sportif and feet were shoved into trainers.

The training shoe had been hip on the fringes for years (the casuals had innovated the idea of trainer as style) but it was dance culture that bounced it bang smack into the centre of culture. Obviously going out dancing is a lot easier in a shoe made for physical jerks. The trainer had got its break and it was going to take it.

As Gary Walker, a trainer-wearing record company boss from Wiija records, points out:

'Trainer culture is a relatively nineties thing. Ten years ago you could walk down London's Oxford Street and think she looks really hip or he looks really hip because they had trainers on but now every has the uniform so it's become really hard to tell.'

In the nation's colleges by the mid nineties the trainer had replaced the Doc Marten as the student signifier. Docs themselves seemed ubiquitous in the early nineties. They gave an air of menace and street tuff to the most unlikely pairs of feet and were swiftly adopted by the indie music-loving student in a quest for authenticity.

The boot has always held an odd position in the clothes hierarchy, worn by both the cops and the skinheads, two sides of the same coin. It was invented as an orthopaedic aid in 1946 by Klaus Marteaens, a Bavarian doctor. The good doctor had broken his foot while skiing and wanted something to make walking easier without the pain of the injury. The boot was an instant succes. It was comfortable, practical and it looked good. In 1959 the British bootmaker, R Griggs was allowed to use the sole on his steel capped workers boot, changing the very stuff the sole was made from to

PVC which was far tougher and resistant to all the sorts of crap that the factory floor would throw at the footwear. The formula was so successful that it has remained unchanged ever since.

It would lurk threateningly on the fringes of fashion for the next few decades.

The Cherry Red, a version of the 'bouncing souls', became the *de rigueur* item in the skinhead's wardrobe in the late sixties before crossing over to British street fashion for the next twenty years.

Although less visible now, the early half of this decade was some sort of peak in the boot's fashionability. With a ridiculous array of colours and styles attached to it in a constant redesigning and, some would say, mellowing out of the boot's once hard-edged appeal.

But even while the Doc Marten was in its ascendancy as the one of the key items of street wear it was being challenged by the now ubiquitous training shoe.

The two companies that really benefited from the explosion in the training shoe were Reebok and Nike, the big two in the shoe wars. Adidas, Converse and Puma are the next level down, not too far behind in the profit wars.

The top dog in the world trainer market, Nike was founded in 1971 as Blue Ribbon Sports by Phil Knight, a middle-distance runner from the University of Oregon. Knight was born in Portland in 1938 and his partner Bill Bowerman was born in Portland in 1911. They set up the company to import the Japanese Onitsuka Tiger training shoe. While on a trip to Japan, Knight had pretended that he was president of the Tiger shoe importing company and fooled gullible shoe manufactures that he was the man they should be exporting their shoes to America through.

After a while he figured he could make better shoes anyway and set up the Nike company. They started manufacturing their own range of shoe called Nike after the Greek winged goddess of victory.

Enlisting the help of Bowerman, his college running coach, Knight set about attempting to revolutionize the design of the training shoe. Bowerman came up with the rubber waffle souls after looking at the rubber rim of his wife's iron. He made himself some rubber waffles and glued them to the bottom of his running shoes. They felt great and the next day he gave a pair to some athletes he was coaching. They raved about the shoe.

The trainer was born. Nike went from strength to strength

with their new revolutionary shoe. Knight started his aggressive sport-star-endorsed advertising campaign by bringing in John MacEnroe the world's No. 1 tennis player of the seventies, which, all helped to make Nike the world's No. 1 trainer by 1979.

The aerobics craze of the eighties knocked Nike sideways with the strongly competitive Reebok taking the lead in the keep fit scene. Nike diversified into other brands. The battle was fierce, with the two companies pegging level in the world market.

That was until Nike upped the sponsorship ante.

Squaring up to Reebok, Nike made its name with the continuous aggressive marketing of its image – a non-stop advertising war featuring superstars of the sport world (a new Michael Jordan trainer has been released every year since 1984). Jordan wasn't even their first choice. They had missed out on Magic Johnson and Larry Bird, the two biggest basketball stars of the period. Jordan, though, has had longevity and his popularity and the boom in the sport, especially on the street, has made Nike the hippest shoe in the world today.

With signed sports stars appearing in adverts that look like aggressive pop videos, Nike has managed to retain a cutting-edge cool for itself. Advertising slogans like 'Just Do It' were hardly pandering to the public and a series of adverts that ran with the slogan 'You Don't Win Silver – You Lose Gold' were criticized by the Olympic committee. Quick on the uptake when sportswear became streetwear in the last twenty years, Nike has carved itself a massive share of the new market. Its distinctive 'swoosh' tick logo has become the designer logo of the whole new boom market.

Reebok, arch rivals, was a company that was started in England by Joseph William Foster, who at the turn of the century made his own shoe to help him in his beloved sport of running. The shoe was so good that his mates demanded them as well. Within ten years most athletes were using the Reebok shoe. Foster by now had turned his invention into a profitable small business. Reebok made a name for itself with its superb design and its reactions to the needs of the athletes, a need that they fully understood, being runners themselves.

The company name Reebok captured this athletic prowess, being named after a small African gazelle, a fast little fucker of an animal. Profits mushroomed in the training-shoe boom and the company moved to a new HQ in Massachusetts to be right at the heart of the world's main shoe market, the United States.

Reebok is currently No. 2 in the cutthroat world market.

Famed for the three stripes, one of the best corporate logos of all time, Adidas is a design classic. Its history goes back more than 80 years when two cobbler brothers Alfred (Adi) and Rudolf Dassler started to make running shoes. Born in Herzogenaurach in Germany in 1900 Adi, a football fanatic started a small company making football and running shoes, the two products that are still the mainstay to this day. Their first major break was in the 1936 Olympics when the black American athlete Jesse Owens, in his gold medal winning, record-breaking humiliation of Hitler's 'super race' athletes at the Berlin Olympics, bagged four golds in a pair of running shoes put together for him by the brothers. The shoes now had prestige, an early case of sports sponsorship! I bet they weren't too popular with the Führer after that.

In 1948, Adi's brother Rudolf split and set up his own Puma company after a row with Adi. Puma has gone on to forge its own idiosyncratic brand, eventually almost challenging its former parent company in the world market.

In the fifties Adidas caught on with footballers, becoming one of the leading brands on the footy pitch before beginning to crossover into the training shoe and then on to the street.

But it was in 1986 as the sportswear boom started to roll that Adidas got its first massive pop cred boost when New York rap trio Run DMC released 'My Adidas', decked themselves out in the company's wears and put the look under the street fashion spotlight. Into the nineties the astonishing rise of the look as more than a sportswear option caught the company on the hop, but they were fast to respond and were locked into a war with rival company Nike. A war that they are currently losing as both Nike's and Reebok's heavyweight advertising campaigns push them further to the front of the market. They may be No. 1 in Europe but even moving the company to America has not helped them break out of this position in the multi-billion world sportswear market.

Around for years but newly hip on the high street were Kappa. The 'Kappa Slapper' became the new high-street look. Glasgow underground band Mogwai emerged as unlikely champions of the label, so enamoured with the logo that they even entitled one of their lo fi moody soundscapes after the crapwear,

'I just like the trackies. I don't like buying clothes. It's just easy to buy. It also gets up the noses of the precious indie kids with their hairclips!' claimed Stuart from the band.

With the swagger typical of a gang of mates in a band Mogwai almost made Kappa look quite cool.

Kappa was an Italian company set up in 1916 in Turin. Initially it made socks and underwear. It changed its name to Kappa from Aquila in the late sixties and made plenty of lire in the youth culture boom of the times, selling jeans with a frankly fairly sexist series of posters of girls' arses in too-tight denims. Its 'Kappa Sports' line became 'kappa' and repositioned itself in the sportwear boom, moving away from the jeans market that had made it so much money.

They made their name sponsoring Italian football teams – Juventus were the first such sponsored Italian side and soon they were working with AC Milan, Sampdoria, ASS Roma and Ajax . . . big European sides with a very high media profile that couldn't harm their brand name.

In 1984 they were being worn by American Olympic athletes and had even moved into Formula One with Justin Villenueve. In 1996 they suddenly seemed to explode on the British streets. From being an occasionally spotted logo they almost seemed to land at the centre of the market.

It was a big-time boom – even Admiral, long thought of as a dead company, revived itself in the late nineties.

The proliferation of sportswear has seen similar stories for all the leading companies who have exploded from small enthusiast roots into major big-time multinationals. Like Converse, once a specialist basketball shoe and now streetwear, or Vans with their careful sponsorship of the skateboard scene and their backing of hardcore thrash tours, these people know their market, react to their market or even go out of their way to create the market in the first place.

The training shoe has become so ubiquitous with nineties culture because it knows the rules. It understands the concept of leisure and comfort and it has learnt the vicious marketing skills of pop culture. It has become one of the decade's key signifiers.

Which brand will dominate the trainers market in the 21st century? You might as well ask who will be the next Oasis . . .

WHAT THE F**K WAS THAT ALL ABOUT?

CHAPTER TWENTY-NINE

ALEC EMPIRE: THE EMPIRE STRIKES BACK

From Berlin, Alec Empire, head honcho of Digital Hardcore records and the outfit Atari Teenage Riot, is cutting techno records that are scarred with the raw power of punk rock and a full-on anarchist politics . . .

It's 1999 and there seems to be a war everywhere you look. The world has gone crazy, riots in China, bombs in Belgrade, Brixton and Soho, the corporate powers are more in control than ever before. There is talk of one known band who had their video sent back to them because it was 'too political'. With its head in the sand, pop is avoiding the deranged pre-millennium debate with a vacuous grin.

It's into this terrifying vacuum that Atari Teenage Riot are stepping in.

They have, of course, been around for ages. Back in the early nineties they released a cover of Sham 69's 'The Kids Are United', a knowing, hyper-electronic maelstrom take on the goofy naive anthem. They were blanked by a UK music scene which had no time for their mental breakbeats and wild-eyed idealistic talk. I hung out with them for a couple of hours in Camden's Roundhouse studios and enjoyed Alec Empire's fast, idealistic take on life. A true believer in a better world and a sonic guerilla lining his band up against the powers that be, Empire seemed to be fighting a tough battle against a hostile media . . .

Seven years later and he's come into fashion. Everywhere you look the Riot are grabbing rave reviews. Their label Digital Hardcore is a conveyor belt of tested demented sonics that sound like truly modern music. Taking the machine-like power of techno and kicking the fuck out of it, they are making the breakbeat sweat for its living. Their tracks are built on a chassis of molten twisted beats with a full-on violent racket built on top.

It's inspiring stuff.

Just a glimpse into a possible future. Berlin-based, Alec Empire sits at the head of a mini empire dedicated to mashing up the machine-like power of techno with the visceral power of punk rock. He is also intensely political, an anarchist who believes in doing things full on.

His band Atari Teenage Riot were dealing fast and furious beats with shouty punk vocals at the beginning of the nineties. Sounds familiar?

The Prodigy went to No. 1 over most of the world dealing in the same sort of palaver. This makes Empire a visionary. He arrived at the same place years before. His uncompromising political stance and desire to crush the big-business corporations that dominate late-nineties culture were never going to make The Riot as big as The Prodge, but their music is percolating slowly through to the mainstream. In America, particularly, they are getting a lot of respect, hooking up with the Beastie Boys and collaborating with everyone on the cutting-edge music scene.

Empire's Digital Hardcore label unleashes a constant flow of like-minded musicians and their cranked electronic music. Exotically monickered electronic terrorists include Shizuo v Shizor, EC8OR, Cobra Killer, Bomb 20 and Christoph De Babalon, among others.

This is nineties music that deals with the nineties. You won't find any lingering nostalgia for the sixties here.

The highly charged technological revolution of the era combined with the ever-fracturing music scene of the times would, you may think, make Empire a happy man. But as he barks away in his rapid machine-gun voice from his HQ in late-nineties Berlin he sounds let down by the vacuousness of pop culture.

'When the nineties started I was euphoric. Everything had changed. I thought everything would go independent and we would be able to wipe out the corporations. At the time I was really into techno and acid house but three years later I got back into punk rock. I wanted to make the music have personality and be more in your face and more political.'

As the nineties have ground on, Empire has become more and more disillusioned.

'I think my generation has not achieved anything. The nineties was a complete revival of every trend and genre recreated in an electronic way. Music totally reflects what goes on in society. It's strange when young people are more conservative than their parents. I mean there has been some great stuff, but it was mainly underground. I really liked The Riot grrrl scene, I thought it was important. It was really like punk rock. The records had a meaning and a lot of energy. They were on the right side. I also like a lot of electronic stuff and noise records from Japan.'

Empire believes that the corporations are now totally in control but sees a thriving underground surviving in their slipstream.

'In the future there will be a divide between their clean elevator music and a new creative underground.'

It was this fierce independence and idealism that marked Empire back in the early nineties when I interviewed him at the genesis of his project.

That first time I hooked up with Empire he was in London mixing the group's debut album, *Delete Yourself*, at Chalk Farm's Roundhouse studios. ATR were a three-piece at the time and very much a creative team. Empire may have been the mouth and the producer but there was a pool of ideas from the whole unit that was getting worked on. They were touting their first single in the UK – the previously mentioned unlikely high-velocity cover of goofy punk legends Sham 69's 'The Kids Are United'. It was one of those ideas that is so naff that it's in fact quite brilliant. The original song is one of those moronic tunes that is actually a slab of great mindless pop. When Empire had turned the song inside out, he had created an apocalyptic, electronic nightmare that was dealing in the vile racism that was just beginning to hit the headlines from his home town of Berlin.

At the time shouting punk style over a heavy-duty break-beat was greeted with derision by hipsters but the seed was planted and when The Prodigy took 'Firestarter' to No. 1 most people pretended that it had never been done before.

Empire, the punk techno animal, was vociferous – laying into the terrifying rise of the right, the power of the corporations and the death of techno. His fellow cohorts in ATR, Hanin Elias and Carl Crack, were barely into their twenties – a good few years younger than the 26-year-old Empire – but they were equally opinionated.

Not that the band were a drab gang of politicos. Their

conversation, like their music, spat a wild humour and they were getting off on the sheer raw power of machines made to sweat for a living.

In 1999 Empire is still fired up with the prospect of making the machine grind out its visceral beat.

'We abuse digital gear. We want to create energy out of the trash of corporations and turn it against them. And then put it through an analogue desk for the warmth. If it stays in digital it loses certain frequencies.'

Producing and sculpting the basic sound of Atari Teenage Riot and being the main motivator in the host of other projects on his Digital Hardcore label when it started, Empire understands noise and how to create one hell of a row.

'I want to make the music more euphoric and move people. I want to make more insane noise stuff, and maybe keep a punk-rock structure so that people can understand us. I want people to sit back and wonder just how a human being can create this.'

Empire still believes in the power of music. And he certainly seems to deal a lot of it out. Mixing and producing his own music as well as a whole batch of stuff on his label. This is a never-ending operation. A constant flow of ideas and a race to create soundscapes that will continually blow your mind.

A band welded to technology like Atari Teenage Riot would seem to be custom-made for the technological explosion that is going on everywhere. But even this seems inadequate for the too-fast mind of Empire who even finds fault with the MP3 files that you can download off the Net to help you play soundclips off websites, an innovation that could potentially shake up the structure of the way music is distributed.

'Computer technology has just not developed. MP3 files just don't sound good enough . . . When I hear my favourite records downloaded with them I can't get the goose bumps I normally get. They just lack the right frequencies. It needs more development.'

Technology just can't move fast enough for the hyperactive Empire. Technology, though, seems to be just another reason to engage the music establishment in a constant baiting and antagonizing. And what better front for attacking the majors than on the grey area of sampling. With his music built on loops and samples and being a collage of sound you'd expect him to have strong opinions on the ever-controversial topic of sampling.

'Fuck copyright. Sampling is free. If someone like Oasis can just rip off sixties riffs and get away with it then why can't you sample those riffs?'

It's the long grinding argument of the samplers but one that holds a great resonance. Groups in the sixties like the Rolling Stones and Led Zeppelin built whole careers on ripping off blues and soul riffs wholesale. Yet if you sample their holy music you'll find yourself slapped into a copyright court. Just ask The Verve!

Empire is a man on a mission. He believes his incendiary music can make a change. A series of great unsettling records, countless side projects, and a label packed with like-minded individuals is the multi-faceted weapon. Fiercely political, he disdainfully stares at the potential political abyss of Europe. Making a strong stand against racism he's appalled by recent laws against immigration in Germany. He also feels saddened by the cultural decline of his home town, Berlin. His conversation constantly turns back towards the isolated bohemian mecca of Kreuzberg in the newly appointed German capital. Typical of many in the city, especially those clustered around the boho nerve centre, he feels the heart has gone from the city.

'It's like a ghost town now. It's full of the bourgeois children of the Bonn politicians. There are no places left where stuff can happen.'

But The Riot are still based there. Maybe the situation makes their music even sharper. The frustration of living in a country struggling to come to terms with its past and still dragging along that undertow of far-right idiocy fires up his music with a righteous power.

Empire cackles and looks to an uncertain future.

'One side of me sees a fascist society with corporations controlling everything worldwide affecting democracy. Everyone is now so cynical. No one believes in politicians any more. Capitalism has failed – just look at Japan and America.'

Empire can paint a gloomy picture but he still believes that there is a way out of the mess.

'The people haven't failed and I'm very optimistic about that.'

Empire, as a self-proclaimed anarchist, believes in the people. He can see a way out of the nightmare.

'Our new record is about that. Revolution is part of evolution. I just don't accept that it's all over.'

It's a hint of optimism flying in the face of the storm and it's that art of self-belief that drives this whole explosive electronic corner of nineties pop culture.

CHAPTER THIRTY

THE PRODIGY

The Prodigy's international success was one of the major surprises of the decade. From the start they had been cutting great records but they sounded parochial and British. When *Fat Of The Land* crashed into the American charts at No. 2 it heralded house music's semi-breakthrough in the States where it was called electronica.

To achieve the breakthrough The Prodigy has criss-crossed their breakbeat power with the raw power of rock. It was an inflammable combination: the two singles off the album, 'Breathe' and 'Firestarter', were massive UK hits. Listen back now and it hits you just how wild and strange these records are.

The Prodigy destroyed musical barriers, bludgeoning their way though the niche nineties with their own vision . . .

The kids are going apeshit.

Jammed into a hall, 5,000 rock fans are freaking out to one bloke and a pile of electronic gear. He's just cranking loops. There is no bass, no guitar and no drums, just this guy with his bag of tricks and these kids, brought up on rock love this shit.

Macedonia in 1996 is a pre-war backwater. Not much happens there but they know their rock and when The Prodigy ride into town they are buzzing with a high-octane excitement. The Essex outfit are well on the way to being the world's biggest rock band and they don't have a guitar between them.

The quiet bloke that got off their tour bus an hour before is busy fiddling with his pile of gadgets and creating a sonic mayhem that has all the right attributes to great rock. It pounds, it goes quiet, then explodes again. It has pounding drums and bombastic overloads. It hits all the correct teen testosterone switches. It kicks ass! This is an electronic show. And no one gives a fuck!

And why should they? Who cares what's making the sounds, what creates the noises as long as you can get lost in the groove. Oblivion, that's all that counts.

The Skpoje kids are very much on message. The atmosphere is electric. This band can rock a house and just to make sure they have brought three MCs with them. Except, being The Prodigy, these aren't three normal MCs but three wild lads who, with dancer Leeroy, rabble rouser Maxim or occasional punk vocals from Keith Flint, intersperse the electronic freak out with crazed gurning and wild looning.

For many kids Keith is the star. His wild tomfoolery is what the majority of punters feel when they get that rock charge. Dressed like a punk rock madman with smeared eyeliner and an inside-out Mohican, Flint has the crowd in the palm of his hand.

Offstage his wild act is dropped and he is by far the most affable member of the crew, handshaking anyone backstage, being just the affable Essex lad out for a good time. The backstage conditions may be atrocious (no light, no toilets, dodgy cables on the floor) but The Prodigy are here to do a job and they don't complain. They literally plug in and play. They take the venue over like an American band. They don't gripe and moan like British bands, they move in, set up, play and take the place.

It's the key to their success.

While most of Europe has no time for the majority of Britpop outfits, complaining that they are too dated, too weak or just too plain boring and precocious to bother with, The Prodigy steamroller is crushing all opposition. Their plug in and play like a sonic juggernaut is going to knock America – the home of guy rock with guitars – dead.

And that's pretty fucking remarkable.

It's difficult now after the impact to understand how revolutionary The Prodigy really are. After all the fuss about 'Smack My Bitch Up' (their greatest breakbeat marred by their dumbest title – irony never works in the mass market where everything is taken at face value) they seem to have been dumbed down, put on the critical backburner, lost their cred edge. But there was a moment when the

Prodigy's astonishing scenario went into surreal overdrive.

When they crashed into the American charts at No. 2 with *Fat Of The Land*, their mission was accomplished. They had taken things full circle, taking the dreaded electronic dance music right into the temple of rock. The most successful amalgamation of the two styles that's ever been attempted. Journalist Neil Davenport pinpoints their crucial crossover.

'A key band in terms of crossing barriers without being clumsy were The Prodigy. They had the dance press and *Kerrang!* in one swing. They also built up most of their reputation live at the festivals. In the end they have become a metal band really – although it must be said that they have very curious taste in guitar music!'

The Prodigy come from Essex, the much maligned county just beyond the huge sprawl of London. Their roots are a perfect summing up of the sort of cultural traits that would constantly bubble up in the nineties. Key creative member Liam Howlett came from Braintree and was a piano-playing prodigy in his youth. Forced to constantly play scales on his piano he became very very good at the instrument. Howlett got his kicks from B-Boy culture, as a bandana'd teen he would be out with a gang of mates bombing walls with graffiti. His tag was perceptively 'fame'.

The first music that really had an effect on him was 2 Tone, but it was Grandmaster Flash's 'Adventures of Flash On The Wheels of Steel' that blew his mind. He completely swallowed the whole of the hip hop culture whole, from the graffiti to the break-dancing (he had a break-dancing crew that would go round the shopping centres on a Saturday afternoon – something that many of his fellow nineties rock stars would cut their teeth on like Kermit from Black Grape, Jason Orange from Take That).

Howlett was also honing his DJ skills, hooking up with Braintree's premier hip hop crew Cut To Kill as their DJ. He spent a couple of years in the crew until the innate gang violence of the scene became off-putting.

They were already falling apart when in 1989 he went to his first rave at The Barn, Essex.

Like most people at the time he had his mind blown. Not really getting off on the acid house so much as the speeded up breakbeat side of the music, he was transfixed. The music suggested a million possibilities and it was shaking up UK street culture like nothing else had done for years.

Also at The Barn are two other wild kids moving to the music, looking for good times, Keith Flint and Leeroy Thornhill. The strands of The Prodigy were coming together.

Keith had been just another kid who had drifted through school without getting anything out of it. When he left he was transfixed by casual culture, expensive label clothes and Ford Cortinas with furry dice, the complete Essex lad. Hooking up with a hippie mate, Keith was introduced to the bohemian life and disappeared round Europe and the Middle East on an eight-month stint. When he returned to Essex he was thrown out of home and was preparing to go back out on the road. This was when he went down to the Barn. Swiftly hooked by the abandon and total energizing lifestyle of acid house he fucked off his travelling adventures and disappeared into an endless loop of raves and mates' settees. It was the life he had been looking for. It was also where he hooked up with Leeroy Thornhill.

Leeroy had been brought up on music. One of his elder sisters had been heavily into punk and the 10-year-old Thornhill hung around with the Braintree punks, checking out Crass, The Slits, early Clash and early Adam And The Ants.

Again it was the hip hop scene that blew his mind. Checking out the key hip hop films of *Beatstreet*, *Breakdance* and *Wildstyle*, he became immersed in break dancing and his BMX. From this he became ensconced in funk and rare groove and eventually ended up digging James Brown.

James Brown is one of the great pillars of pop. His full-on shows, his incredible dancing, his powerful primal music are as hip today as they were when they were released. Brown is one of the most influential figures in pop history.

Moving to Bath, Leeroy would come back to Braintree at weekends and hear his mates go on about acid house and the barn. He didn't like acid house. It didn't have the groove, the sheer rhythmic possibilities of funk, but eventually he was persuaded to do down there. With the added cushion of an E he soon got it and was raving all night. His James Brown fused dance steps blowing the minds of the freaked kids in the building. He was in and was soon a face on the scene.

The final piece of the jigsaw was Maxim Reality – or in the real world Keith Palmer. Again he had ridden roughshod over the key musical phases of the eighties. From Peterborough, he was first fired by 2 Tone (he told Prodigy book writer Martin James that he saw The Prodigy as being like The Specials 'like a gang – untouchable', a key comparison), and via his brother he graduated to the reggae scene. He was soon chatting down the mic and this was where he picked up his monicker.

He recorded a few Go Go tracks with Nottingham producer Ian Sherwood who turned him on to George Clinton. From this point he started digging rare groove and then he moved to London where he fell in with the sound systems scene. Acid house cut across all the various dance scenes but it left him cold. A mate of his from Peterborough rang him and told him that a band were looking for an MC. He answered with not much enthusiasm. He thought he'd give it go. It wasn't that big a deal.

And that's how Maxim ended up in The Prodigy.

The Prodigy had come together out of The Barn. In the old days mates would get guitars and form bands or answer ads in shop windows – all that 'how the Beatles got together' sort of stuff. But now, thankfully, things were changing. The very germ of the outfit getting together goes back to Liam's DJ roots, playing speeded up break beat and rare groove sets. One night Keith Flint asked him about some of the tracks so Liam made him a tape of stuff. One side was his DJ set and the other marked as 'Prodigy' was some tunes he had been working on and was keen to test out on an unsuspecting ear.

Returning from a rave with Leroy, Keith slapped them on to the car stereo. Keith's mind was blown: fast breakbeats and underground techno – it was an aural adventure. The wild pair fell in love with the tape and played it all night, deciding that the next time they saw Liam they would ask if they could be dancers when they played live.

There it was suddenly – there was a band in the strictest most modern sense, everyone had their clearly defined roles. Liam wrote the tunes. He named the band after the moog Prodigy keyboard that he wrote his stuff on and Leeroy and Keith got to dance and show off. They also brought another mate, a girl called Sharky, to come and dance with them. Everyone was happy. A mate of a mate knew of a reggae MC up in Peterborough with wild hair. He sounded interesting. A few calls were made.

And Maxim Reality was in.

And that's how The Prodigy came together. It's a story that encompasses all that's best about eighties pop culture, from the initial stirring of 2 Tone to the final climactic freak out of acid house, from rare grooves to reggae and dubs, strong traditions of MC-ing, sound systems and the cult of the DJ, from hip hop's B-Boy roots of break dancing and graffiti to its powerful breakbeats. It tells the story of everything that was great about the UK youth underground and in The Prodigy a lot of these strands were tied together.

Debut gigs are always weird. You've got the tunes, you've got a rough idea of what's going to happen. But until you hit that stage, you haven't really got a clue exactly what's going to go off.

For The Prodigy their first gig at Dalston's Labyrinth was a nerve-racking experience. They arrived eight hours early a bundle of nerves. The four of them had never met Maxim before. He was turning up for his first Prodigy show without ever having met the rest of the team, and just to compound things they had a set of stage togs in the car boot that no one in their right mind would ever wear.

Keith had come up with the design of green and white harlequin track suits. It made them look pretty ridiculous (although they wore them for for quite a long time) and it was something that they would afterwards regret ever having worn, especially when you compare it to the skater punk hardcore duds that they swaggered around the world in at their 1997 peak.

They ran through eight songs including 'Android' and 'Everyone In The Place'. Maxim was giving it full Ragga MC vibes on the mic, doing what he had always done with the sound systems. It didn't quite click with what the band were attempting and in the two weeks before their next show Liam explained that the Prodge vibe was about communicating with the crowd and not chatting up yourself. Maxim got the drift quick. After all he had never met the Essex Boys before. It sees remarkable that he could just get up there with his mic and go.

Within a month they had scored themselves a deal with XL records after Liam blagged his way on to the label, arranging to play a demo tape to Nick Halkes, the label's A & R man. The sheer strength of his stuff and the obvious quality of ideas landed him the deal with the label he was keen to covet, XL having put out some of his favourite records including Frankie Bones' 'Bones Breaks'.

He had only tried one other label, getting the thumbs down from Tam Tam which had worked the Cut To Kill stuff.

Liam may have been buzzed up by scoring such a swift record deal but it caught the rest of the crew on the hop. They had never even considered getting a record deal. Dancing in The Prodigy was just another excuse for a good time. Keith had even planned to go off on another round the world trip, hanging out in Thailand, but a series of mishaps kept him in the country and the bemused dancers suddenly found themselves in a going concern as The Prodigy's first release, the 'What Evil Lurks' EP, was released in February 1991. A nineties debut for a very nineties band.

'What evil lurks in the hearts of men', the title track's key sample, was taken off a 1940s radio show called *The Shadow* and was the hook line over a mélange of beats that already saw The Prodigy striking out in their own definitive direction. Howlett was influenced by the speeded up breakbeats and flavours of Renegade Sound Wave and Meat Beat Manifesto – two techno pioneers who had been on the fringes of the electronic music scene since pre house days. The two idiosyncratic outfits were never completely swallowed up by the dance boom and remained on the sidelines, cutting their own individual styles.

The single came out and sold a few thousand and The Prodigy celebrated in the pattern that would become a key to their success.

In short, they toured like fuck.

At the time dance music was sneered at for being a no-personality-DJ-led phenomenon that the rock dude couldn't get a handle on. But a great record is a great record – who cares how it's made or how it's presented?

The criticism had some basis in truth and the lack of wild live bands was having an effect on the form's eventual crossover (although being a bunch of dullards with no personality has, strangely enough, hardly affected a good percentage of the guitar band scene!).

The Prodigy would play everywhere. Prancing around in their harlequin costumes you could hardly forget them, no matter how daft they looked. What they really scored on was their energy. They went crazy on the stage. Two wild dancers (Keith and Sharky), one cool dancer (Leeroy) and one up for it MC (Maxim), this was a show and it stood out a mile in a scene that was churning out great records backed with lousy PAs.

They hit a personal peak performing at Raindance before losing Sharky who preferred to go raving instead of fucking around in a group situation. They were now down to the four that would make the gigantic impact.

An impact that they were about to get into with the release of their second single, the classic 'Charly'.

With a sample of the wackoid voice of a cat called Charly (also the slang term for cocaine giving the track an unintentional subversive underground buzz . . . remember this was a full on E crew!) culled from a seventies TV information film, 'Charly' was, ostensibly, a novelty record (and the spate of piss-poor copyists that followed in its wake showed that a lot of people had grabbed this interpretation of the record) .

'Charly' whipped up a whole hornet's nest of controversy on the dance scene. *Mixmag* laid into the outfit in a famous cover a year later with their 'Did Charly Kill Rave' cover. The story looked like a hatchet job on The Prodigy but *Mixmag* were using the releases of the post-Prodge novelty rave record to proclaim the rise of progressive house in the place of the rave scene.

The cover of the piece was a shot of Liam Howlett. The Prodigy may have been getting the blame for killing rave but he was still famous enough to be slapped on the cover!

'Charly' was in fact a stunning sonic assault, a mental speeded up breakbeat it was like the adrenalin rush of rhythm of prime time drum and bass arriving a few years too early. Headbutting the charts, it gave The Prodigy their first Top 5 hit.

Now they were a proposition.

'Charly' was beyond house. The first time you heard it you were blown away with its electric power, its sub bass anchor and its full-on call to energized existence. Liam had once claimed that he was trying to capture the thrill of rave in his records. He had now done this and how!

They turned down *Top Of The Pops*, giving the programme their video instead – a rough, grainy affair of a bunch of people dancing. It may have confused the trad rock bores but it perfectly captured the whole point of most music!

Charting 'Charly' was one thing but following it up was going to be another. The rave scene had thrown up a whole proliferation of one-hit wonders. A lot of the acts were just pseudonyms for engineers or DJs and the fast-moving nature of the form was burning out a lot of outfits. The Prodigy, it was assumed, would be no different. They had had their summer hit with that mad cat song and now they would disappear back to Essex.

But that assumption can only be made if you take Liam out of the equation.

'Everybody In the Place' was a new version of the track from their first EP and its late '91 release saw it capture the new mood of the rave scene. Propelled to No. 2, it caught the MDA-heavy, monged out E vibe perfectly. The rave scene may have been starting to go underground and into its own weird trip of heavy-duty E abuse but there were still enough crazed nu generation freaks out there to buy into The Prodigy.

The rave scene was moving. Its sounds were faster and faster break beats and bizarre sped up vocals. It was a weird wind tunnel that would lead to 'dark' the proto jungle.

The Prodigy themselves were not keeping still. Their next single, the limited edition 'Fire', was built around a sample grabbed from Arthur Brown's classic sixties psychedelic freakout of the same title.

'Fire' was another hi-speed breakbeat collision with a nifty keyboard hook, its flip side, 'Jericho', was a deeper exploration into the dynamics of sound that would eventually become drum and bass. The Prodigy were pushing the envelope of sound while everyone was dismissing them as a novelty band.

By late 1992 all the aspects of The Prodigy were well in place. Their fast as fuck dark breakbeat-driven dark sound, their Essex lad gatecrashing the hip party love of controversy and their non-stop touring ethic.

Their debut album, *Experience*, captured all these strands in a collection that was really a reworking of their singles. It was not the drop-dead statement of an album that defined its times. But with few other records to use as a benchmark, Howlett was on his own.

The album moved deeper into the junglist vibe that was bubbling up out of the underground and was already a flavour in the outfit's tracks. There was also a dub and reggae flavour on some of the tunes. The reggae vibe was best felt on the magnificent 'Out Of Space' which was built around a sample Max Romeo's 'Chase The Devil' with fast and furious breakbeats. The cut was released as a single at the same time as the album and gave The Prodigy yet another big hit. A hit that was a big jump forward in their sound, moving them further away from accusations of being a mere gimmick.

The single's accompanying video saw them taking the piss out of the Vic's Vapour Rub ingesting confused vibe of the rave scene. It was a scene that they felt had little to do with them any more. The Prodigy were now moving away from their rave roots and learning to stand on their own two feet.

Experience had helped them in this quest. Selling 200,000 copies, it hit the album charts at No. 12, starting the crossover into the rock scene and setting up The Prodigy as a band that sold albums – a dream come true for the music business that treated the rave scene built around hit singles as an unmarketable commodity.

Touring their album in November 1992 The Prodigy took a firm step into the direction of the rock scene. They left the rave PA circuit and booked themselves into the same sort of halls that indie bands played, blowing the indie kids away. This was a crucial moment in the nineties music scene. The final non-dance bastion was crumbling and post 1992 the barriers all collapsed. Indie kids had their own version of dance. The Prodigy would start rediscovering their own rock roots and mixing it into their electronic assault combining the two powerful forms into a whole.

It wouldn't be long till there were regular *Kerrang!* front covers for The Prodigy, leading the way for metal bands to mix samples and loops into their trad form. All sorts of possibilities were getting thrown up. It was one of the thrills of nineties' music.

It was a genius move, crashing rock into dance. All the yobbish kick-ass make-ya-wanna-go-crazy music rolled into one. Not just metal. The Prodigy were a collision between hardcore punk and hardcore dance, the two hardcores rolled into one. They looked like an American underground gang of skate punks, a mixture of cool and crazed (Keith by now had cut off his long hair, spiked it into a double Mohican and gone for a demented nineties version of Johnny Rotten).

'Firestarter' is one of the key records of the decade. Now that we are so used to listening to it, it's difficult to remember how freaked out the record sounded when it was first released. The ferocious explosion of breakbeat fury combined with Keith's John Lydon styled screeching vocal was either an exercise in avant garde mayhem or a celebratory piece of pop psychosis. Take it either way, brother.

It was also Radio One's most played record of the year.

The record was a no-messing No. 1, armed with a dark video . . . This was the moment that dance not only met rock in a head-on collision but also tapped into the dark psychotic underbelly of the UK and still managed to make a great pop tune. It was one of those rare No. 1 records that ties all the loose ends together, that captures the moods. Like their heroes The Specials' 'Ghost Town' it was one of those great No. 1s, one of the great pop moments.

1996 was The Prodigy's year. They seemed to be an unstoppable juggernaut. 'Smack My Bitch Up' caused a rumpus with its dumb title which was in fact a sample from Ultramagnetic MCs, which was deliberately provocative. Since then The Prodigy have adopted a more low-key position.

Can there be another twist in their plot?

CHAPTER THIRTY-ONE

APHEX TWIN

One of the most innovative musicians of his generation, Richard James, aka the Aphex Twin, took techno and reconstructed it into something quite startling and different . . . He offers an escape route for anyone interested in trying to fuck with the musical status quo . . .

The story of the Aphex Twin is a story of end-of-the-millennium pop. At no other time in pop's history could someone as deliberately provocative and maverick have been allowed out of their cage. When you get wankers going on about how there could never be another Jimi Hendrix in pop or someone groundbreaking or righteously bizarre warping the form then you've got to point them in the right direction.

Bubbling just beneath the pop surface there is a superb freak show. And they don't come much better than the Cornwall programmer who was one of the first people to put a human (albeit warped) face on to the dance genre.

His first release 'Didgeridoo', released by Warp, seemed to explode out of nowhere. Ostensibly another twist in the wave form of electronic dance music, the EP sounded like nothing that ever went before it. You could of sort of dance to it if you danced like a madman and you could sort of listen to it at home full blast if you were a psycho. It was a dark and dangerous soundtrack and an hypnotic record.

Interviewing the freshly arrived in London Richard James (the Twin's real monicker) was a disarming experience. Not because the bearded James was as freaky as his records but because he was obviously smart and also had a surreal sense of humour. Instead of being a gormless hacker of 12-inch dance singles, here was someone who was pushing the envelope. He lived in a flat stuffed with Kraut rock albums and a scrap heap of electronic equipment with the manufacturers' labels scraped off (odd for someone named after a company that specializes in studio equipment to carve the names of computer companies off his gear but still!). Some of the gear was home-made and it was all held together by a spider's web of wire, leads and masking tape.

The gear mountain spat boffin.

And it was here that he was building the lush and weird sonic soundscapes that were to dominate his next few idiosyncratic releases.

As the music seemed to get lusher and less experimental, his live shows suddenly upped the ante and went for the prime-time weird jugular. Instead of doing the boffin thing and sitting behind his keyboard looking serious as he twiddled a few knobs and passing that off as entertainment, James came up with a live show that was at once funny and totally disconcerting. Giant teddy bears scrapped it out on stage with each other as the Twin sat inside a kennel with a supercilious smirk on his face barraging his audience with a maelstrom of fucked up beats and twisted soundscapes. Female body-builders posed and flexed as the madness was piled on in heaps.

It wasn't meant to mean anything. It was the product of a generation raised on cheap FX horror movie videos. Minds bombarded with the macabre and the freak show world of B-movie slasher films and hilarious cheapo special FX. But if there is one quintessential moment when the Aphex Twin managed to pull all the strands of his nightmare music and visuals together it was with the 'Come To Daddy' video.

Directed by Chris Cunningham, the film clip perfectly matched the song's descending chaotic riff, zigzagging near drum and bass loops and claustrophobic choking vocal from the Twin himself (his first vocal). The pair reunited on 1999's Top 20 hit 'Windowlicker' which came complete with a wicked pastiche of a macho pop video. In both clips James's face is worked meticulously on to other people's torsos.

Scary shit!

A million miles away from boy band plodders and sixties

revivalist guitar bands. The Aphex Twin is one of a clutch of people who are reinventing music into the next millennium.

Where he will go next is anyone's guess.

CHAPTER THIRTY-TWO

ROCK!

Much maligned, constantly misunderstood but permanently on the cutting edge, Rock! in the nineties has been where the real creativity has been at. After a dull eighties when it was dominated by Los Angeles poodle Rock!ers and fading superstars, it exploded into the nineties with a vicious hunger. Cross-pollinating with other forms of music Rock! has never sounded healthier. From nu punk to hip hop crossover, from skatecore to hardcore, from industrial electronic crossover to freak Rock!, from the highly politicized to the superbly dumb metal, in the last ten years Rock! has not let us down at all.

Rock! is dead they always bleat while writing up yet another half-full hip dance night in any given city in the UK. Meanwhile the Rock! clubs are packed with up to a thousand punters freaking out to anything from The Beastie Boys and Ice T to Korn, Limp Bizkit, Rancid, Terrorvision, Offspring, Marilyn Manson, Fear Factory, Metallica and a whole host of other bands that rule the Rock! roost.

Rock! clubs are usually dark, dank holes, packed out, pissed up and with the music cranked to eleven out of ten. Pretension is kicked out of the window and 'having a good time' is the key.

The goth corner are caked in Manson make-up, a garish blur of big coats and sex clothes while the rest of the room is chocker with skatewear, wallet chains . . . baggy Rock! kids share the dancefloor with nouveau punkers, pisshead freaks, long hairs or just multi-coloured follicle explosions. It's a full-on party, a celebration of a world that exists beyond a conventional media outlook.

Rock! is, on the quiet, getting big. One year ago *Kerrang!* quietly moved into position behind the NME. It's now the second biggest selling weekly music paper in the country. If it proved one thing it proved that Rock! was a hugely viable untapped music scene. The magazine has never made any bones about what it covers and it speaks to its readers in the way that they relate to each other about music. There is an air of no bullshit enthusiasm about the magazine, something that the readers appreciate. It's also a reflection of a musical form that has changed dramatically since the eighties.

The eighties in Rock! was pretty naff. A lot of the clichés that haunt the form were forged in that decade. There were signs of a fightback against the poodle rockers with the speed metal bands and even Guns N' Roses but it took a scruffy trio from a small town near Seattle to ram rock right back on stream.

'The defining factor that shaped Rock! music in the nineties was when Nirvana exploded on to the scene at the tail end of the eighties,' explains *Kerrang!* editor Phil Alexander, adding, 'Their influence didn't impact straight away, it took a couple of years to filter through, but by 1992 grunge had totally destroyed the LA cock rock scene. It made it more difficult for rubbish bands to exist. By then Nirvana had totally changed the course of music . . .'

Of course it's been documented a million times, but in the context of Rock! Nirvana were crucial. Not only did they alter the course of Rock! music they completely altered the way that nineties music culture was going. Metal/Rock!, whatever you want to call it, has had big bands before but very rarely has it had a band that would have such a massive effect on all popular pop culture.

It was mass success that pretty well destroyed the band.

'Nirvana were not pretending when they said that they didn't want to be big. They were genuinely not interested in playing to 40,000 people at Reading, they just wanted to play smaller shows to their peers, people that they admired . . . Nirvana realized very quickly how full of shit people were . . . they just wanted to be a cool underground band.'

By '92 there were high-fashion grunge catwalks, indie bands learning to Rock! out, there were hip hop records built out of Nirvana samples, Nirvana records getting played in techno clubs, they were everywhere, in places that they themselves had never intended to be. In the Rock! scene their influence was everywhere as Phil Alexander points out.

'You can see Nirvana's influence borne out through every aspect of Rock! When Marilyn Manson performs he is not regurgitating Motley Crue lyrics, but his own bizarre twisted social consciousness, a social consciousness that roots to Nirvana and even his androgyny thing is from the Nirvana experience. A band like Korn lyrically exorcise their demons, their lyrics are intensely personal. In 1988 they would have probably sung about shagging and riding a Harley.'

Cobain's intense presence hangs like a spectre over Rock! music. Not only did he electrify the scene – he gave it something else to sing about, broadening the very experiences that could be written about in Rock!; he also gave it a consciousness, post-Nirvana Rock! stepped into the real world, a raw real-life attitude that has served it well in a decade where an emotional honesty is demanded.

It's a reality that Phil Alexander feels is at the core of all the best metal/Rock! groups since the inception of the genre.

'Every real classic band is rooted in reality from Black Sabbath to Motorhead, AC/DC even Guns N' Roses who, although they epitomized cock Rock! for many people, were actually going against the grain of their scene by singing about life on the street . . . well, they did in the early days when they were more genuine before the duets with Elton John when it all went a bit pear-shaped.'

This return to rawness and hard-assed reality has seen metal become a far more powerful emotional form of music. No longer a series of wank anthems for confused 15 year olds, it's an increasingly sophisticated form, a music that is more powerful for its new soulful edge. It's also become a music far more confident about itself. It can swallow a whole bag of influences and still Rock!. No longer chasing its own tail and grabbing at the same four or five bands as direct influences, the nineties has seen metal, like a lot of other genres, utilize other forms of music and add their shapes and structures to its ravenous, powerful form. It's something that Phil Alexander applauds.

'There *have* been a lot of different influences. One massive influence has been hip hop. Coming through on to the scene were the first generation of Rock! fans who had grown up with Public Enemy, Run DMC and to a lesser extent The Beastie Boys. This fist-hard rock and hip hop crossover generation has resulted in bands like Korn or Limp Bizkit. In the meantime, over here, there has been the assimilation of techno which has not resulted in a lot of crossover bands as yet but there is a flavour of the style in many bands. The most obvious thing has been the acceptance of The Prodigy by metal fans . . .'

The Prodigy's crossover from being a rave act to a metal act has been one of the important points of the decade. Taking their full-on energy and up-for-it rush of techno, the energy freaks of The Prodge were bound to find themselves fascinated by the Rock! scene. The fringes of both forms were wearing the same baggy clothes, digging the same sort of adrenalin sports, watching the same films and reading the same comics. Culturally they were already there. Musically both techno and Rock! were both digging the full-on energizing rush of their respective forms . . . adrenalin music. The crossover was bound to happen at some point, only it was The Prodigy who had the guts to do it first.

'Prodigy are not hard Rock! by any stretch of the imagination,' says Phil Alexander, 'but they have proven that you don't have to rely on the guitar aspect of this music to get the same amount of aggression in a song. You can get the same sort of feeling from beats and textures. They certainly have the respect of the Rock! bands – everyone from the Foo Fighters to Marilyn Manson has held up their hands and said that they were brilliant.'

Years ago the thought of a band without guitars Rock!ing a festival crowd was a strange one. Admittedly The Prodigy have Giz Butt playing a few six string riffs but they have managed to capture the skullfuck power of great Rock! with an electronic pile-up of sounds. From their formation they had played in raves. Getting off on the energy of their own scene where they checked the sheer raw power of a hardcore band stoking up a crowd of full on nutters, they knew that this was the sort of action that they really required. Phil Alexander can understand why.

'They saw Biohazard at a festival playing to an audience of psychotic total nutters going spastic . . . and they knew that was what they really wanted . . .'

While The Prodigy were going one way from the pages of *Mixmag* to the bowels of *Kerrang!*, the Rock! fans were dragging themselves in the other direction. No longer content with the trad plod of the form, they were demanding different flavours, a reaction to the modern world, and Rock! obliged, pulling itself up by the bootstraps. Phil Alexander has sensed a changed attitude in the fans. Not only have their tastes broadened, basically anything that kicks ass and kicks it hard is welcome, whether it's played on guitars or cranked out of a computer. The whole way that the music is received has changed. A new generation has grown up with a different bagful of influences and expectations.

'There has been a change in mindset and mentality. Instead of using the term heavy metal . . . aggressive music with attitude is far more appropriate. People are a lot less interested in the received opinions. There are great musics out there that people will access if they want. People have realized that punk rock in itself is far more important than the fashionable media would have you believe. It didn't die with The Sex Pistols splitting up. If you're a kid growing up in some nowhere town then the thought of people banging out a punk tune on a guitar can be inspiring. The whole American punk thing has been really important. And it's beginning to have a grass-roots effect on British bands. Countless bands are influenced by Green Day, Offspring or Rancid. They see bands getting somewhere, putting out records and they believe that they can do it themselves.'

Not only has there been a return to the firebrand punk rock roots but there has been a return to melody as well. Rock! bands are writing pop songs and no one is embarrassed. Not the wussy soft Rock! ballads that used to laughably clog up the metal charts but proper ribald pop songs that give you a rush of insane energy, or goofy pop songs that make you feel good. The American punk bands are kings of this form – the holy trinity of Green Day, Offspring and Rancid seem capable of whacking out great tunes – but the British bands are no slouches when it comes to the pop tunes either, as Phil points out.

'To a lesser extent there has been the return of melody as well. People are writing good songs again. Bands like Reef and Terrorvision are knocking out good time pop band songs.'

This return to melody hasn't meant a wussing out. There are bands in the never-ending world of Rock! who are bringing the noise, pushing the sonic envelope and cranking the volumes but are still hooking in the song. A band like Orgy in the States had a big-selling 1999 single with their heavy-duty cover of New Order's 'Blue Monday' and they are just the tip of the iceberg of a whole scene of industrial acts who fuse the heavy-duty noise end of that scene with its curious love of British synth pop and post-punk shenanigans. These are the sort of people who are into Satan, heavy-duty riffs, crazed squelches of feedback and Depeche Mode. It's a bizarre formula but it works. Ask anyone who digs prime-time Marilyn Manson.

The whole of the industrial scene has thrived on such anomalies. It's a scene that is built on the dynamic and power of Rock! It enjoys the same sort of aggressive power and volume-charged energy. Rooting out of the post-punk fascination with the brave new world of synthesizers and electronics, it's taken on a whole new language of its own, a language that was popularized by Chicago outfit The Ministry back in the mid to late eighties.

'Ministry's influence is so understated. They affected so many bands. I guess the reason that they have not got the credit that they deserve is that they have been so inconsistent and bound up in their own problems . . . They haven't got accorded the respect that they deserve . . . Ministry mainman Al Jorgenson can't be bothered to change his image every week like Marilyn Manson who is a lot more calculated, more switched on. Jorgenson has a lack of focus which Marilyn Manson definitely can't be accused of.'

Ministry were carving up huge slabs of industrial sound, great big thick slices of ugly noise that beautifully battered yer head way before Manson or their even more direct descendants Nine Inch Nails, a band who took the industrial schtick and crashed it into the American charts at No. 1, as Phil Alexander notes.

'Trent Raznor, the man behind Nine Inch Nails, took a lot from Ministry. But he took the music somewhere else, he really popularized it. It's the end of the nineties and there is a new Nine Inch Nails album due soon. It could be really influential, really amazing . . . or awful . . . that's what makes it such an intriguing record . . .

'Trent Raznor had a vision and view of the world which was important. He's proved that you can add a load of brooding, menacing textures to hard Rock!, adding a whole new dimension to the way records are made . . . He's been very influential on people outside the Rock! sphere . . . the way he presents his packaging . . . With the Marilyn Manson thing he's had a direct effect.'

Nine Inch Nails took the Ministry thing and made it work in mainstream terms. They took a powerful raw form, dressed it up and sold it through. The next step could only be Marilyn Manson, the last great Rock! star of the nineties.

Manson has been a sensation, a cleverly contrived Rock! star, designed by his own hand, a David Bowie through a meat grinder, a man who fell to mirth and survived rallying his mascaraed shock troops to his glam clarion call. Manson cut a series of dark, unsettling records, lived the decadent devilish Rock! star thing to the full 6 6 6 and finally fell foul of the moral majority after a couple of fans went on the rampage with guns at some backwater American school. Getting the blame for the gunning down of high-school kids was bad enough – after all, it was hardly his fault that people are dumb enough to actually do this kinda thing and it's definitely not his fault that in America you can get yourself a gun collection that would be the envy of tinpot Third World dictators by walking into your local shop. The real problem for Manson was that he cut an album, *Mechanical Animals*, that his fans just didn't like, as Phil Alexander smirks.

'It was just not music to scare the parents with . . .'

A cardinal sin for a shock Rock!er. Actually the record, if not the nihilistic noisefest of his earlier releases, is great and maybe in a few years it will be re-evaluated. It drips with sleaze and bombastic statements, pro anything to piss off those parents if they were listening. It has veered away from the industrial mayhem of earlier works and into the glam trip of Bowie dashed with the screwball sleaze of primetime Iggy.

Not that Rock! has been totally concerned with the downside, the sleaze, the filth and the depravity. All that shit is great in its place but sometimes you've got to wave the flag for righteousness. While the rest of pop music seemed to be consumed by greed and a fear of being accused of being PC and most of its commentators were just too damned comfortable to give a fuck about anything anymore, there was a still an awful lot of shouting and fussing to be made out there. Some bands were still determined to wave the political flag high and proud.

The group that took this anger and righteousness into the mainstream were Rage Against The Machine. Rooting from the intense hardcore scene, they not only kept their beliefs but amplified them, directly influenced by the Washington DC outfit Fugazi. Still one of the greatest bands in the world, every Fugazi album is a revelation and their fierce commitment to a powerful value system is an inspiration. Fugazi are one of the last few groups in the world who could describe themselves as independent and not use the term to describe weedy sixties guitar band rip-offs.

Rage Against The Machine also had that power.

Phil Alexander agrees.

'Rage Against The Machine are important because of the simple fact that what they stand for is important, the social conscience thing. They have a powerful message although I'm not entirely sure if the audience listens to their political stance. Maybe they are more interested in the hard-edged riffs and rapping vocals. Predating them were Faith No More – they really influenced so many bands you would be hard pushed not to find a contemporary band not influenced by them in some way. Just listen to The Deftones or Korn – they've left a huge legacy.'

Korn themselves have become massive. Their blend of hip hop and sharp and angular riffing has made a huge impact on the Rock! audience. In the States they have completed one of the late nineties' biggest grossing tours and a Saturday afternoon T-shirt count in any city centre will see the band's merchandise scoring very highly. Their total success and importance has not escaped Phil Alexander's attention.

'Korn are the biggest hard Rock! band of the late nineties . . . go to little pubs and clubs and watch a band and they sound like Korn. Their combination of a hip hop rhythm section and DC Dischord angular riffs is the key, while they sing about psychotic aspects of life and childhood in an intelligent way.'

Even while Korn are breaking their new styles in the Rock! plot into the higher echelons of the mainstream, grunge is still making its presence felt.

'Soundgarden and Pearl Jam are still really influential. Soundgarden for their riffs, they way that they appropriated the doom sound of Black Sabbath and topped it with strong melodies. Pearl Jam have become important by refusing to play the game after they became famous. It gives them a certain amount of respect and a mystique. I can see them becoming the Grateful Dead for the next millennium . . .'

For me, though, after Nirvana's trip to the dark heart of rock 'n' roll, Pearl Jam just seemed so lightweight, so mundane . . .

While grunge was the year zero for Rock!, the crucial slate cleaner, wiping away all the eighties dullards, its anti-showman schtick has no place in the faster and weirder world of the late nineties. The grunge acts' dour stage schtick was a necessary headbutt to the frankly pretty crap posturing of most of the Rock! Brontosauruses that roamed the stadium swamps of the late eighties but now the punter demands more. It may have been necessary then but, in the new generation of bands starting to find themselves stalking the stadium territory, a very different attitude has been called for. Phil Alexander welcomes the return to the stadium spectacle, but only if it is on new millennium terms.

'One thing that has returned to Rock! is the notion of performance . . . Grunge negated the stadium idea – it forced Rock! back into small clubs. Now performance and shows are back on the agenda. Korn have a massive show in America. The first wave of new bands have resurrected the arena Rock! show without the stupidity . . . It doesn't do anymore to be shuffling around on stage. Now when you get to a certain size you are duty bound to entertain the crowd . . . the entertainment factor is back among us . . . There was a dour hangover for a while . . . The protagonists were not really the original grunge bands who were nowhere near as miserable as they were painted but the copyist bands who came afterwards like Stone Temple Pilots . . .'

Rock! is all-powerful in 1999. It's so used to being ignored by the snobs and the establishment that it has created its own huge world. On Planet Rock! there are bands that sell millions that mean nothing to most people. Such a band is Metallica, the spine and the backbone to the whole scene. Phil Alexander acknowledges their importance.

'Metallica have now maybe lost some of their vitality by being a bit more pompous with stuff like recording with an orchestra. But the fact that they shifted the goal posts by remaining underground was really vital. No-one gave a toss but they were the biggest band in the world and they achieved this by and large on their own terms and own rules.'

Metallica's ongoing success is the story of Rock! No one can tell them to write 'proper songs' or remind them about their 'credibility' they are true Rock! – they bludgeon mercilessly with their riffs and with their attitude. It's a stunning act of selfishness, a selfishness that is at the heart of all great art. Even if you don't like them you have to find some sort of respect for their non-compromising grind.

It's not a simple story, the story of Rock! It sprawls in all directions at once. Pick up *Kerrang!* and you're visually assaulted by fantastically garish groups, full on extroverts with a crossfire of piercings: wild-haired, crazed tattoo maniacs leering at the camera, mixed in with this are gothoid intensities, punkers, skatecore baggied up adrenalin junkies and some of the most fresh-faced teens that are treading the boards in the music scene. It's this diversity that is the strength of the genre. No other form of music (apart from maybe the outer edges of dance) can boast such a broad church. While The Offspring's take on melodic Californian punk turns them into a stadium band, Pantera herald a new age of heavy-duty riff metal with two massive Stateside albums, achieved with no mainstream radio play and no MTV. Then Korn suddenly take the form off into yet another direction.

Every week another bunch of freaks seems to push Rock! up new alleyways. It's a fascinating time for the music, a music that really has come to grips with the dark and violent heart of the nineties.

Rock! is quite definitely, defiantly, not dead!!!!!

CHAPTER THIRTY-THREE

ELECTRO, HIP HOP, HOUSE AND TECHNO

To understand hip hop, house, techno and most of the forms of nineties pop culture you have to understand electro, the grand daddy of a whole bunch of modern sounds.

One of the DJs to pioneer the form in the UK was Liverpool-based Greg Wilson, who was among the first to play dance records at the Hacienda, as well as going on to produce the underrated Manchester rap crew Ruthless Rap Assassins, the band that featured Kermit who would go on to join Black Grape . . .

In the early eighties Greg Wilson was entranced by the stripped down electronic sounds that were coming out of New York where, in one of the weirdest quirks in rock history, black kids in the ghetto started to get hip to Kraftwerk. Taking the atmospheric synth music of the German outfit, they reinvented it as a dance music of their own. It was a truly modern music that matched a modern vibe. The computer age was dawning and here was a music that matched the nu digital times.

The first massive record of the scene was Afrika Bambaata's 'Planet Rock'. This was followed by a whole heap of fab freaky electronics from the likes of Planet Patrol, Whodini and Man Parrish. Greg remembers the emergence of electro into his club night.

'I was already doing Legends. We would be playing soul, disco and funk and at first electro was just part of the playlist, but it began to take over. It had a real impact on kids in Manchester. A lot of the Manchester groups would come down to Legends and check this new music out . . .'

You can hear its echoes in New Order, who utilized the stark electronics and fused it with their minor key indie. You can hear it in early house records and you can quite definitely hear it in hip hop where it was the key source of backing tracks until Run DMC came along and blew it all away with their scratching and breakbeat based workouts.

Down at Legends, Wilson was pushing the boat out in all directions.

'I'd been out in Europe DJing and had time to mess around with things. When I got back to Legends I knew all about vari-speeding the decks, working with technics and mixing. It was stuff that people just didn't do in those days.'

Greg was the first DJ to mix live on TV, appearing on the same *Tube* that came live from the Hacienda as the one in which Madonna performed. Greg remembers the emergence of a whole culture around the music.

'There was the body poppers, people like Kermit used to come down to the club with his Broken Glass crew. They did really well, won competitions and appeared on TV. There was a lot of other crews around at the time as well.'

The emergence of the B-Boy culture was a vital strand in many of the friendships and cultural bonds that were forged into the nineties. So many groups have their roots in this scene. It's infused so many different corners of pop with its flavour, it's difficult to list them all here. From people like Liam Gallagher, who were entranced by this scene, through to more obvious candidates like The Prodigy, hardcore underground punk crosses over on to the B-Boy culture for clothes and music and house took some of the dance steps, some of the DJ mixing skills, and some of the ideas of just what constituted cool.

Electro is one of the key forebears of nineties pop culture . . .

Hip hop

Hip hop has been one of the massive success stories of the end of the century. Starting the decade as an underground form, it swiftly became the biggest selling form of music in the USA, finally overtaking country music in sales in 1998. For the first time in pop music, a black form of music has topped the sales charts – a radical cultural breakthrough.

Late-nineties hip hop is a very different beast than the one that entered the decade. Ten years ago it was an angry underground music, now it's a fat-cat corporate business complete with its own sniping underground critics. Huge crossover successes, that were once the preserve of commercial hits from the likes of MC Hammer and Vanilla Ice, who had knocked the edges off the form, are regular occurrences.

In 1999 Puff Daddy is where hip hop is at, whereas ten years ago Chuck D was the hip hop mainman. Entering the nineties hip hop was still very much under the influence of D's Public Enemy whose radical political stance and powerful message of empowerment was a positive call to arms to disaffected black youth. Public Enemy, along with Run DMC, were the key pillars of the form, linking it back to the days when it was emerging from the clubs, when rappers would do their thing over electro records before constructing their own beats from DJs, scratching records and building drum loops.

Public Enemy not only imparted a powerful message, they also delivered it with a powerful music that was a multi-layered collage of samples and sounds, a dense fat wall of all-enveloping sound put together by their producers – The Bomb Squad, powerful as fuck but still packing the funk. It's not an overstatement to claim that they are one of the best groups that have ever existed – their music and their message is utterly inspirational, 1988's 'It Takes A Nation Of Millions To Hold Us Back' is widely recognized as one of the classics of the genre, a record that was taken as a cue by the next generation of rappers.

Angus Batey, music editor of *Music 365,* has been writing about hip hop for years in various magazines and recognizes the sheer importance of Public Enemy.

'Musically and politically and attitude wise they couldn't be touched by a lot of people who followed in their wake.'

Along with Public Enemy, Run DMC and The Beastie Boys were the first superstars of rap. Run DMC had broken the form through the mainstream with their crucial 'Walk This Way' single that sampled Aerosmith and featured both groups in a classic video.

The rock audience, now awoken to the possibilities of hip hop, were further seduced by The Beastie Boys' first album, a mish mash of AC/DC riffing and monsta hip hop beats that sounded almost like metal drums.

The Beasties' album sold millions and left them with a tough follow-up job. Their second album, *Paul's Boutique*, was a startlingly different affair, a subtler fusion of jazz, great pop, soul and seventies funk, built around hip hop grooves and their trademark brat rapping. It stiffed.

It was a few years till they emerged with *Check Your Head*, one of the key albums of the nineties. The album took eclecticism to a new level, picking up on the sound of *Paul's Boutique* and further refined them into one infectious whole. It broke the Beasties massive and it also opened up a whole new scene in pop.

From there on in, The Beasties spent the decade growing up in public, making political causes hip again (the Tibet campaign) building up a huge business empire, printing a great magazine, *Grand Royal* and still finding time to cut two more albums of the eternally youthful brat infused hip hop.

In the early nineties there was also the pop fused hip hop of the so-called Daisy Age crew De La Soul, whose *3 Feet And Rising* album still sounds as fresh today as when it was released, an upbeat collection of songs that dripped with humanity.

But just in case anyone thought that the form was going soft, a rap crew in Los Angeles were about to bring a meaner, tuffer edge to the party.

Angus feels that the breakthrough gangsta rap outfit NWA may have helped to dissipate some of the righteous steam that dominated hip hop in its early days.

'The biggest thing after Public Enemy was the dominance of the gangsta rap scene. NWA were almost like Public Enemy with loads of beats and noise. *Straight Outta Compton* was the same sort of thing but with swearing, and a lot of nihilism. Their message was "This is where we live and its mutha fucking shit . . ." A lot of people liked the aggressive sound and attitude. It was harder and tuffer and now, looking back, a lot more aggressive compared to Public Enemy, but it was not trying to do anything.'

The template thrown down by Public Enemy was picked up by a whole nation of rappers. NWA had taken the blueprint but knocked all the political and musical edges off it, and simplified the form into what eventually became an unapologetic stew of negativity and violence, reflecting their harsh personal version of ghetto life. They instantly hit a chord.

I interviewed them just after the release of their debut *Straight Outta Compton* album. It gives you a rough idea of the way the band, which was to become the second most influential rap band after Public Enemy, were thinking. At first they told me about their lives.

'We live in Compton which actually looks pretty nice, not too run down, but if you look closer there are people on cocaine, gang members and lots of poor people. At night it turns into a war zone. There's dope dealing, shooting and police helicopters.'

What do the people of Compton think about the way that you have painted their area?

'They love it. Everybody from here knows what we talk about. We're the voice of the people. It's the people who don't understand who give us problems. People who sweep these problems under the rug. They say that we are glorifying the violence, know what I'm fucking sayin', but it's just telling it like it is . . .'

The track that is already raising eyebrows is 'Fuck Tha' Police'. It's got anthem stamped all over it and it could land the group into a whole heap of trouble.

'I don't give a shit. Fuck the police! That's my point of view as a black teenager . . . the police are corrupt. They're not from the neighbourhood. They don't understand what goes on here. Some of them are running the drugs in here. Money is their ultimate goal. That's how they figure it.'

Drugs are the key issue on the streets, ravaging communities and causing gang violence . . .

'There's so much money to be made out of drugs. The government makes billions out of drugs. Young blacks are used as drug prostitutes. They run the drugs in and then the police bust them and sell all their dope . . . it's corrupt. A black man didn't invent free basing. I don't know that many brothers who have got a laboratory! Someone else invented crack. They knew how easy it was to get people hooked. There's drugs everywhere, even politicians are on drugs.'

Are drugs right or wrong?

'No comment. Look they're always gonna be here. I don't use drugs. I know what it does to people, you gotta know what it does to you . . .'

The ghetto life depicted in *Straight Outta Compton* has now become commonplace worldwide. What was pissing NWA off in the early nineties is a common call among the dispossessed at the butt end of a rich society.

'A young black man dressed in a certain way with a baseball cap driving a nice car . . . the police automatically think it's a drug dealer or a gang member.'

NWA were articulating the sheer frustration of their Compton mates.

'You can't go to college, you can't do nothing, you don't have a choice. This country is not even half ours. We live in a white society that don't give you too many options. They just cut you off . . . How am I gonna put food in my mouth?'

NWA talked about touring and how they were surprised by how many different racial groups there *weren't* in the audience . . . they also felt that there was no real political edge left.

'In the sixties with Black power people were willing to die for the cause. Kids don't have the same sort of eagerness or anger anymore. Mind you, I'm not on a crusade to save the world, I'm just trying to live and survive out here.'

What about Public Enemy mentioning that NWA were watering rap down?

'Public Enemy are good friends of ours, we know Chuck D and he's cool. We love each other's music. There is no beef between us, but we don't agree totally with each other. . .'

With their tales of hedonistic violence and of criminal life, NWA offered no answers, just observations. It was a stark reality and one that offered few solutions other than making a big pile of money and getting the fuck out of there. It was also a stark, stunning truth. Anyone expecting pop stars to save the world is as dumb as anyone expecting politicians to do the same.

NWA preferred to rap about what was going down in violent language. At first they were mistaken for dealing out some sort of social political message and were even cautioned by the FBI. Their second album was recorded without Ice Cube, one of their key members, and saw a creeping self-parody. The vocals were handled by Eazy E who saw the group strike an unexpected chord with a white middle-class fanbase. NWA had got out of the ghetto but the ghetto remains, probably a fuck of a lot worse now than when they sang about it.

NWA never got to a third album. Producer Dr Dre left in 1992 and they fell apart.

The post-NWA careers of Ice Cube, Eazy E and Dr Dre would dominate gangsta rap in their own differing ways.

NWA had taken the Public Enemy template and recast it, adding a funkier undertow and with the piling on of the tuff street negativity and criminal flavour they, to all intents and purposes, invented gangsta rap, the genre that would dominate mid-nineties hip hop.

The first key players of the new rap genre were the ex-members of NWA themselves. Dr Dre, who had been the key mover in the move away from Public Enemy's original political noise fused workouts, started moving the sound towards G Funk. He was rap's new key soundmaker, the best producer to emerge since the genius sound manipulators of Public Enemy's Bomb Squad.

With NWA he added the funk to the half-inched multi-textural noise collage of Public Enemy. Further adding the freak phunk of George Clinton's Parliament Funkadelic he forged the whole form into what became G Funk. The music, dominated by whining synth noise, a fat bottom end and funked up grooves, would explode to become the most popular form of hip hop in the mid nineties.

On leaving NWA in 1992 he put together Death Row records with Suge Knight, giving the label its first massive seller in the form of his own *The Chronic* album. His further productions with Snoop Doggy Dogg, Blackstreet and Warren G were huge sellers, making the G Funk form one of the most dominating sounds on the mid-nineties American music scene.

Death Row fell apart in 1996 but not before a whole generation of artists who were either on the label or were inspired by its grooves had scored major selling releases. The G Funk sound was used as basic chassis for the raps of artists as diverse as Bone Thugs N Harmony, Warren G, The Notorious B.I.G., Scarface, Coolio and Snoop Doggy Dogg, who were all affected by the new possibilities that G Funk threw up.

Not everyone was thrilled with the rise of gangsta rap. Chuck D, rap's social conscious, declared that the gangsta scene was the record labels' scene, the authorities promoting it to the negative effect of the ghetto, as Angus points out:

'Chuck D's analysis said that it suited the record companies' purposes to sell and promote gangsta rap . . . They made big money while promoting a negative stereotype – it helps to keep black people down and the white superior, like it's a music business conspiracy to promote the negative side of hip hop culture to the exclusion of all those who have a positive voice . . .'

Snoopy Doggy Dogg was the main benefactor from the whole G Funk scenario. First heard rapping on Dre's *The Chronic*, Dogg made an instant impression with his great distinctive drawled laid-back rapping. His lyrics, that were laced with a certain violence, were rooted in a mean reality. Dogg was eventually arrested on suspicion of being an accomplice in a murder, a charge that has never been made to stick but added a freakish credibility to his street schtick. His life was stuffed with criminal credentials: born and bred on Long Beach in California, he was busted for cocaine and drifted in and out prison. The only escape route he could find was in music. He started making tapes at home with Warren G, another future star of the G Funk form.

His 1993 debut *Doggy Style* was the first-ever debut album in the history of American pop to enter the charts at No. 1. It was an inertia that he couldn't keep up. The 1996 follow-up, *The Doggfather*, saw him lose sales. The delay in releases was hardly helping him keep up his presence, a delay caused by constant court appearances and a real life that often resembled the lyrics of the darkest gangsta rap song.

Digging the early Snoop stuff, Angus Batey feels that the rapper was touching something in the dark and nihilistic hearts of his audience.

'The first album was Snoop and his mates hanging out, having a drink and a smoke, eyeing up rival gangs. In a sense that record exactly represents the same thing to his audience as 'Smells Like Teen Spirit' did to the grunge generation . . . It was for kids from broken homes, the wrong side of the tracks . . . It touched that same aimlessness and dislocation . . .'

The biggest rap star of the nineties and one of the biggest pop stars in the whole world was 2Pac (Tupac Amaru Shakur). He got his distinctive name (from a communist Chilean gang of freedom fighters) from his black panther mother. Shakur was born into a volatile and fucked up world.

Born in New York, he moved over to the west coast at the age of ten. Determined to be a star, he went to acting college and started rapping as a second string rapper with Digital Underground, the outrageous over the top Oakland rappers whose 1990 debut 'Sex Packets' was one of the first releases to pay homage to George Clinton by utilizing his molten funk brew to a hip hop style. It was hardly the glorious rise to stardom that he demanded for himself, but it made a lot of the right sort of connections.

His 1992 debut *2Pacolypse Now* changed the script. The album is a superb series of urban vignettes which, when combined with his highly rated acting debut in the film *Juice*, shot him to stardom. His constant bust-ups with the law added to his outlaw image and further raised his profile. Some were already calling him the James Dean of the rap scene. Angus picks up the tale.

'2Pac was living a fast and furious lifestyle, recording almost constantly, appearing in films, spending a lot of time in jail. He was cramming plenty into a short space of time. The best film that he made was called *Juice* which was directed by Ernest R. Dickerson, Spike Lee's cinematographer. 2Pac played Bishop, a character who was sucked into a criminal life which was ended in a hail of bullets. Some people say that the rapper ended up living that role for real. By 1994 he was head to head with Snoop Doggy Dogg as one of the key two controversial figures in the rap world. In and out of prison, his street credibility was cemented. His 1995 album *Me Against The World* crashed the album charts at No. 1.

One of the tracks, 'Dear Mama', opened up a sensitive, almost poetic side to the rapper, a glimpse of what might just be lurking just below the hoodlum image. In late 1995 he signed to Death Row records, releasing the double set 'All Eyez On Me' the following spring. By now 2Pac was in the big league. With the bright beam of the limelight shining firmly on him he got himself engaged in a public spat with his former friend, the Notorious B.I.G.

His life had taken a turn for the worse when he was given a prison sentence for rape. The day before he was sentenced, he was shot in the foyer of the recording studio where he walked in on a bungled robbery. He turned up in court in a wheelchair and was sentenced to a stretch in Rykers Island prison.

While doing time he did an interview for hip magazine *Vibe* where he claimed the shooting was a set-up organized by his former friend Notorious B.I.G. and B.I.G.'s label boss, Sean Puffy Combs (a.k.a. Puff Daddy), who he claimed were the only people who could have known that he was going to be there. B.I.G. and Puff Daddy were shocked – they couldn't believe what 2Pac was claiming.

It was the first blow in an already deteriorating situation between the East Coast and West Coast rap camps, built around Puff Daddy's Bad Boy Corporation and 2Pac's West Coast connections, and all tied up with Death Row Records, which had been put together by NWA's Dr Dre and former Vanilla Ice publicist and bodyguard Marion 'Suge' Knight.

The schism between the two camps had been rumbling for some time. The New York rap scene was miffed that the gangsta rappers had almost completely taken over what they considered to be their scene – not that that had stopped East Coast scene king Puff Daddy building up a bit of a hip hop empire for himself.

Sean 'Puff Daddy' Combs put together his Bad Boy

Entertainment imprint after being sacked from his previous record label. He quickly established the label and his production skills on all manner of cuts from R & B to hip hop.

Notorious B.I.G. first rapped under the name of Biggie Smalls, sending a demo to the *Source* hip hop magazine. A great review caught the attention of Sean Puffy Combs and B.I.G. was signed to Bad Boy where his career really took off, cutting key tracks and even guesting on a Michael Jackson album. His debut release, *Ready To Die*, was a concept album that ran through his life, using a backdrop of classic cuts to give the record a chronological feel. From 'Superfly' funking it in the background as the baby is born, it tells the story of a man who on release from jail attempts to go straight and dies in yet another hail of bullets.

Life, it seemed, in the rap world really is nasty and short.

The two coastal rap scenes eyed each other jealously. New York had the roots and LA had the stars. There was tension, a tension that had now been exacerbated by 2pac's prison statement.

2pac's outburst had, by now, turned into a festering sore and the two camps would snipe at each other in the press.

The spat blew out of all proportions. It amplified the East Coast-West Coast rivalry which dominated the mid nineties rap scene and it finally resulted in 2Pac's own death when he was shot on 6 September 1996 in a drive-by shooting. He died a week later, a pointless death in a barely fulfilled career.

A rap convention was called swiftly after the murder in an attempt to mend the wounds. The non-attendance of B.I.G., who was working on his prophetic landmark *Life After Death* album raised eyebrows. Within months he too was gunned down on a visit to LA – some say in retaliation for the death of 2pac, some say he was in the wrong place at the wrong time.

It was the peak of a very nasty episode in hip hop's history and perhaps an underlining of the very fragility of the USA, a country that sometimes seems to be barely holding itself together at the seams.

The past few years have seen an incredible amount of bootlegs and outtakes released from the 2pac canon. The time between his release from prison and his murder was spent almost permanently in the studio, recording track after track. Well over a hundred unreleased songs circulate from the post-jail period where he worked his ass off in the studio piling up the songs, cementing his own legend.

Away from the rap wars, Los Angeles was constantly twisting the rap plot. Apart from gangsta rap and G Funk, the West Coast was also dealing out other important hip hop acts. Cypress Hill were the first Latino rap superstars. Their whole trip was their endorsement of marijuana – their music was fused with the sssstoned vibe of draw, the funk beats were slow and heavy like being stoned and their shows in the UK were filled by the raw heavy-duty heads who liked a smoke. Their slow path groove was a big influence on many hip hop crews.

Ice T came out of Newark California and has become one of the form's elder statesmen. His raps are a mixture of spot-on social commentary and lazy sexism. Taking his name from an Iceberg Slim novel, Ice T has cut some great records, appeared in a whole stack of films and even found time to form his own metal band, Body Count. Ice T astutely pointed out that rap and country, the two biggest-selling forms of music in the USA, were oddly similar in lots of ways. While rap was made for urban followers, country was for rural folk, but they both had the same subject matter of unrequited love, lust and death . . . it was a spot on analysis.

While the West Coast was grabbing the mega sales of the mid nineties and dominating the rap form, the East Coast – and particularly New York, the home town of rap – was beginning the fight back. Busting on to the scene in 1993 from New York's Staten Island, The Wu-Tang Clan put their own weird twist on to the hip hop sound with their own definitive way of working. From the start they were working with a powerful business instinct and a warped imagination. The plan was to release a breakthrough album as Wu-Tang and then establish each of the rappers as their own force.

With influences that ranged from Public Enemy and Lee Scratch Perry to some dark gothic sounds as well as a whole host of kung fu and horror flicks, they were about to embark on their own very personal musical vision.

Taking their name from a mythical kung fu sword, The Wu-Tang Clan were a collective of nine rappers, all working at varying degrees on each others' projects and splitting the royalty cheques. An unlikely working scenario, it was actually working and by the mid nineties it was paying off big dividends. The chief producer behind the clan, the RZA, had surfaced during the early nineties as a rapper in All Together Now which also featured future Wu members Genius/GZA and Ol' Dirty Bastard. After they fell apart he signed to Tommy Boy records under the name Prince Rakeem (wild and wacky nicknames are the forté of this gang). He recorded one EP, 1991's 'Ooh We Love You Rakeem', before joining the Wu-Tang in time to put together their 1993 debut *Enter the Wu-Tang: 36 Chambers*, a record that completely helped to reshape the way hip hop was going. The dark, menacing sound and stripped down beats were seized upon as an alternative to the gangsta styles, and the album gave rap a new direction, a new flavour to infuse its work with.

The key solo albums then started to come thick and fast. It's a whole weird world to get lost in, a myriad of releases, the best of which come from RZA, Ol' Dirty bastard, and Genius/GZA.

Now that it has conquered the world, rap music can afford to launch some wild ass stars of its own. Perhaps the best of the new bunch is Busta Rhymes, who mixes the vocal aggression of ragga with the grooves and commercial possibilities of hip hop. Rhymes seemed to slot into the hip hop loose cannon slot previously occupied by Coolio, who was now starting to go more mainstream. Busta Rhyme's first big hit was 1996's 'Woo-hah!! Got You All In Check'. The Long Island based rapper cut a pretty distinctive shape with his extrovert wild personality and crazy raps. His 1997 album *When Disaster Strikes* was another ambitious hip hop work. A sprawling affair, it was closer to a film soundtrack than a traditional song cycle, a further blurring of the edges between music and film, a reverse of the film soundtrack, a record movie track a merging of two of the key creative cultures of the late twentieth century. . .

By the late nineties rap had fractured into a countless clutch of forms, from jazz rap where it was cut with jazz samples, off to Latin rap, G Funk to hardcore rap, new jack R & B to southern rap, old school rap to underground rap, a never-ending rush of rap stars and controversy. Its attitudes beats and even clothes have dominated and informed nineties culture – a flow of ideas from the USA that has been one of the key stylings of British pop culture in the nineties.

CHAPTER THIRTY-FOUR

NU TECHNOLOGY

When we were kids we were promised a brave new world of super sci-fi. A world of no poverty and people dressed in space suits jetting in from outer space. Everything was going to be made out of plastic and the future would be now. There would be no cars and everyone would fly with little jet packs stuck on their backs . . .

It was quite a dream . . . The future didn't really arrive in an all-encompassing wave.

It's crept in insidiously. Instead of changing the framework of our lives, it's appeared in a whole host of mini gadgets and mobile technologies, some of which are so commonplace now that it seems laughable that ten years ago they would be stared at in the street.

There are mobile phones that will burn your ear off but at least give you the opportunity to tell everyone you know that you're on the train; handheld computers you can cram your whole life into – you can even write a book in one of these amazing tiny units (I should know, I've written a whole chunk of this one into my Psion); they can fly space probes to Jupiter that arrive there exactly on time, down to the last second (but the trains are still always late); there are handheld units that whole films can be played back on; computers that you can talk to; digital cameras that create images you can transfer to your computer and then process them at home; and there are new fabrics for clothes, making them tougher, more comfortable, more chic.

There are computer games that are like alternative realities. You can get lost in freaky worlds, blowing away the opposition with the flick of a wrist. Some blame these computerized nether worlds for fucked-up freaks' taking guns down to schools in the US and blowing away a few classmates. It's the same sort of moral outrage that rock 'n' roll and cinema has had to contend with for years.

Computer games panicked the pop industry. In the early nineties they were getting the blame for declining record sales and the major chains showed their loyalty to pop music by giving up huge amounts of space promoting the games culture. A loyalty that will be reciprocated when pop gets sold on the Net (see the next section, 'The Internet') and bypasses the chains.

By the mid nineties pop record sales were again massive and the games sales continued to go through the roof. The two forms now lived together, in fact sometimes there seemed to be a symbiosis between the two.

Wanna make a record but you can't sing? Don't worry ... There are gadgets in studios that can make you sing in tune. Your song sounds lumped and dreary? You can now speed up a track without you noticing. You can chop up a song and stick it back together at home on your computer, you can be your own electronic orchestra.

Technology is going faster and faster and we're all along for the ride. It's making our lives quicker and it means that we can cram more stuff into our short time on this planet.

But perhaps the one key change that will really affect the way that we live and whose benefits are only just starting to become apparent is the Internet.

The Internet

In years to come when they look back on the nineties, perhaps the proliferation of the Internet will be the real story of the times. Typically like all the best counter-culture ideas, such as LSD, the internet was set up by the US military. In the sixties it was put together as a global computer network, as a hyper-safe communication network to protect their communications from communist infiltration. By the late eighties it was in the hand of the hackers and the computer freaks and its rise seemed to be hand in hand with the explosion of techno.

The digital times had its own music and its own communication system!

If in the punk days we had all been photocopying our fanzines the techno generation were armed with a whole heap of technology to get their message through: mobile phones, video camcorders, e-mail and to make their music there was MIDI and samplers . . . The whole means of musical communication had shifted dramatically, but it will be the Internet that will really revolutionize communications in the next millennium.

'I remember in the late eighties when I interviewed Deee Lite,' recalls former *Loaded* editor James Brown, 'and they were going on about the Web and the Internet. I wasn't that sure what they were going on about. They told me that you could send messages from the top of mountains from computers. I thought they were a bit mad.'

In 1989 the Internet was one of those rumours that was advancing fast from the horizon. Like any life-changing new technology, you hear rumours, you then read about them. You don't quite understand what they are going on about and then you gradually get to grips with it.

Then you suddenly find yourself tinkering about with it at home.

When I first got my Internet set up it was a nightmare. All the local computer heads sat round my Mac battling to get the damn thing up and running. The phone line back ups were useless and the Apple Mac didn't quite sit with the new tech.

It took a week of fiddling with different codes to get the e-mail up and running.

In fact it's been a permanent feature of the Internet that it doesn't make good friends with the Apple Mac.

Once you're up and running, it's a great new world, no more letter writing, no more trips to the post office, instant communications – e-mailing is great – and then there is the Web side of things, tons of information to grab and give out, all just sat there, a never-ending pile of human creativity. If I look up my band Gold Blade on the search engine I find a thousand entries on samurai swords . . . It's incredible how much information is out there, it's almost as if the sum total of human knowledge is being encoded into cyberspace!

For pop music, though, the biggest breakthrough is going to be in the selling of music.

Selling music on the Web

It's the biggest shift in the way that we access music since the advent of the CD, if not bigger. The music industry has been attempting all manner of new formats to squeeze the same amount of mega buck profits that the CD garnered. Factory boss Tony Wilson, always a champion of technology, (the host of the annual music business convention 'In The City' is now hosting a similar get together built around the computer nu tech world) attempted many of these formats at Factory, quite often getting his fingers burned.

'Since the big change in music with the advent of the CD in '83-84 there has been a series of failures. In the early nineties we were in fact the first indie to release new format editions of New Order's "Power Corruption And Lies". Then we got into DAT but that didn't happen either. We never actually pressed any copies of "True Faith" on normal CDs. We also had CD ROM. We just wanted that format, all these formats and none of them have really happened, have they?'

Tony Wilson is still pushing for the big technological breakthroughs and has a fascinating slant on what's normally looked on as a pretty sterile world.

'Five years ago my agent in America listed all the major changes and explained how they were led by sex and his theory was that all technology was pushed forward by sex! We are now on the brink of a big change, music is no longer inhibited by the plastic.'

He sees the advent of the new technologies as a way of improving music, of cutting the crap away.

'We all got used to product with two or four sides. Albums were always padded out. It is dispiriting how many songs are just shoved on for no reason . . . With technology there is no reason why you can't just download the songs that you want. CDs will survive but the prime object is the song. You will download the tunes that you want and bypass our love affair with the plastic.'

What Tony Wilson is talking about is downloading the songs that you want down the Internet, accessing the tunes that you want to hear, bypassing the shops.

The days of the throw-away extra track could well be numbered.

The whole idea of the Web taking over the music scene is something that has been the subject of intense debate over the last few years of the decade. Creation boss Alan McGee, who started the whole debate in 1998, explains:

'The price of digital TV will fall. It will be like when colour TV came in. The price will drop. Suddenly digital will be six pounds a month and you will have an Internet on your TV. TV and Internet will be linked into your stereo equipment. Essentially you'll have a banking system of all the record companies. The record labels will all become libraries . . . Say you want "Anarchy In The UK" and Oasis's "Wonderwall", it will come down the line. It will be encrypted that you wanted the tracks and then come down through the corporation before going through publishing to whoever owns it. You'll be able to download whatever films you want. You'll be able to get every CD known to man by paying a subscription fee to the bank that owns the system . . . The bottom line is why would you want to buy a CD when you can just download it . . . You'll be able to get videos for every track . . . Distributors will be out, but specialist shops will survive because people will always want vinyl. The big record shops will become a thing of the past. Buying records is going to become personal . . . It will be a revolution in the music business and that's why I'm hated. I'm saying that retail is on its way out . . . The people who are making money out of the records are the shops.'

For weeks the music business echoed with replies to McGee's statements. The repercussions of his outburst were being felt everywhere. Rock 'n' roll in the technological era could rediscover its maverick spirit.

Tony Wilson, the man who put the fact into Factory, has peered even further over the edge of the new hi-tech precipice than McGee.

'It may not get rid of record companies but it will get rid of the B-side. It will be like a return to sheet music from the first half of the century. Within three or four years the singles chart will be made up from the downloads. The record shop is going to have to reassess itself . . .'

Not only will punters download the music but they will have a much closer relationship with the records' makers.

'You will get direct marketing, you can directly get to the band's mailing lists and merchandise goes hand in hand. You'll be able to order tickets by seeing where you want to sit in the arena by looking at it on your screen.'

You can do all this now. With an MP3 file the music was yours and with a CD burner you could cut your own CDs with the tracks that you had downloaded from the Web. Suddenly record labels and record shops are starting to look very pointless.

The new technology, far from being a threat to the weird and the wonderful, could actually boost its chances of survival. Surely embracing the new technology is a way of making your culture survive. If you want to make obscure psychobilly crossed with dub or you have a penchant for cranking out Japanese-style speed core you could technically have an equal space in the market place. If you wanted a shot at the charts, you wouldn't have to go cap in hand to a distributor or to pay high-street shops to get a racking place.

Underground indie labels like Gary Walker's Wiiija totally benefited from the new technological twist. In their past life they had been dealing with guitar noise but the possibilities of sampling thrown up in the post acid house world changed the way underground music was made and listened to. It could be someone with a cracked copy of Cubase in their bedrooms crunching distorted beats into their guitars, or it could make a group like Wiiija's Cornershop go from being rank outsiders to No. 1 stars in the UK. Walker likes the new technological shift he has witnessed in the nineties.

'So much has changed this decade compared to, say, the seventies. There has been so much rapid change. A whole generation of kids have no concept of phones being something you just have in your home! When I was at comprehensive only the really brainy ones were allowed on the computers. Now it is for everyone. I have e-mail and a fax modem but someone else sets it all up for me . . .'

Lucky Gary. The new technology is fantastic but setting it up can be a nightmare. Anyone who has ever tried to get their CompuServe e-mail account to work on a Mac and a Psion 5 will tell you, it can be a baffling and illogical process with contradictory advice being given on the helplines. It's like we've got all this fab shiny new tech shit but no one is quite sure how to work it all!

When McGee spoke out he typically put himself out on a limb. But the points he made still spark debate. Gary Walker won't go as far as Alan in his assessment of the new communication revolution.

'That whole Internet thing? I think Alan McGee is going to have to live a bit of that down. But some of what he was saying is already starting to happen. For example, you can now license tracks to companies for people to download them and make their own compilation albums downloaded off the Net. Some of that stuff is starting to come in.'

The brave new world of digital may just be there to crank more mush at your worn-out senses. Speaking to fellow noise mercenaries on the high-velocity guitar scene sees a discernible split in the ranks. Some are scared of the new hi tech, shunning this 'computer thing', while others are right in there, fanzine terrorist style, throwing up web sites and learning the possibilities of digital communication. Some of us have had to learn it fast . . . This is a hi-tech war and ignoring it is at your own peril. If you want your smart bombs of sound to hit their targets then be vigilant and don't ignore the new ways.

In the nineties the street overcame its fear of the new. What was once derided as yuppie has become the weapon of the outsider. Mobile phones, once the tool of the city-bound, rich, bona fide wheeler dealer, have become the frontline equipment for the inner-city drug dealer or the chat-to-your-mates kids' toy. Everyone seemed to have one, each with their own wacky jangle of sound that no one tut tuts any more.

'Where are you?'

'I'm on the train' has became the national conversation in 1999. Stating the bleeding obvious while frying your brain on the mobile phone's frazzled electronica has become a national pastime.

Clutched to the ear by virtually everyone in the UK it's become a symbol of the times. Ten years ago they were cumbersome brutes but as the price came down with their size the phones hit boom time. It's difficult now to imagine a world without them.

Of course they probably give you brain cancer, they fall apart all the time (my Motorola has to be traded in about once a month, piece of shit!) and they ring at the worst possible times, but in an increasingly mobile random world they can be a godsend.

Now that they have shrunk to the size of a tie clip you can walk along the road without having to hold them in your hands and yell into thin air like a nutter – which means that the mobile phone is truly mobile, the future truly is now in the world of communications.

Nu tech? It simply can't move fast enough. Faster, smaller, louder – that's what we demand from the new millennium . . .

CHAPTER THIRTY-FIVE

THE CHEMICAL BROTHERS

The Chemical Brothers were revolutionary. Instead of taking dance to the rock scene they were reversing the process. They were adding rock to their dance, cutting records that would push forward the musical boundaries. Creating powerful tracks that put the human back into the machine, great slabs of dance noise that fucked with your head and made you want to party. Of all the chemical generation outfits, this pair of mavericks are the key. Originally a couple of indie heads who'd been blown away by dance, they understood the dynamics of both forms and set about creating a music that would easily straddle the imaginary divide . . .

'It's weird how some people still view dance music and rock music as totally contradictory. We don't see any problem at all. We've used vocals on some of our tracks by Noel Gallagher and Tim Burgess and Beth Orton.'

Things were changing in music – indie kids were still digging bands but were also clubbing it. The Chemical Brothers managed to encapsulate this change. For the first time since acid house's astonishing rise in the late eighties and then slump in the early nineties the music was moving on again. With the addition of lifeblood from the rock scene, a crossover music was being made. It would result in what the Americans naffly termed Electronica with the likes of The Prodigy becoming one of the biggest bands in the world.

Riding in the centre of this were The Chemical Brothers

whose eclectic approach was rubbing up purists on both sides of the divide, even when they were putting out their second album.

'I know dance people feel like it doesn't really belong and some people felt it was wrong working with Noel Gallagher or Tim Burgess. Some people have a problem with the fact that our music rocks. With *Dig Your Own Hole* we went after that sort of sound . . . the Chemical beats sound, the acid over the break beats had been done pretty well on the first album.'

The Chemical Brothers live was the perfect combination for this new way, the pair of them would stand poised over their keyboards shaking their heads in time to the massive beats. They were a rock 'n' roll band without guitars. They had the dynamics of the R 'n' R experience and the funk of a dance band.

The Chemical Brothers were two students – Tom Rowlands and Ed Simmons – who came to Manchester University to study history in the late eighties, attracted by the Madchester explosion and the full-on party scene in the northern city. They were attracted by the city's then explosive pop culture as much as the quality of course on offer.

Rooted in mid-eighties indie music, they had been massive fans of The Jesus And Mary Chain and the possibilities of pop noise that the sonic Scottish rascals suggested. This was a tuff music with an edge that the spineless bastards of most eighties pop disgustingly lacked. They also had had their minds blown by Public Enemy, one of the most influential bands of the late eighties.

Public Enemy were the kings of hip. Listen to their records now and they still sound full on and inspiring, crammed with a ridiculous amount of ideas and textures. This was a music of genius. They rode huge fat beats which were scoured with strange noises and spot on cool samples. They had a defiant image and could play live as well. They instantly revolutionized hip hop and then went on to tear pop culture apart.

In Chuck D they had an eloquent ball-busting front man who rapped like no one before or since. With an authoritative rich voice, Chuck D shot the shit across the tracks. His foil was Flavour Flav, a bona fide pop nutter who wore massive clocks around his head just to remind us that there wasn't much time left. Flav would do these mad nasal chants and rhymes that were stuffed full of great catch phrases.

For white kids, Public Enemy were the dons. They really rocked. Whereas most hip hop before had been really good, it didn't seem to tally with what a white kid wanted from a band. They wanted some sort of rock dynamic, some sort of gang thing and some sort of big big sound that replicated rock without paying any lip service to it at all.

Public Enemy were delivering on all fronts. The fact that they could play this shit live, and then some, quickly saw them playing the sort of shows where they were quickly picking up a vast audience of people who had never listened to this type of music before. They were the starting point for a whole host of key players in 1990's UK dance music . . . and The Chemical Brothers were just two of the mid teens whose minds were blown by the sheer power and ideas of the group.

An inspired Tom quickly found himself in a band playing in Balearic dance combo Aerial, who were one of the several bands hanging around on the edges of the *Boys Own* London scene and who went on to release four singles on Deconstruction.

After meeting up in Manchester, The Chemical Brothers started by DJ-ing at friends' student parties, throwing on whatever record that came to hand, getting a taste for the DJ action. They put on their own night, 'Naked Under Leather', at The Swinging Sporran, a city centre pub venue that was squashed into a corner of a car park and had been better known as a punk venue putting on gigs by the likes of Therapy and The Ex.

The two's Naked Under Leather nights were a great success. They went under the monicker, The Dust Brothers, in tribute to the West Coast production team who had produced the Beastie Boys' *Paul's Boutique*. They were just doing this for fun and didn't have a clue that they could ever take off. When they DJ'd they played dance records and stuff by The Stone Roses. It raised eyebrows in the mutually exclusive dance and rock worlds of the early nineties. They specialized in the eclectic but they also brought in heaps of New York underground hip hop beats to really set the house rocking.

Going to Manc clubs where The Chemicals were DJ-ing in the early nineties restored your humble narrator's belief in a brilliant night out in a club with a wicked soundtrack. You just wanted to own all the damned records that they were playing. Brilliant.

When their course was over they drifted back home to London and released their self-financed debut single 'Songs Of the Siren' ('it was a record of the Naked Under Leather nights, all fuck off sirens and loud noises') to great acclaim and saw the single picked up by

Juniors Boys Own and remixed by Sabres Of Paradise. The buzz intensified and they started on the remix trail, working with the likes of The Manic Street Preachers and getting their name about c/o some heavy-duty rock-solid genius remixes of Primal Scream's 'Jailbird' and The Prodigy's 'Voodoo People'.

Their debut album *Exit Planet Dust* arrived on the crest of a wave, getting hip with the DJ sets at Heavenly Records' Sunday Social. Their fat beats were the backbone to the sound that they would be using on their debut.

They were by now calling themselves The Chemical Brothers after the original American production team of The Dust Brothers complained about them sampling their name. They had been getting calls from the Yank Dust Brothers management who also looked after Ice T – you just don't fuck with these people – and were given 48 hours to change their name. So they came up with The Chemical Brothers, naming themselves after one of their earlier tracks, 'Chemical Beats', which they thought was a terrible name. At first no one was sure about the name but it has become the perfect monicker, a byword for late nineties cutting edge dance music.

Exit Planet Dust had been delayed by some six months before it was released but it was so far ahead of the zeitgeist that when it came out it still turned everyone's heads right round.

This was what pop music in the nineties should sound like! A real yardstick by which everything else should be measured.

Their new album *Surrender* is a perfect summation of the cross-cultural mishmash of the nineties. Pulling key indie faces to sing on the tracks, messing with the electronics, creating breathtaking post dance new millennium musics . . . it's a breathtaking journey across a whole ragbag of styles but there is that constant Chemical stamp on top.

By the summer of 1999 they were the coolest group in the UK.

CHAPTER THIRTY-SIX

BIG BEAT

Perhaps the true pop of the late nineties, Big Beat is either a revival of late-eighties indie dance or a cross-collision of a multifarious crush of styles. Grab what you want from any style of music and make it yours. The form is perhaps the most honest reflection of the niche nineties.

Cross pollination pop culture. Niche this, niche that: pop had quite definitely eaten itself.

Oasis ruling the roost in the mid nineties gave a false impression. Bubbling underneath the rampaging juggernaut was a fractured scene: all strands of pop were dividing and subdividing. A multi-tracked collection of scenes to be tapped into and out of at will.

Yer average pop fan of the nineties was buying into a whole ragbag of scenes at once. It could be rooted to the Balearic anything goes days of acid house or even further back to the multi-eclectism of the post-punk fallout when dub, funk and punk were mixed and mashed.

Mix 'n' match – it's the story of pop, multi-ethnic, multi-styled pop.

Sampling – cut 'n' paste – it's hardly a new idea in the dance world. It was the sound of the nineties, but a distinct flavour has emerged in the late nineties. It was sort of indie dance revisited, bouncy dance music with just enough rock or pop references to cross over to the lucrative student market.

It's called Big Beat music and it's a soundtrack to hedonistic good times. Its sole purpose is to make you dance.

It rules.

Journalist Neil Davenport succinctly captures the appeal of the form.

'Big Beat manages to appeal to two different crowds. They rely on old nostalgic riffs – reverential samples of rock culture and previous musics which appeal to rock heads and it's well grounded in dance music . . . It's for people who haven't got the confidence to just be into dance, it gives them something to cling on to!'

Big Beat's roots go back all over the joint. You can obviously trace it to acid house, but also into rock, the background of many of its purveyors. Indie kids bringing their own baggage to dance. You can see it in the indie-dance crossover post acid house when the indie bands of the early nineties assimilated acid house into their guitar world. You can feel its big breakbeat power in The Chemical Brothers' huge phat records, and you can see its commitment to past and great records in Heavenly Records' highly influential Sunday Social. Ben Turner, editor of *Muzik* agrees with this.

'The Chemical Brothers played a major part in what is going on, and the Heavenly Social really affected the Big Beat explosion. The Chemicals' first gig at Andrew Weatherall's Sabresonic, the dark and dingy railway arches in south London, was really important. In a night of a 1,000 bpm techno, these broken beats came along and everyone was going "Where's this coming from!" It really changed the way everyone thought about things. The NME adopted The Chemicals and the scene exploded. The Social as well helped put the music back into the pubs again. The Chemicals were listening to hip hop and rock and making dance music out of it. They were really instrumental in changing things . . .'

Its seeds were getting sewn everywhere. That it finally coalesced and blossomed in Brighton is no shock. In the nineties Brighton has become bohemian central, without the attendant gangsta vibe of the big northern cities, and with the student dollar washing around the town and a big creative boho scene of dropouts from London, Brighton is the perfect place for something to kick off. The faded Victoriana and the never-ending beach are a perfect backdrop to the good times. You wander though the town and its eclectic shops and you feel like you're in the UK's answer to prime time San Francisco. In the eighties it was looked on as a middle-class dropout town; in the nineties it has became party E-central and, perhaps, the hippest place to live in the UK, capturing everything that late-nineties living is all about.

And the king of the (sand) castle is Norman Cook, aka Fatboy Slim.

Fatboy Slim captured this perfectly. In one of the key albums of the late nineties Norman Cook made a pop record out of a load of bits and pieces of pop he'd sampled off a dog-eared heap of records. Displaying a vinyl fetishist's nous, Cook was turning obscure records from the past into slivers of hits on his excellent album.

A teenage punk in 1977, Cook joined The Housemartins when he heard that they needed a bass player. The Housemartins' bittersweet guitar pop made them chart regulars between 1986 and 1988. Cook was never comfortable with the outfit's commitment to indie guitar pop and seemed relieved when the band fell apart right at the start of acid house. Housemartins' vocalist Paul Heaton went on to form The Beautiful South. One of the biggest bands of the nineties, their greatest hits compilation has gone on to be one of the best-selling albums of all time in the UK. Heaton, with fellow late-period Housemartin Dave Rotheray, still sings bittersweet vignettes that touch on the kitchen-sink drama of real life over lush trad pop-soaked backings.

After The Housemartins split, Cook moved back to Brighton and hit No. 29 in 1989 with MC Wildski's 'Blame It On The Bassline' and scored a No. 1 in February 1990 with his next project, Beats International and their Clash sampling (it's the bass line from 'Guns Of Brixton') 'Dub Be Good To Me', before scoring another Top Ten hit with 'Won't Talk About It' that May and another four smaller hits throughout '91.

It was a hell of a start.

Lying low for a couple of years DJ-ing or remixing under the Pizzaman monicker, Cook returned to the fray in 1993 with the acid-jazz-soaked project called Freak Power whose 'Turn In Turn On Drop Out' single hit No. 2 after being used in a TV ad.

Project after project, Cook proved that he had the pop touch, assimilating dance music but never wandering too far away from his pop roots. Fatboy Slim was the culmination of all this activity.

Signing to local Brighton label Skint, Cook was about to become the national vanguard of a new twist in the dance plot – Big Beat.

Skint was put together in 1995 as a subsidiary of Loaded Records by Damian Harris (who would also release stuff under his own Midfield General monicker). Their club, the Big Beat Boutique in Brighton, was the focal point of the scene and lent its name to the loose new movement. Cook DJ'd there under the Fatboy Slim monicker. It was all coming together.

The first release was Fatboy Slim's 'Santa Cruz' in '95, then Harris's Midfield General and Hip Optimist. Already there was a different flavour here. Concentrating on upbeat witty good time tunes, the Brighton mob were Saturday night out exemplified. The *Brassic Beats Volume One*, released in 1996, was a statement. It including the aforementioned bands and also newcomers to the scene like Cut Le Roc, Req and Bentley Rhythm Ace.

A further two compilation albums came out in 1997 and '98. Skint was a definitive genre. The various outfits may have felt that they were working in isolation from each other, but their funky breakbeats and salutes to pop history with their smart-ass samples linked the whole vibe together. Big business stepped in and in 1998 they were bought by Sony.

For the big beat breakthrough Cook had been the battering ram. Within months he had gone from being the house DJ at the Big Beat Boutique to reluctant pop star. Two low key hits, 'Going Out Of My Head' (May '97, No. 30) and 'Everyone Needs A 303' (Nov. '97, No. 34) had put Cook on the verge of the big time with his seventh project.

His remix of Cornershop's February 1998 No. 1 'Brimful of Asha' sent him back into the mainstream. Legend has it that Cook volunteered to remix the track for nothing after playing the Shop's version which had come out the previous August and scraped the bottom of the charts. Cook speeded the track up and gave it that fat and funky Big Beat feel. It was infectious as fuck and started its non-stop run to No. 1.

The smash seemed to bolster his career more than Cornershop's. The Anglo-Asian band's following release fell outside the Top 20 while Cook went big time.

His June '98 'Rockefeller Skank' was a Top Ten and the follow-up 'Gangster Tripping' a Top Five. Since then you can't escape Cook: his album *You've Come A Long Way, Baby* is glued to the Top Ten, every TV trailer seems to have a piece of his music squeezed in and America is welcoming him.

The album *You've Come A Long Way, Baby* is one of those milestone releases. It captures everything that's great about its surrounding culture. Inventive, bubbling, funny, catchy as fuck,

You've Come A Long Way, Baby is a run of tracks, each one sounding like a Top Five smash. It's got to be the soundtrack to student bedsit life in 1999.

Big Beat Boutique itself went from strength to strength, the great soundtrack and never-ending name drops in the style press made it one of the meccas of club life in 1997/98. A hip club run by people who didn't give a fuck about being hip. It was a fab night out.

On the prom at Brighton, the Big Beat Boutique has found itself one of the best homes in Britain. The Concorde is perfect. It's got that saucy seaside feel and when it shuts you can stagger down to the beach and just party on.

We did.

Inside it's hot, sweaty and packs an electric punch. The music is great. There's no attempt at any suffocating hipness. It's like the Heavenly Social. Just good time music for good time people. DJ Punk Roc is there one of the nights I'm in there and he's kicking out the jams, playing great tunes and MC-ing at the same time.

While the club was going from strength to strength, the attendant 'bands' were also basking in the limelight. Bentley Rhythm Ace took their 'Bentley's Gonna Sort You Out' in the Top 20 in 1997 and became festival faves with their wackoid stage show and dope-fused booming good-time tunes. Formed by Richard March, who had once played bass in Pop Will Eat Itself (who are not such a strange connection in this long and sordid tale since they were fucking about with dance indie crossover, a sort of post Beastie Boys midland pop party in the late eighties and, arguably an unintentional precursor to big beat), Bentley Rhythm Ace (BRA for short!) flavour their big beat stomp with an eclectic mush of daft samples culled from car boot sales and decades of purchasing ridiculous pop records.

By 1999 Big Beat had become another sales pitch, another remix to bolster someone's flagging career, the prime protagonists of the scene were forging their own path and the chancers were diving in with their copycat records. It's the history of pop music as handed down since its big bang back in the fifties.

The form itself survives because its best outfits cut great records (Fatboy Slim's album is one of the best chart albums of the year), using their imagination and not giving a fuck about the tedious rules of good taste. They are making that greatest of stuff, pure pop music . . .

CHAPTER THIRTY-SEVEN

VIVE LA FRANCE

Acid house removed the international language barrier. Now there can be cross-continental hits. After years of domination by the Anglo-American pop axis, European nations were having their own say. French house made a massive inroad into the British pop scene in the late nineties . . .

For years we Brits, the smug Rostbifs displaying the sort of lack of knowledge crucial to having these sort of opinions, have looked down our noses at French pop. Sure our Euro cousins across the channel were *très chic* and had a thing about architecture; their food was always famous but their pop was always, well, er crap.

They got off to a good start. In always digging Gene Vincent over Elvis they understood the innate rawness of rock 'n' roll. They even made fellow rock 'n' roller Vince Taylor a star, which shows a nation with a connoisseur touch when it comes to picking rock 'n' roll stars. They always liked the best of everything but rock 'n' roll was something that other people did and the French seemed to leave the dirty business to the dominating Anglo-American axis.

The home-grown stuff, the theory goes, was always thin on the ground. But there will be no sneering here at Charles Aznavour and Sacha Distel – every country has these oily buffoons singing their middle-aged knicker-wetting dross, and we've churned out plenty of them. Two words, oh smug children.

Cliff.

Richard.

While everyone else was ignoring them the French just got on with their own idionsyncratic cool pop. In the sixties there was Jean-Jacques Perrey doing EVA and Pierre Henry and Les Yper Yper playing psyche rock. There was also an early fling with Electronica that throws up some obvious parallels with the current scene.

Despite the quality of the music it looked like the French were never going to be big players on the international pop scene. This was a pop scene now dominated by the English language – an exclusive club pretty well closed to outsiders. With a music culture rooted deep in jazz, their own innate sophistication would just get in the way: pop was plying a simple groove and the French were being too smart for their own good. Their bands mainly featured rhythm sections schooled in jazz trying to play it straight and dumb and then letting the great god 'noodle' escape again. Early-seventies French funk has rhythms that are so complex that it can almost sound like drum and bass a quarter of a century too early.

The French were also far more futuristic in their leanings. Françoise Hardi's records always had that futuristic taint – 'Voyage' recorded in 1966 sounds more like Stereolab than Stereolab. She went on to collaborate with Jean-Michel Jarre (the worst taints of futurism gone mad?) in the mid seventies and to bring things round full circle, with Air last year.

Françoise Hardi's husband, Jacques Dutronc, is looked on as the head honcho of French pop, with a series of songs co-written with the editor of *Lui* (the French *Playboy*) and, therefore, having 'saucy' lyrics.

The most famous French singer is Serge Gainsbourg, who was a national hero in France. I was in Paris the day that he died (1991) and the city was virtually at a standstill – stunned by his death. Gainsbourg celebrated everything that was lusty and devilish about life in song and in person while cutting some great pop. His musical influence still lives on, with the likes of David Holmes 'borrowing' Gainsbourg's 'Histoire De Melody Nelson' on 'Don't Die Just Yet' among others.

MC Solaar sampled a whole heap of his stuff including 'Bonnie And Clyde', a murder duet that Gainsbourg shared with Bardot singing a darkly Teutonic reply. You can even hear echoes of his sound in Daft Punk – some crazy folk even claim to hear his fingerprints on the sound of 'Da Funk's' glorious fat riff.

Jacques Morali, the man who masterminded the magnificent Village People, came from Paris and still holds the world copyright to his camp creation, raking in millions from the massed ranks of Village People covers bands on the planet. How hip is that!

In the punk days there was Plastic Bertrand who remains stateless to this day, dismissed by French hipsters as being Belgian and laughed out of Belgium and into Switzerland by the Walloons. His eternally scoffed at 'Ça Plan Pour Moi' actually sounds pretty cool these days in a kitschy kinda way. On the other hand there was also Metal Urbaine, a mid-seventies experimental punk-rock outfit whose schtick lay close to the Suicide way of music making. They were great but ignored: rampant international snobbery relegating them to the also rans.

By the eighties all the French seemed to be doing was keeping The Cure in the big time, making the Brit goths their biggest-ever band. Not only this, they were returning the compliment with Jean-Michel Jarre – thanks but no thanks.

On the other hand there was a great hiphop scene in France, with French rappers making their mother tongue sound like the natural compliment to the beats, but the French hiphop story is a localized one and we are dealing with an international picture here. For the rest of the world French pop was either a joke or something that didn't really exist.

Outside France it was only the true hipsters who knew about the beating heart of great French pop.

A curious state of affairs that would have remained the status quo. Suddenly, though, in the mid to late nineties there were murmurings of some sort of hip Gallic action. By 1999 this had blossomed into a fully blown scene.

Sparked by acid house and a new slate that saw all the international pop boundaries collapse in the wake of huge crossover instrumental hits, being able to sing in American became less important, and the doors were opened all across Europe.

Even if it was going to open up their pop scene, acid house was not exactly welcomed by the French authorities. With a much meaner police force declaring war on the new club scene, key clubs were slammed shut in Paris, a city that had thrived on its bawdy reputation but was in fact a place for middle-aged people to go on holiday to. The authorities glared at the new scene with piggy jealous eyes, seeing other people having a better time with a different soundtrack. The new drug scene that had been imported with the scene only compounded this mutual stand-off: it was cultural war and a generational clash.

In 1998 a small scene that had been bubbling underground for years exploded into the mainstream. A huddle of artists, including Motorbass, Daft Punk, Scan X, DJ Cam and labels like F Communications, Yellow and Source, were meddling in the late-seventies disco flavours of Cerrone and Patrick Hernandez and cranking it bang up to date into the brave new world of techno.

The beauty of techno, of course, is its mainly instrumental status. All of a sudden the Anglo-American pop axis was redundant. American was no longer the language of rock 'n' roll. After all, now there was no language in rock 'n' roll at all. Post acid house, most countries started to build up their own music scenes and France was no exception to the new rule.

This cauldron of new talent started to coalesce around the two previously mentioned labels. Source documented all the new activity in its excellent series of SourceLab 1-4 compilation albums, while F Comm and its previous incarnation FNAC Communications had been on the case since the early nineties, releasing cuts by French DJ Laurent Garnier and A Reminiscent Drive.

Laurent Garnier was already a known name in the UK. His DJ-ing stints at the Hacienda, where he spun records at night while working as a chef in the city during the day, had given his name a status on the circuit. In his footsteps other French DJs such as Etienne de Crécy and Dimitri would tentatively follow.

FNAC, set up by Eric Morand, a former radio programmer and DJ, is the spine to the French house scene. He traces the French house scene to the nascent rave parties thrown at the Pyramid in the Palace and the Jungle at the Rex which were both organized by Brits looking for an excuse for a knees-up across the pond. In fact it was at the Rex that Garnier cut his DJ-ing teeth before moving to the north of England.

In January 1992 FNAC put on Paris's first mega rave inside La Grande Arche at La Defense, Garnier made a hometown return and Warp's techno pioneers LFO played a set. Months later Morand officially announced that there was life in the French dance floor when he released the *Respect For France* compilation. In 1994 he renamed the label Fcomm, releasing key tracks and putting the fire into the belly of the French scene.

The lynch pin to the whole palaver is Daft Punk. The duo smartly tagged as 'disco pogo' by *Jockey Slut* magazine, broke the late nineties French pop to the mainstream and personalized all the different strands inherent in the French disco fallout. The genius named duo were swiftly adopted in the wake of The Chemical Brothers' success as a French version of the duo's expert mashing of the break beat.

Their breakthrough hit 'Da Funk' (released in February 1997 and a Top Five hit) was a stunning slab of meaty dancefloor pop. Its coffee-thick slab of crunching synth riffing sounded awesome in clubs. The album *Homework* from which it came was a non-stop workout of intelligent twisting of the disco rule book. The follow-up single 'Around The World' was the song's title, chanted through a vocoder over a hypnotic pulsing backbeat.

Both singles came armed with great videos: 'Da Funk' had the broken-down half-man/half-dog staggering round the chaos of New York streets. It was a funny/sad film clip and one of the coolest videos ever put together for a pop song.

These guys were obviously smart.

Born in the mid seventies, Thomas Bangalter and Guy-Manel de Homem-Christo met at school in 1987. Bangalter was brought up in a pop environment. Bizarrely enough his father, Daniel Vangarde, wrote the mega hits 'Cuba' for the Gibson Brothers and 'D.I.S.C.O' for Ottawan.

How cool is that!

At school they got hip to Jimi Hendrix and sixties music from soul to funk and rock. They formed their first band, Darling, in 1992. They just wanted to be in a band, go on the road and find girls. Plying a left-field indie-drone with Bangalter playing bass and de Homem-Christo guitar, they were heavily influenced by the Beach Boys, naming themselves after the surf rockers' song. Their only release was on a compilation single on Stereolab's Douphonic label. A review in *Melody Maker* of a gig supporting Stereolab claimed that Darling were 'just daft punk music'. Being the wags that they are, they picked up their monicker from the review and renamed the band. Thomas got a sampler for his eighteenth birthday and they rebuilt their sound.

'We didn't know what we wanted to sound like. We only found out by making the records. And then we thought, it sounds like us,' they told *Spin* magazine, explaining their shift from esoteric indie to the dance floor.

Turned on to house by S Express's 'Theme' they moved hungrily through Andrew Weatherall, Primal Scream and The Orb. They were on the crash course for the ravers. The record that really turned their heads was Andrew Weatherall's mix of 'Loaded' – it was their dance epiphany. Like many musicians, the inspirational warm chug of that classic song was the turning point that turned them on to dance.

In 1992 the new-look duo met Scottish dance label, Soma records at the Eurodisney rave in Paris; digging the Slam DJ's turntable skills, a rapport was built up. They gave Stuart McMillan from Slam a demo of 'Alive'. Six months later it was their first release on Soma, backed with 'New Wave', a sly dig at the 'New Wave Of New Wave' scene trumped up by the UK rock press.

A press campaign, launching them as the new 'teen techno sensation from Paris', found little favour in the music press, apart from a piece in ever hip *Jockey Slut.*

The following year they released the breakthrough 'Da Funk' flipped with 'Rollin' and Scratchin'. The song slotted neatly into the space created by The Chemical Brothers: a remix of the Chemicals' 'Life Is Sweet' underlined their role, to many, as the French version of the Brothers. It was a neat comparison but not one that did them total justice. Daft Punk had slabs of funk slapped on to their disco and were not dealing in the huge hiphop breakbeats of The Chemical Brothers.

Although not a hit first time round, it got the band the attention of the underground.

In January 1997 they released their debut album *Homework* and the following month broke through to the mainstream with the re-release of 'Da Funk' backed with 'Musique'. It was a Top Five hit, broke the band across Europe and opened the doors on a French scene. The spotlight fell on to Paris and a previously untapped supply of bands came onstream.

'Around The World' swiftly followed in April and was Top Ten as well. Daft Punk were one of the bands of the year.

Not that they ever forgot their indie ethic. They have their own label, Roulle. Their whole operation is built like a cottage industry. They design their own sleeves and make their records on low budgets. It's like someone had bothered to learn something from the last twenty years of indie wars.

With the pop scene reeling from the fact that the French had given us a cool international group the sucker punch was delivered by Air.

Fuck, two great groups in a year!

Air's light, moody pop is perhaps closer to the classic French pop canyon than any of their contemporaries. They can sound like original French groups like JMJ and Space (not the scousers but the group that released 'Magic Fly', a massive hit in 1997). The French Space plied an electronic-northern soul crossover in the seventies, years before it became trendy indie fodder over here . . . how hip is that!

Continuing their love of French roots, Air are also big fans of Michael Polnareff, an eccentric French freak who was on the Bowie trip. Decorating his music with Arp string machines, Polnareff had an enormous perm, leotard and massive plastic sunglasses obscuring his face. Cool.

The eccentric singer eventually went blind and mad and has lived as a recluse in a hotel for the past fifteen years.

Just to underline how much the great genius of the French pop scene has lost it, he mixed a compilation album put together by the likes of Pulp and St Etienne (surely the two British bands who spiritually are closest to the French pop ideal), reworking his long-lost songs. The record never came out as Polnareff declared 'Who are these people covering my songs? where is Phil Collins? where are the Eurythmics?' He now had even worse taste than in his leotard-wearing days!

Air is built around another duo, Nicolas Godin and Jean Benoit Dunckel. The pair are from Versailles, the very nice town of mansions and castles and the royal palace of the Sun King Louis to the west of Paris. They met at college through a mutual friend Alex Gopher who has also moved on to become a producer. Alex and Jean Benoit had their own band and asked Nicolas to join as a guitarist. They named the band Orange and plied an indie-rock style, the starting point of most of the current wave of French popsters.

Nicolas had been encouraged to play guitar from childhood by his hip parents, while Benoit was classically trained at the keyboard. Recording for Source, the Bastille-based label that ran in tandem with FComm building up a French dance profile, Air at first sighting were some kinda sister band to Daft Punk, but on closer inspection their music is very different. Playing a bright and breezy, almost classic electro pop, they are that very nineties thing: dance music that you can't dance to.

Their first recording, the effervescent 'Modular Mix', was released in 1996 and it firmly placed them in their own eccentric pop world. The song was about the legendary French architect Le Corbusier (inventor of the tower block – not so chic when you have to live in one!) and how it was his idea of the perfect inhabitant for his new-fangled hi-rise world; everything, that is except for the music and the track, was written to that void.

With this track Orange became Air, a part-time on-and-off project while the two main protagonists went to university. It was while at university that Teissier du Cross who worked at Source suggested they release 'Modulator Man' for the label and for one of their 'Sound Lab' compilations; it was then licensed to Mo Wax in the UK.

Encouraged by the good reception that their track got, they recorded a follow-up – the languid 'Casanova 70'. It was a further exploration of their pastoral electro pop, recorded in their own studio which they had constructed in the leafy retreat of Versailles – a million miles away from the tuff urban concrete that backdrops most of the electronic music of the times.

Their big hit, 'Sexy Boy', was a lush roller-coaster of a song. A slice of perfect timeless pop, riding on a breathless vocal and a great bass line. It also came armed with a strange video that was part camp and part childlike and part sharp in its observations of crazed capitalism. It was also very funny. Their debut album *Moon Safari* was an international bestseller. The record captured their breathless pop perfectly. A snapshot of fluffy melodies and oozing textures. It sounded perfectly modern.

Air feel closer to a little celebrated long-forgotten but important clutch of French electronic composers who have an important part to play in this story, like Jean-Jacques Perrey and Gershon Kingsley. There was also Pierre Henry who, frustrated by the lack of instruments that could realize the sound that he wanted, built his own sound generator in the early fifties. A couple of years ago Henry's track 'Psyche Rock' was remixed by Coldcut, Fatboy Slim and William Orbit.

The Air duo also, like Daft Punk, met at school where they also knew Etienne De Crécy, a French DJ.

In more ways than one Daft Punk and Air encapsulated the tradition of French disco which is very different from its Brit counterpart. Sure there is the dancefloor flavour in there, but there are huge slabs of easy listening, the experimental electronic doodlings of Joe Meek and a pure pop consciousness. The closest Anglo outfit to this *très chic* combination is the constantly underrated and quite fab St Etienne.

With Air and Daft Punk fully established, there were other

outfits getting looked over. Pills, who came from the side of Paris that the tourists never see and the rest of the bands certainly didn't live in, plied a tougher meaner workout that rocked many a Euro festival. Sounding closer to the electronic punk world of The Prodigy, they made harsher music from a harsher climate.

In 1999 came the final breakthrough for Cassius, formed by underground mixers Hubert Blanc-Francard (alias Boombass) and Philippe Zdar, two 31-year-old underground mixers who had spent the nineties remixing a whole heap of stuff from Motorbass's *001* (1992) and 1993's *Transfunk* before spending the mid nineties reworking La Funk Mob's releases on Mo Wax. They returned to Motorbass in 1996 and went big time with the Neneh Cherry 'Woman' remix and then on to Björk and Depeche Mode.

They were also spending their time DJ-ing at London's Basement Jaxx (who have gone on to put out 1999's breakthough album, *Remedy*) and Scaramanga and Paris Respect. Getting top rips with the real dancefloor dynamic, they were at the heart of the nu French scene remixing both Daft Punk's 'Around The World' and Air's 'Sexy Boy'.

Cassius's whole vibe was putting in the funk on their French disco workouts and crossing this with hiphop – a hiphop scene in which they had strong roots, remixing the likes of French rap superstar MC Solaar before going on to produce three albums for the French rap superstar including his only (minor) hit in the UK, 'Bouge De La'.

In fact it was hiphop that formed the basis of their musical taste. The knock-on effect of rap music on the nineties cannot be overemphasized: fashion, music, slang, attitude, the whole art of pop was heavily indebted to the American street form, as they explained in an interview.

'We were into music before but it wasn't our music. Hip hop was ours. It wasn't our parents' records.' In an era in which the generation gap seems to have finally vanished then maybe hiphop and techno are the last vague battle lines that can be drawn in pop.

Not that Cassius were exactly street kids slugging it out in the ghetto. Typical of most of the nu French pop they came from the affluent west Parisian suburbs. Boombass's father was a top French record producer. Influenced by his father he started working in a recording studio at the bottom rung as a teaboy, By 1991 he was producing MC Solaar's debut album.

Philippe was brought up in the Alps. He moved to Paris where he was working with Buburt's father – the pair's partnership was then inevitable. Both sharing the same hip interests, Philippe became Boombass's engineer and then by the mid nineties they were a team.

After helping to shape MC Solaar's sound, they went all eclectic on the La Funk Mob's excellent musical journey. Then Philippe's mind was blown after going to a rave in 1992: now he had the techno bug. The future had arrived and he was grabbing it.

Hooking up with French DJ Etienne De Crécy he cut the *Pansoul* album which is acknowledged as one of the key influences on the French dance scene along with Daft Punk's *Homework* and Dimitri From Paris's 'Sacreblue'.

He still had to convince Huburt about his techno conversion and eventually talked his partner into doing a house collaboration for a laugh. The song they came up with, 'Foxy Lady', was released under the monicker L'Homme Qui Valait Trois Millards (French for six million dollar man!), the track becoming a standard for underground DJs on both sides of the Channel.

Inspired by this, they put together Cassius proper.

And yet there are pockets of creativity that still haven't managed to hop over the Channel. There is the Tricatel label, the producer/writer/arranger Bertrand Burgalat (mate of Air whose fuzzed-up garage jokey version of 'Sexy Boy' was the B side of the ubiquitous Air hit in Japan). Not that Burgalat hasn't got any cards close to his chest: the album he recorded with American April March (aka Elinor Blake, an illustrator on the *Ren and Stimpy* show and pal of Jonathan Richman) is tipped to be the breakthrough record for him if it could only get the proper release that it craves.

By the end of the decade the French were laughing at us. They had a hip pop scene and they had a film industry that was just managing to survive the excessive attack of the Hollywood scene. French films may generally be art house or mawkish but they showed the Brits a thing or two about tuff street realism with *La Haine* (1995), a brutal movie that reset Scorsese's *Mean Streets* in the crumbling concrete of the Parisian suburbs.

And to underline this new French mastery of popular culture, instead of the highbrow, they went and won the World Cup in 1998. For years they had ignored football, treating it as a minor interest but the night they won the World Cup in Paris the country went wild. Millions celebrated. The right-wing Front Nationale were made to look even dumber by the victory of a multi-racial side and the French were kings of the world's most important sport.

The French were now even giants of footy.

Très bon.

Popular culture had never seemed so easy.

CHAPTER THIRTY-EIGHT

JOCKEY SLUT

***Jockey Slut* captured the sheer fun of clubbing with the trainspotters' thrill of checking the new records that were flying out. Its editors moved to Manchester in the baggy boom chasing a pop dream and were quickly converted to the city' dance fixation. Getting it down on paper, they put together their own magazine which has become one of the key frontline mags on the dance scene . . .**

The story of *Jockey Slut* magazine is the story of the second generation of house kids coming to terms with the new pop culture. If the first wave had been an all-encompassing rush of hedonistic craziness, the nu generation were keen to assimilate the hedonism and put it into context. They arrived a couple of years after the event and started to build a strong robust culture from the ruins.

Acid House, like punk, had exploded into the mainstream with no real game plan.

Paul Benney and John Burgess of *Jockey Slut* are typical of the next generation.

Too young to really get the initial rave, they were indie kids who dug a bit of hip hop. Like most people who were 18 in 1989 they saw Manchester as the pop mecca.

In 1990 there wasn't a hip teenager in Britain who didn't want to move to Manchester and grab on to the coat tails of the endless party. Paul and John were no different.

'I'd always liked the whole Manchester scene,' remembers Paul. 'I moved to Manchester because of The Smiths, New Order and Joy Division. It was a great time to be there with The Stone Roses and all those bands happening. When I was at college the whole thing just seemed to blow up big time.' There is nothing better than being right there at the epicentre of the party and the pop-loving pair were living out their last teenage months in a pop nirvana.

Acid house was leaking out of every crevice of the city but they were still indie boys at heart. The dance music, though, was insidiously pulling them in.

'I saw The Stone Roses in Northampton in 1989 and I got there at about 6.00. As they piled out of the van I could hear "Good Life" getting blasted out, I thought they must be joking!' remembers Paul. 'But I really liked it.'

Living in a shared student house, Paul started to notice his housemates weirding out. They would come home later and later and look more and more spaced, bringing back monged out mates. It was something that he was going to find very difficult to avoid.

The early nineties are littered with people's first E experiences. For Paul, it was one of the Tuesday nights at the Academy with Dave Booth Dj-ing. Out of his box, he wallowed in the good-time ooze of the drug and floated back home for a cool comedown to Primal Scream's *Screamadelica*, the perfect soundtrack of the times for music heads whose tastes lay between indie and dance but were buzzing on the new drug regime.

John had come from a more dance-orientated background – Prince, Public Enemy, S'Express, Baby Ford.

'I used to go to the Nude nights at The Hacienda on Fridays with this group of mates that included Tom and Ed from the Chemical Brothers.' (The nascent electronic mavericks were also up in Manchester, attracted to the university that had the best club backdrop in Europe on offer.)

'When I first went to The Hacienda I couldn't understand why everyone was so mental in there,' observes John. 'But I certainly understood why in the end!'

He bumped into Paul in a lift at the university and the pair bonded over a Happy Mondays album. It was one of those records that could unite the indie and the dance factions and was a bible for the dance culture of the times. They took over the university magazine, dominating the pop pages.

Paul lived with the soon to be name DJ James Holroyd and watched him learning his trade. Like countless other teens in the country, Holroyd was finding his musical expression in dance E culture. No longer was it necessary to get a guitar or a sampler or even a song together to rock a house. Just get a pile of vinyl. In the nineties the sales of conventional instruments would slide as the DJ became king.

Holroyd started to lend Paul heaps of American house records. It would have a profound effect on his hungry mind – and was to be the start of a life-long passion.

The first club in Manchester that really coalesced the new converts was Most Excellent.

In the fallout from the mass phenomenon of house there was a yearning for specialist clubs. Get the music back to its roots. None of that thousands of people herded around everywhere. Clubs for your mates. Clubs where everyone dug the same sort of thing. Clubs with a schtick. Clubs like Most Excellent were dealing in the glam end of house, backing off from the lad-infested mini-gangster freakouts that were starting to encroach on the other club. Run from the Wiggly Worm club it introduced a new sort of DJ into the fray. People like Justin Robertson and David Holmes, people who were prepared to fuck with the form. Who were prepared to push the eclectic thing just that bit harder.

John and Paul were regulars. They now felt totally at home in this environment. In the Balearic tradition, in house they would play anything. DJs would think nothing of dropping Nirvana into the middle of a bangin' set of house and sit back and watch the place explode. It was a great admission that dance music didn't just belong to the boys with the break beats, that great rock 'n' roll can move yer ass as well. Mix it up, mish and mash, let's not get bogged down in genres.

Inspired into a creative frenzy, Paul and John started making T-shirts. The first one that they designed was 'Factory fucked', a touching comment on the local label's struggles. They then came up with 'Jockey Slut'.

'We were really into The Manics at the time. We'd seen them play and met them at a party that Heavenly Records threw at the Brickhouse afterwards. We loved their slogans and their shirts sprayed with "Culture Slut". We thought that was great so we took it and used the idea for a shirt. It was a comment on the sort of people that hung around with DJs.' It was a neat monicker and one that they wouldn't waste on just a T-shirt.

It was from the new progressive house scene that Paul felt that

DJs, although already icons, were starting to get more on to an even higher platform.

'It was about that time that DJs started to get taken seriously as artists.'

They also spotted another new trend.

'It seems like in 1991 that students started to take drugs. Everyone went home for the summer holidays and when they came back everyone had had a separate experience of getting into E. They had literally come back from all over the UK and everyone had taken drugs.'

The house scene was storming the last bastions of guitar rock. The early nineties student population were soon to be packing away their Doc Martens and Smiths records and buying into the new party scene. It was to change the flavour of the clubs. By the mid nineties there were the first real divisions in the house scene as everyone kept rewriting the rule book to suit themselves.

'If for the purists the late eighties was the year zero in house music, for your average kid 1991 was the real year zero,' observe the *Jockey Slut* team.

John and Paul had spent that summer partying at Shine at the Hacienda. 'I remember the squirty water bottles,' they laugh. 'There was no element of threat then, it was just total fun.'

Also inspired by Most Excellent, which by now had gone by the wayside, The Chemical Brothers, or The Dust Brothers as they were then known, put on a couple of nights at the Swinging Sporran pub called Naked Under Leather. The nascent DJ team were taking their bedroom DJ skills, which they had only unleashed at parties before, into the public spotlight for the first time. They were taking their first steps on a highly influential trail.

Feeling that the likes of *Mixmag* and other dance magazines were not covering the new explosion of dance floor talent, Paul and John started *Jockey Slut* magazine. Within a couple of issues it was getting a nationwide support. A year later they were promoting their own night – 'Bugged Out' at Manchester Sankeys Soap. Bugged Out perfectly reflected their schtick as written about in the magazine. Dedicated to stripped-down techno from the pioneering Detroit school they were bringing in some of the key names from the first city of techno (the Detroit legends, themselves loved playing there – the boarded-up area and the smashed glass all over the road must have reminded them of home!) Bugged Out became one of the key Manc clubs, waving the flag for some sort of maverick party spirit way into the nineties after the rest of the city reverted to handbag house. Now moved to Liverpool's superclub Cream, Bugged Out is a monthly extravaganza, a big-time big-league affair. The magazine is not doing badly either. With a proper distribution its circulation is on the up in a generally depressed specialist music magazine market.

Jockey Slut is probably the most successful of a new breed of specialist underground magazines that have gone from strength to strength in the late nineties. Armed with home computers, it's conceivable to produce a magazine that is the match of any big-time publishers.

The *Slut* proves this, resisting any big buyouts from London. They remain independent of the mainstream. The editorial is done from the north and the magazine oozes the club experience.

It's a triumph of fans over the music machine. A case of the lunatics taking over the asylum.

CHAPTER THIRTY-NINE

PECS APPEAL: BOY BANDS – JUST WHO WON THE POP WARS?

Watching *Top Of The Pops* in the late nineties was a painful experience. The programme itself was always balanced precariously between naff and inspiring. I guess that's the beauty of the show. It perfectly reflected what was going on in pop at the time . . .

And by the late nineties there was a severe tightening of taste belts going on. The indie guitar boom of the mid nineties had been reigned in, the last great wave of guitar pop had run aground. At the end of the decade there is an unprecedented pop boom. Every week another squeaky clean bunch of nobodies crashes in at No. 1. Prancing dullards that worship at the altar of Bucks Fizz are ruling the roost. It's created a sales boom that puts the combined UK record sales ahead of the German record market for the first time ever. It has also created a pop period that will be laughed at in years to come. Outside of this perma-grinning conveyer belt only the strong were going to survive. Some bands, like Blur, reacted by going for the extreme, moving a million miles away from the teen pop scene that they had once flirted with.

Previous champions of guitar music like Radio One had gone swing beat and pec pop, major labels were signing up well-behaved clean-faced kids desperate for pop success at all costs and groups could be heard talking about 'units shifted' with nil irony.

'Art is dead long live pop!' smirked the cynics as music hit one of its most tedious periods.

The kings of the scene in 1999 were Boyzone, who were ending the decade with a non-stop run of No. 1 hits. With their dumb, too-clean pop faces and strutting their vapid stuff, the Dublin troupe made Take That look like The Sex Pistols. Their forté was piss weak ballads sung by a vocalist who was the pop equivalent of Alan Shearer. They were throwing the same sort of no personality shapes as an eighties pro footballer, boasting the same sort of square blankness.

Fine for a footballer but something that has no place in pop.

The boy band was king and strutted its dull stuff over the land.

While indie fans and serious inkie readers were still locked into the Blur v. Oasis debate, in the real world the boy band and especially its female counterpart, the, er, girl band was king or more precisely queen.

In the mid nineties the gloating was going on. The guitar was king and druggy dance music was ruling the clubs, apart from Take That's pristine pop. Everywhere, though, would-be managers were rehearsing their too clean troops hard. Take That had inspired a whole host of money men and every two-bit pretty boy in town was getting coerced into the action . . .

Yup, the indie scene may have threatened to blow away the major label-dominated eighties pop but within a couple of years the pure pop with plain-looking boys and, increasingly, girls primed to be pure pop beef was the currency.

The warning signs were there early. In the early nineties Take That were scoring huge hits with ease, flowering from a bunch of gloopy looking New Kids On The Block rip-offs to a rather more risqué arse-showing live show. Their gigs even saw them dressed as rubbery devils or sexed up pretty boys dancing the pure pop two step in a full-on live pantomime that was actually a pretty good pop show.

The group, put together by Manchester Svengali Nigel Martin Smith, was built around the much hyped-up songwriting talents of Gary Barlow. You can always spot the one who's meant to be the songwriter in these bands. It's the uncomfortable looking pudge who can't dance properly and gets to sing all the verses in the goofy knicker-soaking anthems.

Barlow was a flatfoot who worshipped Elton John. This was while he was a teenager – at an age when most people are on the warpath he had the tastes of a married-off dead person.

Just like The Beatles in their teenybop prime in the sixties, the band had to have their own 'personalities' glued on to their chiselled faces. They had a cute one (Mark), a grunge one (Howard), and one that could dance and was a bit street (Jason – before Take That, Jason Orange was a champ Manc break-dancer) and a daft one (Robbie).

Robbie Williams at the time was the joker in the pack, the chancer from Burslem who was along for the ride, the diametric opposite of the Barlow star machine. Post Take That Barlow was groomed to be the big star, but Robbie Williams rewrote the script by becoming the biggest UK pop star of the late nineties.

By 1999 Williams has become the consummate pop pro, the Tom Jones of his time, seemingly able to bang out single after single of classic pop. It's been an effortless rise to the very top. Once he got his mega hit 'Angels', lost a few pounds and got his life together, there was no stopping him – two albums of class pop songs were also in his favour. Whenever Williams appears on TV he's a live spark, a consummate show-off and a pop natural, showing those glowering pasty-faced indie boys just what rock 'n' roll is all about. Not one of the indie bands of 1998 managed to knock out a rock 'n' roll record as good as 'Let Me Entertain You', the best guitar anthem record released by a British artist of that dull as ditchwater year. The fact that it came from what had been considered a washed-up matinee idol the year before proved that in pop the only rule that holds tight is that there are no rules.

Williams's surge to the top has rather overshadowed Barlow's putsch. The former front man is now left high and dry. Sure, he sells loads of records but can anyone remember how the hell they go? Has his faithful audience of old-before-their-time knicker-wetters got themselves locked into the Cliff Richard scenario . . . ferociously supporting a mediocrity for the rest of their lives.

And the rest of Take That? Well, Mark Owen had a big solo hit and an album that filled upbargain bins; I once bumped into the affable Owen during a *Melody Maker* feature where we all had to pretend that we were actors in an acting school. He was charming and modest and found it difficult to come to grips with the fact that he was once in one of the biggest band of his times. Retired at 23 – that's life in pop. The other two mooched around trying a bit of acting. Jason Orange has recently been cropping up on stage, getting notices as a cred actor. An ex pop star exists in that strange nether world that lies beyond pop fame. A place where you spend the rest of your life with people saying 'Oooh they look a bit older, don't they?', like it's a surprise that anyone famous could actually age.

Take That's pop rivals were East 17, the street version of the cuddly Manc five-piece who sang similar saccharin ballads but with a sneer. With hit singles provided by their songwriting member Tony Mortimer, East 17 (named after the postcode of their home base Walthamstow) had a more erratic chart career than Take That. In spite of hits like 'Stay Another Day' and 'Everybody In The House Of Love', the outfit fell apart when lead singer Brian Harvey mouthed off about taking a whole bunch of Es in one session. Boy bands don't – just don't – take drugs! well, that's the official line.

The media hypocrites in the middle of their anti-E frenzy went for the jugular of the vocalist, stirring up a hornet's nest that went to the House of Commons. Harvey, who was sacked from his band, looked set for pop oblivion but when the rest of the band fell apart he regrouped them without Mortimer as E17 and crept back into the charts with a run of swing-beat-influenced hits.

Take That's pole pop position was stolen by The Spice Girls – another manufactured and quite brilliantly pre-packaged outfit who went beyond hype when their first video was the most requested film clip of all time on *The Box* cable TV show. *The Box* was a series of video clips that were shown in direct relation to the number of times the viewers requested them.

Five pop chicks in tight skimpy pants giving the camera plenty of groin was not going to hamper the new outfit's career, neither was the fact that they seemed to be a brilliant cross section of the cliché idea of just what the girl next door in the UK *actually* looked like.

There was something there for everybody. They were plain enough and clumsy enough to appear human (check Geri Halliwell's clodhoppered dancing). Mel B had a great Leeds accent – maybe the first one ever in pop. They were also over the top Saturday night on the town glam enough to be sexy in a beery belch in yer face kinda way.

It didn't take long for them to have nicknames thrust upon them by a tabloid press which couldn't believe its luck – it was a Fleet Street dream cum true – page 3 girls running riot in the charts, big-busted supa girls with a series of catchy singles and a loose master plan that they were touting under the monicker 'Girl Power'.

It was drooling over page 3 at breakfast time sold back as emancipation and it made perfect sense in the nineties where radical chic has become the norm and a pierced eyebrow was hardly ever raised about anything.

Their pop formula was simple but effective – you know, the three of them tuneless, grappling with the verse and then Sporty Spice letting her really good voice handle the difficult melodic takeoff on the chorus. All was going swimmingly for The Spice Girls until half the group decided to tell everyone that they had Tory sympathies. At one time in pop history this would have finished them. There was a swift debate and then it was all forgotten about. Most of the music industry was probably Tory anyway and if they wanted to vote for the bastards that had wrecked the country in their never-ending years in power then that was their problem.

Typically the northern girls in the band – the two Mels, one a scouser and one from Leeds – recoiled in horror at the thought of being labelled Tories, but it didn't end the band. Stuff like that didn't seem to matter any more. In the mid nineties politics was like football but without the passion.

From the start of their ascent everyone seemed to be predicting the end of The Spice Girls' career but every day they just seemed to get bigger and bigger. Their album was No. 1 and then they took America, Ginger Geri left . . . again the end was predicted but they just got bigger and bigger. A second album sold millions. By 1999 their solo careers were beginning to kick off . . . Mel B (now Mel G after her hi-profile wedding) was on the R&B tip with a couple of sparse stripped to the groove singles, Mel C was singing with Bryan Adams, Baby Spice was appearing solo live and Posh was a full-time media celeb in cloud *Hello* land.

As the nineties ended The Spice Girls were one of the biggest groups in the world. When The All Saints came along they were reckoned to be a cooler version of the consummate nineties girl band and would easily finish The Spice Girls off. All Saints were marketed as the sassy, smart, streetwise version of the Spice Girls – none of the clumpy rubber-soled platforms for these combats and trainer girls. They were hip hip hip showing hip. Their songs were really good as well, classic slices of timeless pop that included a cover of the Red Hot Chilli Peppers' 'Under The Bridge'.

The late nineties sees the pure pop band reign supreme. The too-clean dream dominates the teen scene. Boyzone bring along their pals B*witched and, lo and behold, we have another girl band mashing up the charts. Boyzone manage a band, Westlife and they grab a No. 1. Every week, Saturday morning's *CD UK* sees another bunch of chancers coyly stare at the camera and chug through yet another sub-Bee Gees workout, another dance routine, another raid on the pre teen piggy banks . . . every now and then a great tune is thrown into the equation, like Britney Spears' debut No. 1. But for every high there are a million lows. . .

If this is the real sound of the late nineties – help!

CHAPTER FORTY

WE'RE FOOTBALL CRAZY, WE'RE MONEY MAD

If sport is the key activity in the leisure age then football sits right at the top of the tree. In the nineties the sport broke all records. Awash with money and hype, the game went from being the lame duck of the previous couple of decades to being a full-on exhilarating multimedia operation. The battle now was not just to stay in the Premier League but for the soul of the game, as TV and multinational multimedia predators stalked clubs sniffing out the huge profits which just sat there just waiting to be collected . . .

The streets are awash with emotion, beer and sweat. It's packed. Man United are bringing their silverware back to the north and the city has gone mad. There are half a million people lining the streets, singing the same old songs, blasting their infernal whistles. Cars drive round and round the city centre cranking their horns in an endless parade.

Manchester United's dramatic 2-1 victory in the European Cup Final over Bayern Munich opened the floodgates. After years of losing, someone in the UK had won something. It's that feelgood factor that they talk about. This is what it's like to be top of the world or at least win the European Cup. Football in the nineties really is more than a game, it's become the key populist pastime of the nation.

All through the nineties, popular culture has been leading this way – from lad culture being hip to the casual sports boom that has been the undertow of everything. Football has replaced pop as the key leisure activity of the times. And its most public faces – the players – have become the hip young knights of the realm.

'Where did it all go wrong, Mr Best . . .'

The late nineties sees the bunch of pampered superstars earning ridiculous amounts of money, poncing around like selfish demi godz, wearing daft clothes, swaggering up catwalks, denying cocaine rumours, dating models and occasionally making terrible records and talking shit.

The new brats on the block, the new role models from hell.

Footballers have truly stolen the pop stars' crown . . . doing all the wacky stuff we used to love the rock 'n' rollers for.

Football tells the story of the decade better than almost any other popular art form. As a moral tale for the nineties it's a seething chronicle of the power, corruption and lies of the era. The money men and Stock Exchange cynics prey on the blind faith and passion of the fans. Meanwhile the sheer terror of the old skool, feeling their ancient power slip away from them, is terrifyingly obvious.

Greed, greed, greed . . . The same story could be told in the music and film industries. It can even be told in the food industry where poisonous chemicals are pumped into food to crank profits. It's a story of any industry ripped apart by the new money men cutting corners to make profits. It's also a quest for survival, rebranding the product for the hi tech nu millenium. Changing the nature of the product. Seeking the 21st-century world market.

This is the late nineties and the corporations are well and truly in control. Football itself is at war with its own fans as this new breed stomp over everything in their paths.

It's an ugly struggle for big profits and a crass ripping off of the grass-roots lifeblood of the game – the fans. But after the debacle of the game's decline in the seventies and eighties, it is, perhaps a necessary and brutal revamping of the 'product'.

In the post World War II era the game had been in sharp decline. The fifties had seen a massive resurgence in all forms of popular culture as people felt the weary weight of combat lifted off their shoulders, and football was one of the main beneficiaries. Several clubs could easily boast 50,000 plus gates. It was boomtime and the money rolled in. The abolition of the maximum wage saw the first real split in the football class system. The small-town teams who had been able to afford the wages of their best players were sent into a spiral of terminal decline. Once-proud clubs like Preston North End and Burnley could hardly compete in the new wage wars with the big city clubs like Liverpool or Manchester United.

The days of an open competition were slowly coming to an end.

The new money sloshing around in the game saw the players get richer and richer. Running hand in hand with the boom in the music scene, several of them were coming on like pop stars. The king of them all was George Best, 'El Beatle' to the Spaniards.

Flash, sexy and hip, George Best broke the mould in the football world. The old Stanley Matthews greased-back-hair role model was a thing of the past. Football players lived fast and hard. They bought sports cars and stupid-looking flats and had a dolly bird on each arm. It was the working-class dream come true: an escape from the grim, a dash into the limelight.

Famously, George Best was once asked by a hotel porter – who barged into his room by mistake and saw the soccer star in bed with three blonde bombshells surrounded by bottles of champagne – where it all went wrong. Best's casual smirk was the only possible answer.

By the late sixties the sinister, darker side of football had also reared its ugly, shaven head when hooliganism became fashionable. Not that it was an invention of the times. It had been there for years. Football had always had a rough element. It was just that now it was easier to identify and it was becoming the stuff of headlines. Late-sixties hooliganism was more obvious and it was, for a generation quite literally looking for kicks, cool as fuck.

The seventies were marred by the constant battling. Gates declined and the stadiums, many built in Victorian times, were in a state of neglect. Competing against mass-market pop, colour TV and the cinema, football was sliding down the lifestyle scale.

It was also sliding down the taste scale. In the eighties the players sported perms and hilarious moustaches and wore strange, too tight shorts – it was no wonder the fans started to stay away in droves. Liverpool won everything and the fighting went on. The grounds were ever more dilapidated and the fans drifted away en masse. You couldn't pick up a paper without some bizarrely moustachioed and sheepskin-wearing pundit going on about soccer's crises. The game stumbled from one bad decision to another with the men at the top seemingly incapable of sorting their house out. In the eighties things got worse. Many feared that the game could be on its last legs. The powers that be seemed pretty happy about this state of affairs.

The Tory government hated the game, seeing it as an unruly working-class pastime. Compared to the rest of popular culture, the game seemed old-fashioned. Difficult as it is to believe in 1999, football in the early 1980s was a joke. Only the foolhardy, the loyal or the plain daft were still into it.

The game was in a slumber and it was going to need a nasty shock to kick it back into the real world.

In the late eighties it received several, almost inevitable, nasty sickening jolts that put a full stop to the rot. The fact that any of these incidents happened at all is an indictment on the greed and small-mindedness of the men at the top who treated the fans like cattle. The grounds were fenced up and the punters were herded in and imprisoned behind the mean barricades. Ostensibly to prevent pitch invasions, it made football grounds look like prisons.

The first shocking blow came in the mid eighties with the Heysel stadium disaster. The crumbling grounds and negative attitudes that surrounded the game were disasters waiting to happen. When Liverpool and Juventus fans started fighting at the European Cup final, a wall in the crap crumbling Heysel stadium in Belgium gave way and Juventus fans were killed.

Watching the event on TV in pubs up and down the country, people were sickened. The fighting had been out of order but it was the shitty stadium and the crumbling dividing wall that caused the disaster. The sheer weight of fans who were crushed against the wall made it collapse.

Things would have to change.

Of course they didn't.

The authorities blamed the fans and tried to carry on as before. Even after many fans were killed in the fire in Bradford's dilapidated wooden Valley Parade stadium when they stood stock-still like rabbits trapped in the glare of the spotlights. It seemed that football couldn't sink any lower.

It had the status of a despised game. The only headlines it grabbed were about death and violence.

The final turning point was the 1989 Hillsborough disaster when 96 Liverpool fans were crushed to death after, unbelievably, the police had corralled them into the too small Leppings Lane End of Sheffield Wednesday's Hillsborough Stadium. The fans were pressed up against the wire fences that hemmed them in, their faces contorted by the agony of the sheer weight of bodies crushed against them. It was football's worst nightmare come true. It took ages before anyone got a grip of the situation. Fans streaming into the ground were being crushed on to the human scrap heap.

It couldn't get any worse than this.

Outrageously, some of the authorities and the *Sun* blamed the fans' drunkenness but everyone else knew the truth.

As the bodies were laid out on the pitch, the shocked, stunned faces of the fans were flashed around the world's TV.

Football had hit an utter rock bottom. No other form of entertainment had treated its fans with such contempt and no other form of entertainment had reaped what it had sewn in such a miserable fashion. From that afternoon football was on trial.

The public perception was that the game was in a dire mess. Poor facilities, crap grounds, violence and now mass death all contributed to putting the sport totally out of fashion.

Typically, the ruling Tory party's knee-jerk solution was the unworkable. ID cards were mooted, perhaps as a prelude to giving them out to everybody. Authoritarianism was not the answer. Knee-jerk reactions were not enough.

Football was in a mess. It needed a light at the end of the tunnel. As the game entered the nineties the whole game was fucked.

It took the World Cup in 1990 to kick-start the football revolution. A whole host of factors were conspiring to pull the game up by its bootstraps. One of the first signs that things were stirring was something as trivial as the song picked for England's World Cup bid. By choosing New Order to record the song for England, the football authorities were making an, in context, revolutionary move.

Football songs are, by nature, crap. Usually it's the oafish team flatly singing along to some turgid singalong slapped together by the likes of Chas and Dave. Tuneless witless dirges relying on the stubbornly loyal fanbase to push them up the charts. Picking New Order, a cool band at the height of their powers, to record a football song was a stroke of genius. The Manchester outfit teamed up with comedian Keith Allen to write the lyrics. They put together the cheeky anthem 'World In Motion' with its 'E For England' refrain. The song managed to join football and cool pop with the E culture that was bubbling everywhere in the UK in a series of double entendres.

It was hip and it spoke in street terms. Here was a football song that seemed to address the party state of the nation. The song helped to put the game back on the agenda making it look hip, making it pop – it's an association it's run with ever since. The ecstasy revolution had been massive – it had even created a partial truce on the terraces. Loved up in the clubs and buzzing on a cheeky half at the match, the whole flavour of those terraces had changed for a short period of time. Violence was off the agenda as lager was replaced by smoking pot.

Suddenly football seemed to be getting hip again. After the tragedies the game had been forced to put its house in order. The Taylor Report had made radical recommendations. Realizing that the very grounds that the sport was being played in were dire shitholes the Report forced the clubs into all-seater stadiums. The new grounds were not welcomed by everyone. Fans had been standing since the birth of the game: Liverpool's Kop, Manchester United's Stretford End or Manchester City's Kippax were legendary. They were the boisterous riotous ends of the grounds that were worth a goal start to the clubs. The new all-seater stadiums lacked the atmosphere of the old grounds. Unheard of years ago at Man United, Alex Ferguson is always urging the fans to chant.

All-seater stadiums were claimed to eradicate the problem of football violence. But rising in tandem with the increasing sophistication of the football authorities, the violent element embraced new technology in organizing their argie bargey. E-mails and websites would set up battles away from the grounds and mobile phones were used to coordinate fights. And that's notwithstanding the good old rumpus when rival fans would clash in the city away from the ground almost by accident. Unreported in the press, who were too worried about besmirching football's new clean regime, brawls in the street and running battles between rival fans can still be seen across the city when a big match takes place.

The England fans' constant riots in the 1998 World Cup in France were a case in point but it took the Germans' one-off highly organized brawl coordinated by mobile phones to underline the vicious hi-tech right-wing jackboot of neo-fascist violence that bubbles just below the surface of our safe European home.

Couple this with the never-ending stream of hip paperbacks detailing footy violence and you just have to admit that people dig this yob stuff.

The Taylor Report also recommended closed-circuit TV and

the breaking up of the crowds into smaller, more manageable units. It was a far reaching document and many of its changes have had a profound effect on the game. The clubs started to build their all-seater stadiums. There was talk of getting a 'more Americanized' atmosphere. Smart chairmen saw the Taylor Report as an opportunity to make more money. They took a safety report and decided to turn football into the big bucks Americanized showbiz spectacle that they had been talking about for years.

The switch to all-seater stadium was coupled with better facilities and executive boxes, clubs now went out of their ways to attract a richer clientèle. Amidst snarls of gentrification football was going for the middle-class wallet. The game was getting fashionable with the chattering classes. A new hipness that was reflected in *Fever Pitch*, Nick Hornby's best-selling account of growing up as an Arsenal fan.

Other sports attempted to keep up with football's new commercial nous. There was an attempt to make Rugby Union a shiny new sports product with professional players. Despite press coverage way out of proportion with the actual support of the clubs, the game has lurched from one financial crisis to another while it searches for its soul in the wreckage of the money-mad new millennium. Other sports like cricket are faced with virtual extinction because they seem incredibly dull compared to the glitzy modern world of football.

Nineties sport is cut-throat, it has to be sexy enough for TV or it will find itself sliding into the deadzone. Football's bigtime ambitions in the UK were boosted by the 1990 World Cup. The scene had been set with New Order's hip single but now the most unlikely thing happened – the England team woke up and got themselves on a good run in the finals, taking the game to a dramatic centre stage. The World Cup of 1990 captured the imagination of the nation. England had one of their rare good runs.

They swaggered into the semi-finals of the competition. Their titanic struggle with the old rivals Germany when they got there and the eventual defeat was played out in front of one of the biggest TV audiences ever in the UK. It had put the sport back on the front pages.

It was one of those moments frozen in time when everyone can remember where they were. In Manchester we had to break up the Boo Radleys' debut interview for *Sounds* while the match was on. It was a packed front room sat there in nail-biting tension. England played brilliantly but slid out of the World Cup on penalties after extra time. It was so near and yet so far. The TV shots of the disconsolate players and ultimately Gazza's tears were some of the key images of the year.

Those damn tears were the most idiotically poignant symbol of the brave new world of football. The goofy maverick mid-fielder blubbed after picking up a booking that would have ruled him out of the potential final. Football at last had a human face. Hard-assed men across the nation moistened their eyes along with Gascoigne. Football had another front page and a new hero – and it wasn't a violence story but a fat bloke blubbing, a giant baby in tears. Bizarrely enough it made the sport hip. Football wasn't rampaging yobs any more, it was Pavarotti wailing out opera – or in this case Gazza wailing out.

It opened up the market to the lad revival as everyone seemed to rediscover their long lost love of the game. The defeat by Germany hardly dampened the new enthusiasm for the game. It had made it hip, even chic. The weeks of the World Cup had seen people talking football in a way that they hadn't for years. People rediscovered their love of the game. In the following years the middle classes started to drift back.

The stage was set for a mass revival and with a few more factors the game was about to go big bucks.

The sport suddenly found itself marketable, It was no longer the last refuge of the pissed-up yob, there was a craving for it. The TV rights for the sport were up for grabs and they were getting sold for a lot more money.

The big clubs sniffed the wedge. TV meant big money and it was going to have a profound effect on the game.

As Adam Brown, a football expert from Manchester University social research panel, says: 'The big five clubs and especially Martin Edwards' Manchester United and David Dunn's Arsenal started to push for the creation of the Premier League. It was set up primarily to get all the TV rights. Alex Finn who did the consolatory job on the project said that the sport was not making the most of what it had got.'

It was a key moment in the brave new world of football. The Premier League broke away from the Football League, the organization that had been set up from the game's original days. The clubs in the new Premier League could keep all the TV money to themselves. They no longer had to share it out with the smaller clubs.

The Premier League spearheaded football's social shift. Fans were now coming from, in the cynical parlance of the marketing man, the A and B social classes instead of the Cs and Ds. In other words the working man's game was getting posh. This also meant another interesting twist, as Brown points out.

'The audience for football is getting older. As it becomes more money orientated it's becoming a sport for the moneyed in their thirties; there are a lot less teenagers at the games now than there used to be.'

Just like everywhere else the rich were going to get a damn sight richer and the poor were going to really suffer for it.

Behind the scenes was the nascent cable channel, Sky, set up by Aussie media mogul Rupert Murdoch who saw sport and primarily football as the main route to global media profits and influence. It was inevitable that he was going to get involved in the brave new world of football.

The Premier League picked up the Sky contract in 1992.

They had hit pay dirt.

The football revolution in the UK was now moving at an incredible pace. Within three years it had gone from the marginalization of the eighties to being a superslick product packaged for the Murdoch era. In Europe things were changing too but not as fast. Berlusconi at AC Milan had been pushing for the reformation of the European Cup. Instead of a straight knockout competition, the plan was for the second round to be turned into mini leagues. It was the prelude to a planned European Super League. It was a way of maximizing profits. It wasn't the only rule change that Berlusconi planned, as Adam Brown explains.

'He was up for the mini leagues because, as he said at the time, "It was inconceivable for a club like AC Milan to get knocked out of the cup. It just wasn't modern thinking."'

Moves like this will institutionalize success. Many of the big clubs feel that they should have an atomic place in the Super League, negating the fact that they have to win the championship, which would suit a team like AC Milan whose 1999 form saw them out of the championship race.

Perhaps the game would be more honest if it just gave the championship to the richest club. It would save a lot of pissing about.

With football going big business, big business methods were soon going to be employed in the running of the sport. Clubs floated themselves on the Stock Exchange, forming PLCs, raising millions of pounds.

Clubs like Manchester United were finding themselves climbing into bed with some unlikely bedfellows. The club's shares were now split 16 per cent for the board, 23 per cent small shareholders and the rest were big investors that most fans would never have heard of like Phillips & Drew, the pension fund organization and not the sort of people ever to be seen on the old Stretford End.

When you sell your soul to the (red) devil it comes at a price. The new breed of money men in football were seeking a payoff. TV was bringing in piles of ackers. The companies wanted to make sure that their investments were going to work. Cash could be squeezed from putting the entrance prices up (at the start of the nineties a season ticket at Man U was £75 and at the end of the decade it was £350) and having a new strip every year or even every six months at a vastly inflated price meant more money for the coffers.

Merchandising was one of the biggest earners for the nineties super club, with a quarter of the clubs' profits expected from that source. TV may have been calling the shots but it is only worth 20 per cent of the clubs' income while the newly inflated ticket prices were pulling in the rest of the money.

In the nineties, squeezing every last penny from the fan was tantamount. Preying on the loyalty of the supporter was the name of the game. Clubs built superstores at their grounds selling heaps of tat decked out in the club colours and it sold by the bucket load. The nation's high streets were full of wobbling lager-swilling people who had never run more than ten metres in their lives stuffed into their favourite club's latest shirts.

It was claimed that the only people gullible enough to buy the kits were kids but 85 per cent of the shirts were sold to adults. Money-making had never seemed so easy.

And the fans kept coming. Football was on a roll. People just couldn't get enough of the new product. The higher the prices went the more people wanted to squeeze in. The all-seater stadiums had dented the capacities of clubs but new schemes saw many of the bigger clubs expanding their stadiums and a lot of the smaller clubs downsizing, perhaps realizing that in the new world of football, where money talks, they would never get into the Premier League.

The money men, though, still see TV as the game's real future and with the box dictating when matches can be played (it was behind the switch to Sunday football) they see the whole future of the game geared towards the telly. And football makes for sexy TV: it has drama and excitement and it means something to people's lives, but the further it is removed from the clutches of the true fan, the less of a great spectacle it will become on television. As the stadiums lose atmosphere the spectacle will gradually be reduced, and as the money men keep pushing for what they see as the big European games, the more disassociated the fans will become.

Football thrives on local rivalries and the public only get interested in the European competitions in the later stages. The biggest scalp is still over local rivals – some European matches have no atmosphere and, what's worse, no crowd.

Attempts to broaden football's base with the Euro glamour matches may be falling on deaf ears, as Adam Brown explains.

'What the bosses don't seem to realize is that most of the people who watch football on the TV are the people who go to the matches as well. The grass-roots supporter fears that the men at the top of the sport have learnt to turn it into a soulless spectacle like Grand Prix racing where there is no fan rivalry, just the spectacle pure and simple. No feeling but plenty of profits to be channelled from the game.'

The situation is spiralling out of control. Football is heading for the 21st century fast. It embraces new technology and new money, TV rights and Websites, big money deals, incredible transfer fees, competitions rigged to keep the big money clubs at the top, fewer and fewer teams winning stuff (just check the double in this country, once a rarity it's becoming the norm. In 1999 Manchester United waltzed to the treble, adding the European Cup to the domestic double, a feat that would have been unimaginable in years gone by). European and world leagues are in the pipeline. The sport, for so long the working man's traditional Saturday down the park outlet, has now detached itself from its roots and, despite the complaints of individuals like Brown, it's going to be the big money boys who win. After all, it's always been a business – it's just that now the business has gone into hyperdrive.

And for the radical fans, the ones who still want to stay grounded with their club, it's becoming too much.

The whole debate hit a new level in early 1999 with the Sky attempt to buy out Man United. Owning the TV rights is one thing but owning the best-supported club in the country is another. People like Brown feared that the amount of control that Murdoch would have had in the game would have been way too much. 'He' was looking at the emerging Far East market. Places like China and Thailand, places where he could sell his satellite dishes, and 'he' was using football and Man United as the battering ram.

They could have done all sorts of crazy things, like change the times of the matches to suit the new audience. It could have ended up being a ridiculous situation. But when did the people running football clubs ever take the best wishes of their fans to their mean hearts, or were they always just looking for a quick buck? Martin Edwards at Man United has attempted to sell the club on several occasions, once to Michael Knighton, a football fanatic way out of his depth in the world of superclubs who almost managed to buy the club at an outrageous knock-down price. In the Sky scheme of things the only way you could have seen Man United would have been by paying up front and watching it on a TV channel owned by the boss of the club.

The attempted Sky takeover of Manchester United provoked an outcry among the fans, who campaigned intensely against it. And with some success. The government blocked the takeover and Man United still remains in the hands of long-time chairman Martin Edwards. One nil to the fans! But it can only be a matter of time before the big takeovers kick in.

British football is a worldwide concern. You can walk the streets of Thailand and check out the British football shirts. You can sit in a bar in Africa and watch English league matches as a Man United fan in Zimbabwe Dr Alastair Robb (a relative of mine) describes via email.

'When Manchester United play the bar is packed, everyone's got their shirts on. The night of the European cup final the place went mental . . .'

Adam Brown takes a look at the fans' quandary. The love of the club that's basically ripping them off is one hell of a predicament!

'You can't "go underground" in football. In music you can release tracks on the Internet, take on the record companies like [Public Enemy's] Chuck D has. Football's underground is going to the match. Smaller clubs have more fan power like at Northampton Town. When they were bailed out by the local council they insisted that they put a supporter on the board. And this was not as a token gesture like a similar scheme at Man City. They had direct access to all information at the club.'

It's a new era and an era for clubs with an attitude vicious enough to take advantage of the new wealth: Man U have been at the forefront of the merchandise and TV moolah, making themselves hated in the process but also paradoxically becoming the best-supported club in the UK. In 1999 you can sit in a pub in Cornwall watching United on TV with fans decked out in the club's over-priced merchandise, their loyalty to the club as fierce as any Manchester Red but none of them has even been north of Birmingham let alone to Old Trafford. Local rivalries, though, are still intense. But even that is changing now: with Man U seen as the big rivals to most premiership clubs, the visit of the club takes on a fierce, almost derby match-like proportion in the new borderless world of football support.

Alongside United, the clubs that are making big strides in the new scheme of things are London sides Arsenal and Chelsea. Taking advantage of all that money sloshing around in London and the south, they were always going to benefit from the new moolah-mad world of football. In contrast, Liverpool, the giants of the domestic scene in the eighties despite having the second largest support in the country, seem to be falling behind in the superclub stakes. Adam Brown wonders if, perhaps, they are not quite ruthless enough to survive in the new world of soccer.

'Maybe the rise of Manchester in fashion and music as well as the football has helped to eclipse Liverpool. The club's ownership hasn't changed, I mean that's a good thing. It gives them a sense of tradition, like Everton, another potentially massive club. They're both definitely both falling behind.'

Football is now a world away from the actual elements that make/made the game work, the huge grass-roots support that is still there in love with the basic simplicity of the game. These are fans that pay through the nose for the privilege of supporting their team; they are the ones paying the joke wages of the superstar players, because in the brave new world of football the players have all the best cards. After the Bosman ruling the players grabbed a big slice of cake for themselves. Post Bosman a player who is out of contract can walk out of the club for nothing – his new club doesn't have to pay a fee for him. For small clubs it was a disaster: what's the point of nurturing local talent when a big club can just get the player free when his contract runs out? It gave the players ultimate power: the clubs, desperate to keep their stars, have cranked up the wages and it's going out of control. Players can earn up to £60,000 a week for playing football while other people in our society can be starving. This is a sure sign of a fucked-up society.

Despite all this football as a product, as a game it's far better than it's ever been before, pulling itself up by the bootstraps, coming to terms with new-millennium technology and media. The money in the game has made it flash. It has become a spectacle – and an engrossing one at that.

Not since the chariot races in ancient Rome has Europe seen such great and intense sport!

CHAPTER FORTY-ONE

FROM LO FI TO SCI-FI: HOW THE UNDERGROUND SURVIVED AND PROSPERED IN THE NINETIES

Underground overground wombling free . . . Post the big bang of 1989, indie music was left with two stark choices: it could either go overground into the stadium scene or it could retreat back into its bunker. Some bands opted for the big league while others found solace in the world of lo fi, a clandestine, fiercely independent world of uncompromising music . . .

Geeks, nerds, freaks and fanatics . . .

When Nirvana burst out big and turned the label that they were on, Subpop, into a multimillion-dollar operation with their back catalogue, they kicked off an undignified major label scramble for the scalps of the leftover bands. It looked like the days of the underground were over.

Even now in the late nineties the corporations are very much in control. Initial cheers about the underground's going mainstream have been met with a deep gloom about the state of the indie nation, as Luke Haines, the Auteurs' frontman, starkly notes:

'One of the key things about the nineties has been the loss of indie labels large and small. The whole music scene is now a lot more careerist than when I started. Bands have five-year plans and the stakes are a lot higher. People are looking for their pension plans out of music. Obviously times change but the stranglehold of corporate labels makes it difficult to get forthright opinion across.'

Haines may be correct in painting the general picture of corporate greed stifling the cutting edge that makes for great art action. But there has been plenty of freaky stuff and plain weirdness on the fringes of the music scene.

The key trait of the nineties underground was the struggle to come to terms with technology, either embracing it or ignoring it completely. While some groups moved on to raw lo fi, keeping it real with analogue recorded guitar workouts, others embraced sample culture . . . some even fused the two into a combustible whole. It was a fascinating struggle between musician and the machine. Some of the best records were made by mavericks who didn't have a clue what they were doing with their samplers and Cu base. Attempting to make a drum and bass record, they came up with something utterly different.

In the purist guitar scene post Nirvana, rawness was on the agenda. Trying to strip away the gloss of eighties rock and get to the real raw roots of the guitar, bass and drums was the battle plan. Producers like Steve Albini became key figures in getting the sound of a band as it really was down on to tape.

Instead of using the studio effects Albini would get his sounds from careful mic placement, utilizing the studio's ambience to get the reverb for the drums and using ancient mics for their clarity and warmth. Armed with a reputation for grabbing hard as fuck sound with his band Big Black the vociferous Albini arrived with his own stark agenda. His big breakthrough came with The Pixies' *Surfer Rosa* album.

It was a key record for Albini as it captured his keen ear and idiosyncratic way of capturing sound for an emergent college radio generation. It also caught the crucial extremes of The Pixies' sound – the stop start explosions of noise and melody, the quiet verse and full-on raging chorus that would go on to influence Nirvana and a whole huge school of emergent alternative rock outfits that would form the bedrock of the nineties' alternative rock scene.

If the underground had gone mainstream, it had gone there screaming and kicking. When Nirvana broke big, the whole geography of rock 'n' roll had been changed. Opinions had to be re-evaluated. Fringe bands were now big bucks. The freaks were in the stadiums and all sorts of possibilities were being uncovered.

The whole spirit of independence was called into question as the big boys swallowed up a culture whole and the underground seemed to disappear overnight. The small labels that had been struggling along in the eighties collapsed.

It was time to get organized.

In the early nineties underground vacuum, it looked like inventive music was going to be destroyed by its own success. Quickly assimilated into the mainstream, the quirky were now being told how to play their own music. Major labels had their own versions of indie labels, like indie vanity labels.

Thank God there are those wild-hearted spirits who are not prepared to play the game, a game that was going to take a few twists and turns throughout the decade.

One of the key factors in the new musics was the availability of cheap technology. While guitar heads were mastering four-track recorders in their bedrooms, the fallout of acid house had thrown up the same sort of home-based possibilities. Samplers combined with Cu base and computers made a whole mess of possibilities available. You could put together incredible soundscapes in your back room.

When the indie heads, the guitar freaks and the new dance generation combined, the options were endless.

Lawrence who runs the key Domino label (releasing stuff from the likes of Pavement and Sebedoh), puts it all neatly into perspective.

'To me, the two most interesting things in the nineties were the DIY-flavoured guitar music or what is more badly termed lo fi or kids in bedrooms with samplers rejecting staid studio technology. The meltdown between the two styles has created some great music. That's what I'm interested in . . . the places where the boundaries get blurred.'

Gary Walker, who runs the Wiiija label (Cornershop, Bis, Huggy Bear, Brassy), says, 'Electronic music allows you to work under lots of different personas. It frees you up from the rigours of the band thing.

'When Wiiija started it was known for its heavy-duty noise shit. Groups like Bastard Kestrel and Terminal Cheese Cake cranking up incredible dense sonic landscapes. In the late nineties we find Wiiija with a No. 1 record from Cornershop, and a stable of groups that ranges from the chunky pop of Brassy to pure teen pop of Bis. It tells the story of how the expectations and the sheer sound of underground music has changed in the decade.

'The crunch point for me was in 1995 when Cornershop's *Woman's Gotta Have It* album was picked up by David Byrne's Luaka Bop label. Wiiija moved distributors from Rough Trade to Beggars Banquet and I took the label over instead of just working for it.

That was the point when the label changed.'

Gary sees the underground coming to terms with the real world with some key acts embracing the showbiz ethic while keeping their music raw and cutting edge.

'People like Jon Spencer now put on a great rock 'n' roll show. It's not wilfully non-populist any more. Bands are not so scared of success.'

From a cred history releasing Bikini Kill and Silverfish's noisenik excursions to a post-mid-nineties almost pop Wiiija, it's been a long and strange decade. It's a process that Walker fully embraces but with reservations:

'I want us to be accessible and be populist. I want these records on the radio. On the other hand the other side of me still feels alienated by the main pop audience.'

As Gary points out, lurking under the bright new shiny skin of indie crossover those dark hearts of oddness and alienation still beat. The music may have embraced new technology. It may be playing the pop game to a certain extent but there is still an outsider spirit involved in its creativity. And there is still that air of goofy elitism in its operation, as Gary sniffs:

'I worry that if it gets too big the music may lose its power and its meaning. I hate it when a band gets really big! I still have that sad attitude,' he laughs, struggling with the internal battle between realism and idealism. 'I want the label to be special . . .'

The new technology and the influence of sample-based break-beat culture from hip hop has shaken the scene. Applying maverick tendencies to the machine has made American Beck one of the key figures of the period. Landing perfectly in the middle of sample culture, trad guitars and indie lo fi spirit, his influence has touched many next generation bedroom popsters especially in the UK, as Lawrence from Domino has noticed.

'Sampling culture is a lot bigger over here in Britain than it is in America. Which is odd really because the States have got Beck and The Beastie Boys.'

Aaaah The Beastie Boys. Where once they represented beer-stained tomfoolery and a joyous yobbishness of all the best teen Brat pop, by the mid nineties they were cutting clever inventive records that were smartly self-indulgent and fascinatingly inventive. By indulging their own eclectic hipster tastes they had, ironically, gone supa nova. With their smartass raps and a superb collection of samples from seventies funk and soul records married to hardcore punk rushes and damn danceable hip hop breakbeats they cut a very nineties musical mish mash that was a full-on attractive proposition.

They became not only hip but huge, hitting No. 1 both sides of the Atlantic album charts. Their *License To Ill* album became a licence to make money.

Samplers kicked up a whole new set of possibilities for the lo fi songwriter. Instead of aping ancient riffs on barely learned fret-boards, you could sample a bunch of stuff and inspire your songwriting into another direction.

Lawrence positively enhances this new creative way.

'With bands like Sebedoh on my label, they find that they have a whole new inspiration for their songs. The loop is the starting point. Ten years ago bands like that would have been de-tuning their guitars to the key of Z like Sonic Youth . . .'

The underground never stops. Constantly fucking with the form, it throws up countless new bands all the time or just reclaims those that have been overlooked for a long time.

Bands that have struggled for years, ignored and left by the wayside, have suddenly been embraced. 1999 sees Mercury Rev and Flaming Lips, both bands who have been in existence for well over a decade cutting some great records, suddenly become critical raves.

In the late nineties lo fi deconstructed guitar music. The US has been the key to the artistic rush. Bands like Slint with their multi-textural guitar instrumentals have influenced masses of groups looking for a way out from the trad rock way of doing things, while Fugazi and Shellac and Sonic Youth utilized their punk energy in music that almost sounded like free jazz, throwing up possibilities and shapes all the time.

There was Tortoise's angular post rock and Pavement's poppy take on the dislocated college rock guitar pop. In the new-look world of indiedom it's quite possible for the bands to have hits. Unlike the scaredy cats of the eighties these bands can crossover, and crossover they do.

'Sebedoh was great on *Top Of The Pops*. The next generation of 14 year olds can see that there is an alternative way of making music and pick up their guitars and samplers and keep the whole thing going . . .'

The underground debate continues . . .

CHAPTER FORTY-TWO

PETE WATERMAN: POP GENIUS

Disco Pete, the great Satan of the music press-chomping, furrowed-browed, indie crew, the antichrist of the beer-stained Uni boys, the hoofed destroyer of pop music to the obsessive guitar freak, is, perhaps, the one true pop genius of modern times. And he comes armed with a fistful of infuriating pop nursery rhymes.

Oasis v. Blur, that's small fry, mate. The real pop prodigy of recent pop has got to be Pete Waterman, who has scored a whole stack of No. 1 singles and albums in the '80s and '90s.

Being Pete Waterman means knowing just how low to go. It's having the gut feeling for just what sort of pop the great British people really like. Waterman has the knowledge! He realizes just what schlock the great British public dig. It's not beautiful but it's B.I.G. BIG. Years of working in the music business A&R-ing and DJ-ing have given him an intuitive understanding of what moves the public.

Not only that: it's having the nerve to follow through with the sort of ideas that most hip hustlers on the scene wouldn't have the guts to entertain. Waterman is also one of the few people who could claim to be 'doing it for the kids'. Not for him the trad star system. Disco Pete has the knack of making goofy nerds into pop stars.

This guy has to be a genius if he can sell us the likes of Rick Astley, Sonia and The Reynolds Girls. Yup, Waterman has taken the buck-toothed no-marks off the streets and made them rich. It's a part of his whole ethic, as he was keen to point out to me at the beginning of the nineties.

'I believe everybody has the right to be a star, and the press never believed that. They could never forgive me for giving normal people the chance to have a No. 1 record.'

That's Pete the populist for you . . . knowing what makes Joe Normal tick is one hell of a qualification and making Joe Normal into a star is something else. Maybe it's coming from Warrington (the same place as another man of the people, Chris Evans), a nowhere town between Manchester and Liverpool, which has given him a grip on the real world. On the other hand, collecting rare fish and steam trains makes him as eccentric as anyone else who is doshed up in the pop world. He talks non-stop, mixing a boyish pop enthusiasm with a tough northern edge. He looks like your golf-playing uncle, is opinionated, brass and crass, blunt and on the ball. He listens to what goes on around him in the constantly fluctuating world of pop and continues with his own vision of how pop should be.

Pundits thought that they had got rid of the Hitman after his phenomenal run of success in the eighties. But he's back, bigger than ever in the late nineties, with the goonish Steps, a group so flat-footed and awful that only a pop genius could have designed them and got away with it.

They are the classic buck-toothed, smiley-smiley, too pretty pap that passes for mainstream pop in the year of teen scream, 1999. The whole idea of them is so outrageously naff that only someone with an iron nerve could have pushed them through.

They are also a stroke of musical genius. It takes someone who understands how to pull the little levers of pop to understand what the kids (and we're talking about real kids here) really want. Steps prance around at their gigs and six year olds squeal with delight. It's like taking the sweetie money off children. It's pop bullying! A whole new market gives up their pocket money.

It was The Spice Girls who opened up this previously untapped malarkey in the mid nineties. The Spicies tapped into the post-baby pre-teen market, dropping the average age of the pop fan by about ten years. It was the great forgotten marketplace. Sure enough five-year-olds had been into pop before – thinking The Beatles were cuddly toys or believing that Boy George was some sort of rag doll – but this time they were buying into the pop myth just like everyone else. In the wake of The Spice Girls there has been a whole army of gurning pretenders and into this pop void have stepped STEPS.

They play their gigs like cheerleaders stomping around the crèche. A review of one of their gigs reported that before the gig the stage screens flashed 'Are you ready to scream!' milking the kiddie squeals, and then almost laughably underlining just how young this audience is: 'Have you been to the toilet!' Whether they made this up or not is beside the point. It neatly encapsulates just who and what pop is about in 1999.

What makes something as naff as Steps succeed? Creating a band like Steps is like creating pop by numbers. They are bright and shiny, goofy and innocent in that cynical nineties way. They are also an alchemy of classic moments melted into one pop goo. Take the melodies and harmonies of primetime Abba and meld them to a simpleton karaoke house beat, lob in a couple of *de rigueur* Bee Gees covers and you've got prime pop product late-nineties style.

The band is a hotch potch of current pop action.

A rough guide to naff without the irony.

Critics complain that the band is a fake that they are not, 'real'. It's like someone sat down and looked at the pop scene and saw the dominance of girl groups and boy groups and came up with the incredible scheme to put a group together of boys and girls. It's so simple, it's laughable!

So what if Steps are manufactured? All pop is manufactured – from Noel Gallagher superimposing his 'rock 'n' roll master plan' on to his kid brother's scruffy mates, to Malcolm McLaren's meddling with the already raw and exciting young Pistols, to Brian Epstein's dressing The Beatles in their collarless suits, to Blur's casual coercing of current cutting-edge trends into their sharp pop mix. Pop is manipulative. It always has been. It's just that some people are better at disguising it than others.

And some don't care what you fucking well think anyway.

Waterman is laughing his way to the bank. Affable and opinionated, he's heard all the criticism before. He knows the industry and the media will never understand, let alone love what he's trying to do, and yet, in the oddest way, he's been hipper than the smartasses all along.

'I was a DJ for years and I worked for Motown – the press at the time, papers like NME, used to call it Toytown. When I DJ'd on the Poly circuit, the students wanted me to play Spooky Tooth and

Velvet Underground. Things don't change. Nowadays, of course, Motown is hip.'

It was this background on the decks that gave him the crucial understanding of the pop heartbeat . . . the dance floor. Being a DJ, as we have found out in the nineties, is an excellent way of getting the pulse of the nation. There can be no better test of a record than dropping the needle on it and seeing if people connect. Unlike guitar music that is sold on lifestyle and heavy-duty marketing, dance music has to kick on the dance floor. That's its only test. If you can't dance to it then it doesn't work. It's a lesson that was learnt by the Hitman.

'I can spot a hit. It comes from being a DJ years ago. I know what gets people going. I get a buzz off records: one of the problems with the media thing is that people have great press agents and build up a great image, but the records are crap.'

With Steps there is an element of both sides of the marketing coin. The tunes are pumped with a kiddie disco beat that can make the five year olds sway around and the group's lifestyle is sold as a chummy innocuousness that the parents won't mind having spoonfed to their spoilt brats.

Their success pisses off the purists but Disco Pete is the man who don't give a fuck.

For ever the outsider, Waterman relishes his maverick status in the music business. 'They hate it when an outsider has 12 per cent of the market off his own back', he told me back in 1992.

His brushes with pop authority come thick and fast. Like fellow maverick Jonathan King he is one of those figures that the trainspotter loves to hate and is always ready to get embroiled in controversy. His most recent run in with the 'good taste' crowd came when Glasgow lo fi heroes Belle and Sebastian pulled off the scam of the year and got their big fan base to vote them to best new band position at The Brit awards. The second place band, by a handful of votes, was . . . Steps.

Waterman was not pleased. He kicked up one holy row. An argument that was negated when the statistics were checked. The *Sun* newspaper then ran their own poll and Steps crushed Belle and Sebastian. I guess that wasn't the point. Belle and Sebastian had managed to get one over the music biz: surely that should have amused the self-styled outsider. But then this is a man who hasn't got much time for the whiney world of indie, preferring a broad palate of pop but a pop that is about the song as opposed to the lifestyle hard sell which dominates indie music.

Perhaps the argument made him look far more of an establishment figure than he would like to admit but Waterman still feels like he's on the fringes of the music scene.

Unloved, unthanked and pretty damned successful, Waterman is a man who has spent his life wallowing in pop. His actual tastes run far and wide and he's been the shadowy producer behind the most unlikely of bands.

'I've been involved with everything across the sphere of music, from the first reggae hits . . . right across the board. I don't pigeonhole what I like. People forget that I was the man behind The Specials . . .'

Spotting your author's jaw drop, he picks up the tale:

'I was living in Coventry at the turn of the seventies and I was walking past this pub and I heard this great music coming out of the windows. I walked in and it was The Specials. They were broke, so I gave them the money to put out their first single. People don't remember that, they just remember me for Sonia and Jason. They give me the blame. Fair enough. I'm not going to say that some of these records are the greatest records ever made but they are good pop. Pop is wonderful all the way across the board, Johnny Mathis, Steely Dan . . . The Beatles and The Stranglers who I consider to be the greatest British pop group since The Beatles . . . loads of stuff.'

Waterman is pop through and through. He's in love with the showbiz side of it.

'I love camp. I'm as camp as a row of tents. Pop shouldn't take itself too seriously. It should be fun. It shouldn't worry about life. Life needs a fairground. I'm not saying that there shouldn't be space for more serious things, you've got to be aware of poverty and politics to balance things, but you do need a bit of candy floss in your life.'

The king of candyfloss stares – his intensity and self-belief burning through his glasses. This self-made man who has an innate understanding of pop is the one true popular culture genius of our times.

Now for fuck's sake can you turn off that Steps record!

CHAPTER FORTY-THREE

STADIUM INDIE

From small-time outsiders to selling out stadiums, the rise of indie music has been one of the key successes of the decade. It's been a fierce and frantic rise for bands like Oasis, The Verve and Radiohead . . .

So-called indie music used to be the stuff of the Dog And Bucket. Back rooms of pubs, crap PAs and tiny fiercely partisan crowds. The 'big' groups would always get to No. 41 in the charts and that was it.

In the eighties, pre Manchester indie music was strictly small time.

Now 'indie' (isn't that the worst term for music ever . . . rock 'n' roll means fucking, punk at least sounds naughty, heavy metal perfectly captures the form, but 'indie' – it's so nothing, so meaningless) is strictly big time.

Indie bands roll into town playing the big stadia, the huge venues that have been built in the nineties to accommodate the boom in large-scale events, these are venues that laugh at the notion that pop is dead. Packed out with punters, it seems like an endless procession of bands can stuff these places out.

The big-time stadium indie bands of the nineties nearly always rely on the same soundtrack. It seems as though to fill the big 'dromes', you've got to go miserable, tap into the dark undertow of the decade, the suburban sadness. As the indie bands crossed over they slowed down. The music that had once been frenetic and fast became moody and anthemic, looking into the dark heart of rock 'n' roll and fusing it with songs you could whistle while you were cleaning your car on suburban Sunday afternoons.

Selling misery to the masses, stadium indie has been a key feature of the decade, tapping into the melancholic undertow of the times. With mournful tunes and minor key melodies. Songs of desolation and rejection, of confusion, alienation and angst.

All very stirring stuff.

Some see the post Britpop stadium as a great sound track, 'proper music' to get lost in. Some see it as the devil's work and some see it as a moment in time when pop is treading water.

Factory MD and media man Tony Wilson puts it quite succinctly.

'Radiohead and the Manics, that type of music, I call it the dead generation. It's boring. I went to a Verve gig at The Academy. I mean, I like their songs but I couldn't help feeling that the audience, this Radiohead generation, that this lot are ripe to be blown away when the next thing happens. The next cycle. It's like the music scene before punk . . .'

It's a good argument. Rock will always settle down into this big bloated emptiness. Its natural state. It's been here before. Only this time the actual soundtrack is better. Gimme the now disbanded The Verve any day over Simple Minds or Genesis. I can perfectly well understand Wilson's disdain though. There is something rather, well, boring about stadium gigs. On one level it's a celebration of rock community and on the other it's a cunning way to fleece you of every penny. Some bands have the charisma to pull the thing off and some look like a bunch of boring blokes moaning about their dullard lives through massive PAs. Statements of big. Selling stadium misery to the masses.

It's a loose confederacy of bands who have little to do with each other apart from the stadium statement. You can mood swing from The Manics' searing laments to The Verve's melancholic pop, from The Stereophonics' small-town drama landscapes to Radiohead's studied middle-class angst.

All that links them is the fact that their gigs can only be seen on TV screens.

Touching on the moody currents of the nineties, the brooding millennial angst and turning it into best-selling albums . . . that's quite a trick! It's not a new trick but it's one that's beginning to flavour an awful lot of big-time post-indie rock.

*

It's been a trait of rock 'n' roll for years. From the heartfelt howl of the blues onwards. The happy-go-lucky sixties had been painted black by The Doors' dark poetry and The Stooges' garage-band cigarette burn on chest rock 'n' roll. In the seventies it veered into Pink Floyd's sombre neo-classical rock and their lesser contemporaries who attempted to create a dark scenario with their pompous prog. Troubadours like Nick Drake howled their merciless poetry in the fine singer-songwriter tradition of Bob Dylan and Leonard Cohen.

Post punk, Joy Division made the most convincing case yet for soundtracking a fucked-up mind, while everyone got miserable, dressed in black, and thought that we were all going to die in a nuclear war.

The nineties key guitar band The Stone Roses' deceptively light guitar melodies hinted at something darker and more troubled deep inside their glorious songs. And now the pre-millennial fear that stalks just beyond Tony Blair's endlessly grinning New Labour Cool Britannia has found a whole host of ready applicants prepared to fill stadia with their very personal angst.

The biggest of them all were The Verve – the Wigan band who had formed in the slipstream of The Roses and talked up a good fight. A massive breakthrough single, 'Bitter Sweet Symphony', had sent them into the big league. Their album didn't leave the Top Ten for months and they were selling out a huge hometown gig. After years of talking they had finally delivered.

Embrace were a four-piece from Bradford who by 1997 were coming through in The Verve's slipstream with some fast-talking self-aggrandising interviews. Loose talk costs lives and they managed to piss off Oasis with some excitable comments. However, they were also forging a very strong bond with a new fan base that wanted its guitar groups to prove their integrity with their misery. Doleful ballads and big melodies were touching the heart strings of six-string fiends across the UK.

Even the Manics had gone from firebrand punk rock fired outsiders to mournful stadia packers. By 1999 it seemed that nearly every ex-indie band you could think of was capable of selling out the newly constructed big local stadia with a fistful of anthems. Oasis had managed it with ease, Blur had pulled off big shows, Mansun had moody No. 1 albums without ever quite crossing over into the enormodromes, new bands like Marion were talked up excitedly as being 'stadium bands'. Such talk had nearly cost James their careers but they still went about selling the damn places out regardless, going from weird beard outsiders to effortlessly huge . . .

It was a big shift in what people demanded from pop. To sell out in the gig league, there was less of the bellowing U2-styled eighties anthems and more introverted songs played to massive crowds, personal feelings cranked up and played to masses of people in cold concrete stadiums. The flag wavers like Simple Minds had been pushed aside by mournful boys and their big sad songs . . .

Perhaps the most typical of all the nu stadium indie bands were Radiohead, a band that couldn't get any press at all when they started.

The only writer to give them the time of day was John Harris, then of *Sounds* now editor of *Select*.

'Radiohead are more of a pop group than a prog band . . . they are genuinely forward looking, there is no Beatles, Kinks baggage here. Their music has an immense dignity . . . It sounds like no one else . . . In the same way same as The Mondays, you couldn't tell what they sounded like . . .'

Radiohead had committed the early-nineties cardinal sin of signing to EMI instead of paying their indie dues – this meant no cred and no press. They also looked shit which didn't help. Left out of the early nineties rock zeitgeist they built up a big fan base in America, being one of those bands that works hard. They toured like fuck and gradually honed down their sound.

When they released *OK Computer* (1997, which went to No. 1) they suddenly went wham bam big time. It was even voted the 'greatest album of all time' in a *Q* magazine readers' poll in February 1998!

Perhaps their finest hour, *OK Computer* is a collection of chilling songs that are exquisitely produced. Their records are a collection of great guitar sounds, amazing chunks of six-string shrapnel exploding out of freaked dynamics, loud bits that contrast brilliantly with quiet bits, jagged soundscapes and highly distinctive crystalline vocals. Frontman Thom Yorke has the wiry intensity to embody the songs' explosive turbulence. However, the band were not just dealing out avant garde weirdness, these were really good pop songs fucked with by people too smart to play the dumb card.

Superbly played, superbly arranged clever rock, creating a new musical shape, Radiohead look like they will conquer the world in the new millennium.

They came, they saw, they conquered and then they fucked off. The Verve were the last major success of the baggy/Britpop generation. The post Stone Roses band with a fistful of classic rock riffs and a shapeless wardrobe. But they took it so much further. From the start they were dealing in something far more esoteric, far more freaked out than most of their contemporaries. The Verve were definitely looking at the stars and were getting their feet out of the gutter.

Frontman Richard Ashcroft has that rock star thing draped on his skinny shoulders. Tall, lank, long haired and with that Jagger gait he oozes the star swagger. And that's just offstage, put him on the boards and he's a bug eyed rock messiah throwing skeletal shapes that capture the freak rock the rest of the band are kicking up behind him.

Ashcroft's full on intensity and espousal of the great rock 'n' roll dream has seen him portrayed as a spaced out madman because he has dared to get lost in the majestic power of great music. In a too dull world where everything has to be dealt with a cautious irony, here is someone who actually feels something. In the early nineties this had him marked out as a loon – 'mad Richard' – but at the end of the decade its going to pay big dividends.

All they were trying to do from the start was to make music on the same sort of terms as the greats. With songs like 'Bittersweet Symphony' and 'The Drugs Don't Work' and the classic album 'Urban Hymns', their music was a wide-eyed attempt to reach for the supernova. By the time they disbanded in 1999, they had achieved massive cross-over success.

CHAPTER FORTY-FOUR

THE SUNDAY SOCIAL

The Heavenly Sunday Social was one of the key clubs of the decade. It helped to launch The Chemical Brothers into the big time, it put a full-on good-time party vibe back into the clubs. It also had a killer soundtrack that could only come from a gang of vinyl junkies who were the key figures behind the club.

Some say that the whole Big Beat ethic was spawned in its multi-musical styled, having it large, sprawling nights. It's a claim that the 'Socialists' shy away from, but with their eclectic mix of soul, rock 'n' roll, acid house and The Chemical Brothers' massive beats stomping the dance floor, a good case could be put forward that this was the club that helped to revolutionize late nineties' British pop music.

Sunday nights of reckless boozing, wild records, mad characters – The Sunday Social pissed on the creeping cool that was infecting mid-nineties club life. Inside it would be a wild rush of good times. People you hadn't seen for ages would loon out of the gloom, wandering around the cramped stairs of The Albany you would be barraged by the endless sonic assault of great records. The atmosphere was great. Talk yourself hoarse and act the goat, all notions of cool were out of the window, the club was no fashion statement (although, perversely it became one), it was just a great night out.

The whole ethos and idea behind the social came from the frantic post club back to your house routines of its prime movers Heavenly Records' Jeff Barrett, Martin Kelly, *Junior Boys Own*'s

Robin Turner and the two Chemical Brothers themselves. This was a pretty out of it pow wow between a bunch of good-time-seeking music fanatics with an in-depth knowledge of great pop music.

Robin picks up the story of the club's inception.

'I was a lowly press officer at Heavenly at the time doing press for stuff like Primal Scream and The Dust Brothers, as the Chemicals were then known. We would have these mad nights round Barrett's house after clubbing it where we would be sat putting on old records, stuff like The Mondays' 'Wrote For Luck', Love Unlimited, loads of different stuff, it was like a great party. Tom and Ed from The Chemicals would be there digging out really cool tunes, everyone would be sat there listening, asking what the fuck is this? not in a chin stroking rock reverential kinda way, more of a get legless and listen to great records sort of way, and one night I said we should do a club based on this . . .'

It was a great idea. Armed with these records and a genuine love and enthusiasm for what makes great upbeat records, they were on to a winner. They could also tap into a huge pool of friends. Heavenly Records is one of the nerve centres of British pop: they may not dominate the charts in quite the same way as Creation but via their press office, endless nights out and general bonhomie they have become central to many cool groups' lives. The potential for a bit of good time rumble was quite definitely there but Robin's idea for a club took a bit to catch on with his buddies.

'Jeff thought I'd gone too far with the idea but he quickly warmed to it and came up with the whole framework. Once he was on board, Jeff was crucially important. He booked the DJs, people like Andy Weatherall, Justin Robertson and David Holmes, blagging them for fifty quid. That's all we could afford! When the club took off it was easy getting guests. People were desperate to do it.'

Of course they also had an ace up their sleeves – the Dust Brothers were fast rising DJs with their own strong ideas of how music should sound. They were already getting gigs but their radical approach had seen them relegated to the dreaded back rooms of clubs. Robin could see that they were going to be a far more important proposition than that.

'I was listening to Tom and Ed DJ-ing in backrooms of clubs and I'd be there listening to them playing The Beastie Boys' "Sabotage" or Leftfield's remix of "Renegade Soundwave" or mad acid records, with everyone crammed into the backroom snorting amyl or jumping off speaker stacks. I thought, get this into a proper club, do a sort of residency . . . it would be like a logical progression . . .'

The Brothers' DJ sets at the time are the stuff of legend. They seemed to be armed with the best collection of breakbeat records in the land. Massive crunching beats that made techno suddenly look leaden and dull. Their sets at the Social would massively enhance their burgeoning reputation.

'Tom and Ed were really up for it. They would get tracks they were working on whilst they were recording *Exit Planet Dust* from the studio and try it out on the crowd. They'd work on stuff in the studio from Monday to Saturday and on Sunday bring DATS of new stuff. If people went for it they felt that it had worked . . . What they didn't realise was that everyone was so fucked up that any sort of critical power was out of the window.'

They decided to do the club on a Sunday – the dead night, the night when everybody moaned that there was nothing to do and they found a venue that was a long way from the flash club scenario that was dominating the nightlife scene.

'Martin came up with a venue, the Albany, it's now a Firkin pub. He'd seen the venue next door to the White Horse where he'd gone to see bands play. When it started we just told our mates and it took off from there. Jeff was a brilliant mouthpiece. In a few phone calls he got a hundred people to go. Tom and Ed had lots of mates come down . . . Everyone had their own set of people. . .'

The club was a massive success. People would travel all over the country to scramble into the Social. It quickly had its own coterie of celebrity subscribers, the new mid-nineties pop regime championed the place.

'Oasis and Weller turned up. The Stone Roses' Mani turned up before *Second Coming* had come out and everyone was asking him what it was like. At the time it was this legendary record that no one had ever heard. Mani was totally larger than life . . . There would be all sorts of people in there . . .'

The Sunday Social had its own flavour. There was no mellowed-out E vibe here or the harsh edge that coke gives to a club. Being on a Sunday there were different factors at play here, as Robin recalls.

'It was not a big drug club, it was a boozer club. Being on a Sunday meant that people couldn't get so cained. They've got to go to work and they are skint after the excess of the night before, so it was booze instead!'

When Tricky turned up to play a set the ensuing chaos captures the flavour of the place perfectly.

'We started off with David Holmes. He played first set of the night, all floor-shaking northern soul good-time tracks. It was engineered to keep the floor up, there was nothing specialist going on . . . David Holmes refused to go on after Tricky. We thought he would be amazing because of Massive Attack. The first two singles had come out, "Aftermath" and "Ponderosa", and they had blown everyone's minds. We all thought that he would be incredible. We expected a set of booming dub-styled stuff and him toasting over the top . . . What we actually got was like a mobile DJ being thrown down a long concrete staircase . . . he was playing tracks at the wrong speed, picking up the needle and dropping it down again, playing stuff like Jane's Addiction at the wrong speed . . . and it was incredible . . . pure genius!'

The Sunday Social inspired people to have a lot more than just a good time. Through The Chemicals the Sunday Social had a direct line to the Big Beat franchise.

'The Chemicals started to make these records . . . great records . . . People thought "I can do that", because the records sounded deceptively simple . . . You then got a hundred million bands with two decks and a sampler, but they can't do it.'

The people who knew what they were doing, though, really delivered.

'Norman Cook or the Skint People, Wall Of Sound, Jon Carter took it in a different direction. People like Richard Fearless have a much darker vibe. He's influenced by sixties garage, punk, reggae and Can . . . Carter's into reggae and bogle . . . and Norman Cook just makes great pop records . . .'

Some of the key names in late-nineties dance infused pop music and they were all cutting tunes in that eclectic Heavenly Social flavour. Fired by the club's riotous good time vibe you can easily pinpoint the birth of Big Beat to its up for it party vibe.

The Social was about as rock 'n' roll as clubbing got in the nineties.

CHAPTER FORTY-FIVE

R&B SWINGBEAT

Post Britpop, Swingbeat was everywhere. The style has peppered the charts in its own right. It infused most of the boy band hits and has become a pop staple. Its laid-back groove has become the late nineties mainstream pop sound, an urban sophistication, the soundtrack to the new bar culture, a designer pop for designer lifestyles . . .

Pumped endlessly out of hit factory studios in America, American outfits like TLC, TQ, Janet Jackson and key R&B producer Teddy Riley's Blackstreet are the harbingers of the form. It's a catchall phrase that captures a lot of different flavours, ranging from The Fugees' warm enveloping hip hop flavoured workouts to teen sensation Usher's catchy as fuck Spanish guitar lick driven 'You Make Me Wanna' No. 1 and from The Honeyz to Spice Mel B with her divine post Spice Girls joint smash with the talented Missy Elliot (whose career had been in the background writing and producing some well-known rap faces before launching her own solo career with the *Supa Dupa Fly* album) on the taut and sexy 'I Want You Back'.

Swingbeat is a form that has been adopted to most of the smoochy end of the pop market with UK boy bands like Another Level fusing the sound with their bump and grind balladeering. (In fact B&G, bump and grind would be a better term for the sexual chug of the form than the over-used R&B label which has now been attached to some pretty diverse types of music in the past forty years). Meanwhile East 17, returning as E17, picked up on the flavour to give themselves a more sophisticated adult sound.

R&B has become the pop soundtrack dominating the charts thanks to the full-on support of Radio One.

In the mid eighties the national pop radio station suddenly switched its allegiance to Britpop and guitar bands. There was a flurry of six string action in the charts, a whole gamut of big-selling bands and a buoyancy and confidence about home-grown pop. In 1997 new controller Jeff Smith decided to switch to the music that was already the key listening to the young urban teenager, R&B and swingbeat.

Suddenly radio pluggers who had enjoyed a golden period of a couple of years breaking a whole herd of great guitar pop acts were wringing their hands in misery. The key shows were now out of their hands, daytime radio was no longer Doc Marten or even training shoe, it was designer chic and swingbeat.

Ironic when Smith was the man who used to sell your author the meanest sounding punk records he could find out of his under-the-counter box in the local record shop of my teenage years, Cobweb records, in Cleveleys.

R&B has been around for most of the decade in one form or another. The precursor to the form is New Jack Swing, the late-eighties New York style fermented by vocalist producer Teddy Riley (credits include producing Heavy D, MC Hammer and recording hits with Kool Moe Dee).

Its roots lie in soul artists mixing a bit of hip hop in with their schtick, adding in samples and modern production techniques and updating the form. Sometimes it would be a breakbeat or rapped section. It gave soul an edge it had been lacking for years and, conversely, helped to tame the wild heart of hip hop. By 1999 it's become hard to tell most major hip hop or soul releases apart as they have become meshed together in the form.

The other big cheese in the scene's roots as well as in terms of shifting stacks of units was Sean 'Puff Daddy' Coombs who, as Puff Daddy, has found the lucrative middle ground market for his smoothed out hip hop. Breaking through into the major fat wad league, Coombs has also become a big-time producer behind the likes of TLC, Mary J. Blige, Boyz II Men and Mariah Carey. He had his own label, Bad Boy Entertainment, releasing big-selling hip hop and R&B acts like Craig Mack, Notorious B.I.G., Faith Evans and Total.

After his best mate the Notorious B.I.G. was gunned down, a

victim of the East Coast/West Coast rap wars, a shattered Coombs released his tribute 'Can't Nobody Hold Me Down', a eulogy to his dead friend that was a massive US smash. He followed this up with 'I'll Be Missing You', a reworking of The Police's 'Every Breath You Take', that was one of the biggest-selling singles of the decade.

With the music's very nineties dedication to money and full-on professionalism, Puff Daddy could well be the ultimate figurehead. Not only the creative powerhouse behind a stack of records, he is also a businessman par excellence, running his own affairs, keeping control of the operation.

It's the street law but run at the level of a corporation.

CHAPTER FORTY-SIX

ASIAN POP

A new confidence, a new pop music. For years Asian kids had been shoved to the edge of the pop scene but in the nineties they were putting together some of the hippest, most cutting-edge projects in the UK, helping to reshape pop. The outfits are mostly linked by their political edge, an edge that is forced on them by a Britain that still leaks the ugly poisonous stench of racism . . .

At the beginning of the decade I would interview Aki, the motivating force behind Fun Da Mental. His powerful political vision and outspoken views were a key part of the operation from the start. Aki, the former drummer from Southern Death Cult, was outspoken in his Moslem beliefs and anti-racist standpoint. An inspiring ball of energy, he had formed his own record label, Nation, and was organized enough to have created a big fuss for his non-mainstream outfit.

Heading for the breakthrough, Fun Da Mental split while shooting a video in Pakistan. One half of the outfit became De Tri Mental while Aki regrouped under the initial monicker. They have spent the rest of the nineties remaining true to their original vision and built up a massive following in Europe. In the summer of 1999 they were out on a rapturously received big venue tour of Russia and were a permanent slot on the Euro festival circuit.

It's strange that the Asian pop party has started in this country without them, but then prophets are never acknowledged on their home turf.

In the late nineties there is a whole plethora of Asian-rooted outfits cutting some great music and some of them are getting their tunes in the charts. Perhaps the highest profile are Cornershop. The outfit formed at Preston Poly in the mid nineties as an Anglo-Asian indie group inspired by Jesus and Mary Chain feedback pop.

They cut their first single under the monicker General Havoc. A typical one-off indie excursion into the studio, ragged rough, it had a flash of inspiration lurking inside its grooves.

Hooking up with local music fanatic Mark Waring, they changed their name to Cornershop, reversing the tired old cliché about Asian shopkeepers. Waring brought the idea over to my flat in Manchester. We worked out a bunch of press ideas including burning pictures of Morrissey on EMI's steps as a protest against the singer not explaining a couple of songs that could have been (hopefully) misconstrued as being racist.

Within weeks we had a raging letters war going on in the NME and the band a record deal with Wiiija. I cut my producing teeth on their first singles and then was ejected by the band as they switched and went for a more looped-up dance direction.

A direction that's suited them far better than the punk rock shots they were attempting in the first place. On the verge of splitting in 1997 they recorded the 'Brimful of Asha' which hit No. 65 in the charts before Norman Cook picked up on it, remixed it and turned it into one of the biggest selling singles of the year.

Cornershop's album, *When I Was Born For The Seventh Time*, is a great record. Stuffed full of gentle pop tunes, it's witty, eccentric and warped with funky little breakbeats. The record perfectly captures that mix 'n' match post Beck vibe and it turned vocalist Tjinder into an unlikely pop star.

Asian Dub Foundation coalesced all this seething action into one firebrand whole. Playing a series of incendiary gigs, the outfit formed in 1993 at a community music centre. They burned with a righteous indignation and allied it to powerful zigzagging beats. Their 1995 *Fact and Fictions* debut was a dub-drenched workout but with a full-on energized edge that hinted at drum and bass and ragga roots that were reflected in their songs. It also had a crucial political edge that made the record seethe with a barely containable anger. Their follow-up, *Rafi's Revenge*, contained the anthemic 'Free Saptal Ram', a song detailing a miscarriage of justice, as well as several other songs exploring the Anglo-Asian situation.

Live, the band are awesome: they can take apart a venue with their infectious beats and full-on energy. In France they are enormous and in their homeland of the UK they are on the verge of a breakthrough.

There is a whole host of associated outfits from the pop rap of The Kaliphz (whose mini hits don't go anywhere near reflecting what great raw street rappers they really are – a recent break-up may see some elements of the group reclaim their raw edge), Black Star Liner's multi-styled freakout and a whole host of eclectic action.

The Anglo-Asian scene (though barely a scene, more a series of isolated pockets of intense action) is one of the most creative and vociferous seams in today's music and proof of a new confidence in one of the UK constituent communities.

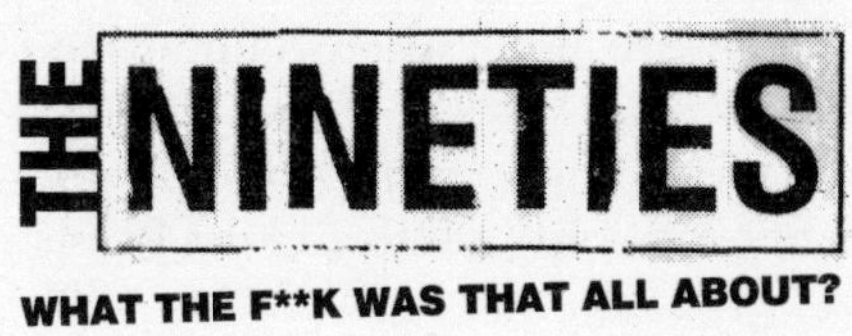

CHAPTER FORTY-SEVEN

THE PRINCE

As *Loaded*'s James Brown put it, the UK was sick of being a nation of losers represented by buffoons like Eddie The Eagle. In the nineties it was Sheffield-born Prince Naseem boxing his way to the big time and world championships who captured the spirit of the decade . . .

The air was thick with smoke and anticipation. You could cut the testosterone and the tension with a knife. In a Manchester city centre underground snooker joint I'm with the Mutoid man Brother Wayne checking the big fight. The Prince, the most sensational sporting hero of the decade, is taking on Kevin Kelly in a bid to retain his world championship belt and also to establish some credibility in the States, a place where he has been all but ignored so far.

In the complex world of nineties boxing there have been few heroes. Big money has seen the establishment of several championship belts. It's hard to define just who is the champ any more. Not that there is any doubt in the Prince's mind – the Sheffield-born boxer has been the world champion in his head since he was nine years old.

Boasting the same sort of swagger as primetime Muhammed Ali but with a tad less of the charm of the greatest, The Prince is none the less a charismatic and inspiring totem in a country too used to being on the losing end.

The snooker club was jammed, there were tough-looking dudes rattling their jewellery and girlfriends, mean-looking little guys with rat like faces arguing over plastic seats, sport heads, cool cats with razor-sharp hair, dealers, fuck-ups, hard bastards and boxing fans. There were also a whole lot of Asian kids who were as intense as fuck.

The Prince was a Muslim and from Yemen. He was hero to whole different sections of the UK. Boxing heads loved him, tired of watching big guys like Frank Bruno get turned into doleful punch bags. They had a grudging respect for Chris Eubank, a grudging respect which would go into overdrive in his last couple of bouts when he took a dreadful pounding but proved that he had the guts to back his proclamations. Now the Asian kids had a role model, at last. They had their very own superstar.

Being Asian had never been so hip: they had some of the coolest bands, the coolest clothes and their own definitive swagger.

And The Prince had taken the swagger on to a higher level. Before the fight he pouted and preened behind a screen, groin thrusting in silhouette and arms raised like he had already won the fight. It took a full ten minutes for him to appear from behind the screen. This was cockiness gone too far. Kevin Kelly stood in the ring, glowing, a bundle of steely hatred. Kelly was street tuff and showbizness wasn't his bag. He was a tough little slugger and you could see his shackles raised.

But The Prince wasn't show boating for the full ten minutes on purpose. The curtain had jammed and he was stuck posing!

The snooker club was boiling over. Even the rat guys arguing over the seats had shut up. They were digging The Prince's incredible cockiness. Instead of the usual humble sportsman crap about the other guy being a great fighter etc., The Prince had talked himself up and behind the screen he was showboating in a way that no British sportsman had done for ages – it was just the way that anyone in the room would have done it if they ever got the chance.

When Naseem hit the ring he oozed an animal confidence and the room erupted into a baying chant of his name. '. . .Naseeeeeem!' The two fighters glared at each other, Naseem was grinning and leering . . . it was cockiness versus pure hatred.

Ding ding the bell went and the Snooker Club crowd fell off their seats, 'fucking this and fucking that', they howled . . . the testosterone was going through the roof. 'He's going to kill 'im', they snarled. The Prince looked good, cocky . . . his guard was down but suddenly he was floored. You could cut the tension with a knife.

The room went silent. It was freeze framed. The guys were half out of their seats. The Prince staggered up, he was shaken. You could see the confidence drained out of his face. The fight recommenced. Naseem was no longer the cocky little brat on the block but was fighting for his career. In the seconds that followed he slowly regained his composure and the room started to relax. One good punch and Kelly was shaken. The room went crazy – the geezers were hugging each other. Three or four of them started to wrestle on the floor. There were shrieks of wild exhilaration.

Kelly then proceeded almost to deck The Prince. Twice more the room was getting tenser and tenser. I felt the sweat running down my back. But Brother Wayne just stood there and smirked.

The room was bog-eyed with tension. They had filled the snooker hall expecting their hero to walk this one. They had surfed on his extravagant optimism. They had been buzzing on his invincibility. Now there were home truths raining in with each of Kelly's punches. The Prince looked sheepish and he looked human and worst of all he looked like he could lose.

But the man pulled himself together, proving that despite all the talk he was also tough as fuck. He was getting the upper hand and with a flurry of punches he had won.

The snooker club went berserk. A couple of fights broke out. There was a whole heap of adrenalin-crazed fans rolling, wrestling on the floor, chairs were flying, grown men were crying and shrieking. It was a good job that he hadn't lost, muttered a bark-faced old guy as he slipped out the door.

The Prince had won and honour was restored.

Britain had a new hero.

CHAPTER FORTY-EIGHT

DANCE SUPERGROUPS

For years in the rock press there was always the tedious argument that dance music was too faceless to be of any interest. Despite the fact that rock was reeling, dance music was ignored.

A whole generation of kids who were either touched by the initial explosion or the second wave of the early nineties were bringing their own agendas to the genre. Because most of them were rooted in rock in their formative mid-teens period, they were quickly reinterpreting the electronic dance to their own agendas.

While Leftfield, growing up in the punk wars, brought the multi-styled experimental flavours of the post-punk fall out to their fab debut album, The Chemical Brothers cut massive hip hop grooves with an innate understanding of rock riffola. The Prodigy's Liam Howlett, growing up on a diet of hip hop and hard rock, fused the two somewhere inside the huge juggernaut of sound that is The Prodigy.

Underworld formed in the early nineties in Romford, Essex. The two key members, Karl Hide and Rick Smith, had previously been in a weird prog sort of band called Freur Juniors. Boys Own signed them up, releasing their 1993 breakthrough 'Mmm Skyscraper . . . I love You' which first hinted at their idiosyncratic approach to electronic music and was a dancefloor smash to boot.

In 1994 they put out their *Dubnobasswithmyhead* album that was hailed as a breakthrough in form. A multifarious combination of styles mashed in with the techno backing, it opened up a whole host of new possibilities in the music. It was the release of the

Trainspotting film that really broke Underworld big, with their 'Born Slippy' cut re-released in 1996 becoming one of the anthems of the year.

With this new added platform of commercial success boosting them up they took their music one step further with the *Second Toughest In The Infants* album which was also a major seller, marking them out as one of the key bands of the electronic forms of the nineties.

Post acid house, the very vehicle for dance music began to change. There were still the DJs and the engineers cutting tracks in studios and keeping a low profile and there were dance projects that evolved into fully fledged groups who went out on tours with big stage productions and light shows.

An early example of this new world was Manchester-based 808 State, who cut some great ground-breaking records at the turn of the eighties. 808 State's debut album still sounds as powerful today as when it was released a decade ago. Full of pile-driving keyboard driven riffs combined with dance rhythms, it was almost like a metal record. At one time they were so massive they sold out Manchester's 10,000 capacity GMex and played a kickass live show, which at the time was astonishing. Apart from Kraftwerk, hardly anyone had pulled off a show like this in almost purely electronic terms.

People like The Orb, whose ambient workouts were underpinned with a rumbling dub undertow, were miraculously dealing their late night comedowns in a live context. If they could get away with it then anyone could!

In their early days, Alex Patterson, a former roadie for post punks Killing Joke, was working with Jimmy Cauty who went on to put together KLF with Bill Drummond. In fact, the original plan was for The Orb to be released by the KLF's own imprint but there was a falling out and The Orb set out on their own path.

KLF are crucial in this story. They have been overlooked in the nineties, but at the beginning of the decade they released some massive records, great slabs of techno criss-crossed with metal pop ideas.

In one of their first ever interviews, Bill Drummond said: 'We are incredibly serious about what we do. Sometimes people think we are faking this, but we are serious. We are to some extent perfectionists-on the other hand if we can't do it fast then we get really bored. Most of the music is accidental. Often people think we are just trying to be clever . . .'

The Propellerheads released their first single in 1996 which was picked up and used by Adidas. A couple of hit records later and they were picked up by the Bond movie, scoring a hit for the soundtrack. Their follow up single 'History Repeating' featuring the divine Shirley Bassey was a massive hit and set their ground-breaking *Decks And Drums And Rocknoll* album.

The duo of Neil Barnes and Paul Daley, trading under the monicker of Leftfield, started their career as remixers before releasing their debut *Backlog* album in 1992. The album was a multi-styled multi-textured slab of post dance music. Leftfield, who had their roots back in the punk days, knew their music and were able to give their album a whole set of distinctive flavours.

Their 'Open Up' single with the former Sex Pistols vocalist John Lydon was their big breakthrough hit, described by many pundits as the best single of 1993. Leftfield's pummelling electronic backbeat was a perfect backdrop to Lydon's distinctive wail. Working with the vocalist was something that the band had always wanted to do, as they told me in an interview at the time.

'When I was a kid, when I was about 13, I hung around with Johnny Rotten, so we always knew him. His band after The Sex Pistols were a big influence on me . . . we wanted to do a track with him on the album and we were tying to track him down. By coincidence I was getting a train to Derby or somewhere and he was on the train, so that was where we sorted it out!'

The single was a massive hit and might have gone higher up the charts if it weren't for the chorus refrain of 'Burn Hollywood Burn' which was considered a touch sensitive due to the single being out at the time of the LA riots.

Their follow-up album, 1995's *Leftism*, set the scene for many of the electronic crossover outfits of the late nineties.

Taking their name from the M25, so central to acid house's myth, Orbital took the potentially stale live situation for ambient electronic music and pushed it into a real live scenario. Improvising instead of relying on backing tapes, the Hartnoll brothers threw an element of surprise into their music. Their four albums in the nineties explored all the possibilities presented by ambient music. An imaginative collage of sounds combined with a political subtext have given Orbital's music an edge that many contemporaries have lacked.

These groups were key to the development of house, taking it from its club-based DJ roots and into the live arena, pushing the boundaries of the music forward, cross-pollinating it with other styles and opening it up to the possibilities of the stadium rock world.

CHAPTER FORTY-NINE

AURAL SEX: DJS AS ROCK STARS

'For years I didn't need to go and see a band. I just went to where the good DJs were playing . . . that was enough for me,' remembers Ben Turner, editor of *Muzik*. 'I grew up with bands and I got into dance music through The Stone Roses and The Happy Mondays, but after Flowered Up disappeared I got massively into DJ culture and even now I would still rather go to a good DJ than a band.'

The rock musician so long central to pop culture was now superceded by 'a bloke who plays records'. It was a major cultural shift and the first change in the focus of attention since the guitar hero phenomenon in the sixties had stolen some of the lead singers' limelight . . .

For old school pop pundits the new pop politic was confusing. The DJ was hardly sexy. You couldn't really seem him (and as usual it was generally a him) and if you did it was generally a balding mid-thirties geezer. They didn't do interviews or have publicity shots. What the fuck was going on?

The totem of pop had changed: the lightning conductor was the DJ (far less hassle than the band), armed with a bag of records and (mostly) an incredible knowledge of how to mix the records with the decks. This was cut and paste culture on the frontline.

Post '88 the relentless message has been that the crowd is the star. It was Ian Brown's key message. It was the unspoken law of acid house and the DJ was the nerve centre.

In a culture where the music is all important, whoever is picking the tracks is the DON! And how much cooler can you get than dropping the track that blows everyone's minds? Or how flash can you get, seamlessly mixing the cuts into an endless whole, dovetailing your set so it builds and drops, pushing the crowd gently to climax.

It was aural sex!

CHAPTER FIFTY

TV TALK SHOWS

The new morality stalks the land. In a world where a president cowers before his people just because he got his cock sucked (and let's face it, what world leader doesn't have groupies?), there was a weird whiff of puritanism in the late nineties. TV talk shows, yer Springers etc., are just the equivalent of getting your head put in the stocks in medieval times. Instead of cabbages, it was abuse that was hurled at the hapless buffoon.

And the whole thing seemed so phoney that it was no surprise when some of the guests turned out to be fake after all. A very nineties thing, the talk show has become massively popular . . .

Jerry Springer is the Witchfinder General, galloping into town with his security henchmen. Dishing out morals to the US white trash. His show, which burst from the terrifying bowels of cable and on to terrestrial TV, first caught people's imagination with its legendary fight scenes. Like a medieval stocks, the programme humiliates anyone from pimps and drug dealers to people who haven't got themselves married off and settled down by the time they are 25 . . . in fact anyone who is deemed to have strayed beyond the vile moral code of post PC America. It's the new moral broom that has swept through the land, telling the people that they have been bad and they will not be redeeemd until they hang their heads in TV shame.

Springer stalks the room, prodding at the overfed freaks sat ripe for the slaughter in front of the baying crowd. The usual scenario is something pretty lightweight: some weasely-looking guy with a bumfluff 'tache and curly perm has been fucking one slab of lard and then has switched to her equally gross out sister.

The first sister is dragged out to the TV stocks and whines about the weasel. It was lurve but now he's run away with sister. Springer looks quizzical and then attempts to look concerned, his arms folded ready for the kill. Cue sista. The next slab of lard wobbles on to the set, spying her own (large amount of) flesh and blood she lays in with her fists. The pair of them have seconds to go for the kill, scratching each other's eyes out, hair flailing. It's like two walruses fighting for beach space. It could be a mean mutha of a fight except one of them is laughing.

The pair are pulled apart and the newly arrived sister spits out her hate for her kid sister and her love of the very shifty-looking weasel whose cocky face is being shown waiting in the wings in a cutaway.

When the weasel gets his cue he walks on to the stage and within seconds all three are fighting. They even throw on the mother for good measure. They argue, cuss and fight. It turns out that they all live in the same house and never fight at home, they save that humiliation for the TV.

The Witchfinder General sums up the show with a sanctimonious speech. It's dripping in that moral wank of the new puritan. Naughty, naughty, he scolds, the audience chant his name and the victims look confused . . . it's another day on the box . . .

The message of these Yank shows and the proliferation of piss-poor UK equivalents is: know your place. Middle-aged women who still dress up to go out are 'mutton dressed as lamb', the two-timing boy/grilfriend is a stud or a slapper, the man with too many tattoos and piercings is a freak of nature, the girlfriend who turns out to be transsexual makes the audience gasp with a stale shock . . .

Springer revolutionized the UK shows. Before him they were stuffy TV twilight zones: mid-morning valium half hours throughout which presenters struggled to stay awake. Post Springer they've all perked up with the same sort of format, except that no one starts fighting. While Kilroy was oozing his oily charm on one channel, Vanessa was ruling the roost on the other side. Astonishingly in her early thirties, Vanessa was the ice queen of ITV's mid-morning schedule. Her show cruised over the usual tittle-tattle of the form.

Flown in from Manchester, your correspondent was once on the *Vanessa* show as a pop pundit. Landing at Norwich Airport (amazingly Norwich has an airport) and getting whisked to the studio and wondering where the battle lines would be drawn in the TV debate, I was there to fend for Oasis at the height of their powers in the ongoing pub argument over whether they were as good as The Beatles.

I'd already run through this debate a fistful of times. Sticking your boot into The Beatles always made for great TV entertainment. I should know – this was about the fifth time I'd been asked to do it on various programmes around the country. The group who had been championless in the eighties had suddenly become a religion. No one could say anything against them. It's always excellent fun to sit in the hot seat and argue with whole audience whose idea of pop music began and ended with the loveable moptops. It had even ended up with a trip down to the Oxford Union and a locking of horns with Jonathan King in yet another Britpop-based row that ended up being debated in the *Guardian*'s question and answer page.

A good pop argument seems to piss people off more than anything. The *Vanessa* people wanted a certain line to be taken. They wanted me to say that I was Oasis's number one fan and to talk like some wide-eyedpoptastic schmuck. Not a fucking chance. There was a bit of a stand-off over the script and the word was that Vanessa wasn't happy and then it was with a hop, skip and jump that I bound on to the show and hit the spotlight running. Sticking up for Oasis was easy. They were in the middle of a run of great singles, their snotty attitude and yobbish stance were a perfect antidote to the too clean liars that always dominate the pop charts, the sort of creeps that claim to be whiter than white but crank as many drugs as the Burnage bruisers.

The *Vanessa* audience of late teens were the sort of terrifying squares that you would have hoped would have died out years ago. They were Thatcher's hellspawn . . . the too-clean squares who were growing away from the pop bohemian zone. Their righteous, priggish faces kept popping out of the crowd whining about Oasis and their drug usage, their mealy-mouthed behaviour or their indulging in the requisite rock 'n' roll carnage, 'it was giving the country a bad name', the punters moaned like the supercilious little brats that they were.

Now a message from your host . . . folks can you quieten down, the Witchfinder General has ten seconds to sum up.

'Watching too much TV can have an effect on an

impressionable mind. There are those out there who profit from these immoral shows, who profit from people who for some bizarre reason will come and talk about their most personal details on the programme, believing that it will make them solve their particular problems, and that I the wise host with the loudest mic will smooth things over in their messed up lives . . . What can I say, apart from . . . thank you suckers . . . and good evening!'

CHAPTER FIFTY-ONE

WHAM BAM THANK U GLAM!

Dressed to kill (quite literally in the case of the Marilyn Manson fans who took their guns to school) the nu glam has flourished at the end of the dressed-down decade. A loose confederecy of the goth revival tied in with the freak metal explosion and the glamour pusses of pop, the boys were starting to put their make-up back on . . . There was a whiff of decadence in the air . . . Glam was back . . .

In a decade dominated by dressing down or the combat pant you would have thought that there was little space for any kinda glam action. Thank fuck some of the skinny young dudes were ignoring the rule book.

I guess the key flag wavers for the she-boy smudged make-up look in the early nineties were The Manic Street Preachers and their fans. Their wanton street glamour meant so much more than the prissy eighties New Romantic school. This was a too pretty take on the punk rock chassis and it had been worn on the streets. Rock 'n' roll classicists to the man The Manics dreamt up their idea of the perfect rock 'n' roll band in their heads and then became it.

A fantasy band made real. At early gigs onlookers would cuss their 'gurly' looks, preferring their musicians to be a bit more he man. Or perhaps they were hooked on the 'authenticity trip' of dress down, you know – the US lo fi scruffy college-boy look. Or maybe they were digging the equation that if you have a beard you must be a genius. Take the sex out of rock 'n' roll and there isn't really an awful lot left.

The Manics inspired a coterie of fans, ghostlike panstick children draped in leopard skin and lace-dressing flash in the pouring rain, taking stick from the passing squares – I mean how British can you get, darlin'? When their totem, Richey Manic, disappeared in February 1995 the nu glam generation were paralysed, The Manics themselves could hardly continue along the same path and, although bass player Nicky Wire still applied the old warpaint for his glam casual crossover look, the band were more likely to be spotted in designer baggy.

I guess it's hard being flash when your best mate has disappeared.

However, once the make-up box had been opened there was no shutting it. Suede may not have got into the panstick but they were glam on the dole . . . you knew they had lived in the gutter but they had always looked up to the stars. The band were hooked into the Bowie myth . . . a skinny ribbed home counties decadence and a sexual ambiguity. Brett Anderson even had the Thin White Duke's vocal mannerisms twisted with the same sort of cockernee as early Adam Ant. Their luscious soundscapes were created by guitarist Bernard Butler and they retained a hard inner core from their pre-teen days of being punk rockers.

For a year they were the press darlings, ready with the media-friendly quip. Anderson was the journo wet dream.

When guitarman Butler quit the group it looked like it was all over for them. But with the addition of the sprightly young Richard Oakes on guitar they were totally rejuvenated.

Their comeback has been swift and ruthless. Their second album saw them a bigger and bolder band, their music was streaked with a far more glam touch, oozing decadence and a menace that was lacking before. They were suddenly muscular and powerful live. Their gigs became sweat frenzies. Being a band with something to prove, they rocked hard. The album spawned a run of Top Ten singles. Each one a flash man vignette of intangible council estate decay . . . hinting at drugs and weird sex. Suede had snatched a decadent and delicious victory from the jaws of defeat.

By 1999 they were scoring No. 1 albums with records that were far far weirder and grittier than that chart slot usually allows. They could also deal out a pretty ballad when one was called for. By the late nineties there were plenty of other would-be freaks and cross-dressing uniques. It looked like there was going to be a full-on glam revival, how could the kagoul clad hordes resist the temptations of the flash? The film *Velvet Goldmine* attempted to be the banner for these theoretical new freaks to march under. The film examined the Berlin burlesque decadence of two rock 'n' roll stars based not too loosely on Iggy and Bowie and like the cold-hearted love scenes in the film it quite literally came and went . . . a neat case of wham bam thank U mam, perhaps.

The main standard-bearers for all things glammed were the bands themselves . . .

Placebo, a trio fronted by Brian Molko, were dealing out fast 'n' sleazy decadent low life rushes. The first time I saw them at Manchester's In The City where they were in the new band competition I thought they were crap but they won that year's competition along with Kula Shaker and within months they were garnering praise.

Molko, an American with a background in Sonic Youth styled indie pop, skewered his songs with enough guitar weirdness to steer them away from the indie grain. His bass player, the endlessly tall Stefan Olsdal was Swedish and drummer, Steve Hewitt, created a strong unit for his bizarre anthems. Hewitt was once in The Boo Radleys and as a teenager he came round to my house to be interviewed as part of the Boo's first-ever piece of national press. He gave me a lift to town in a car that had a home-made stereo in it that blasted Can out at an incredible volume.

That's good taste.

His brother Nick was also the original Gold Blade guitar player. Family? Not exactly. After 'In the City', like a tosser, I gave them a bad review and was top of their hit list. At a *Kerrang!* party Molko V-signed me. I didn't really know who he was but we shook on it afterwards.

The V-sign was nothing, what really pissed me off was how damn wrong I had been. Placebo's thrilling brace of singles were just the sort of stuff I've always loved, all buzzsaw glam and punk energy and the elfin-faced frontman doing the girl/boy thing with the right amount of smudged war paint. Sometimes you've just got to put your hands up and admit that you made a mistake, I guess, and it's great to be proved wrong.

Their first single, 'Nancy Boy', was a glorious rush of sound. Great sneery pop rattling from *Top Of The Pops*. Molko worked his 'I'm a boy who looks like a girl' routine to the hilt and it was winning them a whole stack of converts, including the old dame himself David Bowie, who invited them to some big-time bash he was throwing at Madison Square Gardens in New York, name-dropped them constantly and, even as I type is recording a single with them.

Their debut album, *Without You I'm Nothing*, was a brattish run of great tunes, waving the flag for late-night bedsit tomfoolery with gender, chemicals and make-up.

He may not have looked as much like a girl as he would have us believe but Molko certainly looked like a pop star, the sort of pop star that the skinny, pale-faced intense kinda girl would swoon for. Late nineties glam is a (not always that) pretty broad church.

There were also neo glam outfits like Chester's Mansun who went through a whole wardrobe of costume changes in their early months before settling on the 'normal bloke' look. Their big soundscapes and impassioned delivery saw them pick up some of the lost Manics fans before they turned into one of those bands that have No. 1 albums without anyone really noticing. Not that they would have it any other way. These days it pays to exist outside the music business on your own terms.

Glam was now rearing its pretty little head in the most unlikely places. A slap of purple eyeliner made REM's charismatic singer Michael Stipe look like a pop star for the night; The Spice Girls clomped around in fat shoes, appropriating a kinda clumsy glam like The Sweet had possessed in the great days of the form. Glam in the late nineties comes in so many different flavours from the underground Brit glam Rachel's Stamp, the Bowie glam of Marilyn Manson, the rock 'n' roll glam of Backyard Babies, the pop glam of Suede.

Separating the men from the boys, if this is the right sort of term in this context, were American glam shockers Marilyn Manson.

The outfit, built around the giraffe-like Marilyn Manson (né Brian Warner) dealt a grinding metallic pop that crossed Bowie and Iggy with New Romantic eighties pop and the sonic grind of Big Black and made it work. They surfed in on an unlikely goth revival. Goth, the much maligned movement, had been in existence since the mid eighties. Existing in its own world, it was never a media-friendly scene and was either ignored or sneered at.

By the mid nineties it looked as if it was dead, leaving the sort of pale-faced corpse that most of its aficionados had always craved. But then most observers never go to rock clubs. Goth was a big underground scene without a figurehead. When Manson came along he provided the figurehead, capturing the bleak nihilistic heart of the nineties in a series of smart anthems that touched all the correct controversial buttons.

With a run of albums through the decade his band swiftly became the world's biggest industrial outfit, building on the foundations of the likes of Ministry and Nine Inch Nails.

Industrial music has virtually been ignored in the UK but in Europe and America it's enormous. The harsh grinding chug puts metal on the dance floor and is a club staple abroad. Nine Inch Nails had been massive in the mid nineties but it was Marilyn Manson who sent the whole scene mega.

Manson was the scene's first proper star. He looked like an alien, was the devil's right hand man and knew how to rub up the stiff-assed conservatives with a few well chosen comments.

He wrote an autobiography that is a great read and looked almost set for that sort of crossover that you always get no matter how fucked up you appear to be.

That was until a couple of his fans took the whole schtick too damn seriously and turned up in school with shooters, taking out some of their classmates. That's the problem Manson was always going to have. Over here no one took him seriously. Outrage doesn't mean much in the UK. Not much gets to us nowadays. However, in America they were taking the man at face value. Deadly seriously. Seriously enough for fans to pick up guns and deadly enough for them to use them.

Manson appealed to the outsider, the so-called nerds, the freaks, the bullied. Getting off on the freak music that appalled their classmates and then digging deeper into the satanic side of the music. Already ostracized by their classmates they felt like they had the only answer. One day someone somewhere was going to break. The outcasts in their heavy black coats, the late nineties industrial goths, the trench coat gang, picked up some of their guns that were shockingly easy to buy and wandered into the school and started shooting.

The media backlash threatened to engulf Marilyn Manson. Controversy sells records but some types of controversy even the anti-Christ wouldn't want to court. The gun laws in the US are loose and are obviously to blame in these instances. Still, you reap what you sow and talking up the dark side will always find some willing disciples.

After all, the devil will always make work for idle hands.

CHAPTER FIFTY-TWO

DRUM AND BASS

Drum and bass appeared on the scene in the mid nineties – an explosion of wild ideas and brilliant music. The form itself had roots going back for years. You could hear echoes of its sound in the breakbeats so beloved by the late-eighties B-Boys. Cranking these electronic slices of drum loops, they ended up with a frantic energized rush of kinetic rhythm. Allying these to the deep bottom end bass culled from the dub experience, they went for a bowel-shaking woomph by cranking the bass end even more, creating a voluminous subsonic bass that would rattle the speakers . . .

A crash collision of dub plates, sound system clashes and speeded up breakbeats, drum and bass couldn't fail to be anything but great if it was going to be sourcing some of the best musics made in the last thirty years for inspiration. A culmination of three decades of technology-based black musics mixed together.

You could hear echoes of ragga in the inner-city energy and the occasional bursts of MC activity on top, or the fluid freeform of prime-time jazz in its inexhaustible supply of rhythmic possibilities. It's miraculous that the electronic-based music could actually capture some of the spirit of jazz – perhaps the ultimate in played music.

But drum and bass is a miraculous style. It's thrown up so many possibilities that nobody seems to have got their heads round them yet. The one true new musical form of the nineties, it knocked you sideways the first time that you heard it, as Radio One's Mary Ann Hobbs remembers.

'Drum and bass is really important. It's like when punk first came along. The first time you heard these records you had to completely relearn a way of listening to the music. There was so much energy and excitement, at first you couldn't dance to it. You'd just jump up and down. When I listened to it I thought "Fucking hell, it's so energizing." The records totally squeezed your adrenal glands, it was really challenging. I thought "I don't know how to absorb this." I remember going out to a drum and bass club for the first time. I couldn't dance to it at all but you could feel the massive energy in the club.'

There's nothing like a new form of music to blow your mind, make you feel invigorated and, like Mary Ann says, drum and bass did just that. Instead of looking backwards the music was looking totally forwards.

As a music, drum and bass has had a curious history. Arguments rage over where it exactly came from. There is a heated debate over where it got its original 'jungle' monicker from . . . It could have been Johnny Jungle and his sped up breakbeat white label or it could have been hardcore outfit Top Buzz who were calling their music 'jungle techno' or it could be a 1991 Rebel MC cut, which featured a sampled chant 'Alla the junglist', grabbed from a Jamaican sound system mix tape. It could have been all these roots and a lot more. In the murky world of bedroom technology and white labels, the fast-moving flow of ideas can see the same point arrived at so many times.

And it's not that anyone ever seemed happy with the term 'jungle'. Most of the prime purveyors on the scene hated the word. But while some saw it as a way of capturing the inner-city vibe of the music, the concrete jungle was what they were trying to capture in the music.

Drum and bass was the logical conclusion of the fallout of acid house, from the happy hippie days of the Second Summer of Love and on to the speeded-up breakbeats of the police siege mentality of the hardcore era. The music was getting more linear, more stripped down, especially in the rusting industrial belt of the Midlands which turned its back on house for the fatter and harder sound – becoming a stomping ground for southern DJs like Mickey Finn, Jumping Jack Frost, Fabio and Grooverider who would lay alongside local DJs like Doc Scott, seeking faster, harder, leaner and meaner cuts.

Back in the smoke Fabio and Grooverider were pushing the form at a club called Rage, fucking with their decks to crank their records faster and noisier. The club was packed and the music was hot. This was the cutting edge where people like Goldie and Kemistry and Storm found the sparks of inspiration that made them run with their own version of events.

Outfits like Shut Up And Dance were dropping ragga into the equation and were shocked to find that they were being picked up by the rave crowd who were looking for a cranked up reggae vibe to mix in with the frenetic hardcore that they were digging. Hits for SL2 and the Ragga Twins on the same sort of tip opened up a whole new universe of ideas.

The Prodigy dropped 'Charly', a record that at one level could have been easily dismissed as a novelty record but was in fact a ground-breaking clatter of breakbeats and insane detail.

Meanwhile the authorities were crushing the rave scene. It was winter and in the inner cities it was pretty grim. The novelty records were a million miles away from this harsh reality, so it was inevitable that the music was going to shift to match the nu mood. The style was called 'dark' and it's the one true precursor of the drum and bass explosion.

Built around minor key melodies and with a brooding atmosphere around its grooves, dark is best captured on Goldie's 'Terminator', a ground-breaking record that opened up the possibilities of time stretching for the first time. Speeding up the beats without altering the pitch, this made the records really fuck with your head. Along with cuts from 2 Bad Mice, Doc Scott, and 4Hero, Goldie was soundtracking something darker and bleaker than the happy hardcore scene could ever have dreamt. They inspired a whole host of copycat cuts.

It was time to move on.

The post-dark scene saw the emergence of jungle and hip hop culture and ragga started to infuse the culture of some clubs, bringing with it the attendant downside of crack cocaine and macho posturing. It added a mean edge to the new form of music and it was fodder to a press looking for a negative angle to write up the new style of music.

From these troubled roots jungle started to find its own feet as a musical form. It broke out into bigger venues like Brixton Academy and the Jungle Fever tour. The vibe was dark, the music was serious and the DJs brilliant. From there it moved into clubs, mainly around London with a few enclaves dotted around the country.

Mainly an underground form, its profile was enhanced by Goldie, the charismatic first superstar of the form. With his heavy metal jewellery and extroverted presence Goldie was inevitably going to grab column inches. Born in Wolverhampton, Goldie had drifted through Bristol and Miami returning to the UK as a street graffiti artist he was involved early in the drum and bass scene. Rooted in hip hop he always had a big musical interest. He'd cut a few tracks before but when drum and bass came along he was one of the scene's first people to get a record out.

As the Metalheadz, Goldie and collaborator, Rob Playford cut the debut album, *Goldie presents Metalheadz:Timeless*, *The Shadow* and then *Saturnz Return*. The first two albums were really well received but *Saturnz* was slated. In fact it's a great record, stock full of great ideas, stretching drum and bass as far it will go.

With a high-profile relationship with Björk and a tabloid presence, Goldie has sold a mass of records and has raised the form's profile.

The other big star of the form was LTJ Bukem whose atmospheric drum and bass broke a whole new flavour, ambient drum and bass. It was just the beginning of the form's swift shattering into a whole host of forms as drum and bass was cross-fertilized with a whole pile of other musics.

By the late nineties cynics were claiming that the form was a musical cul de sac. It was hardly ram-raiding the charts but that's the way its main protagonists preferred it, keeping it underground away from the pop conveyer belt. In the meantime the music was no longer the preserve of the clubs. Within a couple of years of its appearance you could hear it pumped into wine bars or on TV adverts selling corn flakes.

Drum and bass has had a curious history. The nearly music of the nineties, it's still a breathtaking form, explosive in its potential and awe-inspiring in its daring and ideas. Remaining just below the surface, its influence is still perceptible. As journalist Neil Davenport points out:

'It may not have broken through itself but its influence is definitely perceptible. Pop records are adorned with drum and bass trimmings. It's the classic case of a hardcore sound filtering into mainstream pop. Music would die without avant garde existing on the outskirts, influencing recording techniques etc. It's had a curious progression, starting off as music of black oppression. Originally techno excluded black music but mixed with ragga it created drum and bass . . .'

Davenport is right. Instead of becoming a major force per se, drum and bass filtered through into the mainstream, feeding other forms with its explosive ideas. It's done what an underground music always does when the mainstream attempts to squash it out. It's sneaked in through the back door, one foot in the mainstream and one quite firmly remaining underground – and that's just the way the prime protagonists prefer it.

EPILOGUE: RU READY FOR THE 21ST CENTURY?

The nineties has been a fast ride. It's thrown up some bizarre possibilities: diverse musics mixed up and sparking off new styles; new pop heroes and some unlikely crossovers (who would have guessed that Leeds anarchist band Chumbawumba would be one of the biggest selling bands in the world in the late nineties, even outselling Oasis at one point!).

As I read back through this book, it hits me just how complex this nineties beast really is. It zigzags in a lot of different directions. There's so many different strands of pop, all running concurrently.

This fracturing of styles is going to continue: everyone is going to get their own version of pop, grabbing all the different pieces of pop history and making something new out of them.

Add to this the new technology, the explosion of the Internet and you've got some wild possibilities coming up.

One thing's for sure: the noughts or whatever the next decade is called (what the fuck is it called?) is going to be an even wilder and weirder ride . . .

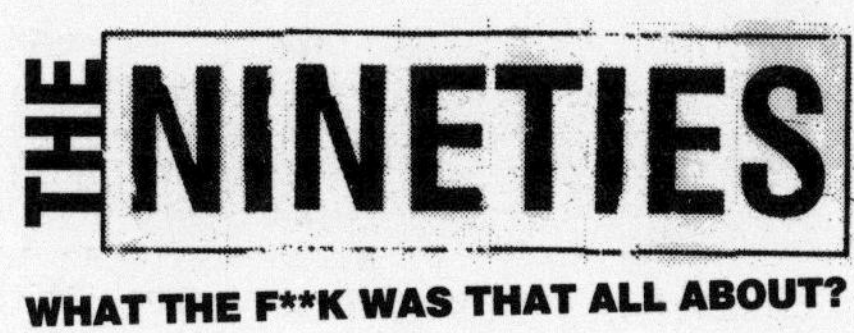

INDEX

INDEX

INDEX

INDEX

INDEX

INDEX

INDEX